VISUAL QUICKPRO GUIDE

UNIX

FOR MAC OS X

Matisse Enzer

 Peachpit Press

Visual QuickPro Guide
Unix for Mac OS X
Matisse Enzer

Peachpit Press
1249 Eighth Street
Berkeley, CA 94710
510/524-2178
800/283-9444
510/524-2221 (fax)

Find us on the World Wide Web at: http://www.peachpit.com
To report errors, please send a note to errata@peachpit.com

Peachpit Press is a division of Pearson Education

Editor: Howard Baldwin
Production Coordinator: Myrna Vladic, Lisa Brazieal
Copyeditor: Elissa Rabellino
Compositors: Phyllis Beaty, Myrna Vladic, David Van Ness
Indexer: Julie Bess
Cover design: The Visual Group

ISBN 0-201-79535-3

9 8 7 6 5 4 3 2 1

Printed and bound in the United States of America

Dedication

This book is dedicated to David Hawkins, {apple|decwrl|hplabs}!well!dhawk

It was David who taught me my first serious addition to a Unix command line:

command | awk '{print $3}' | sort | uniq -c | sort -nr

and this quote from Horace—

To know all things is not permitted.

—to which David's response was

...But you can still go deeper...

David died on July 24, 2000. There is an online memorial
at www.river.org/~dhawk/memorial.html.

Acknowledgments

Creating a book is like creating software—
if it is any good, it is almost certainly a team
effort. Here's a list of the people who made
this book happen, and if we've left anyone
out, it is entirely the author's fault.

Marjorie Baer brought the author in on this
project and instigated the whole effort.
Without her, it wouldn't have even started.

Cliff Colby and Victor Gavenda helped with
the basic outline of the book.

Howard Rheingold, Freddy "Are We Really?"
Hahne, Pilar "Power P" Johnson, and Eugene
Alexander provided the sort of encourage-
ment that makes life worth living.

Ron Liskey made the priceless suggestion
that we set a schedule for how much to write
each week and *stick to it*. Tim Pozar provided
help with the history of BSD and open-
source Unix. The crew that hangs out in the
Macintosh and Unix conferences on The
WELL provided numerous valuable contributions, especially Chris Carroll, Paul Bissex, and
Sean Harding, along with Barrett Brassfield,
Joel Westerberg, John F. Whitehead, Mark
Binder, Matthew Hawn, Michael C. Berch,
Tara L. Andrews, Thomas Armagost, and
James Waldrop. Waldrop and Ken Hipschman
tackled the technical editing and attempted
to correct the author's more flagrant mistakes.
Elissa Rabellino provided kind, careful, and
thorough copyediting. Myrna Vladic, Phyllis
Beaty, David Van Ness, and Lisa Brazieal han-
dled the production challenges with aplomb.

And finally, Howard Baldwin, the editor, provided priceless encouragement and patient
support to a first-time author who probably
caused more trouble than he knows. Thanks,
Howard.

TABLE OF CONTENTS

TABLE OF CONTENTS

TABLE OF CONTENTS

INTRODUCTION

This book is a small part of a big revolution. The revolution is the introduction of the Unix operating system into the everyday computing environment of regular computer users. Never before have so many people had access to a common, powerful, and stable platform that is open to being reshaped through the collaborative efforts of all who wish to contribute.

Mac OS X is now the world's most common version of Unix on the desktop, and you are among the first Mac users to dig into the tools that await you below the surface. If you're not a Mac user and are thinking about Mac OS X, jump right in—you'll be able to follow the book just fine. If you are an experienced Unix user wondering about Mac OS X, take it from us, it really is Unix—not almost, not sort of, but actual, real Unix with the Lovely Mac Interface.

This book is intended to help you, the adventurous Macintosh user, explore the power and variety of the Unix substructure upon which Mac OS X elegantly builds.

Unix is an operating system, and obviously you have used other operating systems in the past—at the very least, you have used the Macintosh operating system, and perhaps Windows, or even DOS. Unix is different. The other operating systems have a sharp distinction between the operating system itself and the applications you use with it. In Unix, the distinction is much less clear.

In learning Unix, you will use a collection of separate applications to do things like copy files, create new folders, view information like file size and date modified, and perform all the tasks that in other operating systems are part of the one big application that is the "operating system."

It has been said that if Unix were an airplane, it would have been built by all the frequent fliers who over the years showed up at the airport with new and/or improved pieces for the airplane. Each time someone had a better, faster (and sometimes even easier) way of doing something, all the other frequent fliers—along with the engineers working for the airplane manufacturer—would crowd around and argue over the benefits of the new tool.

In many cases a new tool (or toy) became a standard part of the airplane. Unix was invented in 1969, but it wasn't until the early 1980s that engineers at the University of California at Berkeley added the code for communicating on the Internet directly into the core (or *kernel*) of Unix. The tools for viewing files and monitoring the operating system have evolved constantly over the years.

New tools are added frequently. Each of them is a separate piece of software, with its own collection of features, options, and tricks for using it; and all of them (or almost all) are designed to be combined with each other in the way that words are combined to make a sentence.

All this means that Unix has evolved organically over the past 30-plus years, and continues to evolve, very much as a language evolves. In this book, we teach you how to think and act in Unix step-by-step, providing you with both a sequential learning process and a reference you can return to in the days to come as you become more and more adept.

Learning Unix is like learning a language—it all comes together to make some kind of sense, but there are idiosyncrasies and bits of historical stuff that pop up. It is not smoothly monolithic, but rather it is gloriously rich and complex. Instead of words, though, Unix has tools.

In Unix we call these tools *commands,* and you will start thinking about "which command to use" just as if you were some kind of authority figure, or wizard, which indeed you are on your way to becoming. Unix experts sometimes speak of "invoking" commands, as if they were magic spells. Perhaps that is not far from the truth.

You will see more similarity between Unix and language as you recognize that Unix commands achieve much of their value from the ways in which they can be combined with each other and even modified as the need arises.

This book teaches you how to perform the tasks necessary to accomplish traditional actions with your computer. Performing a task in Unix is frequently a matter of using two or more commands in a particular sequence. For example, you will use one command to create a new folder, another command to move within that folder, then another command to create a file, and still another command to set the permissions on the file so that you can control who is allowed to use it.

Unix is a world where a string of commands displays a specificity so unique, it results in an exact execution of your intention. Although such an incantation may seem obscure to a novice, the experienced user will see only directness, simplicity, and precision. We'll help you move from the former to the latter.

Who Is This Book For?

This book was written primarily with three audiences in mind:

◆ Experienced Mac users who want to learn Unix.

You are the folks who we expect will actually read and use this book.

We don't expect you to know anything at all about Unix before you read the book (but you will know a great deal about it when you are done). We'll teach you all the basic Unix skills and provide you with a solid reference book to turn to in the future.

We assume that you are adventurous, creative, and curious (hey, you *are* a Mac user, after all).

We also assume that you have experience with the Macintosh and have become comfortable with the new Aqua interface introduced in Mac OS X. If you are new to Mac OS X, we suggest that you also read Peachpit Press's *Mac OS X: Visual QuickStart Guide*, by Maria Langer. (www.peachpit.com/books).

◆ Beginning Unix users who are excited about using Unix on the Macintosh.

If you are a new Unix user who has learned a little Unix already, you'll find this book a thorough reference for all the basic Unix skills. It will probably teach you a few things you haven't learned yet.

◆ Expert Unix users. You have installed and configured Unix systems in your sleep. You know the differences between the System V and BSD versions of the ps command. You have a favorite in the vi versus emacs debate. Your Unix-novice Mac-using friends keep calling you for help with cd and ls.

If you already know your way around Unix, the simple fact is that you already know your way around 90 percent of Unix on Mac OS X. As we describe in Chapter 1, Mac OS X includes a complete Unix system, Darwin, that is based mostly on FreeBSD 4.4 and that you can use just like any other Unix system. Yes, there are a few differences (marked in this book with the Darwin mascot, Hexley),

but mostly it's the same as other Unix systems you have used.

We hope you'll buy this book by the caseload and give copies to friends who are new to Unix, so they'll stop pestering you with basic questions.

What's in This Book?

Simply put, an introduction to Unix.

We give you instructions on how to perform dozens of tasks using standard Unix tools. At least 90 percent of what you will learn from this book applies to other Unix systems, such as GNU/Linux, FreeBSD, and Sun Microsystems' Solaris.

The book consists of 15 chapters, containing more than 400 specific tasks that cover everything from the basics of using the Unix command line to Unix system administration and the installation and configuration of Unix software.

An introduction to Unix

We start off by introducing you to Unix itself in Chapter 1, "What is Unix, and Why Is It Good," in which we explain what Unix is, and describe the relationships between Mac OS X, Unix, Darwin, and Aqua.

The basics of the Unix command-line interface

In Chapter 2, "Using the Command Line," we teach you the basics of the command-line interface. This is the primary interface to Unix, and almost every task in the book is performed using only the keyboard; the mouse is hardly used at all.

In Chapter 3, "Getting Help and Using the Unix Manual," we teach you how to find and read the Unix documentation and how to get more help.

In Chapter 4, "Useful Unix Utilities," we give you instructions for the most common and useful Unix utility programs, including file compression and searching for text, as well as for a set of utilities that are unique to Mac OS X.

Chapter 5, "Using Files and Directories," provides more detailed instruction in the fundamental Unix skills of moving around your disk, and of viewing, creating, copying, and renaming directories and files (*directory* is what Unix calls a folder).

Beyond the basics: editing, permissions, and programming

Chapter 6, "Editing and Printing Files," is devoted to the use of Unix tools to perform these functions. We teach you how to use the standard Unix editor (called vi), which is a keyboard-only editor (no mouse!) that is available on virtually every Unix system in the world.

In Chapter 7, "Configuring Your Unix Environment," we teach you how to create shortcuts (*aliases* in Mac-speak) for commands and change settings (called *environment variables*) that many Unix programs use.

Chapter 8, "Working with Permissions and Ownership," teaches you how to work with one of Unix's more complex facets. We show you how to view the permission settings on files, how to change them, and what each of the dozens of possible settings means.

Chapter 9, "Creating and Using Scripts," is an introduction to simple Unix programming. We teach you about the fundamental building blocks of all programming and how to use each of them: variables, arguments, expressions, control structures, user input, and functions.

Using the Internet

Chapter 10, "Connecting Over the Internet" covers several different methods for interacting with other machines over the Internet. These include logging in to other machines using a command-line interface, and transferring files between machines.

Intermediate skills—system administration and security

Chapter 11, "Introduction to System Administration," is a hefty introduction to managing Unix systems. We show you how to use the all-powerful "root" account, add and remove users, back up essential files, run commands automatically, monitor system use, and perform some basic repairs using Unix tools.

In Chapter 12, "Security," you'll learn about the security of your machine and how to improve it, and we pay particular attention to measures that can protect your machine from attacks that come across the Internet.

Installing and configuring software

The last three chapters take you deeper into Unix by teaching you about the installation and configuration of Unix software.

Chapter 13, "Installing Software from Source Code," gives instructions on how to download and install the vast collection of Unix software that is available in *source-code* form. This is software for which the underlying programming code is available for download, and which you then turn into usable software though a process called *compiling*.

Chapter 14, "Installing and Configuring Servers," continues the theme of software installation by concentrating on *server* software. This is software that runs on your Mac to provide services to other machines over a network (typically over the Internet). Chapter 14 teaches you about servers that enable your Mac to be a Web server, an email server, a file-sharing server for other Macs *and* for Windows machines, and more.

Chapter 15, "More Open-Source Software" (on the Web at www.peachpit.com/umox) introduces you to eight more packages, selected for the diverse range of features they offer.

Glossary and where to learn more

Finally, we provide a glossary to help you quickly find the meanings of many terms that are found in the book (we also explain each one as it appears, of course!), and an appendix listing places to get even more help, including a summary of most of the Web sites we refer to throughout the course of the book.

WHAT'S IN THIS BOOK?

How to Use This Book

Unix for Mac OS X: Visual QuickPro Guide is designed so that each chapter builds upon the skills and understanding taught in the preceding chapters. So before we teach you how to edit files using Unix tools (in Chapter 6, "Editing and Printing Files"), for example, we show you how to work with files in general (in Chapter 5, "Using Files and Directories").

◆ If you are completely new to Unix, we recommend that you work your way through the book chapter by chapter, at least through Chapter 12, "Security."

◆ If you already know a bit of Unix, take a few minutes to skim through the first six chapters, and if you already know the skills we cover, see if you want to work through them in detail. Then decide if you want to work through the book chapter-by-chapter or use it as a reference as you poke around Mac OS X on your own. You'll find instructions on getting to the command line in Chapter 2, "Using the Command Line."

◆ If you are a hotshot Unix expert, gift wrap the book and give it to your favorite Mac user.

Most of this book consists of specific tasks laid out in a step-by-step fashion, with accompanying illustrations and examples of your input and the computer's output. The chapters and tasks are intended to be used as a tutorial, to teach you how to perform and understand the particular tasks and larger concepts. The book is also meant to be a reference work you will come back to as you continue to learn Unix, and you find and create more uses for Unix.

Graphic conventions

We use the following graphic conventions throughout this book:

Keyboard symbols

Where we want to indicate that you must press a particular key, we use special symbols such as Return and Control.

Whenever we show you a command or line of text to type into the computer, we assume that you will press Return at the end of the line unless we tell you not to. To avoid visual clutter and repetition, we do not put the Return symbol at the end of every line.

bold

Used for figure and table references. For example, "**Figure 0.1** shows the 'layers' of Mac OS X, with the Aqua user interface on 'top' and the Darwin Unix layer at the foundation. **Table 0.1** is an example of a table."

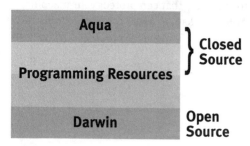

Figure 0.1 Diagram showing the large-scale software layers of Mac OS X with the Aqua user interface on top and the Darwin Unix layer at the foundation.

```
[g4-cube:~] matisse% cal 05 2023
      May 2023
 S  M Tu  W Th  F  S
       1  2  3  4  5  6
 7  8  9 10 11 12 13
14 15 16 17 18 19 20
21 22 23 24 25 26 27
28 29 30 31


[g4-cube:~] matisse%
```

Figure 0.2 Example of using the Unix command line. The `highlighted text` is typed by you, the user; all the `other text` comes from the computer.

Table 0.1

Example of a Table

TABLE ENTRY	MEANING/DESCRIPTION
Unix	A multiuser, multitasking operating system available in more than 100 different versions.
POSIX	A standard for Portable Operating System Interface for Unix.

About "vanilla"

Throughout this book we use the made-up user name "`vanilla`" (and sometimes another one called "`puffball`").

Whenever you see `vanilla`, you should substitute your own short user name. Your home directory has the same name as your short user name.

code text

Used for Unix command-line text, including Unix commands and filenames. Basically, if you see something in code text, that means it is literally what would be typed into or would come out of the computer. If a line of text is too long for this book's margins, a gray arrow indicates that the code should be typed on a single line.

code highlight

Used in figures to distinguish text you type in from text that comes from the computer. **Figure 0.2** is an example of how code text and `code highlight` appear in a figure.

code italics

These indicate text that you type into the computer but where you must substitute the appropriate value for the italicized text. For example, if you see

`ls -l` *filename*

then you would type the `ls -l` part literally, and then the name of a file instead of *filename*.

body-text italics

Used for emphasis and also to introduce words and phrases that are likely to be unfamiliar to Unix novices. For example, "The Unix concept of the *working directory* is similar to the GUI concept of the active window."

case-sensitivity

In Unix, filenames and command names are case-sensitive. The Macintosh preserves the case when it stores filenames, though they're case-insensitive. This means that there are some situations in which COMMAND and command are the same, but because those are exceptions and because case-sensitivity is the Unix standard, we assume that all commands and filenames are case-sensitive unless otherwise noted.

Darwin-specific features

The image in **Figure 0.3** is Hexley, the mascot/logo for Darwin, which is the name of the Unix part of Mac OS X (see www.hexley.com). We use Hexley to indicate features of the Mac OS X's Unix environment that differ from most other Unix versions. Most of the Unix features of Mac OS X do *not* differ from other Unix systems.

The Hexley Darwin OS mascot is © 2000 by Jon Hooper, all rights reserved. Used with permission. Permission to use the mascot may be obtained from Jon Hooper, 646 Luton Drive, Glendale, CA 91206, or via email at jonhoops@mac.com.

Mac OS X–specific feature

The icon at right is used to indicate a Unix feature that occurs only in Mac OS X. For example, there are some Unix tools included with Mac OS X for dealing with files created by older Mac applications, but these tools are not standard parts of any other version of Unix.

Figure 0.3 This is Hexley, the mascot/logo for Darwin. Darwin is the name of the version of Unix used as the foundation of Mac OS X.

Figure 0.4 This icon is used to indicate a Unix feature that is available in Mac OS X and is not a standard part of other versions of Unix.

Developer Tools folder

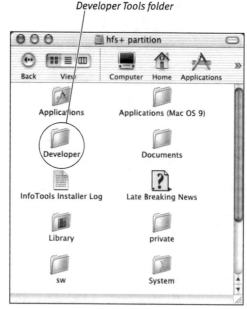

Figure 0.5 A Finder window showing the top level of the system disk. The folder containing the Developer Tools is highlighted.

Requirements

There are a few requirements for effectively using this book. Odds are, you already have all of them covered.

Adventurous and enthusiastic attitude

This is the most important requirement. If you meet this one, you will be able to master the others or do without them. Learning Unix is about learning a richly diverse collection of tools that are part of a lively ecosystem of software development. Unix is an environment for collaborative computing, and by stepping into it, you become part of an ongoing human phenomenon.

OK, enough philosophy. Here are the technical requirements:

Mac OS X 10.2 or later

This book is based on Mac OS X version 10.2 (Jaguar). If you have an earlier version of Mac OS X, then a few things will be different from their descriptions in this book.

Be an administrator

You must be logged in as an "administrative user" for many of the tasks covered in this book, particularly for installing software and conducting system-admin tasks. If you aren't sure what an administrative user is, go to the Help menu in the Finder and search on "administrative user."

Have the Developer Tools installed

Several parts of this book require that you have the Mac OS X Developer Tools installed. This is a collection of software included with Mac OS X but not always installed by default.

Depending on which version of Mac OS X you have, the Developer Tools may already be installed. If you have a folder called Developer at the top level of your hard drive, then the Developer Tools are installed. **Figure 0.5** shows a Finder window with the Developer folder highlighted.

The Developer Tools may be on a separate CD that you must install. If you don't have the CD, there may be an installer application in your Applications folder (in the Installers folder). Also, you can find links to download the Developer Tools from http://developer.apple.com/tools/ or http://connect.apple.com.

Connection to the Internet

Many of the tasks in the book assume that your machine is connected to the Internet, particularly those tasks involving interacting with other machines over networks.

WHAT IS UNIX, AND WHY IS IT GOOD?

Mac OS X is the most significant advance in desktop computing since the introduction of the original Mac interface. It provides users with unparalleled stability, flexibility, and openness—arguably necessary additions to the Macintosh operating system. Each of these features will help users take their Macs to new creative heights. Mac OS X provides these features by virtue of having been built on top of Unix. So if you're using Mac OS X, you're using Unix.

You probably already know that Unix is an industrial-strength operating system. It's specifically designed for always-on, network-connected computers that run multiple applications and are shared by many users. Since its creation in 1969, Unix has evolved into one of the world's most popular operating systems. Moreover, Unix is an excellent environment for creating new software. Apple built Mac OS X on top of a version of Unix called Darwin. If you're a Mac user who wants to push the boundaries of what you can do with your computer, here's what Unix can do for you.

The Advantages of a Unix-based Mac OS

While Unix is best known as a server operating system—most of the servers on the Internet run Unix—it's also been the desktop operating system for engineers, software developers, and system administrators. But Mac OS X is placing a Unix-based system on millions of desktops. With Unix under the hood of OS X, Macintosh users will now be able to take advantage of software developments beyond the boundaries of Apple Computer, while still enjoying the elegance and ease of use the Mac OS is famous for.

Basing Mac OS X on the Darwin operating system gave it three important features that, for all its advantages, the Mac OS had not previously had: stability, flexibility, and openness.

Stability

Even the most devoted Macintosh user will admit that system crashes have been an unfortunate but predictable part of everyday life. Unix systems, however, are extremely difficult to crash. Thanks to *protected memory*—the memory each application uses that is unavailable to any other application—with OS X your Macintosh will continue running even when one or more applications crash. You can simply restart the crashed application without having to restart your Mac.

If your system doesn't have protected memory, a badly behaving application can disturb the memory space of another application, or even of the operating system itself—often with nasty results. Macintosh operating systems before OS X didn't include protected memory—which explains all those system crashes!

A feature called *preemptive multitasking* allows the operating system to limit the amount of computational resources devoted to each application by prioritizing between

tasks. Before Mac OS X, the Mac OS employed *cooperative* multitasking—in which each application is *supposed* to behave and play well with the other applications on a machine. You can guess what happens when cooperatively multitasked applications don't cooperate.

Flexibility

Unix was designed to allow different programs to be connected in an almost infinite variety of ways. Because thousands of utilities are available for Unix (and because they work together so well), Unix users can customize their work environments relatively easily, building their own tools when the need arises. Mac OS X itself comes with around 500 utilities, most of which can be easily combined with other programs (see Chapter 4, "Useful Unix Utilities," for a roundup of the ones you're most likely to use). Because of this (and its portability), Unix is the ideal environment for developing new software.

Openness

Darwin, like other open-source versions of Unix, such as Linux, is open—that is, the inner workings are open to examination and change. You can download, study, and alter its programming source code at will. (In fact, versions of Darwin other than Apple's already exist.) Say you want to create a server that enables you to synchronize an iPod with

What's in a Name?

Strictly speaking, Unix is a trademarked term that's been variously owned by AT&T, Novell, and now the Open Group (www.opengroup.org). Only Unix versions with the correct legal pedigree can use that name. In reality, though, most people casually refer to all of the various "flavors" as Unix.

any computer over the Internet, or one that sends faxes on demand from a catalog of files: Whatever software you create is likely to use an existing piece of Unix software as its starting point.

By allowing people to examine and change their operating systems, open-source software is central to the ongoing evolution and spread of Unix, resulting in a software-development environment that will continue to increase in stability, flexibility, and power.

Unix's ability to connect different programs together provides almost infinite flexibility. Combine this with Unix's built-in support for TCP/IP (the networking protocol that defines the Internet) and other networking tools, and you have an operating system—Mac OS X—that's ready to take you into a future in which you can build your applications, and every computer has the ability to be a server.

Whatever capability you want to add to an application, you can probably do it in Darwin. As a Mac enthusiast, you may have had limited exposure to any kind of programming, but you'll be able to expand your horizons by accessing the Unix underlying Mac OS X. Even if you're brand-new to programming, delving into Unix is the best way to start.

From Multics to Unix

Unix wasn't actually named until about a year into its development—at which point the wordplay on the preceding Multics project was intentional (*uni,* meaning "one," as opposed to *multi,* meaning "many"). The tradition of puns and word games in Unix software continues to this day, as you'll see in later chapters when we introduce programs such as less, which is an improvement on an earlier program called more. More became less, you see.

Becoming a sophisticated user

Thus, you should read this book because you want a deeper understanding of your computer, and to get your fingers and hands and mind inside of it. Using Unix is about moving from being a consumer of software and systems to being a creator of software and systems. This means pushing the envelope of how you interact with the operating system, delving into areas where most users don't go, in order to develop capabilities that most users don't have. Mac OS X makes this possible now because Unix is an operating system for developing and building, for getting into the nitty-gritty.

Since much Unix software is created by volunteers, you're benefiting from the hard work of thousands of users. But using Unix means you will always tweak, modify, and configure to get the software to do what you want. By bringing an industrial-strength server to your desktop, Apple has taken desktop computing to another level—in much the same way that Macintosh-plus-PostScript laser printers brought high-quality print publishing and graphics tools to the desktop. None of this is automatic, though, and using Unix places a greater burden on you. If you're coming to Unix expecting the shrink-wrapped experience of the Mac OS or Windows, you're bound to be disappointed.

You will work with Unix primarily from the command line in the Terminal application (more about that in the next chapter). You will put together lots of odd-sounding commands, creating tiny and not-so-tiny scripts and programs to give the machine capabilities it never had before. You will not only be customizing your machine and creating software, you will be customizing your world, and indirectly the world the rest of us live in.

Most people won't really notice that Mac OS X is Unix-based. In fact, most people will use their Mac OS X Macintoshes just as they always have—writing in their word processors, creating images in graphics software, and editing sound and video.

Furthermore, some of the Unix tools in Mac OS X were available in some form for Mac OS 9, but the Unix versions are included with Mac OS X (for example, a Web server and an email server). With Mac OS X, you are more likely to work with these applications, for a couple of reasons. Mac OS X is so stable that you won't be afraid of messing up your computer. More important, if you use a "pure" Unix tool, like the Apache Web server, then the skills you learn, and the system you build, will be transferable to almost any other Unix environment with little effort.

Unix will always be more hands-on than the graphical user interfaces you're accustomed to. However, if you're ready to experience new heights of computing creativity, you'll find that you have a more personalized and robust system on your hands by the time you finish this book.

Other Versions of Unix

Over the years, many versions of Unix have been developed—some by large corporations (for example, Sun Microsystems' Solaris and Hewlett-Packard's HP/UX), and some by small companies and individuals working for their own pleasure. The most famous of the latter is the open-source GNU/Linux operating system, which combines the work of hundreds of programmers from around the world and has been adopted by thousands of companies. (For example, IBM announced in January 2002 a mainframe computer designed specifically for Linux.)

A good list of dozens of versions of Unix is available at www.ugu.com/sui/ugu/show? ugu.flavors

But First, a Little History

What we wanted to preserve was not just a good environment in which to do programming, but a system around which a fellowship could form. We knew from experience that the essence of communal computing, as supplied by remote-access, time-shared machines, is not just to type programs into a terminal instead of a keypunch, but to encourage close communication.

—Dennis M. Ritchie, coinventor of Unix
From "The Evolution of the Unix Time-Sharing System,"
AT&T Bell Laboratories
Technical Journal 63, No. 6, Part 2, October 1984
(http://cm.bell-labs.com/cm/cs/who/dmr/hist.html)

How did Unix end up as the underpinning of the Mac OS? In 1997, after a series of unsuccessful attempts to update the Macintosh operating system—remember Pink and Copland?—Apple bought NeXT, the computer company that Apple cofounder Steve Jobs had started 12 years earlier after he was forced out of Apple. NeXT had developed a powerful operating system with an elegant user interface but had failed to become commercially successful. (Of course, commercial success is not the only way to gauge the quality of a product. None other than Tim Berners-Lee, inventor of the World Wide Web, used a NeXT machine for his development work on hypertext.)

When Apple bought NeXT, it got the code for NeXT's operating system, development tools, and user interface. But more important, it got Steve Jobs and a culture of Unix-based development. The NeXT operating system, while largely written from scratch, was a version of Unix, and the NeXT engineers were used to a Unix culture—that is, employing powerful, flexible tools and systems in an environment of creative engineering. Given the effect on Apple's operating-system development, some people say that, culturally, NeXT bought Apple.

Since Mac OS X is based on a new version of Unix called Darwin, by the time OS X was released, the percentage of NeXT-derived code was small. Still, that cultural influence has played a huge part in moving Apple toward the values of openness, flexibility, and stability.

Where did those values come from? They were part of Unix from its beginnings. Unix was born in 1969 from the efforts of a small group of scientists working at AT&T's Bell Labs to create an operating system that would allow the group to continue the kind of collaborative programming they had been doing on an earlier project called Multics. Thus, from the very

continues on next page

Unix Pioneer: Bill Joy

Perhaps most recognizable to the general population as the chief scientist and cofounder of Sun Microsystems, Bill Joy is known in the Unix community as the primary designer of the Berkeley Software Distribution (BSD) version of Unix.

Among Joy's many contributions are the NFS (Network File System) protocol, the open-source version of TCP/IP, and the vi text editor.

After its introduction in 1983, BSD Unix became the first widely distributed open-source version of Unix and is the basis for numerous later versions of Unix, including Darwin, the core of Mac OS X.

Bill Joy's official Sun Microsystems biography is at www.sun.com/aboutsun/media/ceo/mgt_joy.html

beginning, Unix was conceived as both a multiuser and a multitasking system—that is, one that many people and many programs could use simultaneously and harmoniously.

In the late 1970s, the University of California at Berkeley used Unix extensively in its computer science department, several of whose

members contributed features to the operating system. A key contribution: building in support for TCP/IP (the networking protocol suite that defines the Internet), added in the early 1980s. Virtually all current versions of Unix use the Berkeley networking code or its derivatives. Eventually, the version of Unix that came out of the university was dubbed the Berkeley Software Distribution (BSD)—from which the Darwin core of Mac OS X is a direct descendant.

Thus, when we refer to Mac OS X's Unix features, we're almost always talking about Darwin. And although you can run Darwin by itself, it won't look like Mac OS X without the proprietary components Apple provides.

Think of Mac OS X as having several layers: The bottom, or foundation, layer is Darwin (**Figure 1.1**). On top of Darwin are a number of proprietary software components Apple has added. Above it all is the layer users see—the graphical interface called Aqua. You can use Mac OS X for traditional Macintosh tasks without ever being aware of the layers underneath Aqua, including Darwin.

Figure 1.1 Apple built the latest version of its operating system, Mac OS X, on top of a version of Unix called Darwin. Between the Aqua interface and the underlying operating system are two layers of Apple-specific programming layers.

Unix Pioneer: Linus Torvalds

Linus Torvalds is widely known as the inventor of Linux, a completely open-source Unix-like operating system. Torvalds wrote the core of Linux, called the *kernel*, and released the first version in 1991.

Besides the Linux kernel, Torvalds's most significant contribution to Unix has been his ability to gently and productively facilitate and coordinate the efforts of literally hundreds of programmers whose work comprises the current version of the Linux kernel.

Torvalds made a key decision when he released the code for the Linux kernel under a software license called the GNU General Purpose License (GNU GPL), which requires anyone making changes to the source code to make those changes freely available to the world. Most installed versions of Linux come with hundreds of other pieces of software also licensed under the GNU GPL, and so the name GNU/Linux is usually more accurate when speaking of Linux.

The unoffical Linus FAQ is at www.tuxedo.org/~esr/faqs/linus/.

Linus's own home page is at www.cs.helsinki.fi/u/torvalds/.

Unix History Timeline

Some key dates in the development of different Unix versions:

- **1970:** Ken Thompson suggests the name *Unix* for the fledgling operating system born in 1969 at AT&T Bell Labs.

- **1973:** The kernel (core) of Unix is rewritten in the C language, making it the world's first operating system that's "portable"—that is, able to run on multiple kinds of hardware.

- **1977:** First BSD (Berkeley Software Distribution) version is released. Licensees must also get a license from AT&T.

- **1983:** Version 4.2 BSD is released. By the end of 1994, more than 1,000 licenses are issued. AT&T releases its commercial version, System V.

- **1983:** AT&T releases System V release 3. IBM, Hewlett-Packard, and others base their own Unix-like systems on this version.

- **1991:** Linus Torvalds releases version 0.02 of Linux, an open-source, Unix-like operating system.

- **1992:** Bill Jolitz releases 386/BSD, a full version of Unix with no AT&T code.

- **1992:** Sun Microsystems releases Solaris, a version of Unix based on System V release 4, incorporating many BSD features.

- **1994:** BSD4.4-Lite is released by the University of California at Berkeley. It is entirely free of legal encumbrances from the old AT&T code. Version 1.0 of Linux is also released this year; Linux incorporates features from both AT&T's System V and BSD versions of Unix.

- **1999:** Apple Computer releases Darwin—a version of BSD Unix and the core of the Mac OS X.

Unix Pioneer: Dennis M. Ritchie

Dennis M. Ritchie has been a computer scientist with Bell Labs for 35 years. He is most famous for having assisted Ken Thompson in inventing Unix and for being the primary creator of the C programming language (with Brian Kernighan in 1972).

Ritchie is also a parent of another operating system, called Plan 9, that is well-known to the community of people who develop operating systems. He is currently head of the System Software Research Department at Bell Labs, where he is working on a new operating system called Inferno.

Dennis M. Ritchie's home page: www.cs. bell-labs.com/who/dmr/.

BUT FIRST, A LITTLE HISTORY

For More on Unix History

- **CrackMonkey** (http://crackmonkey.org/unix.html)—A history of Unix, including a discussion of its important flavors.
- **"The Evolution of the Unix Time-sharing System"** (http://cm.bell-labs.com/cm/cs/who/dmr/hist.html)—Coinventor Dennis M. Ritchie offers a technical and social history of Unix.
- **"Overview of the GNU Project"** (www.gnu.org/gnu/gnu-history.html)—A history of the Free Software Foundation's efforts to create an open and free version of Unix.
- **Open Source: Darwin** (www.opensource.apple.com/projects/darwin/)—Apple's official Darwin Project site, where you can download source code and find links to other related projects.
- **Darwinfo** (darwinfo.org)—General-purpose site about Darwin, including links to mailing lists.
- **The GNU-Darwin Distribution** (http://gnu-darwin.sourceforge.net)—Web site that "aims to be the most free Darwin-based Unix distribution."

Beyond Unix: Other Open Systems

Other open-source technologies are also helping to revolutionize the information infrastructure of society.

- **HTML**—The ease of creating documents using HyperText Markup Language drove the growth of the Web. Anyone viewing a Web page can see, copy, and modify the underlying HTML. The HTML standard is coordinated by the World Wide Web Consortium (www.w3c.org/MarkUp/).
- **Apache Web server** (www.apache.org)—By far the most popular Web server in the world, Apache provides a huge variety of configuration options and can be altered easily to add new ones. Mac OS X comes with Apache (see Chapter 14, "Installing and Configuring Servers").
- **Perl** (www.perl.org)—This powerful scripting and programming language (which comes with Mac OS X) is used in scripts as short as 20 lines and in large object-oriented applications with thousands of lines of code.
- **C**—The programs listed in this sidebar and those included in every version of Unix are written—with few exceptions—entirely in the C programming language. To learn more, check out *The C Programming Language,* by Brian W. Kernighan and Dennis M. Ritchie (Prentice Hall, 1998; http://cm.bell-labs.com/cm/cs/cbook/)—the fundamental book on the topic—or "The Development of the C Language" (http://cm.bell-labs.com/cm/cs/who/dmr/chist.html).
- **ssh**—The **s**ecure **sh**ell tool facilitates secure connections between computers. The open-source version is maintained by the OpenBSD project (www.openssh.org).
- **gcc**—The **GNU c**ompiler **c**ollection translates programming source code into machine-executable applications. It's maintained by the Free Software Foundation (www.gnu.org/software/gcc/gcc.html).
- **Sendmail** (www.sendmail.org)—Mac OS X comes with a version of this common mail server software, which you can use to set up your Mac OS X computer to be your own mail server.

How Mac OS X's Unix Differs from Mac OS 9

The immediate, obvious difference between Unix and Mac OS 9 is the user interface. Until Mac OS X, the various graphical interfaces available to Unix users all fell short of the elegance and polish to which Macintosh users are accustomed.

It is a tribute to the architecture of Mac OS X that you can use it as the next Macintosh operating system and never have to see any significant Unix underpinnings. Never, that is, unless you want to learn Unix.

From a more technical point of view, when OS X is compared with OS 9 (and earlier Macintosh operating systems), several important differences stand out. As we noted earlier, Unix uses protected memory and preemptive multitasking, and has other capabilities that let applications share memory, processors, and applications in a stable and reliable way.

As a result, it is hard for one misbehaving application to affect any other application or the operating system itself. Yes, applications can still crash in Mac OS X, but rarely do they take the whole OS down with them. Not only will you suffer fewer crashes, but they'll impact your other work less.

Unix, and thus Mac OS X, is also a multiuser operating system. It's designed from the ground up with the assumption that many people will be using the computer, often simultaneously. Just as the applications' activities are kept separate, so too are the actions of each user kept separate. Even if 50 people are using the Macintosh, it is hard for any one of them to mess up the other ones.

Another way Mac OS 9 differs from Mac OS X is the arrangement of files and folders (called *directories* in Unix) and the way information about each file is stored.

You will also see something called Home show up as a shortcut in the Finder navigation dialog box, the Save File dialog box, and so on. This concept of each user's home directory as the only place where you normally create files is a thoroughly Unix idea arising directly from Unix's nature as a multiuser system, and is a major change from Mac OS 9.

Apple has strived to mask these differences in Mac OS X, but they are still there, and you must be aware of them if you want to do serious Unix work (or even just be a Mac OS X "power user").

In your day-to-day use of Mac OS X, you'll find that many of the ways it differs from Mac OS 9 have more to do with the new Mac interface, Aqua, than with Unix. For example, the Dock is new to Mac OS X, but it isn't a "Unix change." In this book, we'll focus specifically on the Unix characteristics of Mac OS X, not the differences that come from Aqua.

What You Can Do with Mac OS X and Unix

What do you want to do? Do you want to create movies with iMovie and make them available over the Internet? With the Unix-based Mac OS X, that task is easy: You simply drag the movies into the Sites folder in your Home directory, then enable Web sharing. Would you like to run your own radio station? You can easily use your Mac OS X machine to run the Icecast server, which provides powerful streaming-audio capabilities. Do you want your schedule to be constantly available to friends and family, your résumé always accessible to potential employers? You can provide all those things with greater reliability on a Unix platform.

Beyond the foundation of increased stability, flexibility, and openness, Unix brings a number of more specific features to Mac OS X that are fundamental to the way you will use it. Key among these is the way it supports multiple users and multiple processes.

Accommodating multiple users

As we've said earlier, Unix is a multiuser environment and intentionally keeps each user's actions separate to create a more stable environment.

On a Unix system you are never alone (unless you started the machine in single-user mode, which we'll discuss in Chapter 11; if you already know what that means, keep quiet until the others have a chance to catch up). Unix assumes there are going to be many users running programs on the system.

When you log in to a Unix system, you identify yourself with a user name and password that have already been entered into the system by an administrator (if you are working on your own Mac OS X system, you will have

created at least one account for yourself when you installed the operating system). This enables the operating system to keep your files and actions separate from everyone else's, and is a major factor in Unix stability and security.

✔ Tips

- You can see a list of who is logged in to your system using the command-line w and who commands. See Chapter 11, "Introduction to System Administration," for more information on using the w and who commands.

- You can see a list of all the user accounts on the system with the Netinfo Manager application (also covered in Chapter 11).

All of the files you create in the normal course of using the system are "owned" by you. Every file and every running program (known as a *process*) on a Unix system is owned by a user. All of the important system files—that is, the ones that make up the actual operating system—are owned by a special super-user called *root*. The root account is all-powerful, and you must exercise great care when using it (see Chapter 11 for more on root).

Not every user account on the system is intended for use by a human. Unix systems, including Mac OS X, come with a number of special user accounts with names like "nobody" and "daemon." The system uses these accounts to own processes that should not have the power of the root account.

Each regular user account on a Unix system has its own area on the file system called its *home directory*. This is where all of the files a given user creates and owns are stored. Unix keeps track of who owns each file and allows (or disallows) various operations based on the ownership of files.

Preemptive multitasking

On Unix systems, you might not only have multiple programs running, but you might also have multiple copies of the same program running. Even with just a single person logged in, running a few applications, several dozen processes will be running at any given moment, each with its own separate memory allocation. In fact, the operating system keeps a number of different processes running even if you are not doing anything.

When the machine starts up, the initial process (called *init*), which is owned by the super-user root, begins. The init process then starts many other processes, which are also owned by root.

✔ Tip

■ You can see a list of all the processes on your system using the **ps** and **top** commands. See Chapter 11 for more information on monitoring system usage.

Applications vs. Programs

All applications are programs—the terms are synonymous. In this book we use the term *application* to refer to complex programs used for a variety of related tasks—for example, Adobe Photoshop is an application for graphics manipulation. In Unix you often see the term *command,* which can refer either to an application that handles some specific task (such as copying files) or to a built-in feature of a larger program or application. For example, the command for copying files is the **cp** command, which is in fact a small program. The command to move from one folder into another folder (*directory* in Unix terms) is the **cd** command, which is actually part of a larger program called the shell. See Chapter 5, "Using Files and Directories," for more on the **cp** and **cd** commands.

Parents and children

Every process in Unix is the child of some other process, except for that first process, init, which is the mother of all processes. This concept of processes having parents and children comes up frequently in Unix.

When you log in to a Unix system, you start a process that you alone own. The exact program depends on which Unix system you are using, and how you log in to it. This process will be the parent (or grandparent, or great-grandparent) of every process you start on the system.

When you log in using the Mac OS X graphical user interface, you start a process called WindowServer, which you own.

Every program you run will have the Window-Server process as an ancestor. In other words, if you start up an application such as BBEdit, a popular text editor, then BBEdit's parent process will be WindowServer. If you start up the command-line interface (the Terminal application), you might then start more programs using the Terminal application. Those programs will have Terminal as their parent, and WindowServer as their grandparent, and so on.

So, using your Mac as a single-user system, you might have several dozen processes running.

Files and the filesystem

Unix brings a number of changes to the Mac OS with regard to files and the filesystem (see the sidebar "What Is a Filesystem?" for its definition).

From the user's point of view, the most prominent changes (as compared with Mac OS 9) involve the handling of file security, storage of files, and the use of a different syntax for describing a file's location.

Files and security

On an old Mac OS system, you could alter or delete any file. You could put files from the System Folder in the Trash and cause all kinds of trouble, even accidentallly. On a Unix system, every file is owned by some user. The operating system restricts the ability to create, change, or delete files based on ownership, so that one user cannot alter or delete files created by another user, and you are unlikely to cause any serious damage to the operating system (the exception: the root user can do anything).

Folders are called directories

What Mac users call a *folder* Unix users call a *directory*. A directory that is inside another is called a *subdirectory*. It is important to know which directory you are "in," because when you're working from a command line there is no visual cue, such as an active window. Know the concept of the "current directory" in Unix—that's where you're currently working.

File paths use / instead of :

In Mac OS 9 and earlier, file path designations use colons. In Mac OS X, Unix uses the / (slash) instead of the : (colon) to separate the parts of a file path. In Mac OS 9, then, the path of the FileMaker Pro application would look like that in **Figure 1.2**.

In Mac OS X, the same path would appear as shown in **Figure 1.3**.

Notice that the name of the hard drive doesn't show up anymore. In Unix, drives don't have names. The Mac OS X Aqua interface does have names for drives, and they do show up in the Finder, thanks to some tricks of the Mac OS X Finder, but at the underlying Unix/Darwin level, even in Mac OS X, drives don't have names.

Unix treats the entire filesystem as if it were one big disk. There are ways to see which disks contain which files, but usually when dealing with files in Unix, you only pay attention to the *full pathname* of the file. See Chapter 5, "Using Files and Directories," for more about using pathnames.

Even with the differences cited above, the Unix filesystem is organized similarly to what you are used to on a Mac. Use / instead of : in your pathnames, and think of your system as a Macintosh that has only one disk. Think of that disk as being named /, and then you're close to the way Unix thinks of files, directories, and subdirectories.

```
MyBig Disk:Applications (Mac OS 9):FileMaker Pro 5 Folder:FileMaker Pro
```

Figure 1.2. This is how the path of the FileMaker Pro application would look on the Mac OS 9 file system.

```
/Applications (Mac OS 9)/FileMaker Pro 5 Folder/FileMaker Pro
```

Figure 1.3 This is how the path of the FileMaker Pro application would look on the Mac OS X filesystem.

What Is a Filesystem?

In Unix the term *filesystem* (Unix's terminology for file system) is used in two ways. The first way is more informal and refers to the complete hierarchy of directories. The second way refers to a single storage area that has been formatted for use by the operating system. The "single storage area" is often, but not always, a single disk partition. Filesystems contain directories and files but never other filesystems.

Example of the first form: "/ is the root directory of the filesystem."

Example of the second form: "It is common to have two or more filesystems on the same physical disk."

Get used to filename extensions

Another difference between Mac OS 9 and Mac OS X is in OS X's use of filename extensions—you know, those things at the end of all the filenames on the Web and on PCs, such as .html, .txt, and .jpg (this is no surprise given which operating system the original Web servers used and the one most Web servers still use today).

From the very start, the Mac OS has cleverly kept track of a file's characteristics: what type of file it is, what application opens it, if the file is being used by another application, if the file is locked. Unix doesn't store as much information about each file along with each file. In particular, Unix has no fundamental concept of a file's "type" or "creator" (Mac OS X does, but only for files that were created with Mac file information).

Unix's filename extensions indicate a file's type. This is not as powerful as the Macintosh approach, but it is the standard in the Unix world. Mac OS X tries to have it both ways, and in the Mac spirit uses the old Mac approach in some cases and the standard Unix approach in other cases. But in order to play well with others, Mac OS X incorporates filename extensions. You can decide whether to display them in the graphical interface, but when you use the command line they will always be there.

Files created by Macintosh applications will have the Macintosh creator and type attributes, but files created by non-Mac applications, including all non-Mac Unix applications, will have only the filename extension (if any) to indicate what kind of file they are.

How You Will Be Working with Unix

You are probably already using your Macintosh for a variety of tasks, working in applications that take advantage of the lovely Aqua interface. As you dig below the surface and start using the Darwin layer of Mac OS X, you will be performing operations that are either unique to Unix or better suited to the Unix environment.

Working from the command line

The command line is the primary user interface in Unix. Most Unix software packages are designed to be installed and configured from the command line.

It is from the command line that you will be installing software and manipulating files (copying, moving, renaming, and so on). You might even start editing files using the command-line tools.

One of the most powerful aspects of the command line is in how it allows you to connect a series of commands together to accomplish some task. **Figure 1.4** shows an example of connecting three commands together in order to find all the files in a folder that contain the word *success* and email the resulting list of filenames to yourself.

The command line in Figure 1.4 is composed of three major parts separated by the vertical bar (|) character. (Note: this command line requires that you have activated the email server as described in Chapter 14, "Installing and Configuring Servers.")

The first part uses the `find` command to produce a list of the names of all the files (not folders) in the current folder (by using the `-type f` option) and all those inside it. The output of that command is passed (*piped*) via the | character to the next command, `xargs` (*arguments*). This applies the `grep` (*search*) command to each filename in turn, searching the file for the string "success" and producing a list of the filenames where the string was found. That second list is piped to the third part, the `Mail` command, which sends the list to the specified email address. The final ampersand (&) tells Unix to do all this "in the background," which means that we do not have to wait for the processes to finish before issuing a new command—we can go on with our work at the command line. Chapter 2, "Using the Command Line," takes you further into the details of using the command line.

Under Mac OS X, the most common way to get to the command line is through the Terminal application (found in the Utilities folder under Applications).

```
find . -type f -print0 | xargs -0 grep -l success | Mail address@hostname.com &
```

Figure 1.4 This command line shows how to connect commands together—in this case, finding all the files in a folder that contain the word *success* and then emailing the resulting list of file name to yourself.

Editing files from the command line

In order to really harness the power of Unix, you will want to learn how to edit files using a command-line text editor. Unix is file-centric and uses text files to control almost every aspect of software configuration. Although it's difficult for most Mac users to learn at first, editing files from the command line lets you change files without leaving the command-line environment in which most of your Unix work will occur. Furthermore, the ability to edit files from the command line will make it easy for you to work on other Unix systems besides Mac OS X, something you are almost certain to do once you get further into Unix.

Unix Commands Have Strange Names

Unix commands often have very terse obscure and/or arbitrary-sounding names. Examples: awk, grep, and chmod.

This contributes to Unix's (justly earned) reputation as a difficult operating system to use, requiring users to memorize a great deal in order to become proficient.

Because you are probably itching to know how those three commands got their names, here's the story: awk, a text-processing system, got its name from the initials of the three people who created it. grep, a command for searching inside text, got its name from the commands used in an earlier program to "globally find a regular expression and print." chmod is a command to change the permissions associated with a file and means "CHange MODe."

Programming and scripting

Developed *by* programmers *for* programming, Unix is—not surprisingly—an excellent programming environment, and many of its strengths (and some of its weaknesses) stem from that heritage.

Although you don't need Mac OS X or Unix to create software, if you're using Unix, you'll probably at least poke around with programming—perhaps first modifying existing programs and then moving on to create new ones. In addition to its terrific stability, Unix provides an environment in which it's easy to connect varying tools in an equally various number of ways. And when you need them, you can create new commands, extending your tool kit as you work.

You can also write simple scripts to automate tasks—for example, to perform backups, automate the transfer of files to other systems, calculate the rate of return on an investment, or search text for certain phrases and highlight them. You could write scripts to create a small database-backed Web site, or to convert batches of images for use on the Web, or to analyze voter-registration or campaign-contribution records. Some users never stop creating new applications: We call them *programmers*.

Mac OS X comes with tools to create and run programs in AppleScript, Perl, Bourne shell, and a couple of other Unix scripting languages. The Mac OS X developer tools include software that allows you to create programs in C, C++, Objective-C, and Java as well. (Throughout this book we assume that you have in fact installed the Developer Tools.) With the exception of AppleScript, none of these programming languages were available to Mac users in the past unless they installed third-party software (such as MacPerl or the CodeWarrior compiler). The Mac OS X

continues on next page

Developer Tools also include the Project Builder and Interface Builder applications, which are graphical interfaces for developing software projects written in C, Objective-C, C++, and Java.

Shell scripts

The vast majority of Unix scripting is done using *shell scripts*. These are written using the language of a Unix *shell*. A Unix shell is the program that provides the command-line interface you will be using. A shell accepts typed commands and provides output in text form; it is a "shell" around the operating system. The Bourne shell is one of the oldest command-line interpreters for Unix (see Chapter 2, "Using the Command Line"). Virtually all of the scripts that control what happens when Unix machines start up are written in the Bourne shell scripting language, including most of the Mac OS X startup files.

If you are excited or impatient, you probably want to take a look at one of the Mac OS X system startup scripts right now! Here's how to do it:

To view a system startup script:

1. Open an OS X (not Classic) text editor— for example, the Textedit application, which you can access through Textedit in the Applications folder.

2. Open the file /System/Library/ StartupItems/Network/Network.

   The file will be opened read-only, so you need not worry about damaging it.

You are looking at the script that configures your network connection on startup (**Figure 1.5**).

```
#!/bin/sh

##
# Apache HTTP Server
##

. /etc/rc.common

StartService ()
{
    if [ "${WEBSERVER:=-NO-}" = "-YES-" ]; then
        ConsoleMessage "Starting Apache web server"
        apachectl start
    fi
}

StopService ()
{
    ConsoleMessage "Stopping Apache web server"
    apachectl stop
}

RestartService ()
{
    if [ "${WEBSERVER:=-NO-}" = "-YES-" ]; then
        ConsoleMessage "Restarting Apache web server"
        apachectl restart
    else
        StopService
    fi
}

RunService "$1"
```

Figure 1.5 The script /System/Library/StartupItems/Network/ Network configures your network connection on startup.

Figure 1.6 on the next page is an example of a script you might use in Mac OS X to make a group of files open in Photoshop when they're double-clicked from the Finder. Using this script and some additional Unix commands, you could instruct your machine to find every file ending in .jpg within a directory (folder) and have those files launch Photoshop when double-clicked from the Finder. And by altering the script, you could do the same thing for just those files that already have the Mac type code for JPEGs, GIFs, and others. (The

```sh
#!/bin/sh
# This a comment. Comments help make the code easier to read.
# This script takes one or more file names as arguments and
# sets the Creator Code for each one to Photoshop.

GETINFO="/Developer/Tools/GetFileInfo"
SETFILE="/Developer/Tools/SetFile"

#  8BIM is the Creator Code for Photoshop
NEW_CREATOR="8BIM"
changed_files=0
total_files=0
for file in "$@" ;   # All the command-line arguments are in $@
do
    total_files=`expr $total_files + 1`;  # keep track of total
if [ -w "$file" ];  # If the file is writeable...
    then
        creator=`$GETINFO -c "$file"`; # Get the Creator code of this file
        if [ ! "$creator" = \"$NEW_CREATOR\" ]
        then
            # Set the file to have the new creator code
            $SETFILE -c "$NEW_CREATOR" "$file"
            changed_files=`expr $changed_files + 1`
        fi
    else
        echo "skipping '$file' - not writeable"
    fi
done

echo "Checked $total_files files"
echo "Set $changed_files files to have creator $NEW_CREATOR"
skipped=`expr $total_files - $changed_files`
echo "Skipped $skipped files"
```

Figure 1.6 You might use this script in Mac OS X to make a group of files open in Photoshop when they're double-clicked from the Finder.

type code is a four-character code that identifies the type of each file. It's a pre–Mac OS X feature that many Mac applications still use.)

This example may look scary now, but don't worry—once you learn some Unix, it will make more sense. For now, just let it wash over you, and understand that when you've read this book (and thus know a bit of Unix), you'll be able to create this sort of script fairly easily. (See Chapter 9, "Creating and Using Scripts," for more on creating shell scripts.)

Perl

Perl is one of the most popular programming languages in the world. Although you can use it to build large, complex programs, it is easy enough to learn that most people begin using it to write small utility programs or CGI programs for Web sites.

Because Perl excels at text processing and can easily interact with SQL databases, it's ideal for building Web pages as well as other data-manipulation projects.

Figure 1.7 is a code listing of a Perl script that outputs plain text files in reverse—the

last line comes out first. This would be difficult, if not impossible, using traditional Macintosh applications.

Java

Although still fairly new, Java has already spread far and wide—partly because it's powerful and partly because its creator, Sun Microsystems, has promoted it very hard.

Programs written in Java can run on only one kind of machine, but that machine is a *virtual machine*—a piece of software. Because a virtual machine is software, it can be written for different hardware platforms. Java virtual machines exist for every major operating system, and an increasing number of small hardware devices (such as cell phones) are able to run Java code. Programs written in Java can often run without changes on many different platforms. The Mac OS X Developer Tools come with a Java compiler and a Java virtual machine. The Java programming language has a large set of tools for creating graphical user interfaces and for communicating across networks.

```
#!/usr/bin/perl
# This a comment. Always use comments.
#
# This script takes one or more file names as arguments and
# outputs the files one line at a time, in reverse order.
# I.e. The last line of the last file comes out first.

while ( $file =  pop(@ARGV) ) {
    open FILE, "$file"; # Open the file for reading
    @lines = <FILE>;    # Read the entire file into @lines
    close FILE;
    while ( $line = pop(@lines) ) {
        print $line;
    }
}
```

Figure 1.7 This Perl script code listing outputs plain text files in reverse, with the last line first.

C

The C programming language is to programming what Greek is to literature—the language of heroes. C is the language in which Unix as we know it was written, and most of the utility programs used with Unix were written in C. In the Unix world, the people who invented Unix could be thought of as heroes, and they wrote their great works in C.

The core of every Unix operating system (the *kernel)* is written almost entirely in C, as is virtually every common Unix utility program, such as ls, pwd, and grep. Many important Unix applications, such as Sendmail and the Apache Web server, are also written in C. In addition, C++, Objective-C, and a number of other important languages stem from or are related to C.

Because so much Unix software is written in C, you're likely to at least modify existing C code if you spend much time working on the Unix platform.

Interacting with other Unix machines

Much of what people do with their Unix systems involves connecting to other Unix systems—for example, logging on to a machine that hosts a Web site to edit files and install software, or arranging to automatically transfer files between two Unix machines.

To ease this process, Mac OS X comes with a widely used program called ssh (Secure *sh*ell) that facilitates secure (encrypted) connections to other machines over the Internet. With ssh you can connect from the command-line interface to other Unix machines and the information exchanged is protected from being read if intercepted. Other programs also use ssh to work over encrypted connections.

Running servers

One of the biggest differences between Mac OS 9 and Mac OS X is that the latter allows you to *reliably* run servers (such as a Web server or an email server) on your computer. You could run these types of servers on Mac OS 9, but because OS 9 was much more likely to crash, you probably wouldn't consider it for serious use. Also, most of the software available for these kinds of servers on Mac OS 9 was closed-source proprietary software, so if the vendor changed its business plan or went out of business, you were left with unsupported software. With Mac OS X, you can use the widely installed, open-source applications that most servers on the Internet use.

You might run a server to provide a service to the rest of the world. Or you might run one because you're developing a system that uses it—for example, a shared calendar/event-planning system—and you want to test it on your local machine and/or network before deploying it. There are all kinds of servers; the following are just a few of those available to you as a Mac OS X user.

Apache Web server

Apache is the most popular Web server in the world—that is, more Web sites use Apache servers than any other. Apache is highly configurable, so it can be adapted to many different situations and specific requirements. Apache comes installed in Mac OS X.

Icecast audio server

Icecast (www.icecast.org) is an open-source audio-streaming system for the Internet. Fairly easy to install and configure, Icecast allows you basically to turn your Mac into an Internet radio station.

Using other Unix applications

In addition to the specific applications mentioned above, there are thousands of Unix applications available. Most are free, some are commercial packages, some are open source. With Mac OS X you can use many of these existing applications to monitor network status, analyze data such as Web-server log files, run mailing lists, create Web publishing systems, and more.

Because there are so many, we can't list even a tenth of them. Below are a few that give some sense of the variety available, plus links to places where you can find more.

Samba Windows file-sharing software

Samba lets you share files from your Macintosh with Windows users over a network. The name Samba comes from SMB (Server Message Block), which is the Windows file-sharing protocol.

SQL database engines

If you are a Mac database user, you have heard of FileMaker Pro, which is a great database with a great user interface. But FileMaker Pro doesn't understand SQL (Structured Query Language), which is what all the big serious databases use. Most database-backed Web sites use SQL databases.

A number of SQL database engines are available for Mac OS X, including MySQL, PostgreSQL, and ProSQL.

Image manipulation with GIMP

GIMP (GNU Image Manipulation Program) (www.gimp.org) is a bargain-basement Unix version of Photoshop. Even though GIMP is not as powerful as the main commercial alternative, it is free, open-source software, and runs on many Unix platforms. Using GIMP requires that you install X Windows (see below).

X Windows

X Windows (www.osxgnu.org/software/Xwin/) is the underlying mechanism for providing a graphical user interface on most Unix systems. Mac OS X uses a different method, Apple's proprietary Aqua interface, but many Unix programs were built for X Windows, so if you install it, you can use these other programs (such as GIMP).

You can use X Windows to provide a graphical display for Unix programs that are running on other machines over the Internet. That is, if you are running X Windows on your Mac, and you have an account on another Unix machine somewhere on the Internet, you may be able to run software on the remote machine and see the graphical display on your Mac.

Email list management with Majordomo

Majordomo (www.greatcircle.com/majordomo/) is a free, open-source application for managing multiple email. To use it, your Macintosh must be set up as an email server. With Majordomo, you can run dozens of mailing lists, with different configurations for each one. For example, one list may require that new subscribers be added by the list owner, while another may allow anyone to self-subscribe via email. Majordomo, which was written in Perl, supports list archives and digests as well as many other features.

HOW YOU WILL BE WORKING WITH UNIX

Where to find more

Thousands of Unix programs are available, with more being created every day. A couple of places to look:

The FreeBSD Ports Collection

This collection (www.freebsd.org/ports/) offered more than 6,700 open-source applications as of spring 2002. These are all Unix programs that work on a number of different Unix versions. Because the Darwin layer of Mac OS X is based largely on FreeBSD, most of these programs should work on Mac OS X.

The easiest way to install many of the FreeBSD programs (and other Unix programs) on Mac OS X is to use the Fink program, which is covered in Chapter 13, "Installing Software from Source Code."

Mac OS X Apps

This Web site (www.macosxapps.com) provides a large and growing collection of Mac OS X applications, most of which have graphical interfaces and can be installed in a manner familiar to Mac users. Many of these programs are not "pure" Unix programs in that they make use of proprietary Mac OS X features such as the Aqua interface. Still, many take advantage of the Unix core of Mac OS X, and so this site is a good place to explore.

How You Will Be Working with Unix

USING THE COMMAND LINE

The command line is the primary interface to Unix. While there are many graphical interfaces for Unix systems, the command-line interface gives you the greatest control over the system. Furthermore, the command-line interface is virtually identical on every Unix system you are likely to use, from Mac OS X to Linux, to FreeBSD to Solaris. Of course there are differences, but there are far more similarities. Once you learn how to use the command line on Mac OS X, you will be comfortable using it on any Unix system.

A reminder before we go further: Whenever a task in this book asks you to type something, always press (Return) at the end of the line unless the task description specifically tells you not to.

Getting to the Command Line

The primary way to get to the command line in Mac OS X is with the Terminal application.

Terminal is an Aqua application that allows you to open multiple windows, each of which provides a place to enter commands and see output from those commands.

Because Terminal is running in the Aqua layer of Mac OS X, you can do anything you'd expect from a Mac graphical application—you can print, copy text and paste into other windows, and adjust preferences such as color and font size.

Practically all of your command-line work in Mac OS X will be done using Terminal.

To open Terminal:

◆ Locate the Terminal application in the Finder by going to the Applications folder and opening the Utilities folder.

◆ Double-click the Terminal application icon. A Terminal window containing a shell prompt opens (**Figure 2.1**).

✔ Tips

■ Put the Terminal icon in the Dock. You will be using it often.

■ When adjusting your Terminal preferences (under Window settings in the Terminal menu), always stick with a mono-spaced font like Monaco (the default) or Courier. Command-line software assumes you are using a mono-spaced (also called fixed-width) font, and proper text layout in Terminal depends on this.

■ Experiment with different colors and font sizes for the text and background in Terminal. For example, we prefer 12-point bright green text on a black background because it looks like the screen on an "old-fashioned" computer terminal.

■ Open more than one Terminal window (by clicking on New Shell under the File menu), and give each one a different color scheme as a way to differentiate them. You can have as many Terminal windows open as you like.

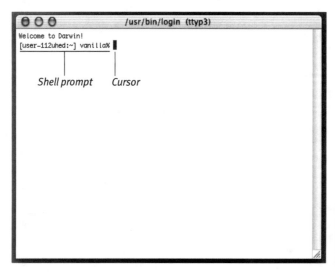

Figure 2.1 This is a screen shot of a window opened in the Terminal application.

Other ways to get to the command line

Using Terminal is by far the most common way to get to the Mac OS X command line, but there are other ways that are useful after you have become proficient in using Unix.

One way is to log in directly to the command line instead of going through the Terminal application in Aqua. **(Note: If you do this, the Aqua interface will not be available until you log out of the command line.)**

To log in to the command line:

1. Enter >console as your user name in the log-in screen. Leave the Password field empty (**Figure 2.2**).

2. Click Login or press [Return].

   This switches you directly to the Darwin layer of Mac OS X. A command-line log-in prompt appears, in white text on a black background (**Figure 2.3**).

   To go back to the Aqua log-in screen, press [Control][D]. Otherwise, proceed to log in to the Darwin layer.

3. Type your short user name, and press [Return] (remember to press [Return] after typing each task item). Note: On every

other Unix system in the world, this would be your user name, but Mac OS X uses the concept of *short user name* to distinguish it from the regular Mac user name.

A command-line password prompt appears.

4. Type your password at the Password prompt.

   Nothing appears on the screen as you type. If you get it wrong, you get another Login prompt, and you are back at step 4.

   If you get it right, the shell prompt appears on your screen.

5. Type logout to return to the Aqua log-in screen.

   There is a long pause before Aqua starts up—as much as a minute. Be patient.

Another way to get to the command line is to start up the machine into *single-user mode*. This boots the machine directly into the Darwin layer so that the command line comes up instead of Aqua. You cannot start Aqua from this mode without rebooting. You should only boot to single-user mode if you are extremely comfortable using Unix. See Chapter 11, "Introduction to System Administration," to learn how to boot into single-user mode.

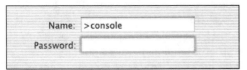

Figure 2.2 You can use the name ">console" to log in to the command line instead of Aqua.

```
Darwin/BSD (yourhostname.domainname.com) (console)
login:
```

Figure 2.3 When you click the Login button, you are switched directly to the Darwin layer of Mac OS X and see the Darwin log-in prompt.

Understanding the Shell Prompt

The first thing you see in the Terminal window is the shell prompt (as we saw in Figure 2.1). The *shell* is a program that sits between you, the user, and the actual operating system. You type commands to the shell, and the shell reads the input, interprets its meaning, and executes the appropriate commands. This is similar to the way the Finder accepts your mouse clicks, interprets their meaning (single click? double click? drag?), and then performs an appropriate action (select item, open item, move item). The shell prompt is a string of text telling you that your shell is waiting for a command line.

The Shell window (in the Terminal folder under Preferences) allows you to specify which shell the Terminal application will use —but don't change the default until you have mastered the material at least through the end of Chapter 5, "Using Files and Directories." Throughout this book we assume you are using the default shell (tcsh) unless noted otherwise.

Now that you know what the shell is, let's start using it.

A Variety of Shells

There are many different shell programs available. The default shell on Mac OS X is called tcsh. Other shells available on Mac OS X are sh, csh, and zsh.

The sh shell is the oldest commonly used shell—sh just means "shell." It is also called the Bourne shell after its principal author, Steve Bourne of Bell Labs. Many important system files are actually small programs (scripts) written using sh commands (see Chapter 9, "Creating and Using Scripts").

The csh shell borrows some of its command syntax from the C programming language (hence the c) and was designed to be an improvement over the sh shell for interactive use. The tcsh shell is a more advanced form of the csh shell (the t comes from two old DEC operating systems). Many Unix experts consider the csh shell a poor tool for creating scripts. A classic essay making

that case is at www.faqs.org/faqs/unix-faq/shell/csh-whynot/.

You can learn more about the tcsh shell at www.tcsh.org.

The zsh shell was designed as an improvement on another shell, ksh (which doesn't come with Mac OS X). It has a command syntax very different from csh and tcsh. You can learn more about zsh at www.zsh.org. If you find out why it is called zsh, let me know.

Another common shell worth mentioning is bash (for "Bourne Again Shell"—one of those Unix puns we warned you about), an improved version of the old standby sh. Although bash doesn't come with Mac OS X, it is easily installed. See Chapter 15, "More Open-Source Software" (at www.peachpit.com/vqp/umox), to learn how to install bash.

Using a Command

To use commands, you type them into the shell at the prompt. The shell executes the command line and displays output (if any), and then gives you another shell prompt. When the shell prompt comes up again, even if there's no other output, your shell is ready to accept another command.

Many command lines (but not all) produce output before returning a new shell prompt. It is quite common in Unix for a command to produce no visible output if it is successful (if it fails, a command should always produce output). In Unix, silence implies success.

To run a command:

◆ ls /Developer/Tools

This is the ls command, which lists the names of files and directories. The output of the command—a list of the tools installed in the Developer/Tools directory —appears and then a new shell prompt follows (**Figure 2.4**).

The command line you just used consists of two parts: the command (ls) and an argument (/Developer/Tools)

```
[localhost:~] vanilla% ls /Developer/Tools
BuildStrings        RezWack             cvswrappers
CpMac               SetFile             lnresolve
DeRez               SplitForks          pbhelpindexer
GetFileInfo         UnRezWack           pbprojectdump
MergePef            WSMakeStubs         pbxcp
MvMac               agvtool             pbxhmapdump
ResMerger           cvs-unwrap          sdp
Rez                 cvs-wrap            uninstall-devtools.pl
[localhost:~] vanilla%
```

Figure 2.4 When you type the command line ls /Developer/Tools, this is what you see.

The parts of a command line

The parts of a command line are separated by spaces. Basic command lines have up to four kinds of components:

◆ The command (required)

◆ *Options* (or *switches* or *flags*) (optional)

◆ *Arguments* (optional)

◆ *Operators* and special characters (optional)

Figure 2.5 shows the different parts of a typical command line (you'll recognize this as the command from Chapter 1 that searched for all instances of the word success in a particular directory).

Each command may have multiple options and multiple arguments.

About the "command" part of the command line

When you enter a command line, the shell assumes that the first item on the line is a command.

There are two types of commands: those that are built into the shell you are using and those that are separate files somewhere on your disk.

The overwhelming majority of Unix commands are of the latter type—that is, Unix commands are usually individual files that are actually small (or not-so-small) programs that perform a specific function, such as listing the contents of a directory.

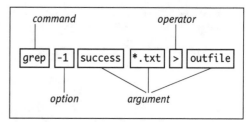

Figure 2.5 The parts of a command line are separated by spaces, and basic command lines have up to four kinds of items in them. This shows the separate parts of the command line.

Unix Commands vs. Mac Applications

Traditional Macintosh applications tend to have a great many features that allow you to accomplish complete projects all from within one application. For example, you can create and manipulate complex documents in a page-layout program. Unix takes a different approach.

In Unix, commands tend to be focused on specific steps you use in a variety of different tasks. For example, where the Mac has a single application (the Finder) for performing many tasks involving files, Unix uses a collection of separate "applications": the ls command lists the contents of a directory, the cd command switches from one directory to another, the cp command copies files, the mv command renames files, and so on.

This difference in approach shows a key difference in philosophy between the traditional Mac and Unix ways of thinking. In Unix, you are expected to combine commands in various ways to accomplish your work; in traditional Mac applications, the program's author is expected to anticipate every kind of task you might want to accomplish and provide a way of doing that.

Unix provides a collection of smaller, "sharper" tools and expects you to decide how to put them together to accomplish your goals.

Your PATH—how the shell finds commands

When the shell sees a command, it evaluates whether it is a built-in command—that is, one that is part of the shell itself (for example, the cd command is built into the tcsh shell). If the command is *not* built in, then the shell assumes the command is an actual file on the disk and looks for it.

If the command does not contain any / (slash) characters, then the shell searches in a list of places known as your PATH for a file whose name matches the command name (see the description of the PATH environment variable in Chapter 7, "Configuring Your Unix Environment"). If the command contains any / characters, then the shell assumes you are telling it not to search your PATH but instead to interpret the command as a *relative* or *absolute path* to the command file. Relative and absolute paths are two ways of specifying Unix filenames on the command line, and we explain relative and absolute paths in Chapter 5, "Using Files and Directories."

About command options

Options (also called switches or flags) modify the way a command behaves. Most commands have at least a few options available, and many commands have a large number of options. As we noted when we talked about Unix's flexibility in Chapter 1, options frequently can be combined.

See Chapter 3, "Getting Help and Using the Unix Manuals," to learn how to ascertain the available options for each command.

To use one option with a command:

◆ ls -s /Developer/Tools

The -s option modifies the output of the ls command, asking for the size of each file. That number (in *blocks*, which correspond to disk space) is now displayed alongside each filename (**Figure 2.6**).

```
[localhost:~] vanilla% ls -s /Developer/Tools
total 1872
  32 BuildStrings      32 RezWack           8 cvswrappers
  56 CpMac             40 SetFile          24 lnresolve
 224 DeRez             40 SplitForks       48 pbhelpindexer
  32 GetFileInfo       40 UnRezWack        40 pbprojectdump
 152 MergePef         336 WSMakeStubs      48 pbxcp
  56 MvMac             32 agvtool          96 pbxhmapdump
  40 ResMerger          8 cvs-unwrap      224 sdp
 232 Rez                8 cvs-wrap         24 uninstall-devtools.pl
[localhost:~] vanilla%
```

Figure 2.6 When you type this command line, ls -s /Developer/Tools, which has one option, the output lists the size of each file in blocks.

Here's a case where we want to combine two options in a command. The -s option gave us file sizes, but using a unit of measurement (blocks) that varies depending on how our disk was formatted. If we add the -k option, the sizes are shown in kilobytes, regardless of the block size on our disk.

To use multiple options with a command:

◆ `ls -s -k /Developer/Tools`

Simply supply both of the options you want.

◆ You can combine two or more options:

`ls -sk /Developer/Tools`

This produces the same output as in the first case and saves typing two characters. **Figure 2.7** shows the output of both command lines. (Unix commands are so short and cryptic because the programmers who invented them wanted to avoid typing.)

```
[localhost:~] vanilla% ls -s -k /Developer/Tools
total 614
  14 BuildStrings    28 MvMac         18 SplitForks     1 cvs-wrap
  28 CpMac           19 ResMerger     18 UnRezWack      3 cvswrappers
 116 DeRez          124 Rez           15 agvtool       22 pbhelpindexer
  14 GetFileInfo     14 RezWack       92 cplutil
  68 MergePef        18 SetFile        2 cvs-unwrap
[localhost:~] vanilla% ls -sk /Developer/Tools
total 614
  14 BuildStrings    28 MvMac         18 SplitForks     1 cvs-wrap
  28 CpMac           19 ResMerger     18 UnRezWack      3 cvswrappers
 116 DeRez          124 Rez           15 agvtool       22 pbhelpindexer
  14 GetFileInfo     14 RezWack       92 cplutil
  68 MergePef        18 SetFile        2 cvs-unwrap
[localhost:~] vanilla%
```

Figure 2.7 This shows there's no difference between what you get when you use the -s and -k options separately and when you combine them in the -sk option.

About command arguments

Most commands accept one or more arguments. An argument is a piece of information the command acts upon, such as the name of a file to display. It's similar to the object of a sentence.

You used a command with a single argument in the tasks above. The single argument was /Developer/Tools, the folder whose contents you wanted to list. A command line can contain multiple arguments.

To use multiple arguments with a command:

◆ ls /Developer /Developer/Tools

You simply add as many arguments as needed on the command line, separated by spaces. In this example, the ls command gets two arguments and lists the contents of both directories (**Figure 2.8**).

✔ Tips

- You can combine multiple options with multiple arguments—for example, ls -sk /Developer /Developer/Tools

- Remember that the shell expects the parts of a command line to be separated by spaces. If an argument has spaces in it, then you need to protect the embedded space(s) from being interpreted as separators. See "About Spaces in the Command Line" below.

Operators and special characters in the command line

A number of special characters often appear in command lines, most frequently the > and & characters.

These special characters are used for a variety of powerful features that manipulate the

```
[localhost:~] vanilla% ls /Developer /Developer/Tools
/Developer:
Applications          Headers              Palettes
Documentation         Java                 ProjectBuilder Extras
Examples              Makefiles            Tools


/Developer/Tools:
BuildStrings          RezWack              cvswrappers
CpMac                 SetFile              lnresolve
DeRez                 SplitForks           pbhelpindexer
GetFileInfo           UnRezWack            pbprojectdump
MergePef              WSMakeStubs          pbxcp
MvMac                 agvtool              pbxhmapdump
ResMerger             cvs-unwrap           sdp
Rez                   cvs-wrap             uninstall-devtools.pl
[localhost:~] vanilla%
```

Figure 2.8 The ls command gets two arguments, /Developer and /Developer/Tools, and lists the contents of both directories.

output of commands. The most common of these operators make it easy to save the output of a command to a file, feed the output of one command into another command, use the output of one command as an argument to another command, and run a command line "in the background" (that is, letting you get a shell prompt back even if the command takes an hour to run).

The use of these powerful features is covered later in this chapter (see "Creating Pipelines of Commands").

Table 2.1 summarizes the most frequently used command-line operators and special characters, with examples of their use.

Stopping commands

Some commands run for a long time, and sometimes they can get "stuck" (perhaps because a command is waiting for some other process to finish, or because of a network problem, or for any number of other reasons) and neither give output nor return you to a

shell prompt. In those cases, you need a way to stop a command once you have started it. Here are two ways to stop a command.

If you are waiting for the shell prompt to appear, then you use ⌃Control⌄C to stop the command.

To stop a command with Control-C:

◆ Press ⌃Control⌄ (usually at the lower left of your keyboard) and simultaneously press ⌃C⌄. This sends what is called an "interrupt" signal to the command, which should stop running and bring up a shell prompt.

✔ Tip

■ If using ⌃Control⌄⌃C⌄ doesn't work, as a last resort you can close the Terminal window, overriding the warning that appears. The stuck command will be stopped. It doesn't hurt Unix for you to close the window; it's just annoying for you.

To stop a command using the kill command:

◆ `kill pid`

You use the `kill` command to stop other commands if you already have a shell prompt. You need to know the *process ID* of the command you want to stop. For details on obtaining process ID numbers, see "About Commands, Processes, and Jobs," later in this chapter.

The `kill` command doesn't always kill a process. It actually sends a signal asking it to stop. The default signal is *hangup*.

Sometimes that isn't strong enough. In those cases you can use signal 9, the kill signal that cannot be ignored:

`kill -9 pid`

Using signal 9 terminates the target with extreme prejudice—the stopped command has no chance to clean up before exiting and may leave temporary files around.

Table 2.1

Operators and Special Characters		
Symbol	**Example and Meaning**	
>	`command > file`	
	Redirect output to `file`.	
>>	`command >> file`	
	Redirect output, appending to `file`.	
<	`command < file`	
	`command` gets input from `file`.	
|	`cmdA | cmdB` (sometimes called the pipe character).	
	Pipe output of `cmdA` into `cmdB`.	
&	`command &`	
	Run `command` in background, returning to shell prompt at once.	
` `	`` cmdA `cmdB` ``	
	Execute `cmdB` first, then use output as an argument to `cmdA` (often called backtick characters).	

USING A COMMAND

Getting help for a command

Most commands have associated documentation in the Unix help system. Unfortunately, Unix help is almost always written for the experienced programmer, not for the novice user, so we have devoted all of Chapter 3 to clarifying it.

You can skip ahead to Chapter 3 and come back if you like, but here is the bare minimum you need to at least begin to explore the help available for commands.

To read the Unix manual for a command:

1. man *command*

This displays the Unix manual for any given command. **Figure 2.9** shows the first screen of the manual for the ls command, displayed by typing man ls.

The man command displays the Unix manual entry for the named command one screen at a time.

2. To move forward one screen, press the [Spacebar] once.

3. To move backward one screen, press [B] once.

4. To quit from the man command and return to a shell prompt: [Q]

You should be back at the shell prompt.

```
LS(1)                    System Reference Manual                    LS(1)

NAME
     ls - list directory contents

SYNOPSIS
     ls [-ACFLRSTWacdfgiklnoqrstux1] [file ...]

DESCRIPTION
     For each operand that names a file of a type other than directory, ls
     displays its name as well as any requested, associated information.  For
     each operand that names a file of type directory, ls displays the names
     of files contained within that directory, as well as any requested, asso-
     ciated information.

     If no operands are given, the contents of the current directory are dis-
     played.  If more than one operand is given, non-directory operands are
     displayed first; directory and non-directory operands are sorted sepa-
     rately and in lexicographical order.

     The following options are available:

     -A      List all entries except for `.' and `..'. Always set for the su-
             per-user.

     -C      Force multi-column output; this is the default when output is to
```

Figure 2.9 When you request help from the manuals, such as man ls, you get an explanation (this only shows a partial amount of output).

Using Common Commands

You've already learned how to perform some basic Unix commands, but now let's run through a series of commands you'll use on a regular basis (we'll go into detail on several of these in later chapters).

To perform some basic commands:

1. cd

The cd command ("change directory") produces no output. Used with no arguments, it tells your shell to set your "working directory" as your home directory.

2. pwd

This command shows your present working directory —where you "are" in the Unix file system. **Figure 2.10** shows typical output from the pwd command.

3. ls

Figure 2.11 shows typical output from ls, which lists the names of files and directories. The actual output depends on what you have in your home directory.

4. echo "Hello there."

The output from the echo command consists of its arguments (in this case, the words "Hello there") (**Figure 2.12**). It also automatically adds a new line (try it with the -n option to not add the new line).

---

pwd—Compare with Aqua

In Aqua, the Finder tells you where you are using the names and positions of windows. One window is always the active window, and the title bar of that window tells you the name of the folder. If the window is the Finder window, then the directory name in the title bar is the equivalent of what the Unix pwd command shows.

```
[localhost:~] vanilla% pwd
/Users/vanilla
[localhost:~] vanilla%
```

Figure 2.10 The pwd command shows your *present working directory*—where you "are" in the Unix file system.

```
[localhost:~] vanilla% ls
Desktop   Documents Library   Movies    Music     Pictures  Public    Sites
[localhost:~] vanilla%
```

Figure 2.11 The ls command lists the names of files and directories. The actual output will depend on what you have in your home directory.

```
[localhost:~] vanilla% echo "Hello there."
Hello there.
[localhost:~] vanilla%
```

Figure 2.12 The output from the echo command consists of two arguments (in this case, "Hello there").

5. echo "Hello $USER, welcome to Unix."

Figure 2.13 shows output from echo, using the $USER *environment variable* in an argument. $USER is replaced by your short user name (the $ usually indicates that the following term is a variable, and the shell substitutes the value of the variable before executing the command; we'll go into detail on *environment variables* in Chapter 7).

6. echo "$USER created this" > file.txt

In this case, the output from the echo commands doesn't go to your screen, but rather it is *redirected* into the file named file.txt, either creating the file with this specific content or copying over anything within it. For more on redirection and output, see "About Standard Input and Output," later in this chapter.

7. ls

Figure 2.14 shows the output from the ls command. The files listed now include file.txt, created in the previous step.

8. cat file.txt

The cat command, derived from the word *concatenate*, displays the contents of the file (**Figure 2.15**), again based on the command in step 6 (*concatenate* actually means "combine"; if you read the Unix manual section on cat with man cat, you will see how it can be used to combine several files).

---

echo—Compare with Aqua

The Aqua interface doesn't really have any equivalent of the echo command. Echo exemplifies a tool that is unique to command-line interfaces.

```
[localhost:~] vanilla% echo "Hello $USER, welcome to Unix."
Hello vanilla, welcome to Unix.
[localhost:~] vanilla%
```

Figure 2.13 This shows the output from echo, using the $USER environment variable in an argument. $USER will be replaced by your short username.

```
[localhost:~] vanilla% ls
Desktop    Library    Music      Public     file.txt
Documents  Movies     Pictures   Sites
[localhost:~] vanilla%
```

Figure 2.14 This output from the ls command now includes file.txt.

```
[localhost:~] vanilla% cat file.txt
vanilla created this
[localhost:~] vanilla%
```

Figure 2.15 The cat command, derived from the word *concatenate*, displays the contents of a file.

cp—Compare with Aqua

In the Finder, you copy files by Option-dragging them, or by selecting them and choosing File > Duplicate. After copying them, you can rename them in a separate operation.

At the command line, you select files to be copied by naming them, and then enter their new names at the same time.

9. `cp file.txt filecopy.txt`

   cp stands for *copy*. You have made a copy of `file.txt` called `filecopy.txt`. Run the `ls` command again to see it (**Figure 2.16**).

10. `rm filecopy.txt`

   The `rm` command *removes* the file. Run the `ls` command again to confirm that it is gone.

11. `mkdir testdir`

   The `mkdir` command creates (or *makes*) a new directory (that's what Unix calls folders), in this instance named `testdir`.

12. Go back out to the Finder (under Aqua) and open your home directory. You should see the file `file.txt` and the directory `testdir` (**Figure 2.17**).

```
[localhost:~] vanilla% ls
Desktop     Library     Music       Public      file.txt
Documents   Movies      Pictures    Sites       filecopy.txt
[localhost:~] vanilla%
```

Figure 2.16 Running the `ls` command again shows you have made a copy of `file.txt` called `filecopy.txt`.

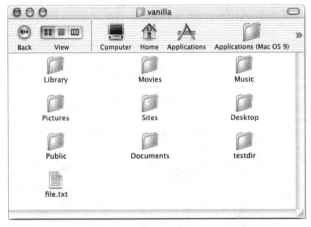

Figure 2.17 The Finder window now shows the new file and directory.

USING COMMON COMMANDS

13. `cd testdir`

You have told your shell to change from the current directory to the directory named `testdir`. Notice that your shell prompt has changed to reflect your new directory (**Figure 2.18**).

14. `pwd`

This confirms that you are indeed in the new directory (**Figure 2.19**).

15. `date`

The `date` command displays the current date and time (**Figure 2.20**); unless you've perfected time travel, your output will be different.

16. `date > dates.txt`

This redirects the output of the `date` command into a file named dates.txt. It is often useful to save the output of a command.

17. `date >> dates.txt`

This time we redirect the output using the >> operator (this redirects the output and appends it to the file instead of replacing the contents).

18. `cat dates.txt`

The file contains the results of both redirects from steps 16 and 17 (**Figure 2.21**).

19. `mv dates.txt newname.txt`

The `mv` command renames (or *moves*) a file. In Unix, a file's name is actually the name of its location, so the same command is used to rename and to move files. Run the `ls` command to see that the file `dates.txt` has been renamed to `newname.txt` (**Figure 2.22**).

```
[localhost:~] vanilla% cd testdir
[localhost:testdir] vanilla%
```

Figure 2.18 After you use the `cd` command, the shell prompt changes.

```
[localhost:testdir] vanilla% pwd
/Users/vanilla/testdir
[localhost:testdir] vanilla%
```

Figure 2.19 Running the `pwd` command again shows your new working directory.

```
[localhost:testdir] vanilla% date
Thu Apr  4 14:56:35 PST 2002
[localhost:testdir] vanilla%
```

Figure 2.20 The `date` command displays the current date and time.

```
[localhost:testdir] vanilla% date > dates.txt
[localhost:testdir] vanilla% date >> dates.txt
[localhost:testdir] vanilla% cat dates.txt
Thu Apr  4 15:00:41 PST 2002
Thu Apr  4 15:00:47 PST 2002
[localhost:testdir] vanilla%
```

Figure 2.21 Using redirection, you get a file that contains the results of both redirects.

```
[localhost:testdir] vanilla% ls
newname.txt
[localhost:testdir] vanilla%
```

Figure 2.22 Running the `ls` command again shows the renamed file.

```
[localhost:testdir] vanilla% ls
dates.txt newname.txt
[localhost:testdir] vanilla%
```

Figure 2.23 Running the ls command again shows the file created with the >> operator.

```
[localhost:testdir] vanilla% ls
[localhost:testdir] vanilla%
```

Figure 2.24 Note that when there is nothing to list, the ls command gives no output.

```
[localhost:testdir] vanilla% cd
[localhost:~] vanilla%
```

Figure 2.25 Your shell prompt changes when you use the cd command.

cat—Compare with Aqua

The cat command not only displays a single file (as shown in step 8 above), but it can be given multiple filenames as arguments in order to display them all, in one long output (hence the name *concatenate*).

The closest thing Aqua has to the cat command is the ability to open multiple files with one application by selecting several files and dragging them all onto an application icon, but there isn't really a direct equivalent.

mv—Compare with Aqua

In the Finder, you move files by dragging them to their new location. Renaming them is a separate operation.

At the command line, you can move and rename files in the same operation.

20. date >> dates.txt

The >> operator creates a file if it doesn't already exist (**Figure 2.23**).

21. rm *.txt

The * operator is used in the command line as a *wildcard* to match all the files ending in .txt. As a result, the rm command actually receives two arguments—dates.txt and newname.txt—and acts on both of them. For more on wildcard operators, see "Wildcards," later in this chapter. Run the ls command to confirm that there are now no files in the current directory; you simply get a shell prompt back (**Figure 2.24**).

22. cd

This takes you back to your home directory. Notice that your shell prompt changes (**Figure 2.25**).

< and >—Compare with Aqua

The Aqua interface has no equivalent to the command lines' ability to redirect output. This is a good example of the difference between the Unix command-line interface and a graphical interface such as Aqua.

The command line is text oriented: Everything is assumed to be text output and can be fed into anything else. (See especially the | operator later in this chapter, in "Creating Pipelines of Commands").

In Aqua, each application is assumed to produce output of a different kind, and applications cannot normally feed their output directly into each other without saving to a file first.

About Commands, Processes, and Jobs

Commands fall into two categories: some commands are built into the shell you are using (for example, the **cd** command), while most are actually separate programs.

To see a list of basic Unix commands:

◆ `ls /bin`

The `/bin` directory contains all of the commands we used in the examples earlier in this chapter. Each command appears as a separate file (**Figure 2.26**). Notice that your shell program (**tcsh**) is included. It, too, is essentially a command, albeit a larger, interactive one.

✔ Tip

■ Other places to see lists of Unix commands are `/usr/bin`, `/sbin`, and `/usr/sbin`. (The *bin* is short for "binary," as most Unix commands are binary files. Not all commands are binary files; some are executable text files or *scripts*.)

```
[localhost:~] vanilla% ls /bin
[          csh        echo       ln         ps         sh         test
bash       date       ed         ls         pwd        sleep      zsh
cat        dd         expr       mkdir      rcp        stty
chmod      df         hostname   mv         rm         sync
cp         domainname kill       pax        rmdir      tcsh
[localhost:~] vanilla%
```

Figure 2.26 The `/bin` directory contains all of the commands we used in the examples earlier in this chapter.

Every time you issue a command that is not already built into a shell, you are starting what Unix calls a *process* or a *job*. You will encounter both terms in Unix literature.

Every process is assigned an identification number when it starts up, called the *PID* (*Process ID*), as well as its own slice of memory space (this is one of the reasons why Unix is so stable—each process has its own inviolable memory space). At any given moment, there are dozens of processes running on your computer.

To see all the processes you own:

◆ ps -U *username*

Fill in your short user name for username. **Figure 2.27** shows typical output with a variety of programs running. Notice how even Aqua programs like iTunes are listed —underneath it all, they are all running on Unix.

The first column of output lists the PID of each process. (Review "Stopping Commands" earlier in this chapter for an example of using a PID number.)

```
[localhost:~] vanilla% ps -U vanilla
  PID  TT  STAT     TIME COMMAND
   68  ??  Ss      0:19.58 /System/Library/Frameworks/ApplicationServices.framew
  366  ??  Rs     99:34.05 /System/Library/Frameworks/Kerberos.framework/Servers
 1065  ??  Ss     14:29.69 /System/Library/CoreServices/WindowServer console
 1066  ??  Ss      0:02.51 /System/Library/CoreServices/loginwindow.app/loginwin
 1071  ??  Ss      0:03.85 /System/Library/CoreServices/pbs
 1075  ??  S       2:05.73 /System/Library/CoreServices/Finder.app/Contents/MacO
 1076  ??  S       0:21.82 /System/Library/CoreServices/Dock.app/Contents/MacOS/
 1077  ??  S       0:28.22 /System/Library/CoreServices/SystemUIServer.app/Conte
 1078  ??  S       0:00.23 /Applications/iTunes.app/Contents/Resources/iTunesHel
 1080  ??  R     493:55.67 /System/Library/CoreServices/Classic Startup.app/Cont
 1081  ??  S       1:56.28 /Applications/Utilities/Terminal.app/Contents/MacOS/T
 1106  ??  S       7:38.94 /Applications/Acrobat Reader 5.0/Contents/MacOS/Acrob
 1142  ??  S     332:09.07 /Applications/Mozilla/Mozilla.app/Contents/MacOS/Mozi
 1357  ??  Ss      0:00.45 /usr/bin/hdid -f /Users/vanilla/Desktop/Eudora 51b21.
 1363  ??  S       0:00.90 /Applications/Preview.app/Contents/MacOS/Preview -psn
 1365  ??  S       0:01.13 /Applications/TextEdit.app/Contents/MacOS/TextEdit -p
 1436  ??  S       1:25.06 /Applications/Eudora/Eudora 5.1 (OS X) /Applications/
 1082 std  Ss      0:00.64 -tcsh (tcsh)
[localhost:~] vanilla%
```

Figure 2.27 When you type ps -U username, you see the variety of programs running, even Aqua programs like iTunes.

ABOUT COMMANDS, PROCESSES, AND JOBS

To see all the processes on the system:

1. `ps -aux`

Figure 2.28 shows typical output from using the -aux options to `ps` (for *processes*).

2. `ps -auxw`

Figure 2.29 shows output when using the -auxw options. The w makes the output wider. **Table 2.2** shows the common options for the `ps` command.

✔ Tips

■ You can use two w's to make the output even wider—for example, `ps -auxww`.

■ Combine the -U option with the -aux options to show a particular user's processes: `ps -aux -U` *username*.

```
[localhost:~] vanilla% ps -aux
USER      PID  %CPU %MEM    VSZ    RSS  TT  STAT   TIME COMMAND
matisse  1142  6.9  12.2  160180  80116  ??  S     333:52.71 /Applications/Mozil
matisse  1080  6.0  18.3 1107988 119684  ??  R     507:33.80 /System/Library/Cor
matisse   366  3.4  0.1    5356    944  ??  Ss     99:54.01 /System/Library/Fra
matisse  1065  0.6  3.9   54776  25692  ??  Ss     14:43.58 /System/Library/Cor
root       72  0.0  0.0    1276    100  ??  Ss      1:49.77 update
root       75  0.0  0.0    1296    104  ??  Ss      0:00.01 dynamic_pager -H 40
root      100  0.0  0.1    2332    372  ??  Ss      0:01.09 /sbin/autodiskmount
root      125  0.0  0.2    3836   1516  ??  Ss      0:03.41 configd
root      163  0.0  0.0    1288    156  ??  Ss      0:03.17 syslogd
root      184  0.0  0.4   20736   2416  ??  Ss      0:00.24 /usr/libexec/CrashR
root      206  0.0  0.1    1580    404  ??  Ss      0:02.03 netinfod -s local
root      213  0.0  0.1    2448    520  ??  Rs      0:08.26 lookupd
root      223  0.0  0.0    1528    304  ??  S<s     1:03.80 ntpd -f /var/run/nt
root      231  0.0  0.3    8964   2040  ??  S       1:15.81 AppleFileServer
root      236  0.0  0.2    3104   1124  ??  Ss      0:08.35 /System/Library/Cor
root      243  0.0  0.0    1288    116  ??  Ss      0:00.00 inetd
root      254  0.0  0.0    1276     84  ??  S       0:00.00 nfsiod -n 4
root      255  0.0  0.0    1276     84  ??  S       0:00.00 nfsiod -n 4
root      263  0.0  0.0    2192    316  ??  Ss      0:00.04 automount -m /Netwo
root      266  0.0  0.2    3740   1148  ??  S       0:00.27 DirectoryService
root      273  0.0  0.1    2432    932  ??  Ss      0:40.56 /usr/sbin/httpd
www       277  0.0  0.1    2432    600  ??  S       0:00.25 /usr/sbin/httpd
root      282  0.0  0.1    2392    960  ??  Ss      0:01.60 /System/Library/Cor
[localhost:~] vanilla%
```

Figure 2.28 Using the -aux options to ps (for *processes*) gives you this typical output.

```
[localhost:~] vanilla% ps -auxw
USER      PID %CPU %MEM     VSZ    RSS TT  STAT     TIME COMMAND
matisse   366  3.2  0.1    5356    944 ??  Rs      99:55.39
/System/Library/Frameworks/Kerberos.framework/Servers/CCacheServer.app/
matisse  1080  3.1 18.3 1107988 119692 ??  S      508:31.05 /System/Library/CoreServices/Classic
Startup.app/Contents/Resources/Tru
matisse  1142  2.1 12.2  160180  80116 ??  S      334:01.62
/Applications/Mozilla/Mozilla.app/Contents/MacOS/Mozilla /Applications/
matisse  1081  1.3  1.6   76212  10168 ??  S        2:04.99
/Applications/Utilities/Terminal.app/Contents/MacOS/Terminal -psn_0_222
matisse  1065  0.3  3.9   54756  25672 ??  Ss      14:46.19 /System/Library/CoreServices/WindowServer
console
root       75  0.0  0.0    1296    104 ??  Ss       0:00.01 dynamic_pager -H 40000000 -L 160000000 -S
80000000 -F /private/var/vm/s
root      100  0.0  0.1    2332    372 ??  Ss       0:01.09 /sbin/autodiskmount -va
root      125  0.0  0.2    3836   1516 ??  Ss       0:03.41 configd
root      163  0.0  0.0    1288    156 ??  Ss       0:03.17 syslogd
root      184  0.0  0.4   20736   2416 ??  Ss       0:00.24 /usr/libexec/CrashReporter
root      206  0.0  0.1    1580    404 ??  Ss       0:02.03 netinfod -s local
root      213  0.0  0.1    2448    520 ??  Ss       0:08.26 lookupd
root      223  0.0  0.0    1528    304 ??  S<s      1:03.81 ntpd -f /var/run/ntp.drift -p
/var/run/ntpd.pid
root      231  0.0  0.3    8964   2040 ??  S        1:15.84 AppleFileServer
root      236  0.0  0.2    3104   1124 ??  Ss       0:08.35
/System/Library/CoreServices/coreservicesd
root      243  0.0  0.0    1288    116 ??  Ss       0:00.00 inetd
[localhost:~] vanilla%
```

Figure 2.29 Using the -auxw options to ps gives you this partial output; adding the w gives you a wider output.

Table 2.2

Common Options for ps

Option	Meaning
-a	Display processes owned by all users.
-u	Display more information, including CPU usage, process ownership, and memory usage.
-x	Include any process not started from a Terminal window.
-w	Wide listing—display the full command name of each process up to 132 characters per line. If more than w is used, adding ps will ignore the width of your Terminal window.
-U *username*	Show process for specified user.

To see a constantly updated list of the top processes:

1. `top`

   The `top` command displays a frequently updated list of processes, sorted by how much processing power each one is using—that is, which one is at the *top* of the list of resource usage (**Figure 2.30**). (The reason they're at 0% is that most processes, at any given time, aren't using that much processor time.)

   Top runs until you stop it by typing:

2. `q`

   This stops the `top` command and returns you to a shell prompt.

✔ Tip

■ If you want to save the output of `top` to a file (such as using the > redirect operator), then use the -l switch and specify how many samples you want. For example, to get three samples use:

   `top -l3 > toplog.`

```
[localhost:~] vanilla% top
Processes:  52 total, 2 running, 50 sleeping... 151 threads          17:44:12
Load Avg:  0.36, 0.51, 0.59     CPU usage:  9.1% user, 90.9% sys, 0.0% idle
SharedLibs: num =  119, resident = 26.0M code, 1.80M data, 6.98M LinkEdit
MemRegions: num = 4441, resident =  203M + 7.88M private,  106M shared
PhysMem:  61.6M wired, 89.8M active,  367M inactive,  518M used,  122M free
VM: 2.49G + 50.8M   17504(17504) pageins, 156(156) pageouts
  PID COMMAND     %CPU   TIME    #TH #PRTS #MREGS RPRVT  RSHRD  RSIZE  VSIZE
 1539 top         0.0%  0:00.24   1   14    15   288K   328K   524K  1.45M
 1436 Eudora 5.1  0.0%  1:25.76   7  113   220  8.14M  14.1M  10.9M   102M
 1365 TextEdit    0.0%  0:01.13   1   66    81  2.20M  7.46M  3.97M  64.8M
 1363 Preview     0.0%  0:00.90   1   62    85  2.38M  7.50M  4.09M  64.9M
 1357 hdid        0.0%  0:00.45   1   11    37   808K   340K   676K  2.05M
 1142 Mozilla     0.0%  5:35:11   7  102   879  59.0M  33.7M  78.2M   156M
 1106 Acrobat Re  0.0%  7:43.54   1   54   183  6.68M  24.6M  18.6M  88.8M
 1082 tcsh        0.0%  0:00.75   1   24    15   480K   656K   960K  5.72M
 1081 Terminal    0.0%  2:07.07   6  120   138  4.20M  11.8M  9.93M  74.4M
 1080 TruBlueEnv  0.0%  8:38:24  18  187   489  90.8M  28.6M   117M  1.06G
 1078 iTunesHelp  0.0%  0:00.23   1   45    39   528K  2.90M  1.00M  38.1M
 1077 SystemUISe  0.0%  0:28.49   2  107   104  1.46M  6.96M  2.60M  61.0M
 1076 Dock        0.0%  0:22.69   3  108   105  2.07M  8.41M  4.60M  63.1M
 1075 Finder      0.0%  2:05.74   3  112   263  13.6M  14.1M  18.9M  83.1M
 1071 pbs         0.0%  0:03.85   1   29    29  1.98M   812K  2.86M  19.4M
 1066 loginwindo  0.0%  0:02.51   7  133   122  2.71M  6.93M  4.50M  51.5M
 1065 Window Man  0.0% 14:52.00   3  182   219  2.13M  23.1M  25.1M  53.5M
  948 httpd       0.0%  0:00.22   1    9    66   140K  1.23M   604K  2.38M
  947 httpd       0.0%  0:00.17   1    9    66   140K  1.23M   604K  2.38M
[localhost:~] vanilla%
```

Figure 2.30 The `top` command displays a frequently updated list of processes, sorted by how much processing power each one is using.

The Danger of a Space Misplaced

A bug in the installation software for an early version of iTunes could cause the erasure of an entire hard drive if the first character in the drive's name was a space.

The installation script did not allow for that possibility and neglected to use quotes where it should have. Even professional programmers occasionally have trouble dealing with spaces in filenames on Unix systems.

About Spaces in the Command Line

As we have seen, the shell uses spaces to separate the parts of the command line. Having two or more spaces separate a command from its options or its arguments doesn't change anything. When your shell acts on your command line, it breaks it into pieces by looking at where the spaces are. The following command lines both do the same thing:

```
ls -l
ls      -l
```

But this one is very different:

```
ls -  l
```

In the first two cases the shell sees two items: `ls` and `-l` In the third case the shell sees three items: `ls`, `-`, and `l`.

But there are times when you have to include a space inside an argument—such as in a filename that itself contains spaces. Consider what would happen if you tried the command line

```
ls /Applications (Mac OS 9)
```

If you don't do something special to handle spaces in command-line arguments, you will have problems. The shell treats the spaces as separators, and you will get unexpected and probably undesired results. (**Figure 2.31**)

Here are two ways to handle spaces safely in command-line arguments.

```
[localhost:~] vanilla% ls /Applications (Mac OS 9)
Badly placed ()'s.
[localhost:~] vanilla%
```

Figure 2.31 When you use unprotected spaces in a command-line argument, you get an error message about the misplaced parentheses.

To protect spaces using quotes:

1. `ls "/Applications (Mac OS 9)"`

When you enclose the argument in quotes, the shell treats everything within the quotes as a single entity.

2. You may also use single quotes:

`ls '/Applications (Mac OS 9)'`

✔ Tip

- Using single quotes around a string of characters eliminates the effect of any special character, including the $ we saw earlier for environment variables. Compare

`echo 'hello $USER'`

with

`echo "hello $USER"`

The first one echoes the exact characters, while the second identifies the user.

To protect spaces using the backslash:

◆ `ls /Applications\ (Mac\ OS\ 9)`

The backslash character (\) is often used in Unix to *escape* a character. This means "make the next character not special." In this case it removes the special meaning of "separator" from the space character. This is called *escaping a character*.

✔ Tip

- Many Unix shells (including the default shell on Mac OS X) provide a feature called *filename completion*. When typing a part of a command line that is an already-existing file, you can type just part of it and then press Tab; the shell tries to fill in the rest for you.

Wildcards

Arguments to commands are frequently file-names. These might be the names of files the command should read, copy, or move. If you want to act on a number of files, you don't want to have to type every filename, especially when all the filenames have some pattern in common.

That's where wildcards come in. Wildcards (often called glob-patterns) are special characters you can type in a command line to make a command apply to a group of files whose names match some pattern—for example, all files ending in .jpg.

When the shell reads a command line, it expands any glob-patterns by replacing them with all the filenames that match. The shell then executes the command line, using the new list of arguments with the command.

To use a glob-pattern to match all filenames starting with Hello:

◆ `ls Hello*`

The asterisk (`*`) is the glob character that matches any number (zero or more) of characters.

The shell finds all the filenames that begin with `Hello` and substitutes that list for the `Hello*` on the command line.

So if the directory contains files with the names `Hello`, `HelloTest`, and `HelloGoodbye`, then the shell changes the command line with the wildcard into

`ls -l Hello HelloGoodbye HelloTest`

✔ Tip

■ You can use more than one glob-pattern in a command line, such as

`rm *.jpg *.gif`

This removes all the `.jpg` and `.gif` files from the current directory.

To use a glob-pattern to match only one single character:

◆ `ls "File?"`

The `?` character matches any single character. So the example above would match files with names such as `FileA`, `File3`, `Files`, and so on. It would not match `File23` because the pattern only matches one character.

✔ Tip

■ You can combine the `?` and `*` glob characters together. For example,

`ls ??.*`

This would list files whose names begin with exactly two characters, followed by a period, followed by anything. (The period is matched literally.)

More specialized glob-patterns

Sometimes you want to use a list of files that matches a more specific pattern. For this you might use a more complex kind of pattern.

To match a range of characters:

1. `ls /var/log/system.log.[0-3].gz`

   would result in output similar to that shown in **Figure 2.32**.

   The `[ ]` characters are used to create a glob-pattern called a *character class*. The resulting pattern matches any single character in the class. A range of characters can be indicated by using the hyphen, so that `[0-3]` is the same as `[0123]`.

2. Ranges may be alphabetical as well as numeric:

   `ls Alpha-[A-D]`

3. Unix files names are case-sensitive. You can match either by including both in the character class:

   `ls Alpha-[A-Da-d]`

✔ Tip

- You can create a character class that is quite arbitrary—for example, the glob-pattern

  `Photo-[AD]`

  matches only `Photo-A` and `Photo-D`.

To negate a character class:

- ◆ Use the `^` character as the first character in the character class.

  When you do this, the glob-pattern `*[^3-8]` matches anything that does not end in 3, 4, 5, 6, 7, or 8 (the `*` matches anything, the `[^3-8]` means "do not match 3-8").

Patterns and rules similar to those described here are used in many different Unix tools, especially in a set of tools called regular expressions. See Chapter 4, "Useful Unix Utilities," for more on regular expressions.

```
[localhost:~] vanilla% ls /var/log/system.log.[0-3].gz
/var/log/system.log.0.gz  /var/log/system.log.2.gz
/var/log/system.log.1.gz  /var/log/system.log.3.gz
[localhost:~] vanilla%
```

Figure 2.32 This shows the output when you use a glob-pattern — in this case [0-3] — for a range of characters.

About Standard Input and Output

Normally, the output from command lines shows up on your screen. You type in a command and press (Return), and the resulting output shows up on your screen. This is actually a special case of the more general-purpose way that Unix handles both input and output.

All Unix commands come with two input/output devices, called `stdin` (for *standard input*) and `stdout` (for *standard output*). You can't see the `stdin` and `stdout` devices the same way you see a printer, but they are always there. You might like to think of `stdin` and `stdout` as valves or hose-connectors stuck on the outside of every command. Think of the `stdout` connector as being fed to your screen, and your keyboard feeding the `stdin` connector.

You have seen redirection of `stdout` with the `>` and `>>` operators earlier in this chapter. In this section, you will learn more about redirecting `stdout`, and also how to redirect `stdin`—that is, to have a command get input from someplace other than the keyboard—and how to connect the `stdout` of one command to the `stdin` of another, creating what is called a *pipeline*. This ability to connect several commands together is one of the most important features of Unix's flexibility.

Besides `stdin` and `stdout`, there is one more virtual connection on each command, `stderr` (for *standard error*), which is output connection for warning and error messages. If a command issues an error message, it comes out of the `stderr` connector, which is normally connected to your screen (same as `stdout`). If you redirect `stdout` to a file (with `>`), `stderr` still goes to your screen. You can redirect `stderr` as well, though.

`stdin`, `stdout`, and `stderr` are often capitalized in Unix manuals and literature. Both upper- and lowercase usage is correct.

Figure 2.33 illustrates the concept of the `stdin`, `stdout`, and `stderr` connectors.

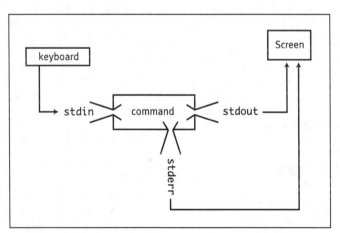

Figure 2.33 Here's how the normal connections of stdin, stdout, and stderr work.

Redirecting stdout

The most common form of redirection is to redirect the output of a command into a file. You will redirect stdout to a file when you want to save the output for later use such as editing or viewing.

To save output in a file:

◆ Add > *filename* to the command line.
For example,

ls /Users > users

redirects the output into the file named users. If the file does not already exist, it is created. If the file does exist, the contents are overwritten.

✔ Tip

■ Sometimes you want to simply throw away the output of a command without ever seeing it. To do this, redirect the output into the special file called /dev/null. For example,

noisy_command > /dev/null

■ Anything written to /dev/null is simply discarded. It's a good place to send insults and complaints.

Sometimes you will want to add the redirected output to a file instead of overwriting the contents:

To append output to a file:

◆ Use >> *filename* at the end of the command—for example,

ls /Users >> users

redirects the output to the file called users, or creates the file if it did not already exist.

Redirecting stderr

Stderr can be redirected as well. One reason to do this is to save errors into a log file. Another reason is to not have warning and error messages clutter up your screen.

To redirect stderr to a file:

◆ Use >& *filename*
In the tcsh shell you cannot redirect stdout and stderr separately, but you can make stderr go to the same file as stdout. For example,

ls /bin >& outfile

puts the stdout and stderr output into the file named outfile. You can use >>& to append instead of overwriting an existing file.

In the bash shell you can redirect stdout and stderr separately.

Redirecting stdin

Sometimes you'll want a command to get its input from a file you have prepared. For example, you might have prepared the text of an email message and want to feed it into the mail command, or you have a list of file names you want to feed into a program.

Most Unix commands allow you to redirect standard input and have it come from a file instead the keyboard.

To take standard input from a file:

◆ Add < *filename* to the end of the command.
For example, if you have a file that contains a list of 30 file names, you might type

ls -l < *list_of_files*

instead of

ls -l *file1 file2 file3*

... and so on.

Creating Pipelines of Commands

Another way to manipulate `stdin` and `stdout` is to have one command take its input directly from the output of another command. To do this, Unix uses the `|`, or *pipe*, character to connect commands together to form *pipelines*, with the `stdout` of each command being piped into the `stdin` of the next one. The enables you to create an almost infinite variety of command lines processing input and output to what are nothing more than miniature custom applications.

To pipe the output of one command into another:

1. Type the first command that produces output, but don't press Return until the last step below.

   This can be any command (along with options and arguments) that produces output on `stdout`. For example,

   `ls -l /bin`

   lists the contents of /bin, where the executable files for many commands are stored (**Figure 2.34**). But let's say we want to know the modification date and the filename. Noticing that this information starts 38 characters into each line, we might pipe the output of the `ls` command into the `cut` command, telling `cut` to show us only character 38 and up from each line.

```
[localhost:~] vanilla% ls -l /bin
total 4208
-r-xr-xr-x  1 root  wheel      13728 Dec 20 22:24 [
lrwxr-xr-x  1 root  wheel         19 Dec 20 22:25 bash -> /usr/local/bin/bash
-r-xr-xr-x  1 root  wheel      13980 Dec 20 22:25 cat
-r-xr-xr-x  1 root  wheel      13852 Dec 20 22:22 chmod
-r-xr-xr-x  1 root  wheel      19012 Dec 20 22:25 cp
-r-xr-xr-x  1 root  wheel     318716 Dec 20 22:25 csh
-r-xr-xr-x  1 root  wheel      14716 Dec 20 22:22 date
-r-xr-xr-x  1 root  wheel      22580 Dec 20 22:23 dd
-r-xr-sr-x  1 root  operator   18660 Dec 20 22:23 df
-r-xr-xr-x  1 root  wheel       9856 Dec 20 22:24 domainname
-r-xr-xr-x  1 root  wheel       9216 Dec 20 22:24 echo
-r-xr-xr-x  1 root  wheel      56304 Dec 20 22:23 ed

(...output truncated for brevity...)
```

Figure 2.34 Running `ls -l /bin` lists the contents of /bin, where the executable files for many commands are stored.

2. Add the | character at the end of the command.

The | character catches the output from what is on its left and passes it to the stdin of what is on its right.

3. Add the command that will receive its input from the pipe. Continuing our example, the command line would now look like this:

```
ls -l /bin | cut -c38-
```

and the result would look like **Figure 2.35**. Now you can press ⎡Return⎤. Or if you wanted to redirect the output of the pipeline to a file, the final command line would be:

```
ls -l /bin | cut -c38- > outfile
```

Before this next task will work on your Mac OS X system, you need to make a small fix; see Chapter 14, "Installing and Configuring Servers," the section "Fixing the Permissions on the Root Directory so Sendmail Will Work." Once you have made the fix, and assuming your computer is connected to the Internet, you can pipe the output of any command into an email message for another user on the Internet.

To pipe the output of a command into email:

◆ *command* | mail -s "*subject*" address
command can be any command line that produces output on stdout. *Subject* is the subject of the email message, and *address* is a valid email address.

```
[localhost:~] vanilla% ls -l /bin | cut -c38-

Dec 20 22:24 [
Dec 20 22:25 bash -> /usr/local/bin/bash
Dec 20 22:25 cat
Dec 20 22:22 chmod
Dec 20 22:25 cp
Dec 20 22:25 csh
Dec 20 22:22 date
Dec 20 22:23 dd
Dec 20 22:23 df
Dec 20 22:24 domainname
Dec 20 22:24 echo
Dec 20 22:23 ed


(...output truncated for brevity...)
```

Figure 2.35 Running ls -l /bin | cut -c38- gives this partial output.

Running a Command in the Background

Some commands take a while to run. For example, a command that searches through a large number of files or a command that must read a large amount of input may take more time than you're willing to twiddle your thumbs.

It is a simple matter to have a command run in the background and get a shell prompt right away so you can keep on working. The command keeps running—you can stop it or bring it to the foreground if you like—but you can let the operating system worry about the command while you do other things.

To run a command line in the background:

◆ Add the & character at the end of the command line.

At the end of any command line, you can add the & character so that the entire command line runs in the background.

The shell shows you the background job number and the process ID numbers for each command on the command line, and gives you a shell prompt right away.

Figure 2.36 shows an example of getting three samples from the top command and sending them in email.

Once the job is finished running, the shell displays a notice the next time it gives you a new shell prompt. That is, the shell does not spontaneously notify you, but it waits and displays the notice along with the next shell prompt (**Figure 2.37**).

✔ Tip

■ If a background job needs input from you, it simply sits and waits patiently—possibly forever. Before putting a job in the background, you should have a good idea of how it behaves normally.

The [1] is the Job ID number

    519 is the process ID of the top command

        520 is process ID of the mail command

```
[localhost:~] vanilla% top -l3 | mail -s "3 samples from top" matisse@matisse.net &
[1]  519  520
[localhost:~] vanilla%
```

Figure 2.36 Running a command in the background, here you've gotten three samples from the top command and sent them in email.

```
[localhost:~] vanilla%
    [1]  - Done          top -l3 | mail -s 3 samples from top matisse@matisse.net
[localhost:~] vanilla%
```

Figure 2.37 The shell notifies you when the job is completed.

You can have several jobs running in the background, and you can bring any of them back to the foreground, or stop any of them by using the kill command, discussed earlier in this chapter.

To see a list of jobs running in the background:

◆ jobs

The jobs command displays a list of background jobs started from the current shell (**Figure 2.38**). If you have multiple Terminal windows open, each has its own list of background jobs.

Even if a job consists of multiple commands (processes), it has a single job number.

To bring a job back to the foreground:

1. jobs

Run the jobs command to get a list of job numbers. Pick the one you want to bring back to the foreground.

2. fg %n

Use the fg command (meaning *foreground*) to bring the job from the background. You identify the job with % and its job number: %1 for job 1, %2 for job 2, and so on.

The job is now running in the foreground.

✔ Tip

■ Once a job is in the foreground, you can stop it with Control C, or with the method shown below.

To stop a background job:

1. jobs

This shows you the list of all jobs running.

2. kill %n

where *n* represents any number, such as kill %2

This is the same kill command we saw earlier in this chapter, only this time instead of the process ID we are using the job ID. The same options apply here. Kill by itself sends a hangup signal to each process in the job, requesting that it quit; kill -9 sends kill signals that can't be ignored, stopping the job in its tracks.

Sometimes you might not realize that a command is going to take a while to finish until after you start it. You might have pressed Return and find yourself waiting for the job to finish. Or maybe you want to temporarily stop a job, get a shell prompt, do something else, and then return to the job that was stopped. You can *suspend* the job and get a shell prompt back right away.

A suspended job will be in the background, but it won't keep running; that is, its memory remains active, but it consumes no processor time. You can bring it back to the foreground, or tell it to keep running in the background, just as if you had started it initially with an & at the end of the command line.

```
[localhost:~] vanilla% jobs
    [1]  + Suspended              vm_stat 5
    [2]  + Running                top -l3 | mail -s 3 samples from top matisse
[localhost:~] vanilla%
```

Figure 2.38 Running the jobs command gives you a list of jobs running in the background.

Compare with Aqua

The Unix concept of putting a command in the background is very much like the traditional Mac or Aqua situation where you have an application running in one window, and you open a window for a different application. The first application continues to run, and you can get on with other things.

To suspend a job:

◆ Control Z

Figure 2.39 shows what happens when you use Control Z to suspend the **top** command while it is running. The shell shows you the job ID and process ID of the suspended job, and returns you to a shell prompt.

✔ Tip

■ You can bring the job back to the foreground as described above using the **fg** command. If the job you want to bring back to the foreground is the one you just suspended, you can use **fg** by itself with no arguments.

```
SharedLibs: num =   93, resident = 22.5M code, 1.57M data, 5.52M LinkEdit
MemRegions: num = 3234, resident =  142M + 7.07M private, 84.3M shared
PhysMem:  60.1M wired, 71.8M active,  245M inactive,  377M used,  263M free
VM: 2.34G + 45.8M   9564(0) pageins, 0(0) pageouts


  PID COMMAND      %CPU   TIME    #TH #PRTS #MREGS RPRVT  RSHRD  RSIZE  VSIZE
  439 Mozilla      1.7% 36:35.72   6    87    437  26.6M  25.4M  43.2M   109M
  396 AOL Instan   1.7% 31:01.89  10   121    170  10.7M  11.0M  16.2M  79.3M
  379 Eudora 5.1   0.0%  7:26.90   7   112    162  6.49M  12.5M  11.2M   100M
  356 httpd        0.0%  0:00.13   1     9     65   140K  1.25M   612K  2.38M
  329 tcsh         0.0%  0:00.61   1    24     17   508K   676K   996K  5.99M
  328 ssh-agent    0.0%  0:01.23   1     9     14    80K   352K   172K  1.29M
  327 Terminal     1.7%  0:51.57   5   114    103  2.89M  7.12M  6.08M  68.5M
  325 sh           0.0%  0:00.01   1    16     13   164K   640K   556K  1.69M
^Z
[1]  +   736 Suspended                  top
[localhost:~] vanilla%
```

Figure 2.39 Using Control Z suspends the top command.

If you have suspended a job and decide you want the job to keep running, but in the background, you can do that, too.

To have a suspended job continue running in the background:

◆ bg %n

For example,

bg %2

tells job number 2 to start running again, but to do so in the *background*. **Figure 2.40** shows an example of starting a job, suspending it, running another command, and then starting up the suspended job again in the background.

✔ Tip

■ If the suspended job is the one you most recently suspended, you can use **bg** with no arguments.

```
[localhost:~] vanilla% find /Developer/Documentation -name "*.htm" > found_files
^Z
[1]  +   743 Suspended    find /Developer/Documentation -name *.htm > found_files
[localhost:~] vanilla% uptime
 9:18AM  up 1 day, 15 mins, 2 users, load averages: 0.08, 0.15, 0.14
[localhost:~] vanilla% bg %1
[1]    find /Developer/Documentation -name *.htm > found_files &
```

Figure 2.40 You can suspend a job, and then restart it in the background using bg %n.

Opening Files from the Command Line

One of the great things about using the Unix command line in Mac OS X is that you are also using a Macintosh. So how do you access graphical Mac applications or AppleScripts from the command line? Apple provides a set of command-line tools to do exactly that.

To "double-click" a file from the command line:

◆ open `filename`

The **open** command performs the equivalent of double-clicking each of its arguments. For example,

open *.doc FunReport

is the same as double-clicking all the `.doc` files in the current directory, along with the file `FunReport`. The default application for each file is used just as if you had double-clicked the icons in the Finder.

✔ Tip

- You can specify which application to use with the *-a* switch (or option)— for example,

  open -a "BBEdit 6.5" found_files

  would open the file called `found_files` using the BBEdit 6.5 application.

To run an AppleScript from the command line:

◆ osascript `scriptname`

The **osascript** command executes the script named by its argument.

✔ Tip

- If you are an experienced AppleScript programmer, read the Unix manual for **osascript** by typing:

  man osascript

  You will also be interested in learning about the **osacompile** and **osalang** commands.

Importance of Editing Text in Unix

Editing text from the command line is a crucial part of using Unix.

Unix system-configuration files, system-startup files, source code for software, and much documentation are all contained in text files, which you will have occasion to edit when using the command line.

While you can certainly use your favorite Aqua text editor or word processor to edit text in Mac OS X, you will need to be able to edit files directly from the command line if you do any serious command-line work.

Also, if you want to be able to use other Unix systems besides Mac OS X, you will need to learn how to edit files using one of the command-line tools.

Chapter 6, "Editing and Printing Files," teaches you the basics of using the most common command-line text editor, the vi editor. In this chapter, you will use the simpler pico editor, which is adequate for the example of creating a shell script but is not appropriate for more complex Unix work such as editing system-startup files.

Creating a Simple Unix Shell Script

A shell script is a text file that contains a series of shell commands. Shell scripts are used for a wide range of tasks in Unix; Chapter 9, "Creating and Using Scripts," covers complex shell scripts that contain loops, functions, and other features associated with computer programming. But here we'll talk about simpler shell scripts, which are often just a series of command lines intended to be executed one after the other.

When you create a script you'll be using frequently, you should save it in a place where your shell normally looks for commands. This way, you can run the script by simply typing its name, as you would for any other command. The list of places where your shell looks for commands is called your PATH, and we teach you how to change your PATH in Chapter 7, "Configuring Your Unix Environment."

The standard place to store scripts for your personal use (as opposed to scripts intended for use by all users) is the bin directory inside your home directory. Mac OS X (as of version 10.2) ships without this directory's having been created for each user and without its being on the list of places where your shell looks for commands (your PATH), so before we have you actually create a script, we show you how to create this directory and add it to your PATH. (See Chapter 7 for more on your PATH.)

To create your personal bin directory:

1. `cd`

   This ensures that you are in your home directory.

2. `mkdir bin`

   This creates a new directory called bin (a standard Unix name for directories that contains commands, scripts, or applications).

✔ Tip

- See Chapter 5, "Using Files and Directories," for more on the mkdir command.

To add your bin directory to your PATH:

1. `cd`

   This ensures that you are in your home directory. (You can skip this step if you have just done the task above, but it doesn't hurt to do it again.)

2. `set path = ( $path ~/bin )`

   This adds the bin directory inside your home directory to the list of places your shell searches for commands. The next step takes care of doing this for all future Terminal windows you open.

3. `echo 'set path = ( $path ~/bin )' >>`
   → `.tcshrc`

   That command line adds a line of code to a configuration file used by your shell. Every new Terminal window you open will have the new configuration.

   Be careful to type it exactly as shown— the placement of spaces and the use of single quotes must be replicated exactly. Be sure to type both greater-than signs.

   The text contained inside the single quotes is added as a new line to the end of the file .tcshrc that is inside your home directory. You may check that this was successful by displaying that file with

   `cat .tcshrc`

   and the last line of the output should be

   `set path = ( $path ~/bin )`

Unix shell scripts can be written for any of the available shells, but the standard practice is to write shell scripts for the sh shell. The sh shell can be expected to behave in the same way on any Unix system.

Here is an example of creating a simple shell script that shows you a variety of status information about your computer.

To create a shell script to show system status:

1. cd

    This makes sure you are in your home directory.

2. cd bin

    This changes your current directory to the bin directory.

3. pico status.sh

    This starts up the pico editor, telling it to edit (and create) the file status.sh (**Figure 2.41**).

    We name the new script with a .sh extension as a reminder that it is written using the sh scripting language.

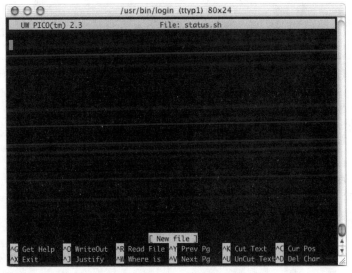

Figure 2.41 This is what you see when you start the pico editor.

4. Type in the script from **Figure 2.42**. Note that the highlighted line uses the *back-quote* character—this is the ⌐ˆ⌐ character, which is usually in the upper left of your keyboard (to the left of ⌐1⌐).

5. ⌐Control⌐⌐X⌐

   Typing ⌐Control⌐⌐X⌐ causes the pico editor to quit. Pico asks you if you want to save the changes you have made (**Figure 2.43**).

```
#!/bin/sh
# This is a comment. Comments are good.
# This is my first shell script.
echo "System Status Report"
date
echo -n "System uptime and load:" ;  uptime
echo -n "Operating System: " ; sysctl -n kern.ostype
echo -n "OS Version: " ; sysctl -n kern.osrelease
echo -n "OS Revision number: " ; sysctl -n kern.osrevision
echo -n "Hostname: " ; sysctl -n kern.hostname

bytes=`sysctl -n hw.physmem`
megabytes=`expr $bytes / 1024 / 1024`
echo "Physical memory installed (megabytes): $megabytes"
```

Figure 2.42 This is the code listing of a system-status script.

```
[localhost:bin] vanilla% status.sh
System Status Report
Sat Apr  6 11:36:43 PST 2002
System uptime and load:11:36AM  up 1 day,  2:33, 4 users, load averages: 0.26, 0.42, 0.55
Operating System: Darwin
OS Version: 5.3
OS Revision number: 199506
Hostname: localhost.localdomain
Physical memory installed (megabytes): 640
[localhost:bin] vanilla%
```

Figure 2.43 The pico editor asks if you want to save changes.

6. y

Type a y to tell pico that yes, you want to save the changes you have made.

Pico then asks you to confirm the filename to save to (**Figure 2.44**).

7. Press Return.

Pico exits, and you are back at a shell prompt.

8. chmod 755 status.sh

The chmod command (*change mode*) sets the file status.sh to be an executable file. See Chapter 8, "Working with Permissions and Ownership," for more on the chmod command.

Now all you have to do is tell tcsh (your shell) to rebuild its database of available commands to include status.sh.

9. rehash

The **rehash** command makes tcsh rebuild its list of where to find commands. Tcsh now knows where to find the new command, status.sh.

You can use the new command as you would any other—just type its name at a shell prompt and press Return.

10. status.sh

Figure 2.45 shows typical output from the command. You have just created your first new command.

Welcome to Unix.

```
File Name to write : status.sh
^G Get Help   ^C Cancel
              ^T To Files
```

Figure 2.44 The pico editor asks you to confirm the filename you're using.

```
[localhost:bin] vanilla% status.sh
System Status Report
Sat Apr  6 11:36:43 PST 2002
System uptime and load:11:36AM  up 1 day,  2:33, 4 users, load averages: 0.26, 0.42, 0.55
Operating System: Darwin
OS Version: 5.3
OS Revision number: 199506
Hostname: localhost.localdomain
Physical memory installed (megabytes): 640
[localhost:bin] vanilla%
```

Figure 2.45 Typing status.sh shows you output from the command you have just created.

GETTING HELP AND USING THE UNIX MANUAL

3

There are four ways to get help when using Unix: from external documentation such as this book, Web sites, and other similar materials; from the extensive Unix reference manuals that come with every version of Unix, including Mac OS X; from the built-in help that comes with most commands; and from other people via online discussion systems, email, and user groups. You are already taking the first approach, so this chapter concentrates on the other three.

The Unix reference manuals are a collection of *man pages,* which are specially formatted files intended to be viewed with the **man** command. Unix **man** pages are written for an audience of experienced programmers, not for novice users, so to understand Unix man pages, you need to understand the conventions used in them.

Mac OS X comes with almost 3,000 Unix man pages. Most of these are copied from the FreeBSD version of Unix, the one used to create Mac OS X's Darwin layer. Some of these pages come from Apple itself, and some come from the software Apple acquired when it bought NeXT. As of this writing (summer 2002), Apple had barely begun to update the man pages to be Darwin-specific. Fortunately, most of the man pages do not require updating; unfortunately, there is no easy way to know which ones do require it.

Command-line programs almost always provide a minimal level of help—usually just enough to show you the options and arguments the command expects. Still, that is often enough to remind you of the proper way to use the command.

Help from other people is the most valuable kind, and it's available from a variety of sources. At the end of this chapter is a list of the best places to look.

Using the Unix Manual

Every Unix command is supposed to have an associated man page that describes the command and the options available for using it. You read man pages using the man command.

Unix man pages are arranged into eight or nine sections, depending on which flavor of Unix you are using. Mac OS X uses the eight sections shown in **Table 3.1.** Wherever you see a Unix command name followed by a number in parentheses—for example, date(1)—the number refers to the section of the manual with which the command is associated. Thus chown(2) refers to the chown documented in section 2 of the manual, while chown(8) refers to the chown documented in section 8 of the manual.

Throughout this book we use the Unix convention of referring to a manual entry by saying "see man *entry*." *Entry* is usually a command name—for example, we might say "see man ls" to look at the manual entry of the ls command. *Entry* can also represent anything else the manual covers; some system-configuration files have manual entries.

To display a man page:

1. The short answer is: man *command*

   For example,

   man man

   shows you the man page for the man command. **Figure 3.1** is a code listing showing the beginning of the Unix man page for the man command. It is probably rather confusing at this point, which is why we have this chapter to explain Unix man pages.

Table 3.1

Sections of the Mac OS X Unix Manual	
SECTION	CONTENTS
1	*User commands* Commands you use most frequently, such as man and grep.
2	*System calls* Commands (actually *functions*) provided by the operating system for use in programming, mostly in the C language, such as man and setuid.
3	*System library functions* Tools for programmers available in a variety of languages (C, Perl, Tcl, and others), such as man Text::Soundex.
4	*System kernel interfaces* More-advanced tools for programmers, mostly in the C language, such as man stdout.
5	*System file formats* Man pages for the most important system-configuration files, describing their use for system administration, such as man appletalk.cfg.
6	This covers games, but Mac OS X does not come with any command-line games.
7	*Miscellaneous items* Character-set definitions, file types, file-system information such as man hier for "hierarchy."
8	Servers and system-administration commands such as the Apache Web server and man httpd.

USING THE UNIX MANUAL

```
[localhost:~] vanilla% man man

MAN(1)                    System General Commands Manual                    MAN(1)


NAME
     man - format and display the on-line manual pages

SYNOPSIS
     man [-adfhkotw] [-m machine] [-p string] [-M path] [-P pager] [-S list] [section] name ...

DESCRIPTION
     Man formats and displays the on-line manual pages. This version knows
     about the MANPATH and PAGER environment variables, so you can have your
     own set(s) of personal man pages and choose whatever program you like to
     display the formatted pages. If section is specified, man only looks in
     that section of the manual. You may also specify the order to search the
     sections for entries and which preprocessors to run on the source files
     via command line options or environment variables. If enabled by the
     system administrator, formatted man pages will also be compressed with
     the `%compress%' command to save space.


     The options are as follows:


     -M path    Specify an alternate manpath. By default, man uses manpath(1)
                (which is built into the man binary) to determine the path to
                search. This option overrides the MANPATH environment variable.


     -P pager   Specify which pager to use. By default, man uses %pager%.
                This option overrides the PAGER environment variable.


     -S list    List is a colon separated list of manual sections to search.
                This option overrides the MANSECT environment variable.


     -a         By default, man will exit after displaying the first manual
                page it finds. Using this option forces man to display all
                the manual pages that match name, not just the first.


     -d         Don't actually display the man pages, but do print gobs of debugging information.
```

Figure 3.1 Typing man man lets you see the man page for the man command itself (this is partial output).

continues on next page

USING THE UNIX MANUAL

Figure 3.1 *continued*

-f   Equivalent to whatis.

-h   Print a one line help message and exit.

-k   Equivalent to apropos.

-m machine As some manual pages are intended only for specific architectures,
            man searches any subdirectories, with the same name as the current
            architecture, in every directory which it searches. Machine specific
            areas are checked before general areas. The current machine type may
            be overridden using this option or by setting the environment variable
            MACHINE to the name of a specific architecture. This option overrides
            the MACHINE environment variable.

-o   Look for original, non-localized manpages only.

            By default, man searches for a localized manpage in a set of
            locale subdirectories of each manpath(1) component.

            Locale name is taken from the first of three environment variables with
            a nonempty value: LC_ALL, LC_CTYPE, or LANG, in the specified order.

            If the value could not be determined, or is not a valid locale name,
            then only non-localized manpage will be looked up.

            Otherwise, man will search in the following subdirectories, in the
            order of precedence:

                 <lang>_<country>.<charset>
                 <lang>.<charset>
                 en.<charset>

            For example, for ``de_DE.ISO8859-1'' locale, man will search in the following
            subdirectories of the /usr/share/man manpath component:

                 /usr/share/man/de_DE.ISO8859-1
                 /usr/share/man/de.ISO8859-1
                 /usr/share/man/en.ISO8859-1

Figure 3.1 *continued*

	Finally, if the search of localized manpage fails, it will be looked up in the default /usr/share/man directory.
-p string	Specify the sequence of preprocessors to run before nroff or troff. Not all installations will have a full set of preprocessors. Some of the preprocessors and the letters used to designate them are: eqn (e), grap (g), pic (p), tbl (t), vgrind (v), refer (r). This option overrides the MANROFFSEQ environment variable.
-t	Use %troff% to format the manual page, passing the output to stdout. The output from %troff% may need to be passed through some filter or another before being printed.
-w	Don't actually display the man pages, but do print the location(s) of the files that would be formatted or displayed.

2. But there is a longer, more useful answer. The generalized syntax of how to display a Unix man page is this:

```
man [-adfhktw] [section]
→ [-M path] [-P pager] [-S list]
→ [-m machine] [-p string] name
```

What does that mean? It is the technical way in which Unix command syntax is described. This format, though daunting at first, is a concise and accurate way to show how a command should be used, and you will see this format constantly in Unix documentation.

The man pages for commands all begin with a synopsis of the command using the format shown above. It is well worth your time to learn this syntax.

Figure 3.2 shows an element-by-element translation of the specification for the man command itself.

According to the specification, the only required argument to the man command is the name of the manual entry you want, but there are several available options. You must read the man page itself to learn what the options mean. In this case the options have the following meanings:

-a Displays all of the man pages that match the command name you supply (the final argument to the man command). Normally the man command shows only the first match (searching the manual from section 1 through 8).

-d Displays debugging information instead of the actual manual page(s).

-f Finds a list of the manual pages that contain the entry in their one-line description. (The entry is the final, and required argument to the man command.)

-h Displays a help message for the man command.

-k Same at the -f option.

-t Produces Postscript out by passing the output of the man command through another program (called *troff*). If you use this option you will almost certainly want to save the output in a file or pipe it to a program that understands Postscript (see "Redirecting stdout" and "Creating Pipelines of Commands" in Chapter 2.)

-w Shows the locations of the actual man page files.

-M You must supply a list of one or more directories (separated by colons) right after this option. The directories are searched for man pages instead of the default locations (which are all in /usr/share/man).

-m You must supply a "machine" name. In this case "machine" refers to the hardware architecture of the machine, for example, "PowerPC". This option is rarely used. It is intended for situations where there are manual pages for different, architectrure-dependent versions of the same command.

-p If used you must supply a string of letters which indicate a series of pre-processor programs that the manual page will be passed through. Each pre-processor program has its own man page, for example `man eqn` to read about the eqn program. The available preprocessors and the letters that designate each one are:

```
e - eqn
p - pic
t - tbl
r - refer
v - vgrind
```

✔ Tips

- Use the man command to read about each new command in this book. Many commands have options that go beyond what we're covering.

- In some cases, man pages in two sections of the manual have the same name. Using the -a switch displays all the entries for a given name.

- Look at the end of most man pages for a "see also" section that lists related commands. A related command might be more useful than the one you first thought to use.

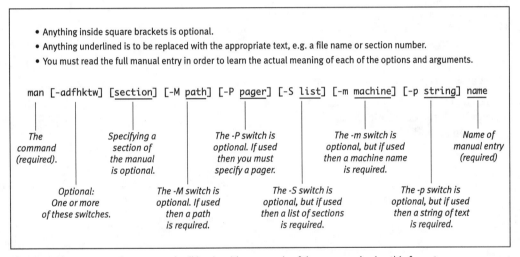

- Anything inside square brackets is optional.
- Anything underlined is to be replaced with the appropriate text, e.g. a file name or section number.
- You must read the full manual entry in order to learn the actual meaning of each of the options and arguments.

man [-adfhktw] [section] [-M path] [-P pager] [-S list] [-m machine] [-p string] name

The command (required).

Optional: One or more of these switches.

Specifying a section of the manual is optional.

The -M switch is optional. If used then a path is required.

The -P switch is optional. If used then you must specify a pager.

The -S switch is optional, but if used then a list of sections is required.

The -m switch is optional, but if used then a machine name is required.

The -p switch is optional, but if used then a string of text is required.

Name of manual entry (required)

Figure 3.2 The man pages for commands all begin with a synopsis of the command using this format.

Sometimes you may not be sure which command you want. The apropos command can be used to search the title lines of all the manual pages.

To search for a man page:

◆ apropos *keyword*

For example, if you are looking for commands related to appletalk, you would try:

apropos appletalk

Figure 3.3 shows the result (reformatted slightly for print). Each entry lists the name of a man page, the section it belongs to, and usually a one-line description of the man entry.

✔ Tips

■ Of course, you can try man apropos to learn more about the apropos command.

■ On many Unix systems, man -k is the same as apropos. This is true on Mac OS X.

■ You can also search for man pages by looking in the directories inside /usr/share/man and /usr/local/man.

```
[localhost:~] vanilla% apropos appletalk
appleping(1)     - exercises the AppleTalk network by sending packets to
                   a named host
appletalk(8)     - enables you to configure and display AppleTalk network
                   interfaces
appletalk.cfg(5)
at_cho_prn(8)    - allows you to choose a default printer on the
                   AppleTalk internet
atlookup(1)      - looks up network-visible entities (NVEs) registered on the
                   AppleTalk network system
atprint(1)       - transfer data to a printer using AppleTalk protocols
atstatus(1)      - displays status information from an AppleTalk device
[localhost:~] vanilla%
```

Figure 3.3 The apropos command can be used to search the title lines of all the manual pages.

Printing Man Pages

Unix man pages are plain text files written using a special formatting syntax (see `man mdoc.samples` for a tutorial). The raw files are not suitable for printing because they contain text that the `man` command uses to produce boldface, underlining, and other text formatting, but in some cases you can translate the man page into HTML or PostScript.

Note that the printing techniques described here work for many, but not all, man pages, simply because some converters may not be able to handle certain formatting commands (they may have been written at different times). However, you'll always be able to see the text on the screen—on the printed page you may get truncated text or missing paragraph breaks.

See Chapter 6, "Editing and Printing Files" for more on printing from the command line.

To print a man page to a PostScript printer:

◆ `man -t command | lp`

For example, if you want a printed man page for the `date` command:

`man -t date | lp`

You are using the –t option of the `man` command to produce PostScript output and piping that into the `lp` command. If you're using a PostScript printer, you get a nicely formatted result. See the Gimp-Print Web site (http://gimp-print. sourceforge.net/) for software that allows you to print PostScript on non-PostScript printers.

✔ Tip

■ If you wanted to save the PostScript version of a man page, perhaps for use in some future project, then you would simply redirect the output of the `man` command to a file:

`man -t date > date.ps`

Besides converting man pages to PostScript, you can also convert many of them to HTML. This will allow you to view the page in a Web browser and print it to a non-PostScript printer.

To convert a man page to HTML:

◆ Find the raw man page.

Use the -w option to the `man` command— for example:

`man -w tcsh`

`tcsh` is just the name of the command we want the man page for. Even though `tcsh` is your shell, it is still just another command.

`groff -man -Thtml /usr/share/man/`
`→man1/tcsh.1 > tcsh.html`

(You will see some debugging output on your screen from the `groff` command but you can ignore it. The new file `tcsh.html` will not contain the debugging text.)

You can now try viewing the HTML page with your favorite browser, even from the command line:

`open tcsh.html`

✔ Tip

■ Some man pages convert better than others. If you know HTML, you may be able to edit poorly formatted HTML versions to fix conversion problems.

Using Commands' Built-in Help

The most common way to learn about a command is to read its built-in help. Many commands support an option that displays information about the command, and almost all commands display a *usage* message (that is, how it's best used) if it is invoked with improper arguments or options.

Built-in help is terse, often consisting only of a usage message using the format described in Figure 3.2. Still, it is easily available and often reminds you of the available options and required arguments.

There isn't a consistent way to get built-in help from commands, but there are several ways that work.

To see the built-in help from a command:

◆ Try invoking the command with the --help option (that's two dashes).

For example, try:

ssh –help

Some commands (like ssh) provide an extensive listing of available options (see **Figure 3.4** for a partial listing from the ssh command).

For some commands, the --help option is not valid, and for others it looks like a valid option but doesn't provide any help

```
[localhost:~] vanilla% ssh -help
Usage: ssh [options] host [command]
Options:
  -l user     Log in using this user name.
  -n          Redirect input from /dev/null.
  -F config   Config file (default: ~/.ssh/config).
  -A          Enable authentication agent forwarding.
  -a          Disable authentication agent forwarding (default).
  -X          Enable X11 connection forwarding.
  -x          Disable X11 connection forwarding (default).
  -i file     Identity for public key authentication (default: ~/.ssh/identity)
  -t          Tty; allocate a tty even if command is given.
  -T          Do not allocate a tty.
  -v          Verbose; display verbose debugging messages.
              Multiple -v increases verbosity.
  -V          Display version number only.
  -P          Don't allocate a privileged port.
```

Figure 3.4 Some commands (like ssh) give an extensive listing of available options; this is the result when you type ssh –help.

```
[localhost:~] vanilla% ls -help
ls: illegal option -- h
usage: ls [-1ACFLRSTWacdfgiklnoqrstux] [file ...]
[localhost:~] vanilla%
```

Figure 3.5 What you get when you type ls -help.

◆ In some cases, using a single dash gives something useful:

ls -help

Even though -help is not a valid option to the ls command, it still gives you some insight. Most commands give a usage message when invoked with an invalid option or without a required argument. **Figure 3.5** shows the output from ls when invoked with the -help option.

◆ In some cases the -h option will produce a help message.

The man command is an example of a command that will give you a help message if you invoke it with the -h option:

man -h

✔ Tips

■ Try deliberately using an invalid option, such as -XXX and see what happens.

■ If the built-in help is not helpful or is missing, just refer to the man page.

Getting Help from Other People

Unix evolved organically, with features and commands being added piecemeal over the years. Even with all of the books written about Unix, person-to-person interaction remains the best way to become comfortable with using Unix, and often is the only way to learn about new features or the more sophisticated uses of features you already know about.

Becoming connected to other Unix users is your best route to Unix mastery. **Table 3.2** shows several good places to start.

Table 3.2

Human Help Resources	
RESOURCE	WHAT AND WHERE
Mac OS X Hints (www.macosxhints.com)	A Web site devoted to tricks, hints, help, and arcana about Mac OS X. Includes extensive discussion forums. Created and run as a labor of love by Rob Griffiths. If you find the site useful, consider donating $10.
Apple Discussions (http://discussions.info.apple.com)	Apple's official Mac OS X discussion forums. No charge, but you need to set up an Apple ID account.
The WELL (www.well.com, or from the command line `telnet well.com`)	The WELL has been a vibrant online community since 1985. Participants tend to be highly literate and interested in a wide range of subjects. The Macintosh and Unix discussion areas are extremely high quality and worth the $10/month fee all by themselves. Several of the people who helped with this book are WELL users.
Darwin mailing lists (www.opensource.apple.com/projects/mail.html)	Apple hosts a number of email lists on the Darwin operating system. The Darwin-UserLevel and DarwinOS-Users lists are most likely to be useful to a new Unix user.

Useful Unix Utilities

Unix's flexibility arises from its large collection of tools and the ease of combining different tools to accomplish tasks. This idea of combining tools comes up repeatedly in Unix and is a key part of the Unix culture of computing.

When we say utility here, we mean a command or other software that is commonly used in a variety of situations, and that is frequently combined with other commands to perform a useful task. For example, the sort command is usually used to sort the output of other commands.

Unix utilities have been designed to be combined with each other easily. You've seen in Chapter 2, "Using the Command Line," how the output of a command can be piped into the input of another command. This allows you to create an almost infinite variety of command lines using different commands, options, and arguments.

Because there are so many commands, just knowing what is available is a big part of being able to use Unix effectively. This chapter is intended to introduce you to the more common and useful Unix utilities.

In Chapter 3, "Getting Help and Using the Unix Manual," we showed you how to use the man command to search for commands by keyword. Some of the commands in this chapter are covered in detail elsewhere in this book. In each case, we'll refer you to the appropriate chapter rather than repeat the information here.

In any event, it is a good idea to read the Unix manual entry for each of the commands described here. Even if you don't understand all of what you read, you will get a good sense of what is possible and will see references to other related commands (in the *see also* section of each man page). For more on using the Unix manual, refer back to Chapter 3.

Almost all the commands described in this book are found on every Unix system you are likely to use. This is one of the best features of Unix—that even though different versions exist and are constantly being updated, the skills you learn on one Unix system will help you on all Unix systems.

Mac OS X—Specific Utilities

There are some utilities on your system that are specific to Mac OS X. Some of these commands deal with the differences between traditional Macintosh files and Unix files, while others provide connections between the Darwin layer and the Aqua layer. The developer tools in /Developer/Tools are mostly examples of the former, while the open and osascript commands are examples of the latter. (If you haven't installed the Developer Tools, you should do so now; they come on a separate CD from Mac OS X.)

Here are the most important of the Mac OS X–specific commands you are likely to use in day-to-day work:

open—Access files from the command line

The open command in Unix works the same way a double-click on the Mac does: It lets you open one or more files from the command line. And with the -a option you can achieve an effect similar to drag and drop by specifying an application to use when opening a file. See man open for the Unix manual entry and Chapter 2 of this book, "Using the Command Line," for an example of using open.

MvMac and CpMac—Copy and rename traditional Mac files from the command line

The MvMac and CpMac commands provide most of the features of the standard Unix mv and cp commands. Unlike the standard Unix commands, though, these two will not damage traditional Mac files (We'll elaborate on what we mean in Chapter 5, "Using Files and Directories"). Note: These commands do not have Unix man pages.

osascript—Run AppleScript from the command line

AppleScript is the Mac-specific scripting language that allows you to control Mac applications from scripts (see the "Learning AppleScript" sidebar). In Mac OS X you can run AppleScripts from the command line using the osascript command.

To run an AppleScript from the command line:

◆ osascript *filename*

This executes the AppleScript contained in the file represented by *filename*.

For example, if you have a script called playsong that contains

```
tell application "iTunes"

open file "MyDisk:Users:vanilla:
→Desktop:slow_ride.mp3"

end tell
```

then the command line

```
osascript playsong
```

would run the AppleScript, launching iTunes and opening the slow_ride.mp3 file (**Figure 4.1**).

✔ Tip

■ Notice that AppleScript expects files to be described using colons to separate the names of folders. This is quite different from Unix commands, which expect you to use the slash character (/), prevalent throughout this book.

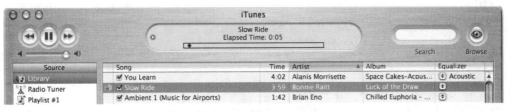

Figure 4.1 iTunes running a file opened from the command line.

Learning AppleScript

AppleScript is a complete language for controlling your Macintosh using scripts. Here are some resources for learning more about AppleScript:

◆ The main Apple Computer Web site for AppleScript is (www.apple.com/applescript/).

◆ If you have installed the developer tools, then you have an AppleScript Language Guide on your computer at Developer/Documentation/Carbon/interapplicationcomm/AppleScript/applescript.html

◆ You can also find the Language Guide on the Web at the AppleScript Scripting Language page (http://developer.apple.com/techpubs/macosx/Carbon/interapplicationcomm/AppleScript/applescript.html).

◆ Peachpit Press has published a Visual QuickStart Guide to AppleScript (*AppleScript for Applications*) (www.peachpit.com/books/catalog/71613.html).

File Compression and Archiving

If you've been using a Mac, you have most likely seen files compressed using StuffIt, Aladdin Systems' popular file-compression utility.

In the Unix world, there is a handful of commands already part of the operating system that are used for archiving and compressing files. It's likely that software you download from the Internet will be compressed using these tools.

gzip

gzip is a program for compressing files. The "g" in gzip is from "GNU" (see the sidebar "What Is a GNU?") and the "zip" is a reference to an earlier program called zip. gzip is not the same as zip though. The older zip program will not only compress files, it will also combine multiple files and/or directories into a single file. The gzip program is more widely used than zip in the Unix world because gzip provides better compression (smaller files) and the Unix tar command is the commonly used program to combine multiple files into a single file.

To compress a file using gzip:

◆ gzip *filename*

Gzip attempts to replace the files named in its arguments with compressed files, adding the .gz extension to the filename (gzip may not be able to replace a file if the file with the new name already exists and cannot be changed, in which case you get an error message). So if the original file is called Picture 1.tiff, the compressed file is called Picture 1.tiff.gz.

Figure 4.2 shows an example of compressing all the .tiff files in the current directory. Notice how gzip did not change the modification times of the files.

```
[localhost:~/Desktop] vanilla% ls -l *.tiff
-rw-r--r-- 1 vanilla  staff  186590 Apr 14 20:49 Picture 1.tiff
-rw-r--r-- 1 vanilla  staff  569553 Apr 15 10:41 Picture 2.tiff
-rw-r--r-- 1 vanilla  staff  517795 Apr 15 10:51 Picture 3.tiff
[localhost:~/Desktop] vanilla% gzip *.tiff
[localhost:~/Desktop] vanilla% ls -l *.tiff.gz
-rw-r--r-- 1 matisse  staff   93648 Apr 14 20:49 Picture 1.tiff.gz
-rw-r--r-- 1 matisse  staff  170010 Apr 15 10:41 Picture 2.tiff.gz
-rw-r--r-- 1 matisse  staff  119743 Apr 15 10:51 Picture 3.tiff.gz
[localhost:~/Desktop] vanilla%
```

Figure 4.2 Compressing a set of files using gzip.

✔ Tips

■ You can use gzip to compress the output of other commands. Just pipe the output of the other commands into gzip and redirect to a file. (See Chapter 2, "Using the Command Line," to review pipelines.) For example:

```
grep root /var/log/mail.log | gzip >
→output.gz
```

That command line runs the grep command to search for the string root in the file /var/log/mail.log. The output of grep (the lines containing root) is piped into the gzip program, and the output of gzip is redirected into the file output.gz.

■ If you use gzip to compress a Mac file that has a resource fork, the file loses both its icon and its association with the application that created it, and thus may become useless. To safely compress traditional Mac files, use StuffIt.

gunzip

Of course, once you have a compressed file, you'll want to know how to uncompress it.

To uncompress a gzipped file:

◆ gunzip `filename.gz`

Gunzip replaces the compressed file with the uncompressed version, removing the .gz filename extension. For example:

```
gunzip "Picture 1.tiff.gz"
```

replaces Picture 1.tiff.gz with Picture 1.tiff.

✔ Tip

■ You can use gunzip in a pipeline. If you want the output of gunzip to go into a pipe, use the -c option:

```
gunzip -c filename.gz | command
```

When gunzip is used this way, it does not replace the compressed file.

What Is a GNU?

GNU is a recursive acronym (that is, an acronym that contains part of itself) that stands for Gnu's Not Unix. The GNU project is the domain of the Free Software Foundation, which coordinates a huge volunteer effort to create a complete Unix-like operating system that has the following four freedoms:

◆ Freedom to run the program, for any eason you want

◆ Freedom to study the internals of the pro- gram works, and to alter it to suit you

◆ Freedom to redistribute copies so you can help other people

◆ Freedom to make the program better, and make your changes available to the public, so that the others benefit from your efforts

There are hundreds of GNU software pack- ages. There is even a GNU-Darwin project: The GNU-Darwin Distribution (http:// gnu-darwin.sourceforge.net/).

There's more information on the GNU pro- ject and the Free Software Foundation at GNU's Not Unix! (www.gnu.org).

FILE COMPRESSION AND ARCHIVING

tar

In many cases you will want to compress an entire directory (folder). Unlike the StuffIt program, gzip does not compress directories. To deal with this, you use another program from the command line, called tar (for *t*ape *ar*chive), which creates a single file from a directory and all of its contents (a *tar file*). Tar was originally used only for making backups to tape systems (hence its name) but is now used far more frequently to create tar files prior to compression.

The version of tar included with Mac OS X can simultaneously combine a directory full of files into one file and compress the result with gzip.

To archive a directory using tar:

◆ tar -cvzf *newfile*.tar *directoryname*

The tar command needs the -c option to tell it to create a new archive.

The v option tells tar to "be verbose" and show you the names of all the files it is processing. You can leave it out if you like.

The z option tells tar to compress the result using gzip. Leave it out if you don't want compressed output.

The f option tells tar that you are specifying a filename for the new archive. Without the f option, tar assumes that you are trying to write to an attached tape drive. The f option must come last.

Figure 4.3 shows a listing of the contents of the code directory and then output from tar when you create a tar file with tar -cvzf code.tar code

```
[localhost:~/Desktop] vanilla% ls -l code
total 16
-rw-r-r-  1 matisse  staff   156 Nov  4 09:57 Changes
-rw-r-r-  1 matisse  staff  1444 Nov  4 09:57 README
drwxr-xr-x 4 matisse  staff    92 Apr 16 12:44 src
[localhost:~/Desktop] vanilla% tar -cvzf code.tar.gz code
code
code/Changes
code/README
code/src
code/src/syntax.c
code/src/syntax.h
[localhost:~/Desktop] vanilla% ls -l code.tar.gz
-rw-r-r-  1 matisse  staff  3203 Apr 16 12:56 code.tar.gz
[localhost:~/Desktop] vanilla%
```

Figure 4.3 Listing the contents of a directory and then archiving it with tar.

Tar does not replace the original directory. Notice that the output from **tar** in Figure 4.3 lists all the files and subdirectories that are included in the archive (a result of the -v option).

✔ Tips

■ Tar has a plethora of options. See **man tar** for the complete list.

■ If you want to use the **tar** command in a pipeline, use the special filename - (a single dash). This is especially useful if you are working on a Unix system where the version of **tar** cannot compress its output. On those systems you might use

tar -cvf - code | gzip > code.tar.gz

Of course, once you have a **tar** file, you want to be able to reverse the process and turn it back into a directory (this is called *unpacking*).

To unpack a tar archive:

◆ **tar -xvzf code.tar**

This produces output as shown in **Figure 4.4**. The -x option tells **tar** you want to extract files from a **tar** file. The v and f options have the same meanings as before: v means "be verbose," and f means "extract from a file, not a tape drive."

Omit the z option if the archive is not compressed.

Unlike **gunzip**, **tar** does not replace the archive when you extract files from it.

```
[localhost:~/Desktop] vanilla% ls -l code
total 16
-rw-r-r-  1 matisse  staff   156 Nov  4 09:57 Changes
-rw-r-r-  1 matisse  staff  1444 Nov  4 09:57 README
drwxr-xr-x 4 matisse  staff    92 Apr 16 12:44 src
[localhost:~/Desktop] vanilla% tar -cvzf code.tar.gz code
code
code/Changes
code/README
code/src
code/src/syntax.c
code/src/syntax.h
[localhost:~/Desktop] vanilla% ls -l code.tar.gz
-rw-r-r-  1 matisse  staff  3203 Apr 16 12:56 code.tar.gz
[localhost:~/Desktop] vanilla%
```

Figure 4.4 Extracting the contents of a compressed tar file.

FILE COMPRESSION AND ARCHIVING

File and Text Processing

As you have probably noticed, the Unix command line is very file-oriented. Almost everything you do involves at least one file, and often several. Here are a few of the most commonly used command-line tools for processing files.

Besides being useful for processing files, all of the tools described here function equally well in pipelines for processing text that comes directly from other commands without being saved to a file first.

wc—Counting lines, words, and bytes

The wc command displays a count of lines, words, and bytes contained in its input. Input to wc can be one or more files specified as arguments; wc also takes input from stdin (see Chapter 2, "Using the Command Line," to review stdin).

To count the number of lines, words, and bytes in a file:

◆ wc *filename*
For example,

wc /etc/hostconfig

counts the contents of the file

/etc/hostconfig

showing 28 lines, 41 words, and 474 bytes (**Figure 4.5**). (The file /etc/hostconfig is one of the many system-configuration files in the /etc directory.)

✔ Tips

■ The -l option displays only the number of lines, -w the number of words, and -c the number of bytes. The default behavior is the same as using the -lwc options together. **Figure 4.6** shows a comparison of output from each option.

```
[localhost:~] vanilla% wc /etc/hostconfig
28       41      474 /etc/hostconfig
[localhost:~] vanilla%
```

Figure 4.5 Counting the number of lines, words, and bytes in a file with wc. Your output will have different numbers.

```
[localhost:~] vanilla% wc  /etc/hostconfig
     28      41      474 /etc/hostconfig
[localhost:~] vanilla% wc -lwc /etc/hostconfig
     28      41      474 /etc/hostconfig
[localhost:~] vanilla% wc -l /etc/hostconfig
     28 /etc/hostconfig
[localhost:~] vanilla% wc -w /etc/hostconfig
     41 /etc/hostconfig
[localhost:~] vanilla% wc -c /etc/hostconfig
    474 /etc/hostconfig
 [localhost:~] vanilla%
```

Figure 4.6 Comparing the results of using different options with wc.

■ If you give wc more than one file as an argument, it gives you a line for each and a summary line adding up the contents of all of them (**Figure 4.7**).

```
[localhost:~] vanilla% wc  /etc/*.conf
     20     90    753 /etc/6to4.conf
     22     47    576 /etc/gdb.conf
     57    361   2544 /etc/inetd.conf
      0      0      0 /etc/kern_loader.conf
     46    199   1160 /etc/named.conf
      1      6     44 /etc/ntp.conf
      2      4     44 /etc/resolv.conf
     21    144    983 /etc/rtadvd.conf
      0     12     52 /etc/slpsa.conf
     50    273   1602 /etc/smb.conf
     18     66    724 /etc/syslog.conf
     12     29    238 /etc/xinetd.conf
    249   1231   8720 total
[localhost:~] vanilla%
```

Figure 4.7 Counting lines, words, and bytes in several files at once.

```
[localhost:~] vanilla% sort data data2
1 cat
1 dog
1 orange
10 fish
100 pears
2 apples
[localhost:~] vanilla%
```

Figure 4.8 Using sort to sort alphabetically.

```
[localhost:~] vanilla% sort -n data data2
1 cat
1 dog
1 orange
2 apples
10 fish
100 pears
[localhost:~] vanilla%
```

Figure 4.9 Sorting numerically with sort.

sort—Alphabetical or numerical sorting

The sort command takes its input either from files or from stdin and produces sorted output on stdout. The default sorting is in alphabetical order. You can also sort numerically.

For the following tasks, create two plain-text files (using the pico editor as described in Chapter 2, "Using the Command Line"). The first file should be called data and should contain three lines:

```
100 pears
2 apples
1 orange
```

The second file should be called data2 and contain three lines:

```
1 dog
1 cat
10 fish
```

To sort alphabetically:

◆ sort data data2

This produces the output shown in **Figure 4.8**. The results are correct, but something looks wrong. The problem is that **100** is alphabetically lower than 2. The next task shows you how to sort numerically.

To sort numerically:

◆ sort -n data data2

This produces the output shown in **Figure 4.9**. (n stands for *numeric*).

✔ Tips

■ Add the -r option to *reverse* the sort order:
sort -nr data data2

■ You can of course use sort in a pipeline:
ls -s /usr/bin | sort -n

■ To save the output, use output redirection:
sort -n data > sorted

uniq—Only one of each line

The uniq command takes sorted text as input and produces output with duplicate lines removed.

To display only the unique lines:

1. Create a file called data containing the following lines:

```
dog
cat
mongoose
cat
bird
dog
snake
cat
bird
```

2. sort data | uniq

This produces the output shown in **Figure 4.10**.

3. But what if you want to know how many of each line there was? Adding the -c (*count*) option to uniq:

```
sort data | uniq -c
```

produces the output shown in **Figure 4.11**.

4. But now the output is no longer sorted numerically. So:

```
sort data | uniq -c | sort -rn
```

Pipe the output through sort again, with the rn options for *reverse numerical* sorting, and you get output as shown in **Figure 4.12**.

✔ Tips

■ If you want to have uniq act on more than one file, use sort to act on them simultaneously:

```
sort file1 file2 file3 | uniq
```

```
[localhost:~] vanilla% sort data | uniq
bird
cat
dog
mongoose
snake
[localhost:~] vanilla%
```

Figure 4.10 Uniq deletes duplicates so that there is only one of each line.

```
[localhost:~] vanilla% sort data | uniq -c
   2 bird
   3 cat
   2 dog
   1 mongoose
   1 snake
[localhost:~] vanilla%
```

Figure 4.11 Getting a count of each entry, using uniq.

■ If you give the uniq command one argument, it will use that as a filename to take its input. If you give it two arguments, uniq assumes that the second one is the name of an output file, and it will copy the results of its output to the second file, overwriting its contents:

```
uniq infile outfile
```

awk

The awk program, a multi-featured text-processing tool, gets its name from the initials of its three inventors (Aho, Kernighan, and Weinberger; Kernighan is Brian Kernighan, coinventor of the C programming language).

A common use of awk is to send to stdout only certain fields from a file or pipeline of data (see Chapter 2, "Using the Command Line," for more about *standard output,* or stdout.) For example, the log files created by Web servers record several fields of data including date/time of request, what the user requested, and how many bytes were sent to the browser. **Figure 4.13** shows a sample from /var/log/httpd/access_log (this is your Web-server

access log if you have enabled Web sharing by going to the Apple menu and choosing System Preferences and then Sharing).

Let's say you want to extract only the URLs that were requested in order to determine the most popular pages. Awk allows you to specify what separates "fields" in each line. The default separator is a *whitespace*, which should work fine in this case. (A whitespace is any blank space in a line, including any run of the space character and/or tabs.) If you look at each line of the data in Figure 4.13, you'll see that the field you want is field number seven; that is, if you break a line into pieces, wherever whitespace occurs, the seventh piece has the URL in it.

continues on next page

```
[localhost:~] vanilla% sort data | uniq -c | sort -rn
    3 cat
    2 dog
    2 bird
    1 snake
    1 mongoose
[localhost:~] vanilla%
```

Figure 4.12 Sorting the counted entries using sort -nr.

```
66.47.69.205 - - [14/Mar/2002:14:53:48 -0800] "GET /~matisse/images/macosxlogo.gif HTTP/1.1" 200 2829
66.47.69.205 - - [14/Mar/2002:14:53:48 -0800] "GET /~matisse/images/apache_pb.gif HTTP/1.1" 200 2326
66.47.69.205 - - [14/Mar/2002:14:53:48 -0800] "GET /~matisse/images/web_share.gif HTTP/1.1" 200 13370
66.47.69.205 - - [14/Mar/2002:14:54:00 -0800] "GET /~matisse/cgi-bin/test HTTP/1.1" 200 25
66.47.69.205 - - [14/Mar/2002:14:54:29 -0800] "GET /~matisse/cgi-bin/test HTTP/1.1" 200 25
66.47.69.205 - - [14/Mar/2002:15:08:27 -0800] "GET /~matisse/upload.html HTTP/1.1" 200 397
66.47.69.205 - - [14/Mar/2002:15:33:48 -0800] "GET /~matisse/images/web_share.gif HTTP/1.1" 200 13370
66.47.69.205 - - [14/Mar/2002:15:33:50 -0800] "GET /~matisse/images/web_share.gif HTTP/1.1" 200 13370
```

Figure 4.13 Example of contents of a Web server log from /var/log/httpd/access_log.

FILE AND TEXT PROCESSING

To print only one field from a file:

◆ awk '{print $7}' /var/log/httpd/
→access_log

This produces output like that shown in **Figure 4.14**.

Each line in the original file represents one request made to your Web server, so each URL is from one request. You might already have realized that we could get a quick count of the requests by using the sort and uniq commands covered earlier in this chapter:

awk '{print $7}' /var/log/httpd/
→access_log | sort | uniq -c |
→sort -nr

gives us output like that in **Figure 4.15.**

```
[localhost:~] vanilla% awk '{print $7}' /var/log/httpd/access_log
/~matisse/images/macosxlogo.gif
/~matisse/images/apache_pb.gif
/~matisse/images/web_share.gif
/~matisse/cgi-bin/test
/~matisse/cgi-bin/test
/~matisse/upload.html
/~matisse/images/web_share.gif
/~matisse/images/web_share.gif
[localhost:~] vanilla%
```

Figure 4.14 Using awk to print one field from a file.

```
[localhost:~] vanilla% awk '{print $7}' /var/log/httpd/access_log | uniq -c | sort -nr
   3 /~matisse/images/web_share.gif
   2 /~matisse/cgi-bin/test
   1 /~matisse/upload.html
   1 /~matisse/images/macosxlogo.gif
   1 /~matisse/images/apache_pb.gif
[localhost:~] vanilla%
```

Figure 4.15 Using awk to feed a pipeline.

✔ Tips

- You can print more than one field:

  awk '{print $1,$7}'
  → /var/log/httpd/access_log

  Figure 4.16 shows the result.

- You can vary the field separator in awk with the -F option (for *field*). This allows you to specify a different field separator than the default (whitespace). If you use a separator of ", then awk will break the line into fields wherever a " appears. For example, in

  awk -F\" '{print $2}'
  → /var/log/httpd/access_log

  the \ is required before the " to remove its special meaning to the shell.

Figure 4.17 shows the result. See how field two ($2) contains a chunk of information that is not easily defined if you use whitespace as the field separator.

```
[localhost:~] vanilla% awk '{print $1,$7}' /var/log/httpd/access_log
66.47.69.205 /~matisse/images/macosxlogo.gif
66.47.69.205 /~matisse/images/apache_pb.gif
66.47.69.205 /~matisse/images/web_share.gif
66.47.69.205 /~matisse/cgi-bin/test
66.47.69.205 /~matisse/cgi-bin/test
66.47.69.205 /~matisse/upload.html
66.47.69.205 /~matisse/images/web_share.gif
66.47.69.205 /~matisse/images/web_share.gif
[localhost:~] vanilla%
```

Figure 4.16 Printing two fields with awk.

```
[localhost:~] vanilla% awk -F\" '{print $2}' /var/log/httpd/access_log
GET /~matisse/images/macosxlogo.gif HTTP/1.1
GET /~matisse/images/apache_pb.gif HTTP/1.1
GET /~matisse/images/web_share.gif HTTP/1.1
GET /~matisse/cgi-bin/test HTTP/1.1
GET /~matisse/cgi-bin/test HTTP/1.1
GET /~matisse/upload.html HTTP/1.1
GET /~matisse/images/web_share.gif HTTP/1.1
GET /~matisse/images/web_share.gif HTTP/1.1
[localhost:~] vanilla%
```

Figure 4.17 Using a different field separator with awk.

FILE AND TEXT PROCESSING

sed

Sed is a *stream editor*—that is, a tool for editing streams of data, whether in a file or the output of some other command.

Create a file called sedtest, using the text in **Figure 4.18**. You can use sed to make it rhyme by changing all the occurrences of *love* to *amore*.

To convert all occurrences of *love* to *amore*:

◆ sed "/love/s//amore//" sedtest

   produces output as shown in **Figure 4.19**.

✔ Tip

■ If you are using sed to change a file and then redirect its output to a new file, check the new file to make sure it's correct, and then replace the old file with the new file.

Perl

Perl is a programming language equally suited to small tasks and large, complex programs.

In this chapter, we are citing Perl in its role as a text-processing utility—a general purpose tool in the same category as awk and sed.

Following is an example of using Perl to create a very small utility program that provides a feature not available from any existing command.

Earlier in this chapter, you learned how to sort data alphabetically or numerically, but what if you simply wanted to look at a file backward—seeing the last lines in the file first? This might come up if you are looking at a file consisting of date/time entries and you want to see the latest ones first.

More About sed and awk

The standard reference for these two venerable Unix utilities is *sed & awk*, by Dale Dougherty and Arnold Robbins (O'Reilly) (www.oreilly.com/catalog/sed2/).

```
There's just no better foray then the one they call love.
When the moon hits your eye, like a big pizza pie, that's love.
When an eel grabs your hand, and won't let go, that's love.
```

Figure 4.18 A sample data file. But it doesn't rhyme very well.

```
[localhost:~] vanilla% sed "/love/s//amore/" sedtest
There's just no better foray then the one they call amore.
When the moon hits your eye, like a big pizza pie, that's amore.
When an eel grabs your hand, and won't let go, that's amore.
[localhost:~] vanilla%
```

Figure 4.19 Using sed to make the data rhyme. (Given the prevalence of puns in Unix, it seems only natural that we should add a few.)

Although Unix provides numerous tools for situations like this, there are still times when you want to do something beyond what the current tools provide. Users of other operating systems look to a catalog of software to see if they can buy a tool that will serve the purpose, or failing that, wait for someone else to create a new tool. Unix users build their own. And often Unix users choose Perl as the programming language in which to build their new tools.

Perl excels at text processing and allows you to do some things very easily that would be difficult or impossible using other tools.

Perl is a complete programming language used for everything from simple utility scripts to very large and complex programs containing tens of thousands of lines of code. Teaching Perl is beyond the scope of this book, but we do want to give you some sense of how useful it is and pique your interest in learning more (see the sidebar "Resources for Learning Perl"). And we cover the basics of Unix shell scripts in Chapter 9, "Creating and Using Scripts."

Our example here is a short script that reverses the order of its input—the last line of input comes out first, and the first line comes out last, regardless of alphabetical or numerical sort order.

The steps are similar to the ones in Chapter 2, "Using the Command Line," in the section "Creating a Simple Unix Shell Script":

```
#!/usr/bin/perl
# script to reverse input
@input = <>;
while ( @input) {
    print pop(@input);
}
```

continues on next page

Resources for Learning Perl

◆ If you have never heard of Perl, a good place to start is Perl Mongers' Perl Fast Facts (www.perl.org/press/fast_facts.html).

◆ If you are looking for online documentation, mailing lists, and other support resources, then go to Perl Mongers Free Online Support (www.perl.org/support/online_support.html).

◆ You can start right on your Mac with man perl.

◆ A primary resource for beginning Perl programmers is *Learning Perl, 3rd Edition*, by Randal L. Schwartz and Tom Phoenix (O'Reilly) (www.oreilly.com/catalog/lperl3/).

◆ The definitive programmer's guide is *Programming Perl, 3rd Edition*, by Larry Wall, Tom Christiansen, and Jon Orwant (O'Reilly) (www.oreilly.com/catalog/pperl3/).

◆ If you are looking to start learning how to use Perl for CGI programming, then check out *Perl and CGI for the World Wide Web, 2nd Edition: Visual QuickStart Guide*, by Elizabeth Castro (Peachpit Press) (www.peachpit.com/books/catalog/73568.html)

FILE AND TEXT PROCESSING

To create a script that will reverse its input:

1. `pico ~/bin/reverse`

   This opens the pico editor and creates the script (called **reverse**) in the bin directory of your home directory, as we did in Chapter 2, "Using the Command Line," with the system-status script. (Make sure you have added `~/bin` to your PATH as described in Chapter 2.)

   The following lines are entered into the `pico` editor:

2. `#!/usr/bin/perl`

   This must be the first line. It tells Unix to use Perl when running this script.

3. `# script to reverse input`

   This line is just a comment, to remind us what the script does.

4. `@input = <>;`

   This line causes all input to go into a variable called `@input`. Each line of input is stored as a separate item in the variable (think of the variable as a storage container for data).

5. `while ( @variable) {`

   This is the start of a loop that will continue as long as there is anything left in the `@input` variable.

6. `print pop(input );`

   This line removes the last item (**pop**) and sends it to `stdout` (`print`)

7. `}`

   This ends the loop. While the script is running, Perl checks here to see if there is anything still in `@input`, and if there is, it executes the `print pop(@input);` line again; otherwise, Perl proceeds to the next line.

   There isn't a next line in this case, so the script stops running when `@input` is empty.

8. You can stop entering text, and exit from the `pico` editor, by pressing Control x .

9. `pico` will ask you if you want to save the changes; you say yes by typing *y*.

10. `pico` asks you to confirm the name you are using to save the file. You confirm by pressing Return .

    You'll be back at the shell prompt.

11. `chmod 755 ~/bin/reverse`

    That makes the script executable so you can run it later (remember that `chmod` means "change mode"; the 755 refers to the mode that sets permissions; see Chapter 8, "Working with Permissions," for more details).

12. `rehash`

    This tells your shell to rebuild its list of available commands to include `reverse`. You're done.

```
[localhost:~] vanilla% cat data
19/Mar/2002:02:13:24
20/Mar/2002:05:03:23
21/Mar/2002:12:23:22
03/Apr/2002:05:10:00
05/Apr/2002:12:03:20
07/Apr/2002:02:12:18
07/Apr/2002:05:17:17
11/Apr/2002:12:34:16
[localhost:~] vanilla% reverse data
11/Apr/2002:12:34:16
07/Apr/2002:05:17:17
07/Apr/2002:02:12:18
05/Apr/2002:12:03:20
03/Apr/2002:05:10:00
21/Mar/2002:12:23:22
20/Mar/2002:05:03:23
19/Mar/2002:02:13:24
[localhost:~] vanilla%
```

Figure 4.20 Comparing the output of cat and reverse.

Congratulations—you've created a new Unix command and written a Perl script.

To display input backward using reverse:

◆ reverse data

This sends the contents of the file data to stdout, last line first. **Figure 4.20** shows a comparison between using cat and reverse on the same file.

You can use multiple files, for example:

reverse data data2 data3

Searching for Text

It is extremely common when using Unix to want to search for specific words or strings of characters inside text files or to search the long output of some command. The main Unix command for this, as we mentioned in Chapter 1, "Why Apple Built Mac OS X on Unix," is grep.

Using grep

To search for a string in a text file:

◆ grep *string file*

For example,

grep memory /etc/rc

finds all the lines in the file /etc/rc that contain the string memory (**Figure 4.21**).

To make the search case-insensitive:

◆ Use the -i option. For example,

grep -i apple /etc/services

Figure 4.22 shows part of the result. Note how both apple and Apple are found.

```
[localhost:~] vanilla% grep memory /etc/rc
# Start the virtual memory system.
ConsoleMessage "Starting virtual memory"
[localhost:~] vanilla%
```

Figure 4.21 Using grep to find the string "memory" in a file.

Not All greps Are the Same

We cover the version of grep that comes with Darwin/OS X. Different flavors of Unix come with different versions of the grep family (grep, egrep, fgrep, agrep), so the exact behavior of each command will vary slightly depending on the version installed on your system. The best way to see the differences is to read the Unix man pages for each command.

```
[localhost:~] vanilla% grep -i apple /etc/services
echo              4/ddp      #AppleTalk Echo Protocol
at-rtmp         201/tcp      #AppleTalk Routing Maintenance
at-rtmp         201/udp      #AppleTalk Routing Maintenance
at-nbp          202/tcp      #AppleTalk Name Binding
.
.
.
appleqtc        458/tcp      #apple quick time
appleqtc        458/udp      #apple quick time
appleqtcsrvr    545/tcp
appleqtcsrvr    545/udp
[localhost:~] vanilla%
```

Figure 4.22 Performing a case-insensitive search with grep. Your output depends on your machine's configuration.

Where grep Gets Its Name

Grep gets its name from g/RE/p, which is a representation of the commands in the old Unix editor **ed** to *"globally search for a regular expression and print."*

Regular expressions make up a complex and powerful system for matching patterns and are available in many Unix programs. We'll cover a small part of regular expressions in this chapter.

The **grep** program is the main Unix command for searching text files or a stream of text (such as the output of another program). The output of **grep** is every line that contains the search string. The default is for searches to be case-sensitive.

To search for a string in multiple files:

◆ Simply add more files to the argument list, perhaps by using wildcards. For example,

```
grep -i network *
```

As we discussed in Chapter 2, "Using the Command Line," the ***** (asterisk) is a special character expanded by the shell to be a list of many files.

This is probably the most common use of **grep**—to find all the occurrences of a string throughout multiple files. When searching multiple files, **grep** adds the filename at the beginning of each line of output so you know which file each line came from:

```
grep reboot /etc/rc*
```

gives output as shown in **Figure 4.23**.

✔ Tip

■ If you give an argument to **grep** that is a directory (instead of a regular file), **grep** gives you an error message saying that the file "is a directory." You can tell **grep** to skip directories by adding the **-d skip** option—for example,

```
grep -d skip NETWORK */*
```

```
[localhost:~] vanilla% grep reboot /etc/rc*
/etc/rc:    ConsoleMessage "Automatic reboot in progress"
/etc/rc:    # We shouldn't get here; CDIS should reboot the machine when done
/etc/rc.boot:      # The root filesystem was checked and fixed.  Let's reboot.
/etc/rc.boot:      # Note that we do NOT sync the disks before rebooting, to
/etc/rc.boot:      ConsoleMessage "Root filesystem fixed - rebooting"
/etc/rc.boot:      reboot -q -n
/etc/rc.boot:# Try fsck -y and reboot if the above fails horribly.
/etc/rc.boot:    fsck -y && reboot
[localhost:~] vanilla%
```

Figure 4.23 Using *grep* to search multiple files.

To recursively search all the files in a directory:

◆ Use the -r option. For example,

`grep -ri network /System/Library`

performs a case-insensitive search (note the -i option) of all the files inside /System /Library/ and all of its subdirectories. This could result in a lot of output, so you might want to pipe the output through the less command (review the less command in Chapter 2, "Using the Command Line"):

`grep -ri network /System/Library | less`

To find the lines that do not match:

◆ Use the -v option.

`grep -v tcp /etc/services`

finds all the lines in the directory /etc/ services that do not contain the string tcp.

To search the output of another command:

◆ Pipe the output of the other command through `grep`.

`last | grep reboot`

shows all the reboots this month.

(The last command shows a history of log-ins to your machine, as well as crashes and reboots.)

✔ Tip

■ Use multiple greps in the pipeline to narrow your request.

`last | grep reboot | grep "Feb 16"`

finds all the reboots on February 16. See how the first grep filters the output of the last command, and the second grep filters the output further, narrowing down the result.

The grep and egrep (e for *extended*) programs have a huge number of options. **Table 4.1** lists some of the more common ones. See the Unix manual for more (type *man grep*).

Table 4.1

Options for grep and egrep	
OPTION	MEANING
-i	Ignore case.
-v	Show only lines that do not match.
-n	Add line numbers.
-l	Show only the names of files in which matches were found.
-L	Show only the names of files without a match.*
-r	Recursively search directories.*
-d skip	Skip arguments that are directories.*

* These options are not as common as the others, but OS X does have them.

Compare with Aqua

Mac OS X provides a nice graphical interface for finding strings of text in files on your Mac, and in some ways it can do a better job than `grep`. In 10.2, you go to File > Find; in earlier versions of Mac OS X, you use the Sherlock application. They both search the names and contents of files. Mac OS X's GUI search tool can also build indexes of files, which speeds up searching. And of course, it is mostly a point-and-click interface.

In practice, `grep` is often easier to use than the Aqua Find command or Sherlock (once you get used to the command line); for example, it is rather hard in the Find command or Sherlock to focus your search on a few specific files, whereas with `grep` you can supply any arbitrary list of files as arguments on the command line.

Using patterns in your search

You will often want to search for something more complicated than a literal string of characters. You might want to search only for lines that begin with a certain string, or for lines that contain a range of dates, such as `Feb 15` or `Feb 16`.

The `egrep` command supports an extremely powerful (and complex) pattern-matching system called *regular expressions*. The `re` in `egrep` stands for "regular expression." (The `grep` command also supports a small number of regular expressions. To avoid switching back and forth, we will stick with `egrep` here.)

Regular expressions are used in a large number of situations in Unix, not only with the `grep` and `egrep` commands. For example, the Unix programs `sed`, `awk`, and `vi` all use regular expressions, as do the C, Perl, Tcl, Python, and Java programming languages. The basic syntax of regular expressions is the same or very similar in a variety of situations, so once you learn how to use them in one area, you have a head start on using them in another.

Regular expressions are built up like mathematical formulas (see the sidebar "Learning More About Regular Expressions"). Still, you can do a lot with the few rules we'll show you here.

An important concept to grasp in using regular expressions is that when you search for "hello," you are really searching for a pattern consisting of six *atoms* (*h, e, l, l,* and *o*). In regular expressions, an atom is a part of the overall expression that matches one character. The most common kind of atom is simply a literal character, so the atom *h* matches the letter *h*. But atoms don't stop there. For example, the atom [*a-d*] matches one letter from the range *a, b, c,* or *d.* So when you see the word `atom` used in the examples below, keep in mind that an atom can be as simple as one character, or it can be a more complex notation that matches one character from a list of possibilities.

Regular expressions have a few major rules, which are demonstrated in the examples below.

Also, note that you always enclose the pattern inside single quotes; this is to prevent the shell from misinterpreting any of the characters used in regexes (as they're traditionally called) that have special meaning to the shell: [] {} . *

To find lines starting with a specific string of characters:

◆ Put a ^ at the beginning of the string;

`grep ^# ~/bin/reverse`

finds only lines beginning with #, and `grep -v ^# script.pl` would find all lines *not* beginning with #. **Figure 4.24** shows the output from both command lines.

The ^ character in a regex is called an *anchor* because it anchors the search string to the start of the line.

To find lines ending with a string:

◆ Putting a $ at the end of the string

`grep today$ logfile`

finds only lines ending with **today**. The $ anchors the search string to the end of the line.

✔ Tip

■ If you anchor a pattern to both the start and end of line—for example, ^word$—then only lines that exactly match will be found.

```
[localhost:~] vanilla% cat ~/bin/reverse
#!/usr/bin/perl
# reverse cat script
#
@file = <>;
while ( @file ) {
    print pop(@file);
}


[localhost:~] vanilla% grep ^# ~/bin/reverse
#!/usr/bin/perl
# reverse cat script
#
[localhost:~] vanilla% grep -v ^# ~/bin/reverse
@file = <>;
while ( @file ) {
    print pop(@file);
}


[localhost:~] vanilla%
```

Figure 4.24 Using a pattern that matches the character at the start of a line.

```
[localhost:~] vanilla% egrep '^[hH]ello'
Hello, nice to meet you.
Hello, nice to meet you.
Say, Hello world
^C
[localhost:~] vanilla%
```

Figure 4.25 Testing a regular expression.

Testing regular expressions

Regular expressions can get quite complex, and learning how to use them takes practice. Luckily there is an easy way to test them to see if they match what you think they will match.

If you use one of the `grep` commands (`grep` or `egrep`) with a pattern but without giving it a filename or input from a pipe, then it waits for you to type input and repeats back to you any lines that match.

In most of our examples we use the `egrep` command because it supports *extended* regular expression. In cases where we don't need extended regexes, we will use plain old `grep`.

Learning More About Regular Expressions

Regular expressions are used not only with the `grep` program but also with multiple Unix programs and programming languages.

Here are a few places to learn more about *regexes* (as they are known to Unix experts):

◆ Learning to Use Regular Expressions (http://gnosis.cx/publish/programming/regular_expressions.html).

   A nice online tutorial, though it assumes you are working with regular expressions in one of the many programming languages that use them.

◆ Steve Ramsay's Guide to Regular Expressions (http://etext.lib.virginia.edu/helpsheets/regex.html).

   An introduction to regular expressions that describes the history and main concepts, and gives examples of their use.

◆ *Mastering Regular Expressions,* by Jeffrey E. F. Friedl (O'Reilly, 1997) (www.oreilly.com/catalog/regex/).

   Considered by many to be the standard in-depth work on regular expressions.

To test a regular expression:

1. Type

   `egrep 'regular expression'`

   For example:

   `egrep '^ [hH]ello'`

   (Using both upper- and lower-case letters means you're looking for both instances.)

   Notice you are not giving `egrep` a file to search. When you press Return , you get a blank line. `Egrep` is waiting for you to type in a line of text, which it will check against the pattern. **Figure 4.25** shows the examples in this task with the text you type highlighted (in `pink`) and the Mac's response in plain (`black`) text. We use this format for the remaining tasks in this section that show examples of testing regular expressions.

2. Type in a line of text that you think should (or should not) match the pattern, and press Return . For example:

   `Hello, nice to meet you.`

   If the shell displays (repeats back to you) the line you typed, then the expression matched (the example above should match). Otherwise, it did not match.

3. Type in another line of text to check.

   `Say, Hello world`

   This does not match the pattern in step 1 because the line does not match the ^ anchor ("look at the beginning of the line").

4. To exit from the test, press Control Return .

✔ Tip

■ In each of the tasks below, try testing the regular expression with several different lines of input to see how each one behaves. Try to predict what will and will not match.

To find lines containing a string in which one character can vary:

◆ Use square brackets to create an atom from a list of characters. For example:

egrep '[FNW]orm A-100'

The atom [FNW] means "One character that matches any of the three atoms F, N, or W." **Figure 4.26** shows examples of testing this pattern with three different matching lines.

To create an atom that is anything *not* in a list:

◆ Use the ^ character as the first character in the list. For example:

egrep '[^FNW]orm A-100'

Figure 4.27 shows examples of testing this pattern (again, you type the text that's in pink). Matching lines will *not* contain any of the following:

Form A-100

Norm A-100

Worm A-100

✔ Tips

■ Notice how the last example is different from the -v option (described earlier). The -v option finds all lines that do not match the whole pattern. The example here finds lines that contain 'orm A-100' but only if the first letter before 'orm' is *not* F, N or W.

■ Notice that the use of ^ here is different from using ^ as the start-of-line anchor. The ^ behaves differently when it is the first character in a square-bracket list.

```
[localhost:~] vanilla% egrep '[FNW]orm A-100'
Worm A-100 is a very virulent worm.
Worm A-100 is a very virulent worm.
Norm A-100 isn't really normal.
Norm A-100 isn't really normal.
Form A-100 must filled out in pink ink.
Form A-100 must filled out in pink ink.
^C
[localhost:~] vanilla%
```

Figure 4.26 Using an atom that matches any character in a list.

```
[localhost:~] vanilla% egrep '[^FNW]orm A-100'
Worm A-100 no longer matches.
Either does Norm A-100.
Nor even Form A-100.
But form A-100 does because of the lowercase f.
But form A-100 does because of the lowercase f.
hello
hello
does this match?
does this match?
how about this?
how about this?
^C
[localhost:~] vanilla%
```

Figure 4.27 Using an atom that matches any character *not* in the list.

```
[localhost:~] vanilla% egrep '.oy'
toy should match
toy should match
so should boy
so should boy
even coy
even coy
but not this line
oy this one doesn't match either!
but oy, this one does.
but oy, this one does.
^C
[localhost:~] vanilla%
```

Figure 4.28 Using a . (period) to match any single character.

To create an atom from a range of numbers:

◆ Use egrep and put square brackets around the range:

egrep 'Feb 1[5-9]' mail.log

The [5-9] means "5, 6, 7, 8, or 9" in regular-expression language.

✔ Tip

■ You can use multiple lists, such as [2-3][0-5] (that means "20-35")

To create an atom from a range of letters:

◆ Use egrep and the square brackets, and a-z for lowercase, A-Z for uppercase. For example:

egrep 'Appendix [B-D]' book.txt

✔ Tip

■ You can make the range case-insensitive by using lowercase and uppercase ranges in the atom:

egrep 'Appendix [B-Db-d]' book.txt

To use a wildcard character:

◆ Use the . character to mean "any single character." For example:

egrep '.oy'

behaves as shown in **Figure 4.28**.

To find lines in which an atom is repeated zero or more times:

◆ Use the * (star) quantifier. For example,

`grep 'Form A-10*'`

behaves as shown in **Figure 4.29**.

In this case the atom is the 0. The * quantifier means "zero or more of the preceding atom." Notice how it found the line in which 0 did not appear at all.

✔ Tip

■ Be careful when using the * character. If an argument contains a * and you don't want the shell to expand it to a list of file names (see "Wildcards" in Chapter 2), then you must make sure any use of * on the command line is either enclosed in quotes or that you escape the * by preceding it with a backslash; for example:

`grep fo\*bar *.txt`

In that case the shell would expand the second * to match all the files names that end in .txt but the shell would pass the string fo*bar to grep as an argument without expanding the *.

```
[localhost:~] vanilla% grep 'Form A-10*'
Form A-100
Form A-100
Form A-10
Form A-10
Form A-1
Form A-1
^C
[localhost:~] vanilla%
```

Figure 4.29 Using * to match zero or more of an atom.

More rules and tools for building regex atoms

The regex examples shown above allow you to perform some fairly sophisticated matching, but there are a lot more ways to create atoms and patterns. **Table 4.2** describes several additional tools you will find useful in constructing more complex patterns. All of the tools and rules in Table 4.2 require egrep. The real key is to experiment using the testing approach described above.

Table 4.2

Rules and Tools for regex Atoms

RULES	TOOL/MEANING
Match 1 or more	Use the + quantifier, "one or more of the preceding atom."
Match 0 or 1	Use the ? quantifier, "zero or one of the preceding atom."
Exact number	Put the number in braces; [a-c]{3} means "any character from the list a-c repeated exactly three times."
Alternatives	Put each alternative in parentheses, and separate them with the pipe character; '(Fox)|(Hound)' means "match lines containing either Fox or Hound."
Match special characters	If you want to match characters that have special meanings in a regex such as [or ^, then *escape* (that is, remove any special meaning) them with a \; for example, \[will match a literal [. Inside a square-bracket list, you do not need to escape anything.
Match ^ inside a list	To include the ^ character in a square-bracket list, put it anywhere except first in the list; for example, [a-c^] matches a, b, c, or ^.

Searching for Files

While grep and egrep are great for searching inside files, they don't look at the names of files or other information about the files such as size or modification date. For that, Unix provides other tools.

locate

Locate searches a database of files for filenames that match its argument. The locate database contains the names of almost all the files on the system (it omits some files for security reasons).

This means that locate can perform a very fast search of practically the whole system, but it only finds files that existed as of the last database update. The database is rebuilt weekly (Sundays at 4:30 a.m. on Mac OS X); see Chapter 11, "Introduction to System Administration," under the section "Running Regularly Scheduled Commands," to learn how to change that.

If you are looking for a file you believe has been around since Sunday, locate is a good way to look for it.

To use locate to search for a file:

◆ locate *string*

Locate produces a list of file paths that include the string. Note that it is case-sensitive:

locate security

and

locate Security

produce different results, as shown in **Figure 4.30** (partial results shown).

✔ Tips

■ locate tends to produce voluminous output, so consider piping its output through grep to filter it or through less to see it one screen at a time. For example:

locate security | grep Library

or

locate security | less

■ Want to count how many files locate located? Pipe it through wc -l:

locate security | wc -l

```
[localhost:~] vanilla% locate security

...

/Library/Documentation/Services/apache/misc/security_tips.html

/System/Library/Frameworks/JavaVM.framework/Versions/1.3.1/Home/lib/security

/System/Library/Frameworks/JavaVM.framework/Versions/1.3.1/Home/lib/security/cacerts

/System/Library/Frameworks/JavaVM.framework/Versions/1.3.1/Home/lib/security/java.policy

/System/Library/Frameworks/JavaVM.framework/Versions/1.3.1/Home/lib/security/java.security

...

[localhost:~] vanilla% locate Security

...

/Library/Receipts/SecurityUpdate10-19-01.pkg

/Library/Receipts/SecurityUpdate10-19-01.pkg/Contents

/Library/Receipts/SecurityUpdate10-19-01.pkg/Contents/Resources

/Library/Receipts/SecurityUpdate10-19-01.pkg/Contents/Resources/BundleVersions.plist

/Library/Receipts/SecurityUpdate10-19-01.pkg/Contents/Resources/da.lproj

...

[localhost:~] vanilla%
```

Figure 4.30 Comparing results for Security and security when using locate. (Your output will differ, but you get the idea.)

find

While `locate` is fast and simple, `find` is more flexible, allowing you not only to search for patterns in filenames but also to specify multiple criteria. You can search by type of file (directory? plain file?), modification date, size, and many more. See the Unix man page (`man find`) for a complete list and several good examples.

The first argument to `find` is always a directory name, which tells `find` where to start looking (it can be . for the current directory). You then specify options to tell `find` which files will match, and finally what to do with each matching filename. The default is to send each matching file name to `stdout`, but you can do other things, such as execute a command using each found filename as an argument.

To search for files based on name:

◆ find *dirname* -name "*pattern*"

For example,

find ~ -name "Pictures*"

would show all the files in your home directory whose names begin with "`Pictures`" (**Figure 4.31**). (Your shell interprets the ~ character as "my home directory." See Chapter 5, "Using Files and Directories.")

To search for files based on type:

◆ Use the -type option to select the file type you want, such as directories.

find ~/Documents -type d

finds all the directories inside your Documents directory (**Figure 4.32**).

To find only regular files, use -type f. See man `find` for a complete list of available types.

✔ Tip

■ Combine the -type option with the -name option to find only files that match both name and type.

find ~ -type d -name "Picture*"

finds only directories whose names begin with "`Picture`."

```
[localhost:~] vanilla% find ~ -name "Pictures*"
/Users/vanilla/Documents/Picture of Susan
/Users/vanilla/Pictures
/Users/vanilla/Pictures/Picture 1.jpg
/Users/vanilla/Pictures/Picture 2.jpg
/Users/vanilla/Pictures/Picture 3.jpg
/Users/vanilla/Pictures/Picture 4.jpg
[localhost:~] vanilla%
```

Figure 4.31 Finding all the files in your home directory whose names start with "Picture."

```
[localhost:~] vanilla% find ~ -name "Pictures*"
/Users/vanilla/Documents/Picture of Susan
/Users/vanilla/Pictures
/Users/vanilla/Pictures/Picture 1.jpg
/Users/vanilla/Pictures/Picture 2.jpg
/Users/vanilla/Pictures/Picture 3.jpg
/Users/vanilla/Pictures/Picture 4.jpg
[localhost:~] vanilla%
```

Figure 4.32 Finding only directories.

A very cool feature of find is its ability to find every file that has been modified after some specific reference file, such as one with a particular date. One use of this feature would be in scripts that perform backups.

To find every file modified after a reference file:

◆ find *dirname* -newer *filename*

 find . -newer "Figure 4.27.doc"

 searches the current directory and all the subdirectories contained inside it for files that have a more recent modification time than the file Figure 4.27.doc.

 Figure 4.33 shows what the output might look like. Notice how the current directory (.) showed up in the list. This is because a directory is considered "modified" whenever a file is added to or removed from it.

✔ Tip

■ Find can also find files that have (or have not) been modified, accessed, or created in the past *n* 24-hour periods, where *n* is any whole number.

```
[localhost:~] vanilla% find . -newer "Figure 4.27.doc"
.
./Chapter 4.doc
./Figure 4.28.doc
./Figure 4.29.doc
./Figure 4.30.doc
./Figure 4.31.doc
./Figure 4.32.doc
./Word Work File D 3702
./Word Work File D 4
[localhost:~] vanilla%
```

Figure 4.33 Finding files modified since a reference file.

One last thing we will show you about find is how to apply a command line to every file that find discovers. That is, the find command produces a list of files, and you may want to use each of those filenames as an argument to a command, over and over. One reason to do this would be to use grep to search each of the found files. Another reason would be to move the found files to a new location, and a third reason would be to remove each of the found files. The possibilities are endless.

Find provides a built-in option for executing a command on each file, the -exec option. However, this option does not handle files with spaces in their names very well. Also, if a large number of files are involved, the -exec option is noticeably slower than using xargs.

The alternative is to pass the output of find, via a pipe, to another command, called xargs. Xargs takes a list of files on stdin and executes its arguments as a command line for every filename it is passed, putting the filename at the end of the command.

To apply a command to each file found:

◆ find . -name "*.doc" -print0 | xargs
  →-0 ls -sk

The first part of the find command should be familiar by now—you are finding all the files in the current directory whose names end in ".doc." The -print0 option tells find not to put a *newline* character at the end of each line of output, but instead to use a special character (called the *null* character), which never appears in filenames.

You then pipe the output of find into xargs. The -0 option to xargs tells it to use the null character as the separator between filenames. Xargs then executes the command line ls -sk *filename* on each filename that it gets from the pipe.

The result will look like **Figure 4.34**, giving us the size (in kilobytes) of every .doc file in the current directory and all of its subdirectories.

✔ Tip

■ You could get just the numbers with:

find . -name "*.doc" -print0 | xargs
→-0 ls -sk | awk '{print $1}'

And if you wanted to add them up, you would create a Perl script called **add** containing

```
#!/usr/bin/perl
while (<>) {
    $sum += $_;
}
print "$sum\n";
```

and then use the command line

find . -name "*.doc" -print0 | xargs
→-0 ls -sk | awk '{print $1}' | add

which

The which command is used specifically to find out which version of a command should be executed. When you enter a command line, Unix looks for the command in a series of directories named in a list called your PATH, and executes the first matching command it finds. (See Chapter 7, "Configuring Your Unix Environment," to learn how to alter your PATH.)

Sometimes there will be more than one command with the same name among the various directories in your path. The which command tells you which one will actually be executed.

To search your path for a command:

◆ which *command*

which ls shows you that the ls command is in /bin/ls, and which cd shows you that the cd command is a shell built in.

```
[localhost:~/Documents/OS X] vanilla% find . -name "*.doc" -print0 | xargs -0 ls -sk
204 ./Chapter 0 - Introduction/Introduction.doc
136 ./Chapter 0 -TOC/Outline.doc
 32 ./Chapter 0 -TOC/Outline_Comments_me.doc
180 ./Chapter 0 -TOC/Outline_v2.doc
260 ./Chapter 0 -TOC/Outline_v2.hb.doc
184 ./Chapter 0 -TOC/Outline_v3.doc
448 ./Chapter 0 -TOC/Outline_v4.doc
 64 ./Chapter 0 -TOC/TOC.doc
 64 ./Chapter 0 -TOC/TOC2.doc
188 ./Chapter 1/Chapter 1 v2.doc
160 ./Chapter 1/Chapter 1 v2beta.doc
204 ./Chapter 1/Chapter 1 v5a/Chapter_1_v5a.doc
 24 ./Chapter 1/Chapter 1 v5a/Figure 1.2.doc
[localhost:~/Documents/OS X] vanilla%
```

Figure 4.34 Finding the size of all the .doc files in the current directory.

SEARCHING FOR FILES

Viewing and Editing Files

All of the commands mentioned here are covered in more detail in Chapter 5, "Using Files and Directories," and Chapter 6, "Editing and Printing Files"; we covered pico in Chapter 2, "Working with the Command Line."

Viewing files

The less, cat, head, and tail commands (described below) are all used for viewing files. For more detailed information on these four commands, see Chapter 5.

less. The less command is a *pager*—a utility for viewing a long stream of text one screen (or *page*) at a time. When you are viewing a Unix man page, you are seeing it *paged* through less.

cat. The cat command is used to combine ("concatenate") files together. It is frequently used to simply display an entire file without pausing.

You can think of cat as a way of displaying short files, and less for displaying long files.

head. The head command is used to show just the beginning of a file or other output.

tail. If head shows the beginning, can you guess what tail does?

Editing files

The three most common Unix tools for editing text files are vi, emacs, and pico. We'll cover these in more detail in Chapter 6.

vi. Vi is a very full-featured command-line text editor. Vi is found on virtually every Unix system and is the primary editing tool we cover in this book.

emacs. Emacs is another full-featured text editor, having far more features than vi (including a built-in adventure game). Many programmers prefer emacs to vi, and the debate over which editor is best approaches religious fervor.

pico. Pico is a fairly simple text editor.

Sending Email

If your Mac OS X system is connected to the Internet, you can easily send email from the command line.

Before you can do this, however, you must fix a configuration problem with Mac OS X (unfortunately, as of spring 2002 Apple reported that it had no plans to fix this problem). To do this, see the `sendmail` section of Chapter 14, "Installing and Configuring Servers." If you want your Mac OS X machine to receive email directly from the Internet, you will also need to read the rest of Chapter 14, but you can send email without being set up to receive.

Assuming you have fixed the `sendmail` problem, you can proceed with sending email from the command line.

mail

The `mail` command lets you compose and send email from the command line (`sendmail`, on the other hand, is a server-based command for transporting messages). It can also be used for reading email if your Mac is set up to receive mail, but we don't cover that here. Instead, we cover the `pine` program, a better tool for reading email from the command line, in Chapter 15, "More Open-Source Software" (at www.peachpit.com/vqp/umox).

To send email from the command line:

1. `mail` *username@host.domain*

   You give the `mail` command one argument: the address you want to send to.

   The `mail` command responds by prompting you for a subject. **Figure 4.35** shows the complete process of sending email from the command line.

2. Enter a subject line and press Return.

   `Mail` responds by waiting for you to enter your message.

3. Enter the body of your message.

   Note that `mail` lacks any kind of fancy editing capability. You must press Return at the end of each line (there is no word wrap).

4. When you're done, type a . on a line by itself and press Return.

5. That is how `mail` knows you are done with your message. `Mail` responds as shown in **Figure 4.35** with EOT (*End of Transmission*).

   Your email is on its way, and you get a shell prompt back.

✔ Tip

■ If you use the -v (verbose) option, you can see details of your message being handed off to another machine over the Internet. **Figure 4.36** shows an example of this.

```
[localhost:~] vanilla% mail susan@cool.domain.net
Subject: Is it soup yet?
This is the message body. You must press enter at the end of
each line.


When you want a blank line press return twice.

.
EOT
[localhost:~] vanilla%
```

Figure 4.35 Sending email from the command line.

```
[localhost:~] vanilla% mail -v president@whitehouse.gov
Subject: Keep the Internet Open and Available
The full protections of the Constitution of the United States
should be available in matters involving the Internet
under the jurisdiction of the United States.

Thank you for your attention.
.
EOT
president@whitehouse.gov... Connecting to wh.eop.gov. via esmtp...
220 wh2.eop.gov - Server ESMTP (PMDF V5.2-33 #41062)
>>> EHLO myhost.mydomain.net
250-wh2.eop.gov
250-8BITMIME
250-PIPELINING
250-DSN
250-ENHANCEDSTATUSCODES
250-EXPN
250-HELP
250-SAML
250-SEND
250-SOML
250-TURN
250-XADR
250-XSTA
250-ETRN
250-XGEN
250-RELAY
250 SIZE 102400000
>>> MAIL From:<user@myhost.mydomain.net> SIZE=268
250 2.5.0 Address and options OK.
>>> RCPT To:<president@whitehouse.gov>
250 2.1.5 president@whitehouse.gov OK.
>>> DATA
354 Enter mail, end with a single ".".
>>> .
250 2.5.0 Ok.
president@whitehouse.gov... Sent (Ok.)
Closing connection to wh.eop.gov.
>>> QUIT
221 2.3.0 Bye received. Goodbye.
[localhost:~] vanilla%
```

Figure 4.36 Using the -v option to mail to see the interaction between machines over the Internet during email transfer.

Any command that produces text on stdout can be piped into mail. You can specify a subject on the command line with the -s option (s for *subject*).

A common reason for piping command output into the mail command is to run a command that takes a while to finish, pipe it into mail, and run the whole command line in the background (see Chapter 2, "Using the Command Line"). This allows you to get back to a shell prompt and get on with your work, and eventually get email when the process is done. You might do this if you wanted to find all the MP3 files in your home directory and email yourself a list.

To pipe output from any command into mail:

◆ find ~ -name "*.mp3" | mail -s "My
  →MP3 files" myaddress@host.domain &
  This pipes the output of the find command into mail. The & at the end of the command line runs the whole thing in the background (as we noted in Chapter 2, "Using the Command Line").

Another useful trick with mail is to take the message body from a file by redirecting stdin.

To take the message body from a file:

◆ mail -s "here is the file"
  →address@host.domain < memofile
  This passes the contents of the file message to mail as the message body.

  Unless the message is made up only of plain text (that is, no images or other nontext material), it does not show up properly. The mail command is very old and predates the common use of email attachments. If you want to send anything besides plain-text email from the command line, you should use pine.

Pine

Pine is a command-line email program that takes over your whole Terminal window (though it is a "full screen" program, it won't take over your whole Mac screen, just the Terminal window you run it from). It can handle email attachments.

Pine was developed as an easier-to-use alternative to another full-screen, command-line email program called elm. The name Pine stands for "Pine *is not* elm." (The Pine program is capitalized, the pine command is not.)

We cover the installation and use of Pine in Chapter 15, "More Open-Source Software."

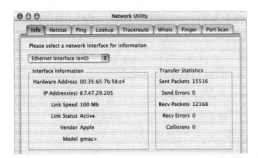

Figure 4.37 The Info panel of Network Utility.

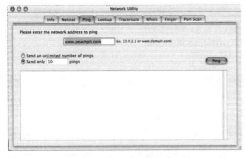

Figure 4.38 The Ping panel of Network Utility.

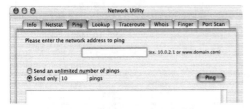

Figure 4.39 Entering a domain name for Ping testing.

Network Analysis

Being a multiuser operating system from its start, Unix has always been intended for use on a network. If your Mac OS X machine isn't already connected to a network, it likely will be at some point. In this section we describe some of the tools for analyzing network activity that come with Mac OS X.

Network Utility

X The Network Utility program (/Applications/Utilities/Network Utility) is an Aqua program that provides a graphical interface for several common network-analysis tasks.

To launch Network Utility:

◆ Double-click the Network Utility icon, or at the command line enter

`open "Network Utility"`

The Network Utility application opens to its Info panel (**Figure 4.37**).

To see if another Internet host is active:

1. Select the Ping tab of Network Utility.
   The Ping panel opens (**Figure 4.38**).

2. Enter a domain name or an IP address to test.

   Figure 4.39 shows a domain name entered for testing. A domain name is the part of a Web address (URL) after the two slashes. It consists of two or more words separated by dots—for example, *www.peachpit.com*. An IP (Internet Protocol) address is a set of four numbers separated by dots. Each number in an IP address is between 2 and 254.

   You can adjust the number of pings (essentially, a request for a response) you want to send.

   continues on next page

NETWORK ANALYSIS

3. Click the Ping button.

Network Utility sends a series of short messages (called *packets*) to the remote machine and expects responses. The results are shown in the lower portion of the window (**Figure 4.40**).

If the packets do not make it to the remote machine and back again, you will see gaps in the icmp seq numbers. These indicate a percent packet loss of greater than 1 percent, especially high time values (that is, the time it took to conduct the ping), or no response at all. (To properly test for packet loss, send at least 100 pings.) Normal time values depend on the nature of your Internet connection. Frequent testing of a handful of remote machines over a period of a few weeks will give you an idea of what is normal for your connection. Some networks are configured to block the kind of packets used in these tests, so in a few cases, a machine or network appears unreachable even though it is functioning normally.

✔ Tip

■ You can run the same test from the command line with:

```
ping -c 10 www.peachpit.com
```

See man ping for many more options.

When your computer connects to another on the Internet, the data being exchanged passes through a series of intermediate special-purpose computers called *routers*. Routers connect networks together (the Internet is an internetwork system, like *inter*state or *inter*national, hence the name).

It is possible to see a list of the routers between your computer and any particular destination you connect to through the Internet. The list can and does vary as networks are added, dropped, and reconfigured.

To trace the route to another Internet host:

1. Select the Traceroute tab in Network Utility (**Figure 4.41**).

2. Fill in the domain name or IP number of a host to test (**Figure 4.42**).

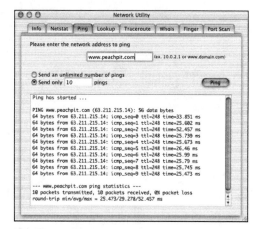

Figure 4.40 What happens when you send ten pings to www.peachpit.com.

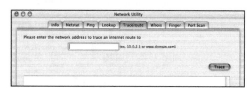

Figure 4.41 The Traceroute panel of Network Utility.

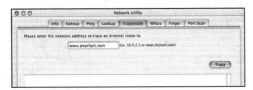

Figure 4.42 Entering a domain name for Traceroute testing.

Figure 4.43 The results of using Traceroute on www.peachpit.com.

3. Click the Trace button.

The trace results appear in the lower part of the Traceroute panel of Network Utility (**Figure 4.43**).

Each line shows one router with the three round-trip times (in milliseconds) for data sent between your computer and the router. If the connection along the way is bad, the round trip time is replaced with an asterisk (*).

✔ Tip

■ You can run the same test from the command line with

traceroute www.peachpit.com

See man traceroute for more options.

Network Utility has half a dozen more features, some of which have a dozen or more options. While they are beyond the scope of this book, you can't hurt your Mac by trying them. **Table 4.3** contains a brief description of the panels other than Info, along with their command-line equivalents.

Table 4.3

Network Utility Features	
FEATURE	**DESCRIPTION**
Netstat	Gives information about raw data that has been sent and received through your network (Ethernet) connection. See man netstat for the command-line version.
Ping	Tests to see if another machine is reachable through the Internet. See man ping for the command-line version.
Lookup	Used to find information about Internet addresses (both domain names and IP numbers). See man dig for the command-line version.
Traceroute	Shows the routers in between your machine and another machine on the Internet. See man traceroute for the command-line version.
Whois	Used to find information about domain names (as opposed to specific machine addresses—use Lookup for that). Finds who owns the domain name and who is responsible for translating addresses in that domain into IP addresses (the "DNS" servers for the domain). See man whois for the command-line version.
Finger	Used to find information about users logged in to other machines on the Internet. Few Internet hosts allow incoming finger requests. See man finger for the command-line version.
Port Scan	Used to see what services a particular Internet host is providing, such as Web server or email server. There is no direct command-line equivalent.

NETWORK ANALYSIS

Using the Internet

The tools described here are the main programs you will use to interact with other machines over the Internet. Although technically speaking anything you do over the Internet involves interacting with another machine, these tools are the ones you will use more intensively for command-line work.

telnet

Telnet is a command for connecting to another machine. Use it to log in to the other machine and get a shell prompt from it, just as the Terminal application gives you a shell prompt on your machine.

Telnet is mostly deprecated these days because it sends data and passwords without encryption, and does not provide the kind of secure connections that ssh provides. See Chapter 12, "Security," and man telnet for more details.

ssh

Ssh (secure shell) is a tool for creating encrypted connections to other machines over the Internet. Like telnet, ssh can be used to log in to another machine. Ssh also can be used to create secure connections between machines for file transfer, or to relay incoming data to a different machine for handling, among other capabilities. Ssh can also provide an encrypted connection for other features such as file transfer (see scp below).

Ssh is the preferred tool for connecting to other machines through the Internet. See Chapter 12, "Security," and man ssh for details.

scp

scp (secure copy) is a tool for transferring files between machines on a network. Scp uses ssh to provide an encrypted connection. See Chapter 12 and man scp for details.

ftp and sftp

Ftp (*file transfer protocol*) is an old tool for transferring files between machines on the Internet. It provides a way of logging in to an FTP server and interactively exchanging files. Because the FTP protocol sends passwords and data without encryption, it shares the vulnerabilities of telnet and is less desirable than scp or a new alternative, sftp (secure ftp). See Chapter 12, man ftp, and man sftp for details.

lynx

Lynx is a command-line, text-only Web browser.

Mac OS X doesn't come with lynx; see Chapter 15, "More Open-Source Software" (at www.peachpit.com/vqp/umox), to learn how to install it.

USING FILES AND DIRECTORIES

5

This chapter is all about showing you how to use files and directories "the Unix way." You have done most of the things in this chapter before, using the Finder. This includes seeing what files and directories are available, copying files, renaming files, and getting information about files. In Aqua, you use one application (the Finder) for many different file-related tasks. In Unix, you use many different applications (that is, commands) to navigate among directories and to create, change, delete, and examine files and directories.

Almost every command you use in Unix involves one or more files or directories. In most cases, when we say "file" when referring to Unix, we mean "file or directory."

All of the tasks in this chapter assume that you have a Terminal window open and that you have read Chapter 2, "Using the Command Line."

Seeing the Whole File System

An important difference between the Unix and Aqua (and Mac OS 9) approaches to files and directories is the way they handle disks and the locations of files.

Aqua locates files in folders, which are in turn located on disks. Each disk has its own hierarchy of files and folders.

In Unix, there is only one hierarchy of directories and files. If you have more than one disk attached to your system, then each disk carries a portion of the hierarchy (as opposed to Mac OS 9, where each disk has a separate hierarchy of files). The beginning of the hierarchy is the *root directory*. **Figure 5.1** shows the hierarchy of your entire file system contained on three disks.

To see the contents of the root directory:

◆ ls /

As discussed in Chapter 2, "Using the Command Line," the ls command (for *list*) shows the names of files and directories. It can be used with any number of arguments. If an argument is the name of a directory, then the contents of that directory are shown; **Figure 5.2** shows the contents of the root directory.

Your first thought may be, "Where did my disk(s) go?"

You may have noticed that the disks you see in the Finder didn't show up in that listing. See Chapter 11, "Introduction to System Administration," for an explanation of how the Unix directory structure is mapped onto your disk(s).

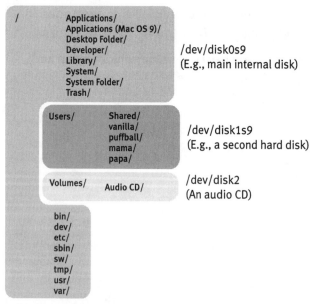

Figure 5.1 There is only one hierarchy of files on your system no matter how many disks you have.

```
[localhost:~] vanilla% ls /
Applications              Network              cores
Applications (Mac OS 9)   Shutdown Check       dev
Cleanup At Startup        System               etc
Desktop                   System Folder        mach
Desktop DB                Temporary Items      mach.sym
Desktop DF                TheFindByContentFolder  mach_kernel
Desktop Folder            TheVolumeSettingsFolder private
Developer                 Trash                sbin
Documents                 Users                sw
InfoTools Installer Log   Volumes              tmp
Late Breaking News        automount            usr
Library                   bin                  var
[localhost:~] vanilla%
```

Figure 5.2 Typing `ls /` shows the contents of the root directory. Your output depends on your machine's configuration.

Compare with Aqua

There is no way to see the contents of the root directory in the Finder. This is probably because Apple doesn't consider the items it has hidden to be useful to an Aqua-only user.

Some Aqua applications will let you navigate to the root directory by typing in the "Go to" field of the Open dialog box, but even then the view you get does not show every file and directory in the root directory. (Some Aqua applications, notably the BBEdit text editor, have an "Open Hidden" choice under the File menu.) The Aqua interface tries to keep you away from the more hard-core Unix files and folders.

If you choose "Go to folder" from the Go menu in the Finder and then type in a / (slash), you will be shown a list of the disks and partitions on your system, along with the Network icon (the globe in **Figure 5.3**).

You *can* use the Go to Folder dialog box to navigate into some of the hidden directories; for example, if you type in /usr you will be shown the contents of the /usr directory. You just can't see the root directory itself.

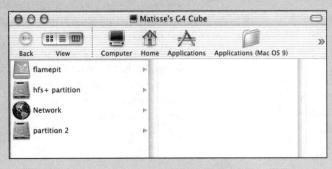

Figure 5.3 You can get a list of the disks and partitions on your system, along with the Network icon, by using the Go to Folder dialog box from the Finder's Go menu.

Seeing Where You Are in the File System

At the Unix command line, you are always "in" some directory in the file system. The directory you are in right now is called your *current working directory* (often abbreviated to either *working directory* or *current directory*).

The current directory is the default directory for commands that read or create files. For example, if you give a command a filename to read, and do not specify where to look for that file, the command will look for it in the current directory.

When you first open a Terminal window, your working directory is your home directory. Your home directory has the same name as your short username. As you perform various tasks, you will frequently change your working directory. You can think of your working directory as being similar to the active Finder window (that is, the active window belonging to the Finder application).

To display the current working directory:

◆ pwd

The **pwd** command "prints" the location of the working directory (**Figure 5.4**). The command doesn't actually print anything—it just outputs the path, and your screen is the normal place for output from commands.

The working directory is the default directory for a large number of actions. For instance, the **ls** command will list the contents of the working directory by default. (Throughout this book we use *vanilla* as an example of a short user name; of course, you will use your own short user name instead.)

```
[localhost:~] vanilla% pwd
/Users/vanilla
[localhost:~] vanilla%
```

Figure 5.4 Typing pwd shows your current working directory. Yours will be different, of course.

Compare with Aqua

The Unix concept of the *working directory* is similar to the graphical user interface (GUI) concept of the active window—the window that currently will be the subject of actions like "close."

Here's another way to compare the Unix working directory with Aqua. Think of what happens when you save or open a file from within an Aqua application. The dialog box that appears starts you off in whatever folder the application most recently used. That folder is similar to the current working directory.

SEEING WHERE YOU ARE IN THE FILE SYSTEM

Understanding and Using Unix Filenames

You use filenames constantly in Unix. Almost every command covered in this chapter, and most commands in Unix, accept one or more filenames as arguments. Those filenames can be entered in two different forms: as *relative paths* or *full paths*.

The difference between relative and full paths is simple but critical. A path tells you not only the name of a file, but also its location in the file system. A path is like a set of directions telling you how to get somewhere.

Full paths *always* begin with a / and give the absolute location of the file in the file system; that is, they give you "directions" to the file starting from the root directory. Every full path is completely unique.

Relative paths *never* begin with a /, and they give you directions to the file starting only from your working directory—that is, from where you are right now. The same relative path can refer to different files, depending on where it is used.

To use a full path as an argument:

◆ `ls /Developer/Tools`

Use a full path as a filename when you want it to refer to the same location, no matter what your working directory is when you type the command (**Figure 5.5**).

The path `/Developer/Tools` means, "Starting from the root directory, look for a directory called Developer, and then inside there look for an entry called Tools."

✔ Tip

■ Use full paths when you are not sure where you are, or when you want to make certain you are referring to a specific version of a file.

To use a relative path as an argument:

◆ `ls Sites/images`

Use a relative path as a filename when you want the path to refer to a location in your current working directory (**Figure 5.6**).

continues on next page

```
[localhost:~] vanilla% ls /Developer/Tools
BuildStrings        RezWack          cvswrappers
CpMac               SetFile          lnresolve
DeRez               SplitForks       pbhelpindexer
GetFileInfo         UnRezWack        pbprojectdump
MergePef            WSMakeStubs      pbxcp
MvMac               agvtool          pbxhmapdump
ResMerger           cvs-unwrap       sdp
Rez                 cvs-wrap         uninstall-devtools.pl
[localhost:~] vanilla%
```

Figure 5.5 Using a full path for a filename means you get the same result regardless of your current directory.

```
[localhost:~] vanilla% ls Sites/images
apache_pb.gif   macosxlogo.gif  web_share.gif
[localhost:~] vanilla%
```

Figure 5.6 Using a relative path as a filename.

The path Sites/images means, "Starting from the current directory, look for a directory called Sites, and then inside there look for an entry called images." If you started from your home directory, then the path would resolve to

/Users/vanilla/Sites/images

If you used that relative path from a working directory of

/Volumes/ExtraSpace,

then the path would resolve to

/Volumes/ExtraSpace/Sites/images

To use a more complex relative path:

◆ ls ../../Developer/Tools

Each .. is a special directory name that means "one step closer to the root directory" (see the sidebar "Two Special Directory Names" for more details). Each .. takes you one step closer to /, so starting from a working directory of /Users/vanilla, the first .. refers to /Users, and the second .. refers to / itself.

So the path ../../Developer/Tools means, "Starting from the working directory, take two steps toward the root directory and then look for a directory called Developer, and then inside that for Tools."

Having the shell type the filename for you

Now that you have been typing some longer paths, you will be happy to learn about the *filename completion* feature of some Unix shells (see Chapter 2, "Using the Command Line," to review shells).

Filename completion is a way of having the shell type most of the filename for you. You can use it whenever you are typing a filename or path that already exists.

To use filename completion:

1. Type any command that will use a filename as an argument.

   For example, to see the long-form listing (the -l option to ls gives the long-form listing) of contents of the /etc/httpd/users directory, type ls -l (make sure to type a space after the command).

2. Type the beginning of the filename. For example,

   /e

   Figure 5.7 shows the command line up to this point.

3. Press Tab.

   The shell will try to fill in the rest of the path for you, or at least as much of the path as is unique. In this case there is only one entry in / that begins with e, so the shell fills in /etc/, and then waits for you to continue (**Figure 5.8**).

```
[localhost:~] vanilla% ls -l /e
```

Figure 5.7 To use filename completion you start by typing the beginning of the filename.

```
[localhost:~] vanilla% ls -l /etc/
```

Figure 5.8 When you press Tab, the shell will try to fill in the rest of the filename for you.

Two Special Directory Names

There are two very special directory names: . and ..

The . directory name always translates to the full path of the working directory. So if your working directory is /Users/puffball/bin, then the relative path ./script.sh translates to /Users/puffball/bin/script.sh.

Anytime you are using a path, you can use the directory name .. to mean "one step closer to the root directory." So if your working directory is /usr/local/bin, then the path ../../sbin translates to /sbin (each .. goes one step closer to /).

The . in script.sh does *not* have any special meaning. The . and .. only have their special meanings when they are used *as a* directory name, not as *part of* a directory or filename.

```
[localhost:~] vanilla% ls -l /etc/h
hostconfig     hosts.equiv     httpd/
hosts          hosts.lpd
[localhost:~] vanilla% ls -l /etc/h
```

Figure 5.9 If there is more then one possible match when you press Tab, the shell will beep. If you then type Control D all the available matches will be displayed. The list in this Figure may be a little different from your system.

4. Type a little more of the filename.

   In this case, just type an h, so your command line now looks like this:

   ls -l /etc/h

5. Press Tab.

   In this case there are many entries in /etc/ that begin with h, so the shell will beep. If you then type Control D, the shell displays all the entries that match (**Figure 5.9**). You should see the one you want among the entries listed.

   Notice how the shell repeats the partial command line after showing you the possible matches.

6. Type just enough of the filename to make it unique. In this case that would be a t, so your command line now looks like this:

   ls -l /etc/ht

7. Press Tab.

   The shell fills in some more, so now your command line looks like this:

   ls -l /etc/httpd/

8. Press Tab again.

   The shell shows you everything in /etc/httpd/ (**Figure 5.10**) and repeats the partial command line.

   continues on next page

```
[localhost:~] vanilla% ls -l /etc/httpd/
httpd.conf.bak      magic           mime.types.default
httpd.conf.default  magic.default   users/
[localhost:~] vanilla% ls -l /etc/httpd/
```

Figure 5.10 Another example of the shell's displaying possible matches after you press Tab and Control D.

9. Repeat the process of typing a little more of the filename and pressing Tab until the filename you want is filled in.

   In this case it should be sufficient to type a u, and then press Tab. That should fill in the whole filename you want:

   ls -l /etc/httpd/users/

10. If there are more arguments, type them in.

    In this example, there would not be any more arguments. In other cases you might have more filenames, or other arguments to add to the command line.

11. Press Enter when the command line is complete. **Figure 5.11** shows the final result. (You should see a line for each user on your system.)

✔ Tip

■ Use filename completion as much as you can, as it will help avoid misspellings.

A Special Name for Home

The ~ (tilde) character has a special meaning when used on the command line in a path. It translates to "the home directory of the user" whose username follows the ~. So ~puffball translates to /Users/puffball.

If the ~ is used without a username, for example, in ~/Documents, then it translates to the home directory of whichever user is running the command.

The actual locations of users' home directories are different on different Unix systems, and in some cases different users on the same system may have their home directories in nonstandard places. For example, in Mac OS X, regular users have their home directories in /Users, but the root user's home directory is /var/root.

Using the ~ character lets the shell do the work of figuring out where a user's home directory is, so you can use ~puffball without having to know exactly where puffball's home directory is, and you can use ~/ to refer to your own home directory regardless of your working directory.

```
[localhost:~] vanilla% ls -l /etc/httpd/users/
total 32
-rw-r-r-  1 root  wheel  142 Mar 14 14:50 howard.conf
-rw-r-r-  1 root  wheel  207 Mar 14 14:52 matisse.conf
-rw-r-r-  1 root  wheel  141 Jan 28 13:16 noway.conf
-rw-r-r-  1 root  wheel  143 Dec 26 12:48 vanilla.conf
[localhost:~] vanilla%
```

Figure 5.11 The result of the final, completed command line. Your output depends on the user accounts you've created on your system.

Moving Around in the File System

When using Unix, you will frequently want to change your working directory because the current directory is the default location for many commands (the terms *current directory* and *working directory* are used interchangeably in Unix documentation, as discussed above in "Seeing Where You Are in the File System"). For example, the `ls` command lists the contents of the current directory if given no arguments. If you never changed your working directory, you would often need to type very long paths and would be more likely to make mistakes.

To change your working directory:

◆ `cd Public`

The `cd` command takes one argument and produces no output (unless it fails to work; remember that in Unix, "silence means success"). The argument to `cd` is the path of a directory that will become your new working directory (in this case, "Public"). You can see where you are with `pwd`.

Notice how your shell prompt changes to reflect your new working directory. **Figure 5.12** shows the shell prompt before and after the `cd` command. See the sidebar "A Special Name for Home" for an explanation of the ~ character.

In this example, Public is a relative path, but quite often you will use a full path:

```
[localhost:~] vanilla% cd Public
[localhost:~/Public] vanilla%
```

Figure 5.12 Using `cd` to change your current directory. Your prompt also changes.

◆ `cd /etc/httpd`

takes you to /etc/httpd regardless of where you were.

✔ Tip

■ You can use the special directory name `..` with the `cd` command:

`cd ../..`

To move back to your home directory:

◆ `cd`

If you use the `cd` command with no arguments, it will take you back to your home directory.

Filenames Are Case-Sensitive

Unix systems, including Darwin, use case-sensitive filenames. So at the command line, a file or directory named Public is not the same as one named public.

Your Mac uses a format for its disks called the Macintosh HFS+ file system. The HFS+ format is a "case-preserving, case-insensitive" file system. Apple has done a very nice job of dealing with this in Mac OS X.

If you are working at the command line on an HFS+ partition (HFS+ is the normal way a Mac OS X partition will be formatted), then file and directory names are case-insensitive.

If you are working in a UFS partition (a common way of formatting in the Unix world), then file and directory names are case-sensitive, and if you look at a UFS folder from the Finder, you will see that you can have two files whose names differ only in case—for example, FOO and foo.

Seeing the Contents of Directories

We normally think of a directory as "containing" files, but in reality a directory is just a special kind of file. A directory contains a list of entries. Each entry is the name of a file or another directory. This is an important concept. In Unix, the only place where a file's name is actually stored is in the directory. Filenames are not stored inside the files themselves. When you rename a file, you are changing the entry in a directory, but not changing the file. And when you remove a file, you are removing the file's name from a directory. The operating system removes the file if there are no other directory entries for that file. This becomes very important when trying to understand "hard links," which are

described below in the section "About Links (the Unix Version of Aliases)." (Hard links are a way of having more than one directory entry that all refer to the same actual file.)

To list the contents of the current directory:

◆ ls

You will see all of the nonhidden entries in the current directory (see below for listing hidden entries).

To list the contents of any directory:

◆ ls *path*

If *path* is a directory, then the contents of the directory will be shown. The *path* is always optional with the ls command. If omitted the default *path* is . (the current directory).

```
[localhost:~] vanilla% ls /bin /sbin
[           csh          echo        ln       ps       sh        test
bash        date         ed          ls       pwd      sleep     zsh
cat         dd           expr        mkdir    rcp      stty      zsh-4.0.4
chmod       df           hostname    mv       rm       sync
cp          domainname   kill        pax      rmdir    tcsh


/sbin:
SystemStarter   fsck_msdos    mount_cd9660    mount_webdav   restore
autodiskmount   halt          mount_cddafs    newfs          route
badsect         ifconfig      mount_devfs     newfs_hfs      routed
clri            init          mount_fdesc     newfs_msdos    rrestore
dmesg           ipfw          mount_ftp       nfsd           rtsol
dump            kextload      mount_hfs       nfsiod         service
dumpfs          kextunload    mount_msdos     nologin        shutdown
dynamic_pager   mach_init     mount_nfs       ping           slattach
fastboot        md5           mount_smbfs     ping6          tunefs
fasthalt        mknod         mount_synthfs   quotacheck     umount
fsck            mount         mount_udf       rdump
fsck_hfs        mount_afp     mount_volfs     reboot
[localhost:~] vanilla%
```

Figure 5.13 Supplying multiple arguments to ls to see the contents of more than one directory.

You can list the contents of several directories by specifying multiple paths on the command line. **Figure 5.13** shows the output from the command line

`ls /bin /sbin`

(Each the files listed is actually a command. Use the `man` command described in Chapter 4, "Useful Unix Utilities," to learn about each of them.)

Hidden files

Unix normally does not show you files whose names begin with a . (a period, or "dot" in Unix-speak). These *dot files* are typically configuration files that are used by programs such as your shell when they start up. Dot files are something like the preferences files that littered your System Folder in pre–OS X versions of the Mac OS. See the sidebar "More About Hidden Files" for details.

To see hidden files:

◆ Use the -*a* or -A option to `ls`.

Unix (and the Mac OS X Finder) hides files whose names begin with a . (dot).

Adding the -*a* option shows all dot files (-*a* for "all files").

The -A option is the same as -*a* except that the two special directory names . and .. are not shown. In this case, it's -A for "almost all."

Figure 5.14 compares the output of

`ls`

`ls -a`

`ls -A`

```
[localhost:~] vanilla% ls
Current Projects   Library        Pictures        bin
Desktop            Movies         Public          system-status
Documents          Music          Sites
[localhost:~] vanilla% ls -a
.                  .exrc          Documents       Sites
..                 .login         Library         bin
.CFUserTextEncoding .ssh          Movies          system-status
.DS_Store          .tcsh_history  Music
.Trash             Current Projects Pictures
.bash_history      Desktop        Public
[localhost:~] vanilla% ls -A
.CFUserTextEncoding .login        Documents       Public
.DS_Store          .ssh           Library         Sites
.Trash             .tcsh_history  Movies          bin
.bash_history      Current Projects Music         system-status
.exrc              Desktop        Pictures
[localhost:~] vanilla%
```

Figure 5.14 Using the -*a* and -A options to `ls` reveals dot files. Your output will be different.

Getting more information from ls

The -l option to ls gives the "long" form of its output, listing one line for each entry and giving information about the file's sizes, date of last change, and other information.

See "Getting Information About Files and Directories" later in this chapter for more on the -l option.

Sorting the output of ls

The default for ls is to sort its output alphabetically. By using the -t option you can cause the output to be sorted according to the *time* the file was last changed.

To sort the list by time instead of name:

◆ Use the -t option to ls.

This is most useful when it's combined with the -l option (for example, ls -lt *.jpg),

because the -l option causes the modification date and time to be displayed.

Figure 5.15 compares the output of ls -l with ls -lt.

To reverse the sort order:

◆ Use the -r option (r for *reverse*).

Figure 5.16 compares the output of ls with ls -r.

✔ Tip

■ If you want to find out which files in a directory were most recently modified, use ls with the l, t, and r options:

ls -ltr

That will put the most recently modified files at the bottom of the list, so even if the list of files is very long, the last thing on your screen will be the most recently modified files.

SEEING THE CONTENTS OF DIRECTORIES

```
[localhost:~/Documents] vanilla% ls -l
total 48
-rw-r--r--   2 vanilla  staff    55 Jan  2 17:37 foo
-rw-r--r--   1 vanilla  staff   331 May  8 19:04 novel.txt
-rw-r--r--   1 vanilla  staff   134 May  8 19:06 report.txt
-rw-r--r--   2 vanilla  staff    55 Jan  2 17:37 test1.txt
-rw-r--r--   1 vanilla  staff    87 Jan  2 17:38 test2.txt
-rw-r--r--   1 vanilla  staff    62 Jan  2 17:38 test3.txt
drwxr-xr-x   3 vanilla  staff   264 May  5 13:39 vi-practice
[localhost:~/Documents] vanilla% ls -lt
total 48
-rw-r--r--   1 vanilla  staff   134 May  8 19:06 report.txt
-rw-r--r--   1 vanilla  staff   331 May  8 19:04 novel.txt
drwxr-xr-x   3 vanilla  staff   264 May  5 13:39 vi-practice
-rw-r--r--   1 vanilla  staff    62 Jan  2 17:38 test3.txt
-rw-r--r--   1 vanilla  staff    87 Jan  2 17:38 test2.txt
-rw-r--r--   2 vanilla  staff    55 Jan  2 17:37 foo
-rw-r--r--   2 vanilla  staff    55 Jan  2 17:37 test1.txt
[localhost:~/Documents] vanilla%
```

Figure 5.15 Adding the -t option causes ls to sort by the time of last modification.

To list only files matching a pattern:

See the entry on command-line wildcards in Chapter 2, "Working with the Command Line," or pipe the output of ls through grep (review Chapter 4, "Useful Unix Utilities," or man grep).

Sometimes you will want list the entries of a directory—its own directories and their subdirectories, and so on. This is known as a *recursive* listing. There is an easy way to do this:

To recursively list the contents of a directory:

◆ ls -R *path*

If *path* is a directory, then ls will recursively list the contents of *path* and its subdirectories (in this case, *R* is for *recursive*). **Figure 5.17** compares the output from

ls ~/Sites

and

ls -R ~/Sites

Notice how with the -R option, the listing shows the contents of the two subdirectories.

```
[localhost:~/Public] vanilla% ls
cgi-bin     dancer      images      index.html   upload.html
[localhost:~/Public] vanilla% ls -r
upload.html  index.html  images     dancer       cgi-bin
[localhost:~/Public] vanilla%
```

Figure 5.16 Using the -r option causes ls to reverse the sorted order of its output.

```
[user-112uhed:/usr/local] vanilla% ls ~/Sites
images      index.html test
[user-112uhed:/usr/local] vanilla% ls -R ~/Sites
images      index.html test

/Users/vanilla/Sites/images:
apache_pb.gif    macosxlogo.gif  web_share.gif

/Users/vanilla/Sites/test:
second_test.txt test_one.txt    third_test.txt
[user-112uhed:/usr/local] vanilla%
```

Figure 5.17 Using the -R option tells ls you want a recursive directory listing.

Viewing the Contents of Text Files

Because Unix uses text files for so many things (a few examples are system configuration, source code, log files, and documentation), you will frequently want to view the contents of text files. Unix provides many tools to do this, and we've described the more common ones here. To learn how to edit text files, see Chapter 6, "Editing and Printing Files."

All of the tools shown here apply not only to viewing text files but also to seeing the output of other commands; that is, you can pipe the output of commands into the tools shown here. (Review Chapter 2, "Working with the Command Line," the section "Creating Pipelines of Commands.")

The two most common ways to view text files are with the commands `cat` and `less`. We have seen these commands in earlier chapters, but we will go into more detail about them here.

The `cat` command (short for *concatenate*) combines all of its input and sends it without any pauses to `stdout` (review Chapter 2, the section "About Standard Input and Output," for more on `stdout`).

Remember that the `less` command is a *pager*, a program that displays one page or screen of a file at a time, waiting for your command to show the next page.

Using a pager

The two most common pager programs are called `more` and `less`. The `less` program is an advanced version of the `more` program, so that is the one we describe here. (The `more` program was invented first, and gets its name from the fact that you have to keep asking it to show you *more* of a file. The `less` command's name is the sort of recursive word game that Unix programmers love: `less` is an improved version of `more`; thus `less` is more.)

To view a file one screen at a time

1. `less` *path*

   If your Terminal window is 24 lines high, then each "page" is 23 lines long—that is, one line less than your Terminal height. `less` uses the bottom line of the window to display status information and to accept some commands from you.

2. If you want to go forward one page, press the `Spacebar` .

3. If you want to good backwards one page, then press `B` (for "back").

4. If you want to skip forward to the next occurrence of *string*, then type:

   `/string`

   and then press `Return` .

5. If you want skip backward to the prior occurrence of *string*, type

   `?string`

   and then press `Return` .

6. If you want to go directly to line 23, type 23G (that's an uppercase G).

7. If you want to go directly to the end of the file, type g (for *go*).

8. If you want to exit from `less`, type q (for *quit*).

✔ Tip

- Pipe the output of other commands into `less` so you can see their output a page at a time. For example,

  `grep Copyright *.c`

  searches all the `.c` files in the current directory for the string `Copyright` (see Chapter 4, "Useful Unix Utilities," or `man grep` for details on `grep`).

  The resulting output could be very long, so you pipe it through less:

  `Copyright *.c | less`

Sometimes you want to see an entire file without pausing. Perhaps you know the file is very short, or you want to use the Terminal window's scroll bars to move up and down. You might want to select the text with the mouse to copy or print it.

Another reason to see an entire file is to join two or more files together. Unix provides the cat tool for this purpose.

To see an entire file without pausing:

◆ cat *path*

The cat command gets its name from *concatenate*, and in fact that is what it does—it concatenates (or combines) all the files in its argument list and sends them to its output. For example,

cat *file1 file2 file3*

results in the contents of all three files appearing on your screen without a break.

✔ Tips

■ Use cat to concatenate several files into one new file:

cat *file1 file2 file3* > newfile

■ Use the -n option to number lines. For example:

cat -n script.pl

Figure 5.18 shows an example of using cat -n to see a file with line numbers. (The example uses the script you created in Chapter 2, "Working with the Command Line.")

■ Use the -s option to "squeeze out" blank lines, resulting in single-spaced output. For example:

cat -s file1 file2 > newfile

```
[user-112uhed:~] vanilla% cat -n bin/system-status
     1  # This is a comment. Comments are good.
     2  # This is my first shell script.
     3  echo "System Status Report"
     4  date
     5  echo -n "System uptime and load:" ;  uptime
     6  echo -n "Operating System: " ; sysctl -n kern.ostype
     7  echo -n "OS Version: " ; sysctl -n kern.osrelease
     8  echo -n "OS Revision number: " ; sysctl -n kern.osrevision
     9  echo -n "Hostname: " ; sysctl -n kern.hostname
    10
    11  bytes=`sysctl -n hw.physmem`
    12  megabytes=`expr $bytes / 1024 / 1024`
    13  echo "Physical memory installed (megabytes): $megabytes"
    14
[user-112uhed:~] vanilla%
```

Figure 5.18 Using cat -n adds line numbers to the output of cat.

Seeing just the beginning or end of a file

Sometimes you want to see just the first (or last) few lines of a file. You might want to confirm that the file contains what you expect, or to see the last lines added to a log file.

The Unix commands head and tail show you the beginning or end (respectively) of their input.

To view just the beginning of a file:

◆ head *path*

For example:

head /conf/config.txt

The head command will show you the first 10 lines of a file.

You can control the number of lines to display by giving the number as an option. For example,

head -15 /etc/rc

displays the first 15 lines of the system-configuration file /etc/rc (**Figure 5.19**).

To view just the end of a file:

◆ tail *path*

For example:

tail /var/log/mail.log

The tail command works just like the head command, but it shows you the end of a file. For example,

tail -100 /var/log/mail.log

displays the last 100 lines of the system mail log.

```
[user-112uhed:~] vanilla% head -15 /etc/rc
#!/bin/sh


##
# Multi-user startup script.
#
# Copyright 1997-2002 Apple Computer, Inc.
#
# Customize system startup by adding scripts to the startup
# directory, rather than editing this file.
##


##
# Set shell to ignore Control-C, etc.
# Prevent inadvertent problems caused by interrupting the shell during boot.
##
[user-112uhed:~] vanilla%
```

Figure 5.19 The head command shows the specified number of lines from the start of its input.

VIEWING THE CONTENTS OF TEXT FILES

✔ Tip

- The head and tail commands can both be used on multiple files; add as many file names as you need on the command line. For example:

  `tail file1 file2` or `head *.html`

  The output will have each file's name.

We've mentioned system log files several times because Unix systems keep a variety of log files to record system events (startup and shutdown, email being sent or received, and Web pages served by a Web server, to name a few).

Checking the addition of new lines to a log file is very useful. You might be debugging a piece of software or watching to see the effect of some change to your network. You could continuously run the tail command, but it is far more useful to tell the tail command to simply keep showing you any new lines as they are added.

To view the end of a file while it is growing:

1. Use the -f option to tail.

   `tail -f /var/log/system.log`

   shows all lines being added to the main system log file as they are added.

   The -f (for *follow*) option shows you the end of the file and keeps displaying new lines as they are added. Unix experts call this "tailing a file."

More About less

The less program has a large number of options and an even larger number of commands for moving around inside a file. Type man less at a shell prompt to read the Unix manual entry on less for a complete (if rather technical) description of its capabilities and features.

---

2. When you want to stop `tail -f`, press Control C .

✔ Tips

- Keep an extra Terminal window open when you need to run `tail -f`. That way, you can see the file you are tailing in one window and do your work in the other one.

- Pipe the output of other commands through head or tail to see just the start or end of the output. For example,

  `last | tail`

  shows just the last 10 lines of output from the last command (which shows all logins, crashes, and reboots in the current month; see man last).

More About Hidden Files

Mac OS X uses a variety of files and directories that are hidden from casual view. In most cases you will have no reason to mess with these files, but as you get further in Unix, you will want to know what they are and why there are there.

A good summary of the hidden files and folders used by OS X is at "Mac OS X Hidden Files & Directories" (Westwind Computing; www.westwind.com/reference/OS-X/invisibles.html).

Also, see Chapter 7, "Configuring Your Unix Environment," for a discussion of how to make some hidden files appear in the Finder.

Creating Files and Directories

There are many ways to create files and directories from the command line. The method you choose will depend on your purpose. Two common purposes are to capture the output of a command into a file, and to create a new, empty directory. Chapter 6, "Editing and Printing Files," covers the more complex tasks of editing files from the command line, but we'll go over the basics here.

To create a new directory:

◆ mkdir *path*

The mkdir command (for "make directory") takes one or more arguments, each of which is a *path* of a new directory. The path (as with all path arguments) may be relative or absolute. The mkdir command produces no output unless an error is encountered.

✔ Tip

■ Use ls to check that your new directory was created (**Figure 5.20**).

To create a series of nested directories:

◆ Use the -p option to mkdir.
For example,

mkdir -p test/*dir1*/*dir2*

makes all the directories in the path if they do not already exist (**p** for *path*). So if **test** already exists, only **dir1** and **dir2** will be created.

To create an empty file:

◆ touch *ath*

The touch command takes one or more paths as arguments. If any of the files do not exist, they are created. The touch command updates the file access time on each file. You could create several empty files at once:

touch file1 .../test/*file2* /tmp/*file3*

Creating a file from command output

The output of most commands can be sent into a file instead of your screen by adding > path/to/file at the end of the command line. If the file already exists, the old contents are replaced. Use >> to append or create instead of replacing the old contents. (Review the section "To save output in a file" in Chapter 2, "Working with the Command Line.")

```
[user-112uhed:~] vanilla% ls
Current Projects    Library       Pictures        bin
Desktop             Movies        Public          system-status
Documents           Music         Sites
[user-112uhed:~] vanilla% mkdir "My Projects"
[user-112uhed:~] vanilla% ls
Current Projects    Library       My Projects     Sites
Desktop             Movies        Pictures        bin
Documents           Music         Public          system-status
[user-112uhed:~] vanilla%
```

Figure 5.20 Use the ls command to check that mkdir really created a directory. (What you see will be different.)

Copying Files and Directories

In the Finder, you select files to copy by clicking and option-dragging them or by choosing File and then Duplicate.

In Unix, you select files to copy by typing their names and/or paths as arguments to the cp command (cp for *copy*). You can use wildcards (see Chapter 2, "Working with the Command Line"), and the files need not all start in the same directory.

The cp command behaves differently depending on its arguments. For example, it will behave differently if its last argument is a directory rather than a file. The cp command produces no output unless it encounters an error.

To copy a file in the same directory:

◆ cp *oldfilename newfilename*

If *newfilename* is an existing nondirectory file, then cp will attempt to overwrite the file, replacing its contents.

To copy a file into a directory:

◆ cp *oldfilename directorypath*

If the last argument to cp is a directory, then the file is copied *into* the directory and the copy will have the same name as the original.

cp /etc/appletalk.cfg .

will create a copy of /etc/appletalk.cfg in the current directory (represented by .), and the copy will also be named appletalk.cfg.

To copy a file from one directory into another and change its name:

◆ cp oldfilename *directory/newname*

Simply make sure that the last argument to cp is a path to a file, not to a directory. For example:

cp /etc/appletak.cfg /tmp/atalk.copy

To copy more than one file at a time:

◆ cp *file1 file2 directorypath*

For example:

cp script.pl config.pl bin/

When cp is used with more than two arguments, it assumes that the last argument is a directory (you'll get an error message if it is not). All the files are then copied into the directory.

The source files need not all be in the same directory. The following example would copy all the .mp3 files from the /tmp and Public/ directories into the Music/ directory:

cp /tmp/*.mp3 Public/*.mp3 Music/

To copy an entire directory:

◆ cp -R directory destination

For example:

cp -R /etc/httpd .

copies the entire /etc/httpd directory into the current directory.

With the -R option, cp will recursively copy directories' names in its arguments. The *destination* must be a directory.

cp -R *file1 dir1 dir2 dir3*

copies *file1* and all of *dir1* and *dir2* into *dir3*.

continues on next page

✔ Tip

- Add the -p option to tell cp to attempt to preserve the file-modification times and permissions on the file(s). For example,

  `cp -Rp /etc/httpd .`

  We say "attempt" because some information about the files may not be preserved unless you execute the command as root, using the sudo command described in Chapter 11, "Introduction to System Administration."

To copy (only) the contents of an entire directory:

- ◆ cp -R *directory/ destination*

  If you append a / to the path of a directory you are copying, then the *contents* of that directory are copied. This is tricky. These two command lines are *not* the same:

  `cp -R /etc/httpd .`

  `cp -R /etc/httpd/ .`

  The extra / in the second one changes its behavior. With the trailing / on the source directory, cp will copy only *the contents* of the directory and not the directory itself.

Table 5.1 shows more options for the cp command.

Table 5.1

More Options for cp

Option	Meaning
-i	*Inquire* before overwriting existing files.
-f	Attempt to remove files that cannot be overwritten. Ignores -i.
-p	Attempts to *preserve* file permissions and modification dates.
-r	Similar to -R, but *symbolic links* (similar to aliases) are followed, not copied, and certain special files are copied instead of being re-created (see the section "About Links," later in this chapter, for more detail).
-H	Symbolic links on the command line are followed (overrides some of the behavior of -R). The symbolic links in the copied directory are still copied, not followed.
-L	Used with -R, this causes all symbolic links to be followed, not copied.

Shorter paths for CpMac and MvMac

The CpMac and MvMac commands (along with a few others) are installed with the Developer tools in a place where your shell will not normally find them, which is why you have to use the full paths of these commands, unlike other commands such as cp and mv (whose full paths are actually /bin/cp and /bin/mv).

See Chapter 7, "Configuring Your Unix Environment," to learn how to "teach" your shell about the /Developer/Tools directory so you do not need the full paths to use CpMac and MvMac.

Note: You can find the full path of any command that your shell *does* know about with the which command:

`which mv`

Old Mac Files in an OS X World

When the Macintosh operating system was introduced in 1984, one of its many innovations was the fact that files "remembered" which application created them. They did this by storing extra information about each file (metadata) in a *resource fork,* which is essentially a second file invisibly attached to the main file. Early Macintosh applications stored a wide variety of information in their resource forks.

As useful as the resource fork feature is, it simply has not been adopted by any other commonly used operating system. As a result, Mac users have often had trouble when sending Macintosh files to non-Macintosh systems because the files lose the resource fork, which in some cases renders them useless.

Not all pre–Mac OS X files store data in the resource fork. For example, applications that are intended to be shared with non-Macintosh systems create files that don't use the resource fork. Nonetheless, some Macintosh applications still use the resource fork.

Standard Unix programs such as cp and mv do not know about resource forks. If you are using Unix command-line tools to manipulate files that may have been created by traditional Mac applications, you need to be aware that you will lose the resource forks. In some cases an alternative will be available, such as the CpMac and MvMac tools described here.

Copying files and preserving the Mac metadata

Many Macintosh applications built before Mac OS X, and applications that use the Carbon libraries, store some information *(metadata)* in files in a way that Unix programs do not recognize. (The Carbon libraries are software components that Apple provides to make it easier for developers to convert pre–Mac OS X software to run on Mac OS X without using the Classic environment.) If you use the standard Unix tool (cp) to copy those files, then some information will be lost, specifically the Mac creator and type codes. Among other things, this means that the Finder will not know which application to open if you double-click the file, and it will lose its icon.

The Mac OS X Developer Tools include tools for dealing with Mac files from the command line.

To copy files and preserve the Mac metadata:

◆ Use the command /Developer/Tools/ CpMac instead of the cp command.

/Developer/Tools/CpMac only supports the -r option, which is essentially the same as the -R option to cp. None of the other options for cp will work.

For example, to copy a FileMaker Pro file named Open Source DB from the current directory into your Documents directory:

```
/Developer/Tools/CpMac "Open Source
→DB" ~/Documents/
```

Renaming or Moving Files

As we mentioned previously, a file's path is both its name and its location, so renaming a file is really the same as moving a file. In Unix, to move is to rename, and to rename is to move. When you move a file from one directory to another, you are removing the file's name from the first directory and adding it to the list of files in the second directory. You are actually modifying the directory, not the file.

To move or rename a single file or directory:

◆ mv *oldpath newpath*

If *newpath* does not exist, then the old file will be moved/renamed to the new path.

If *newpath* is an existing directory, then the old file will be moved into the destination directory.

If you add a trailing / to the destination directory name, mv will make sure that it is in fact a directory (you will get an error if it is not).

If *newpath* is an existing file, then mv will attempt to overwrite the old file. You cannot overwrite directories. If there is an existing directory where you want to move something, you must rename or delete the existing directory first.

To move several files at once:

◆ mv *path1 path2 path3 destinationpath*

The mv command handles arguments in a manner very similar to that of the cp command described above.

If the mv command is used with more than two arguments, it assumes that the final argument is a directory name and moves all the earlier files into that directory. **Table 5.2** shows the options for the mv command.

To move files and preserve the Mac metadata:

◆ Use the */Developer/Tools/MvMac* command instead of mv.

As with the CpMac command described above, there is a MvMac command:

/Developer/Tools/MvMac oldpath newpath

Unlike mv, the MvMac command does not support the -i or -f options.

Table 5.2

Options for mv	
OPTION	MEANING
-i	*Inquire* before overwriting existing files.
-f	*Force* no warnings when overwriting files (that is, you don't want to be notified about files being changed).

Deleting Files and Directories

In Unix, when you remove a file or directory, it is gone forever.

In Unix, when you remove a file or directory, it is gone forever.

In Unix, when you remove a file or directory, it is gone forever.

Are we clear on this?

The file is not moved to the Trash, where you can go back and retrieve it later, and recovering a deleted file is extremely difficult (see the sidebar "To Use the Trash from the Command Line").

To remove a file:

◆ rm *path*

You can *remove* multiple files by supplying multiple paths as arguments; for example:

rm *file1 file2* *.jpg

To remove an empty directory:

◆ rmdir *path*

If the directory named by *path* is not empty, you will get an error message. As with many commands, you can supply multiple file paths.

To remove a directory and everything inside it:

◆ Use the -r option with rm. For example:

`rm -r file1 directory1/ file2`

Table 5.3 shows the options for the rm command.

✔ Tips

■ Be extremely careful with rm. Consider moving the file(s) to ~/.Trash instead.

■ Be especially careful when using wildcards in arguments; for example, rm * would remove every file (except dot files) from the current directory. Think twice before doing that.

■ Some people like to configure their shells so that rm is always used with the -i option. See Chapter 7, "Configuring Your Unix Environment," to find out how to create an alias of rm in your shell so it becomes rm -i.

Table 5.3

Options for rm	
OPTION	MEANING
-d	Remove empty *directories* as well as files.
-r	*Recursively* removes directories and their contents; implies -d.
-f	*Force* attempts to override permission restrictions, and does not report errors.
-i	*Inquire* before removing each file; type a *y* to confirm.

To Use the Trash from the Command Line

When you use the Finder, the files you put in the Trash are actually moved into a "hidden" directory in your home directory, called .Trash (in Unix, files whose name starts with a . are not normally displayed).

Instead of deleting files, you can move them to the Trash with

`mv -i filename ~/.Trash`

The -i (for *inquire*) option will prompt you before overwriting a file with the same name in the .Trash directory. This is different from the Finder behavior in which the filename of the newly trashed file gets changed, instead of the older trashed file of the same name being deleted. (See Chapter 9, "Creating and Using Scripts" for a script that emulates the Finder behavior.)

You can use MvMac instead of mv, but MvMac does not support the -i option.

Getting Information about Files and Directories

Besides its name and its contents, you probably want to know many other pieces of information about a file. The main kinds of metadata you want are

◆ File sizes

◆ File types

◆ Time and date last modified

◆ Who owns the file

◆ The *permissions* on files

(See Chapter 7, "Configuring Your Unix Environment," for more on permissions and ownership.)

Using the ls command to get file information

You have already used the ls command to list the contents of directories. The command is also used to obtain many kinds of information besides filenames.

To see file type, size in bytes, date modified, owners, and permissions:

◆ ls -l *path*

Use the -l option to the ls command (-l for "long form").

ls -l /

shows you a long-form listing of your root directory (**Figure 5.21**).

Figure 5.22 shows what the different parts of the output mean.

To show file sizes in kilobytes:

◆ Use the -s and -k options together:

ls -sk *path*

The -s option means "list sizes," and the -k option means "list sizes in kilobytes." If you omit the k option, the size is listed in *blocks,* which vary in size depending on the version of Unix and how the disk was formatted. On our disk in OS X, each block is one half-kilobyte.

```
[user-112uhed:~] vanilla% ls -l /

drwxrwxr-x   46 root      admin       1520 Apr 28 14:01 Applications
drwxr-xr-x   36 matisse   unknown     1180 Apr 28 13:56 Applications (Mac OS 9)
drwxr-xr-x   34 root      wheel       1112 Dec 20 22:25 bin
lrwxrwxr-t    1 root      admin         13 Apr 28 19:52 cores -> private/cores
lrwxrwxr-t    1 root      admin         11 Apr 28 19:52 etc -> private/etc
lrwxrwxr-t    1 root      admin          9 Apr 28 19:52 mach -> /mach.sym
-r-r-r-      1 root      admin     563960 Apr 28 19:43 mach.sym
-rw-r-r-     1 root      wheel    3160824 Apr 10 09:28 mach_kernel
lrwxrwxr-t    1 root      admin         11 Apr 28 19:52 tmp -> private/tmp
drwxr-xr-x   10 root      wheel        296 Sep  2  2001 usr
lrwxrwxr-t    1 root      admin         11 Apr 28 19:52 var -> private/var

(Partial output)
```

Figure 5.21 Using ls -l to get metadata about files. (Your output will differ.)

Discerning different types of files

Not all files are the same. For example, some files are directories, while others are special files the operating system uses to interact with disks and other devices.

Even among regular files there are differences. For example, some files are images, others consist of programming source code in various languages, and some are compiled applications. Among files created with traditional Mac applications, there are attributes such as *stationery* (if a Mac file is marked as stationery, then it is a sort of template— a read-only document you use as a starting place for creating new documents) and *creator*.

There are several ways to find out a file's type, each showing different kinds of information.

To see file types using ls -l:

◆ Examine the output from ls -l.

The first character of each line tells you what kind of file it is. **Table 5.4** summarizes the meaning of the first character in the output.

◆ If you want information about a directory, then add the -d option:

ls -ld *directorypath*

The ls command reports information about the directory file itself, and not its contents.

Table 5.4

File Types from ls -l	
FIRST CHARACTER	**MEANING**
-	Regular file.
d	Directory.
l	Symbolic link. A special kind of file that contains the path of another file, similar to a Mac alias.
b	*Block special files* represent physical devices that deal with blocks of data, such as disks (or drives).
c	*Character special files* represent devices that deal with streams of characters, such as modems.
s	*Socket links* (also called *named pipes*) are special files that connect to programs. Writing data to the file actually "pipes" the data to the program.

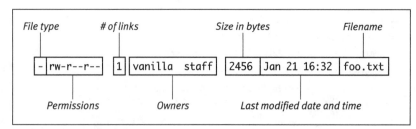

Figure 5.22 This diagram shows what the output of ls -l means.

To see basic file-type information:

◆ Use the -F option to ls:

ls -F *path*

The -F (for *file type*) option distinguishes directories, executable files (Unix commands), and symbolic links by adding / after directories, @ after symbolic links, and * after executables. **Figure 5.23** compares ls / with ls -F /.

To guess file types from hundreds of possibilities:

◆ file *path*

The file command attempts to figure out what kind of file each argument is. It uses a set of tests defined in the /etc /magic file. The file command can recognize more than 100 file types, but it is not 100 percent accurate. Some of the file

continues on next page

```
[user-112uhed:~] vanilla% ls /
36035726                    Network                 bin
Applications                Rescued Document        cores
Applications (Mac OS 9)     Rescued Document 1      dev
Cleanup At Startup          Shutdown Check          etc
Desktop                     System                  mach
Desktop DB                  System Folder           mach.sym
Desktop DF                  Temporary Items         mach_kernel
Desktop Folder              TheFindByContentFolder  private
Developer                   TheVolumeSettingsFolder sbin
Documents                   Trash                   sw
InfoTools Installer Log     Users                   tmp
Late Breaking News          Volumes                 usr
Library                     automount               var
[user-112uhed:~] vanilla% ls -F /
36035726                    Network/                bin/
Applications/               Rescued Document        cores@
Applications (Mac OS 9)/    Rescued Document 1      dev/
Cleanup At Startup/         Shutdown Check          etc@
Desktop                     System/                 mach@
Desktop DB                  System Folder/          mach.sym
Desktop DF                  Temporary Items/        mach_kernel
Desktop Folder/             TheFindByContentFolder/ private/
Developer@                  TheVolumeSettingsFolder/ sbin/
Documents/                  Trash/                  sw@
InfoTools Installer Log     Users/                  tmp@
Late Breaking News*         Volumes/                usr/
Library/                    automount/              var@
[user-112uhed:~] vanilla%
```

Figure 5.23 Adding the -F option to ls adds characters to some filenames showing file type. (Your output will differ.)

types that `file` will try to recognize are image formats (such as .JPEG, .GIF, and .PNG), programming languages (C, Perl, and Java), and compressed file formats (StuffIt archives, zip files, and Unix compress format).

As with most commands that deal with filenames, you can supply as many paths as you like.

`file /etc/*`

applies the `file` command to everything in the /etc directory.

Most of the files in the /etc directory are text files, but the `file` command is able to look inside them and make an educated guess about what *kind* of text file each one is (**Figure 5.24**).

Working with Mac metadata

The challenges of integrating pre–Mac OS X files with a Unix system are numerous and difficult. Apple has done quite an amazing job of providing backward compatibility for files created with older applications, while allowing thousands of Unix tools to operate. Still, there are some issues a command-line user should be aware of. (An excellent paper on some of the technical problems Apple has had to deal with is available online at www.mit.edu/people/wsanchez/papers/USENIX_2000/.)

```
[user-112uhed:~] vanilla% file /etc/*

/etc/appletalk.cfg:      ASCII text
/etc/authorization:      can't read `/etc/authorization' (Permission denied).
/etc/daily:              Bourne shell script text
/etc/dumpdates:          empty
/etc/inetd.conf:         C program text
/etc/localtime:          symbolic link to /usr/share/zoneinfo/US/Pacific
/etc/magic:              commands text for file
/etc/mail:               directory
/etc/pwd.db:             Berkeley DB Hash file (Version 2, Big Endian, Bucket Size 4096, Bucket
→Shift 12, Directory Size 256, Segment Size 256, Segment Shift 8, Overflow Point 3, Last Freed 2,
→Max Bucket 7, High Mask 0xf, Low Mask 0x7, Fill Factor 32, Number of Keys 18)
/etc/services:           English text
/etc/shells:             ASCII text
/etc/weekly:             Bourne shell script text

(Partial output)
```

Figure 5.24 The `file` command attempts to figure out what kind of files are in the directory. (Again, your output will differ.)

Options for the ls Command

The ls command has more than two dozen available options and can show many kinds of information about files. The Unix manual page on ls (man ls) is where you can see all of them.

Traditional Mac applications, and some Mac OS X applications, use an older system of storing information about each file that is not understood by standard Unix commands. For example, the Finder can mark a file as "locked," and Unix command-line programs will not be able to alter the file, but neither will they tell you why you can't change them—you'll just get an error when trying to delete or rename a locked file. (You can use the Darwin/ Mac OS X version of the ls command with the -lo options:

ls -lo *filename*

to show if a file is "locked": the notation uchg will be added to the output for locked files.)

The GetFileInfo command (provided as part of the Mac OS X Developer Tools collection) will show you this Mac-specific information.

To see the Mac metadata for a file:

◆ /Developer/Tools/GetFileInfo *path*
  For example,
  /Developer/Tools/GetFileInfo/
  → Developer/Documentation/QuickTime/
  → PDF/QuickTime5.pdf

  is shown in **Figure 5.25**.

```
[user-112uhed:~] vanilla% GetFileInfo /Developer/Documentation/QuickTime/PDF/QuickTime5.pdf
file: "/Developer/Documentation/QuickTime/PDF/QuickTime5.pdf"
type: ""
creator: ""
attributes: avbstclinmed
created: 02/18/2002 14:49:24
modified: 02/18/2002 14:49:24
[user-112uhed:~] vanilla%
```

Figure 5.25 The GetFileInfo command will reveal Mac-specific metadata.

The attributes line lists a series of file attributes. Each letter represents one attribute that is either On (upper case) or off (lower case). See **Table 5.5** for the meaning of each attribute.

Unlike many other Unix commands, GetFileInfo does not handle multiple filenames as arguments.

GetFileInfo is installed in a directory where your shell will not normally find it, so when you use the command you must use its full path: /Developer/Tools/ GetFileInfo. For instructions on how to teach your shell to look in more places for commands, see Chapter 7, "Configuring Your Unix Environment."

✔ Tip

■ If a file is locked, then you can unlock it from the command line using the SetFile command, described below.

To set the Mac metadata for a file:

◆ /Developer/Tools/SetFile -a letter
→path

For example,

/Developer/Tools/SetFile
→-a l "My File"

unlocks the file "My File."

/Developer/Tools/SetFile
→-a T ~/Documents/Letter

turns the file Letter into stationery.

See Table 5.5 for the meaning of each option/attribute.

✔ Tip

■ Check that the attribute was set with the GetFileInfo command described above.

Table 5.5

File Attributes from GetFileInfo	
OPTION/ATTRIBUTE	MEANING
a or A	Alias file
v or V	Invisible*
b or B	Bundle
s or S	System (name locked)
t or T	Stationery
c or C	Custom icon*
l or L	Locked
i or I	Inited*
n or N	No INIT resources
m or M	Shared (can run multiple times)
e or E	Hidden extension*
d or D	Desktop*

*Note: Upper case means on, lower case means off.
Options or attributes with * are allowed with folders.

About Links (the Unix Version of Aliases)

A Mac alias is a special file that "points to" another file. Unix has its own way of doing this, using *links*. Actually, Unix has two kinds of links: *symbolic links* (or "symlinks" in the Unix vernacular) and *hard links*.

Both symlinks and hard links are created with the ln command (**Table 5.6**).

Symlinks are more similar to Mac aliases than hard links are, so we will address them first.

Table 5.6

Options for ln	
OPTION	MEANING
-f	Force the link to remove any existing file at the target location, if possible.
-h	If the target path is a symbolic link, do not follow it. Use with the -f option to replace a symbolic link with a hard link.
-s	Create a symbolic link instead of a hard link.

Using symbolic links

Symlinks are special files that contain the path (relative or absolute) to another file.

When seen from the Finder, symlinks look and behave (mostly) like Mac aliases. (When Mac aliases are examined from the command line, they look like empty files.)

Mac aliases still point to the original file even if the alias and/or the original file is moved. Unix symlinks are less intelligent.

For instance, symlinks that use full paths can be moved around and still work, while symlinks that use relative paths will stop working if the they're moved (unless the link and original file move together and maintain the relative relationship). This is because symlinks point at a path, not at the actual file's data. This is different from Mac aliases.

If you look at a symbolic link with ls -l, you see the path the link points to. **Figure 5.26** shows that the /etc directory is actually a symlink to /private/etc and /mach is actually a symlink to /mach.sym.

The first example shows a symlink that points to a relative path, and the second example shows a symlink pointing to a full path.

You use the Unix ln command to create links, and the -s option to create symbolic links. (Notice that the syntax of the ln command is similar to that of the cp command, covered earlier in this chapter.)

continues on next page

```
[user-112uhed:~] vanilla% ls -ld /etc
lrwxrwxr-t  1 root   admin  11 Feb 25 17:40 /etc -> private/etc
[user-112uhed:~] vanilla% ls -l /mach
lrwxrwxr-t  1 root   admin   9 Feb 25 17:40 /mach -> /mach.sym
[user-112uhed:~] vanilla%
```

Figure 5.26 You can see that symlinks can be made by using either full or relative paths.

To create a symbolic link:

1. Type `ln -s` but don't press [Return].

2. Type the path to the existing file or directory.

   Think about whether you want to use a relative or full path for the existing file.

   These are different commands:

   ```
   ln -s /Users/vanilla/Documents/
   →letter.doc .
   ```

   ```
   ln -s ../Documents/letter.doc .
   ```

   They both create a symlink called `letter.doc` in the current directory, but the first one points to an absolute path, while the second one points to "one step toward the root directory, then down into Documents, then letter.doc."

   Remember, a full path will continue to work even if the symlink is moved, but a relative path will continue to work if the original *and* the symlink are moved together—say if you copy a collection of directories and files to another computer.

3. Type the path or name of the symlink, and press [Return].

   If the path you type is an existing directory (for example, the current directory), then the symlink will have the same name as the original file and will be created in that directory.

   ```
   ln -s ../file.txt .
   ```

   creates a symlink called `file.txt` in the current directory (remember `..` is just another name for the current directory; it is a perfectly valid path).

   If you want to give the symlink a different name than the original, just type a path name that ends in the new name (or more simply, a new filename). The symlink will be created with that name:

   ```
   ln -s ../file.txt newname
   ```

✔ Tips

- Use symlinks when you want it to be obvious where the links point to. Anyone can use `ls -l` to see where a symlink points.

- Use symlinks whenever you want to make a link to a directory.

- Use symlinks when you want to link to a file on a different disk or partition.

- Do not use symlinks when you want the link to keep working when the original file moves.

- Unix tools deal with symbolic links in different ways, sometimes acting upon the symlink file itself, sometimes acting upon the original. For example, the `-H`, `-L`, `-P` and `-R` options to `cp` all affect how `cp` handles symlinks. For this reason, it is important to be aware of the presence of symlinks even if you did not create them. For instance, the `rm` program never follows symlinks; it will remove them but not follow the link to remove the original file.

- If you remove the original file, a symlink will stop working—you'll get a "File not found" error if you try to use it. But if you put a new file at the location that the symlink points to, then the symlink works, regardless of what file is there (even if it's not the original).

Using hard links

At the beginning of this chapter, we described how Unix directories are special files that contain a list of file and directory names. Filenames are stored as entries in directories. These entries are "links" between the filename and the actual physical location on the disk partition where the file is stored (called an *inode*). Every file has at least one hard link. A hard link is essentially an extra name for a file, so the file's actual data occurs only once on the disk (at the location specified by its inode), but it can appear in more than one directory, or even twice in the same directory but with different names.

Hard links are used partly for the same reasons as symbolic links (for example, as a space-saving mechanism), but more important, they are used so that any of the links can be deleted and all the other links will still work (contrast this with symbolic links, where if the original file is deleted, the symbolic links will no longer point to anything).

Hard links differ from symbolic link in some important ways:

♦ You cannot make a hard link to a directory.

♦ You cannot make a hard link to a file on a disk that is different from the one containing the link.

♦ Hard links continue to work even if the original file and/or the link are moved around on the disk.

♦ If you move a hard link to a different disk or partition, it becomes a new file, no longer connected in any way to the original. That is, if you edit the link after moving it, the original file is not affected at all, and vice versa.

♦ Perhaps most interestingly, hard links continue to work even if the original file is deleted. Now how can that be?

While symbolic links are actually tiny files that contain the path of the original, hard links are extra names for the original file. Every time a hard link is created or deleted, the operating system makes a note about it in the data stored on disk about the file.

Keeping in mind that filenames are actually hard links, when you use rm to remove a file, you are actually removing a link, not a file. The "link count" is reduced by one. The file itself is not actually removed until the last hard link is removed. As long as at least one hard link for a file remains, the file will still exist.

You can see the number of hard links to a file with ls -l. Figure 5.22 shows where to find the number of links in the output from ls -l.

Because a hard link points to the actual location of a file on the disk (to the inode for the file), you cannot create a hard link on one disk that points to a file on another disk (or partition). For that, you need to use symlinks.

To create a hard link:

◆ ln *existingpath newpath*

With hard links, it makes no difference if the paths you use are relative or full. In either case, a new directory entry is created.

If the new path you enter is an existing directory path, then the link will be created inside that directory and will have the same name as the original.

✔ Tips

■ Use a hard link when you want the link to keep working even if the original file is moved or removed.

■ Just as with cp, if you supply ln with more than two arguments, it assumes the last argument is a directory and creates links inside that directory for each of the earlier arguments.

EDITING AND PRINTING FILES

Learning how to edit text files from the command line is the second most important Unix skill, right after learning how to use the command line itself. That's because text files form the basis of many activities we'll cover later in this book. Unix uses text files to store the vast majority of system configurations. Most system-administration tasks involve editing text files. Installing Unix software almost always requires you to edit a text file or two. And finally, the scripts you create are also text files.

Text files in Unix are all stored as plain files. That is, there is no font, color, sizing, style, or alignment information stored in the file. Unix text files are intended to be displayed using a monospaced font so that every character takes up the same amount of space on the line. Unix uses a different end-of-line character than Macintosh programs, so a text file created in a Macintosh word processor will look strange when viewed in a Unix text editor. (Some Macintosh programs such as BBEdit offer the option to save files with Unix-style line endings.)

In Chapter 2, "Using the Command Line," you used a simple Unix text editor called pico to edit a file from the command line. Pico is a fine editor for casual editing of text files, but for a variety of reasons (such as difficulty in handling very long lines), pico is not a good choice for performing serious Unix administration work, such as editing system-configuration files. In order to properly perform Unix system-administration tasks, you need to use a more powerful text editor.

There are two standard powerful Unix text editors, vi and emacs. Mac OS X comes with both of them. In this book we are going to show you some basic vi skills because vi is more widely available on different Unix systems. (See the sidebar "BBEdit— an Excellent Text Editor," for a useful Mac-centric solution.)

Once you know how to create and edit files from the command line, you will of course be curious about how to print them. At the end of this chapter we'll show you a couple of ways to do this.

Editing Files with vi

The vi editor is the *visual interface* to an older and even more basic editor called ex. Ex only displays a single line at a time, because it was created for use on typewriter-like terminals. Vi added *full screen* capabilities for use on video display systems. Full screen means that vi takes up the entire Terminal window. Vi uses the last line of the Terminal window, called the *status line*, to display information to you .

In order to keep your files neatly organized, start by creating a new directory in which to practice editing files (you might want to review Chapter 5, "Using Files and Directories").

To create a directory for use in practicing with vi:

1. `cd ~/Documents`

   This takes you to the Documents directory in your home directory.

2. `mkdir vi-practice`

   This creates the new directory, called vi-practice.

3. `cd vi-practice`

   This sets your current directory as ~/Documents/vi-practice.

Super quick start

Vi is a complete application, with dozens of options, features, and commands. In order to work with vi, though, you have to have a file, so here is a quick task to start vi, enter some text, save it, and quit from vi. Later in the chapter, we will go into the details of each step.

To create a file using vi:

1. `vi path`

   Path is the path to the file you want to edit and will typically be the name of a file in the current directory. For example:

   `vi shopping-list`

   This will bring up the vi editor and fill your Terminal window (note that the name of the file appears on the status line at the bottom of the window) (**Figure 6.1**).

Figure 6.1 This is what you see when you start up vi.

If the file does not already exist, it will be created when you first save from within vi. This is very similar to the procedure with word processors familiar to you, except that you are specifying the new filename when you start vi.

The highlighted rectangle at the top left of the window is the *cursor*, which is similar to the insertion bar you see in a regular Macintosh word processor, except that this type of cursor always sits *on* a character, not in between two characters. (Your cursor might look different. You can select a different cursor in the Terminal application preferences; in this book we assume you are using the default *block cursor*.)

You also see a series of tilde (~) characters running down the left side. They are vi's way of telling you that those lines are empty lines at the end of the file.

2. The next step is to switch to *edit mode* and enter some text:

i

Do *not* press Return.

That is just the lowercase letter *i*. (There are many ways to enter edit mode in vi—we'll go into detail on them in the section "About vi's Two Modes.")

Now that you are in edit mode, you can:

3. Type in at least five lines of text. You must press Return at the end of each line (see the sidebar "Word Wrap in vi," below).

Figure 6.2 shows what happens after you have entered several lines of text.

continues on next page

Figure 6.2 Our shopping list entered into the file using vi.

4. Next, save the file. To do that, you must switch back to *command mode,* so press [Esc] .

There is no need to press [Return] after pressing [Esc] .

If you are unsure whether you switched back to command mode, then press [Esc] again. Terminal will beep if you are already in command mode. There is no harm in pressing [Esc] several times (that is, if you don't mind the beep).

5. Now you can save the file:

    :w

Notice how the cursor drops to the status line as soon as you type the colon character (**Figure 6.3**).

6. :q

You are back at the shell prompt, and you've created a file using vi.

7. cat shopping-list

Run the cat command to verify that the new file exists and contains what you typed into it (**Figure 6.4**).

Obviously, there is a lot more to vi than this example. Now that you have created a file, we will explore vi's different modes, as well as how to move around inside a file, change and delete text, copy and paste, and search and replace.

✔ Tip

■ You can tell vi to show you which mode you are in by typing (from command mode)

    :set showmode

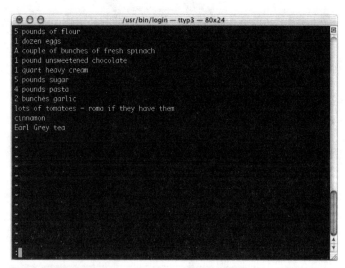

Figure 6.3 When you type a colon in command mode, the cursor drops to the vi status line.

Starting vi

The vi command can be started with or without specifying filenames on the command line.

The most common way to start vi is to give it one pathname as an argument. If the file already exists, it will be loaded into vi when you launch the editor. If the file does not exist, it will be created the first time you save from within vi. You can also start vi with no arguments, in which case you must supply a filename when you first save the file.

Vi also allows you to enter multiple arguments and provides a way to edit each file in turn.

To start vi and edit or create a single file:

◆ vi *pathname*

Pathname can be a full or relative path (review relative paths in Chapter 5, "Using Files and Directories"). Most commonly, you simply supply the name of a file in the current directory:

vi *myfile*.txt

If the file does not exist, it is not created until you save your work.

To start vi without specifying a filename:

◆ vi

This will start up the vi program, using a temporary file. (The path of the temporary file will appear on the status line.) In order to save text entered into this temporary file, you must supply a name for the file when you save it.

To start vi with multiple filenames:

◆ vi *file1 file2 file3 ...*

You can supply as many files as arguments as you like. Vi will start up and display the first file in the list.

You can move to the next file with the : n command (from command mode only), but only after you have saved any changes to the file.

You can move to the next file and discard changes with the :n! command.

✔ Tip

■ You can use command-line wildcards to open several files. For example,

vi *.txt

will open all the files in the current directory whose names end in .txt.

```
[localhost:~/Documents/vi-practice] vanilla% cat shopping-list
5 pounds of flour
1 dozen eggs
A couple of bunches of fresh spinach
1 pound unsweetened chocolate
5 pounds sugar
4 pounds pasta
2 bunches garlic
lots of tomatoes - roma if they have them
cinnamon
Earl Grey tea
[localhost:~/Documents/vi-practice] vanilla%
```

Figure 6.4 Using the cat command to verify that the new file exists and contains what you typed into it.

About vi's Two Modes

The most important thing to learn about vi is that it has two modes: *command mode* and *edit mode*.

A good way to start thinking about vi's two modes is to compare vi with any GUI word processor you have used, but imagine that the only way to move the mouse or select text is by typing commands. That presents a problem—how does the software know when you are typing a command, and when you are typing text to go into the file?

Vi handles the problem of distinguishing commands from text by its two modes. In edit mode (also sometimes called *insert mode*), anything you type is inserted into the file. In fact, the only thing you can do in edit mode is enter text and move around inside the file using the arrow keys. In some older versions of vi, you can't even move around in edit mode, but happily Mac OS X comes with a version that does allow you to use the arrow keys while in edit mode.

In command mode, anything you type is interpreted as a command. Saving and quitting involve using commands, and so does moving to the beginning or end of the file, or selecting a range of text to replace, or searching for text, and so on. Anything you would use the mouse for in a GUI word processor is accomplished from command mode in vi.

You must be in command mode in order to save a file, quit, undo, search and replace, copy and paste, and all similar functions.

Typing the same thing will have very different results depending on which mode you are in. This is probably the most difficult thing to get used to in vi, along with the fact that you cannot use the mouse (all moving of the cursor in both modes is done from the keyboard.)

Switching to command mode

Switching to command mode from edit mode is the simplest task in vi—there is only one way to do it.

To switch back to command mode:

◆ Press `Esc`.

The `Esc` key is located at the upper-left corner on most Macintosh keyboards. This is the only way to switch back to command mode from edit mode. If you are already in command mode, you will get a beep.

✔ Tip

■ If you aren't sure whether you are in command mode, go ahead and press `Esc`. Once you hear the beep, you'll know you are in command mode.

Switching to edit mode

When you first start vi, you are always in command mode. In order to enter text, you must switch to edit mode.

Before switching to edit mode, you should see where exactly the cursor is in the file and think about where you want the next text to be inserted (just as with the insertion bar in Mac word processors).

There are several ways to switch to edit mode, and the method you choose determines where the new text will go. For instance, if you want the new text to be inserted *after* (to the right of) the current cursor position, then you will choose one particular method of switching to edit mode. If you want the new text to be inserted *before* (to the left of) the cursor, then you will choose a different method.

All of the one-letter commands shown here for switching to edit mode take effect immediately—that is, you do not press `Return` after any of them.

Initial cursor position before switch from command mode to edit mode.

1 pound unsweetened chocolate
5 pounds sugar
4 pounds pasta

1 pound unsweetened chocolate	1 pound unsweetened chocolate
5 pounds of sugar	5 pounds sof ugar
4 pounds pasta	4 pounds pasta

Result of switching to edit mode with "i", and typing "of"

Result of switching to edit mode with "a", and typing "of"

Figure 6.5 Text will be inserted either before or after the initial cursor position, depending on how you switch to edit mode.

Initial cursor position before switch from command mode to edit mode.

1 pound unsweetened chocolate
5 pounds sugar
4 pounds pasta

1 pound unsweetened chocolate
5 pounds sugar

4 pounds pasta

Result of switching to edit mode with the "o" command.

Figure 6.6 Using the o command to switch to edit mode opens a new line below the one you were on.

To enter edit mode and add text before the cursor:

◆ i

Do not press (Return). The i command (for *insert*) lets you edit to the left of wherever the cursor was when you typed *i*.

✔ Tip

■ This is usually the way you want to switch to edit mode, but be careful—when you want to add text to the end of a line, use the method shown next.

To enter edit mode and add text after the cursor:

◆ a

The a command (for *append*) switches you to edit mode and lets you add text *after* (to the right of) the cursor position. (Compare with the i command, which lets you *insert* text before the cursor position.)

Figure 6.5 compares the results of these first two methods.

✔ Tip

■ The a command is the one to use when you want to add text to the end of a line.

To enter edit mode and add text below the current line:

◆ o

The o command (lowercase *o*) *opens* a new line below the one you were on. New text will be entered on that line (**Figure 6.6**).

To enter edit mode and add text above the cursor:

◆ O

The uppercase O command does the same thing as the lowercase o, except it opens a line above the one you were on (**Figure 6.7**).

Table 6.1 summarizes the most common ways to switch from command mode to edit mode.

Initial cursor position before switch from command mode to edit mode.

Result of switching to edit mode with the uppercase "O" command.

Figure 6.7 Using the uppercase O command to switch to edit mode opens a new line above the one you were on.

Table 6.1

Switching to Edit Mode in vi	
WHERE TO ADD NEW TEXT	COMMAND
Before the cursor	i
After the cursor	a
Below the current line	o
Above the current line	O

Word Wrap in vi

An excellent feature of vi is its ability to deal with very long lines of text, far wider than the 80 columns that are the default display in a Terminal window.

You have to press Return at the end of each line in vi, unlike what you do with paragraph-based word processors you are probably used to.

You can tell vi to automatically insert a return character when you get within x columns of the right edge of the Terminal window. To do this, make sure you are in command mode (press Esc) and then type

`:set wm=5`

for auto returns within five columns of the edge. You can change that number to anything convenient. If you want that option to always be on, put

`set wm=5`

in a file in your home directory called .exrc.

```
shopping-list: unmodified: line 5 of 12 [41%]
```

Figure 6.9 Pressing [Control][G] displays the cursor position on the vi status line.

Navigating Using vi

In vi you do all of your navigation within the Terminal window with the keyboard, and almost all of it from command mode.

Think of your file as having a grid of lines and columns, each one a character wide and high. Your basic cursor movements are "up," "down," "left," and "right."

Figure 6.8 shows the vi cursor on line 5, column 13.

To see which line you are on:

◆ [Control][G]

The status line will display the line number where the cursor is and also will indicate whether the file has unsaved changes ("modified") or not ("unmodified") (**Figure 6.9**).

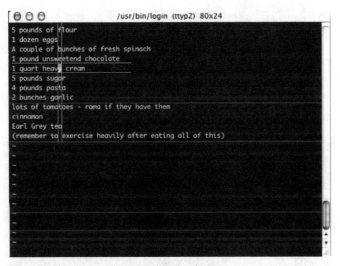

Figure 6.8 The vi cursor is now on line 5, column 13.

Basic cursor movement

Newer versions of vi (including the version included with Mac OS X) allow you to move the cursor by using the arrow keys while in either command or edit mode. But not every version of vi allows this. Some versions support the arrow keys only in command mode, and some do not support the arrow keys at all, regardless of which mode you are in. **Table 6.2** shows commands for moving the cursor that will work in command mode with every version of vi.

You do *not* press Return after any of the commands shown in Table 6.2. In fact, pressing Return by itself in command mode is another way to move down one line.

Navigating by searching for text

Another very common way to navigate within a file when using vi is to search for a string of characters, which moves the cursor to the next occurrence of the string. You may search forward (toward the end of the file) or backward (toward the top of the file). In either case, the search will "wrap" around the top or end of the file.

Table 6.2

Basic vi Moves	
MOVE THE CURSOR:	COMMAND
Left one column	h
Right one column	l
Up one line	k
Down one line	j
To the end of this line	$
To the start of this line	^
Down one screen	Control F (similar to "page down")
Up one screen	Control B (similar to "page up")
Go to line 23 of file	23G
Go to last line of file	G

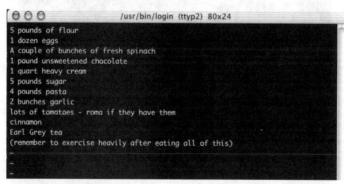

Figure 6.10 The cursor drops to the bottom line as soon as you type a slash to search from command mode.

Remember that these commands must be executed from command mode, and that you can make sure you are in command mode by pressing [Esc] .

To move forward to the next occurrence of a string:

1. /

    The cursor will drop to the bottom line (the vi *status line*) in your Terminal window (**Figure 6.10**).

2. Type the string you want to search for.

    The search string is case-sensitive (**Figure 6.11**). (The search string in Figure 6.11 is Ea.)

3. Press [Return] to execute the search.

    The cursor moves to the next occurrence of the string (**Figure 6.12**).

✔ Tips

■ To repeat the last search and move to the next occurrence of the string, use the n command.

■ To repeat the search in the opposite direction, use N (uppercase N).

To move backward to the previous occurrence of a string:

◆ This is exactly the same as searching forward, except you use [?] instead of /.

    Once again, the cursor will drop to the status line as soon as you press [?].

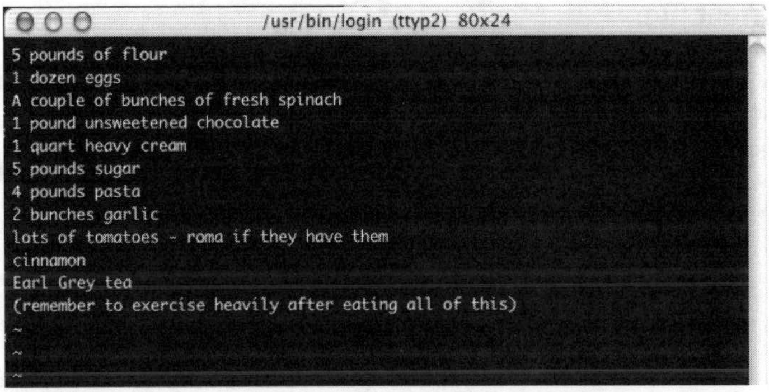

Figure 6.11 Enter a case-sensitive search string, and press [Return].

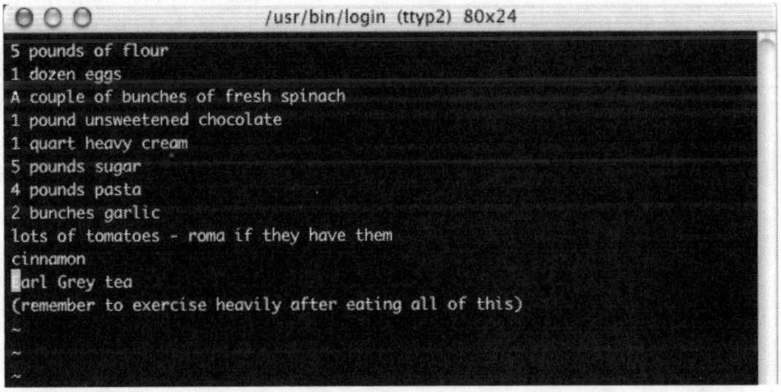

Figure 6.12 The cursor moves to the next occurrence of the search string.

NAVIGATING USING VI

Saving a File in vi

Vi offers features similar to the familiar Save and Save As features found in most Macintosh applications.

To begin, you must be in command mode. All save commands in vi begin with a colon. This drops the cursor to the last line of your Terminal window and tells vi you are about to enter a command that affects the entire file.

You will see that many vi commands begin with your typing a colon. If the cursor doesn't drop to the status line when you type a colon, then you have forgotten to switch to command mode. In those cases, backspace over the colon you inserted and press Esc.

You always press Return at the end of vi commands that start with a colon.

To save the current file:

◆ :w

The :w command (for *write to disk*) saves the current file.

To save the file with a new filename:

◆ :w *pathname*

The currently version of the file is saved at *pathname*.

You will still be "in" the file you started on after the save; that is, using :w *pathname* won't change which file you are editing.

Usually the *pathname* will simply be a filename to save the file in the current directory, but there is no reason why you cannot save to a file somewhere else; you just have to supply a proper (relative or full) pathname. For example,

:w ~/Documents/*newfile.txt*

saves a copy of the file you are editing as *newfile.txt* in the Documents directory of your home directory, regardless of where you were when you started vi.

✔ Tip

■ The :w *pathname* feature is useful if you started vi without specifying a filename.

To save and attempt to override warnings:

◆ :w!

Sometimes you get warnings that vi is unable to save a file when you use the :w command. Often the problem is related to the file's *permissions*— that is, who has permission to read, write, and copy it (we'll cover permissions in detail in Chapter 8, "Working with Permissions and Ownership"). As long as you either own the file or have write permission in the directory containing the file, using :w! will override permission warnings.

BBedit—an Excellent Text Editor

The BBEdit program is a GUI text editor. Available in both "lite" freeware and full-featured commercial versions, BBEdit is a powerful tool for editing plain-text files such as HTML, programming source code, and Unix text files.

The commercial version will allow you to perform all your Mac OS X system-administration tasks. Because it is a commercial version, we did not use it as the primary editor discussed in this book—we don't want you to have to buy something else in order to use this book. Still, we heartily recommend BBEdit lite to anyone who works with plain-text files on a Mac.

BBEdit is available from Bare Bones Software (www.barebones.com).

Quitting vi

As much as you probably love using vi, sooner or later you will want to do something else, maybe anything else. Knowing when and how to quit is one of life's great lessons. Quitting from vi is pretty easy, as long as you have saved all your changes. You can combine saving and quitting if you like. If you try to quit from vi with unsaved changes, vi will give you a warning on the status line (**Figure 6.13**). You can override the warning if you want to quit without saving.

To quit vi if you have saved all changes:

◆ :q

Vi quits and returns to the shell prompt.

If for some reason you forgot to save any changes, then vi will display a warning message in the status line and will not quit.

To combine saving and quitting:

◆ :wq

The file will be saved, and vi will quit.

To quit without saving:

◆ :q!

Vi will quit even if there are unsaved changes to the file.

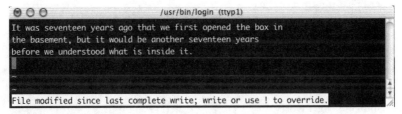

Figure 6.13 Vi gives you a warning on the status line if you try to quit while leaving unsaved changes.

Changing and Deleting Text

Besides the basics of entering text, saving, and quitting, you often use vi to change text that has already been saved. Sometimes you will simply want to delete text, other times you will want to alter existing text.

Deleting text is simpler, so we'll look at that first.

Deleting text

You can delete text from either edit mode or command mode.

The basic rule for deleting text in edit mode is: You can delete text you just entered on the same line by pressing (Delete); otherwise, switch to command mode and use one of the delete commands described below. Since this is Unix, the full explanation is of course more complicated.

In edit mode, you can only delete text you just typed in—not text that was already in the file before you started editing or text that you entered prior to switching into command mode—even if you switched back to edit mode.

The version of vi in Mac OS X *does* allow you to delete back past the start of the line to the previous line, but it doesn't immediately update the screen—the text you are deleting stays visible until you either press (Esc) to switch to command mode or reach the start of the line.

If this seems confusing, don't worry.

From command mode, you may delete any text in the file. Any text deleted while in command mode is saved temporarily in memory (similarly to the traditional Mac concept of the Clipboard) and is available for pasting. See the section "Copy and Paste," later in this chapter.

To delete text from edit mode:

◆ (Delete)

It's that simple.

To delete one character from command mode:

◆ x

The x command (for *excise*) will delete the character under the cursor.

There are many ways to delete text from command mode. **Table 6.3** summarizes the most important methods.

To delete one line of text from command mode:

◆ dd

The dd command deletes the current line (the line the cursor is on).

Notice how most of the methods shown in Table 6.3 follow a pattern consisting of the d command followed by something that indicates how much text to delete.

Table 6.3

Deleting Text from Command Mode in vi	
To Delete This	Type This
Character under the cursor	x
Two characters	2x
From here to end of line	d$
This whole line	dd
Five lines (including this one)	d5 Return
From this line to end of file	dG
From this line to line 27	d27G
From here forward to *string*	d/*string*
From here back to *string*	d?*string*
From cursor to end of word	dw

Changing text

You can change text in either command or edit mode.

To change text in edit mode, backspace over it and retype, but note the limits on deleting text from edit mode (described above).

Changing text from command mode is usually a matter of selecting a range of text with a command that switches you into edit mode; then what you type after switching replaces the selected text. This is very much like selecting text with the mouse in a GUI word processor: As soon as you type something after making the selection, the selected text disappears.

It is important to note that many of the text-changing examples below combine the change-text command (c) with one of the navigation techniques we talked about earlier in this chapter. For example, c24G will actually do the following:

1. Delete all the text from the current cursor position through line 24 (inclusive).

2. Switch you into edit mode.

So whatever you type next will replace the deleted text (which is available for pasting with the p command; see the section "Copy and Paste").

CHANGING AND DELETING TEXT

To change from the cursor position to the end of the word:

1. cw

   Do *not* press Return. Notice how the last character of the word you are on changes to a $.

   You have "selected" the text from the current cursor position to the end of the word for changing, and you have also switched from command mode to edit mode.

Whatever you type next will replace the text from the current cursor position to the $ (inclusive).

Figure 6.14 shows the text before using the cw command, and **Figure 6.15** shows what happens when you type *cw*.

2. Enter the new text.

3. Press Esc to exit change mode.

   Whatever text you enter replaces the word you started on (**Figure 6.16**).

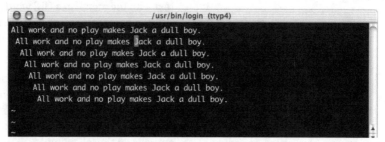

Figure 6.14 Example of text before typing the cw command to change one word in command mode.

```
● ● ●                    /usr/bin/login (ttyp4)
All work and no play makes Jack a dull boy.
 All work and no play makes Jac$ a dull boy.
  All work and no play makes Jack a dull boy.
   All work and no play makes Jack a dull boy.
    All work and no play makes Jack a dull boy.
     All work and no play makes Jack a dull boy.
      All work and no play makes Jack a dull boy.
~
~
~
```

Figure 6.15 After typing the cw command, the last character of the selected word changes to a $.

```
● ● ●                    /usr/bin/login (ttyp4)
All work and no play makes Jack a dull boy.
 All work and no play makes George a dull boy.
  All work and no play makes Jack a dull boy.
   All work and no play makes Jack a dull boy.
    All work and no play makes Jack a dull boy.
     All work and no play makes Jack a dull boy.
      All work and no play makes Jack a dull boy.
~
~
~
```

Figure 6.16 Whatever you type next replaces the selected text.

To change text from the cursor to the end of the line:

◆ c$

The c$ command means "change to end-of-line." Once again, this command puts you into edit mode.

✔ Tip

■ There is a shortcut for this command—C (an uppercase C).

To change text from the cursor to the next occurrence of a given string:

1. c/*string*

You must press Return at the end of the search string. This is a good example of combining the c command with a movement command showed to you earlier (/*string*). Using this command to change text will select all the text from the current cursor position to the next occurrence of *string*, and switch you to edit mode.

2. Type the replacement text.

✔ Tip

■ You can also search backward, so that c?*string* selects text from the current cursor position to the previous occurrence of *string* (toward the top of the file).

To change text from the current line to a specific line number:

1. c5G

Of course you replace 5 with whatever line number you want. This selects the text from the current line to the specified line number—all the lines are included. The screen will update as soon as you type the *G*, showing the selected lines deleted and leaving you in edit mode. **Figures 6.17** and **6.18** show text before and after the c5G command.

2. Type the replacement text.

Remember that you are still in edit mode when you are done.

Figure 6.17 Example of text before using the c5G command.

Figure 6.18 After you type c5G, the selected lines are removed.

Sometimes you want to change just one character. Here is an easy way to change one character without having to go into edit mode and back.

To change just the character under the cursor:

1. r

   The r command selects just the character under the cursor.

2. Type the replacement character.

   Unlike most other editing commands, r lets you stay in command mode as you do this.

To flip the case of the character that is under the cursor:

◆ ~

   Typing the ~ character switches the character under the cursor from upper- to lowercase, or vice versa. This command does not switch you into edit mode.

To undo the last change:

◆ u

   The u command undoes the last edit you made anywhere in the file, even if the cursor has moved since the change was made, and even if you have saved the change.

   Typing u again restores the change.

✔ Tip

■ You may also restore the current line to the last saved version with the U command (uppercase U). This will work even if you have left the current line and returned since making changes to it.

To revert to the last saved version:

◆ :e!

   Then press [Return]. Vi will reload the last saved version of the file.

Copy and paste

Vi supports fairly easy copy and paste functions. Like the commands for changing text, the copy command (y for *yank*) may be combined with many of the movement commands to select ranges of text and copy them.

To copy the current line:

◆ y

   This yanks the current line into the vi equivalent of the Clipboard; it's called the *buffer* and is totally separate from the regular Mac Clipboard.

Once you have yanked text, you can paste it.

To paste the contents of the buffer:

◆ p

   The p (for *paste*) command inserts the contents of the buffer at the cursor.

   If the buffer's content is one or more lines, then the text will be inserted below the current line.

   If the buffer's content is less than a full line, then it will be inserted into the current line to the right of the cursor.

✔ Tip

■ The uppercase P command will also paste, but it will paste either *above* the current line or to the *left* of the cursor.

To paste multiple copies simultaneously:

◆ Precede the p command with a number.

   For example, 10p pastes ten copies of the buffer's content.

To copy several lines into the buffer:

◆ Precede the y command with a number.

   For example, to copy the current line plus four more lines (five lines total), type 4y.

To paste deleted text:

◆ Any deleted text may be pasted using the p and P commands.

There is no separate "cut" command in vi. All deleted text—text deleted using d$, dw (delete to the end of the word), 10d [Return] (delete this and the next ten lines), x, 5x, (and so on) goes into the same buffer as yanked (copied) text.

Search and replace

Search and replace in vi is done in command mode using commands on the status line. Like the commands to save and quit, the search and replace commands all begin with a colon, which drops the cursor to the command line, and all end with pressing [Return].

(To simply search for a string of text without replacing it, see "Navigating by Searching for Text," earlier in this section.)

The general format of the search-and-replace command is:

```
:[optional range of lines]s/Old/New/
→[optional modifiers]
```

You will always type the colon, the s, and the three slashes. "Old" and "New" may be patterns using a simplified set of the regular expressions you learned in Chapter 4, "Useful Unix Utilities."

To create a general search-and-replace command:

1. Type a colon to drop to the vi command line.

2. As an option, you can enter a *range* of lines to be affected. This is a pair of specifiers separated by a comma. For example, 23,57 indicates lines 23 through 57 (inclusive). Use the line specifier . for "the current line" and $ for "the end of the file." For example, use .,23 to indicate the current line through line 23 (either up or down from the current line without wrapping around the top of bottom of the file). Using .,$ would mean from the current line through the end of the file. If you do not specify a range, then only the current line is affected (the same as a range of .,.).

3. Type the letter s (for *substitute*).

4. Type a slash: /.

5. Enter the target (search) pattern.

6. Type another slash.

7. Enter the replacement pattern.

8. Type a third slash.

9. Enter any optional modifiers such as g for *global on each line*.

10. Press [Return] to execute the command.

Here is a series of increasingly complex search-and-replace commands.

To replace the first "Foo" with "Bar" on the current line:

◆ `:s/Foo/Bar/`

This is the simplest form of a search and replace in vi. The first occurrence of Foo on the current line will be replaced with Bar.

To replace every "Foo" with "Bar" on the current line:

◆ `:s/Foo/Bar/g`

In this case you are adding the g modifier so that the change affects the line "globally"; that is, every occurrence of the first string is replaced.

To replace every occurrence in the file:

◆ `:1,$s/Foo/Bar/g`

By adding a range of lines, the change affects more than the current line. In this case the range 1,$ means from the first line in the file through the end of the file. If you leave off the g modifier, then only the first occurrence of Foo on each line will be changed.

✔ Tip

■ The range need not start at line 1. A range of 55,$ would affect lines 55 through the end of the file.

To replace from one line to another line:

◆ `:15,23s/Foo/Bar/g`

Here the range is from line 15 through line 23.

To replace from the current line to the end of the file:

◆ `:.,$s/Foo/Bar/g`

Here the range begins with the . character, which means "the current line"—that is, the line the cursor was on before you typed the colon.

To replace from the current line and five more lines below it:

◆ `:.,+5s/Foo/Bar/g`

The +5 in this range means "the current line plus five more below it."

To replace from the current line and seven more lines above it:

◆ `:.,-7s/Foo/Bar/g`

The -7 here means "the current line plus seven lines above."

To replace text only when it occurs at the start of a line:

◆ Put the ^ character at the beginning of the target string.

This command would replace Foo only when it occurs as the very first thing on a line:

`:1,$s/^Foo/Bar/`

(No need for the g since you are only looking for Foo at the start of each line.)

To replace text only when it occurs at the end of a line:

◆ Append $ to the target string.

This command will replace Foo only when it occurs as the very last thing on a line:

`:1,$s/Foo$/Bar/`

Table 6.4

More vi Commands

COMMAND	WHAT IT DOES
J	Joins the next line to this one.
%	Finds the matching closing parenthesis or brace. Position cursor on an ( ) { } [ ] first.
:set ruler	Displays row#,column#.
:set all	Shows current settings.
:set ai	Turns on auto-indentation.
:set noai	Turns off auto-indentation.
:set number	Shows line numbers on left.
:set nonumber	Turns off line numbers.
:set wm=5	Sets wrap margin to five characters from right edge.

Vi Cheat Sheets

There are hundreds of vi cheat sheets on the Web. Here are a few in different styles.

◆ **vi Editor Cheat Sheet** (K Computing; www.kcomputing.com/vi.html). Has a link to an excellent PDF cheat sheet that is very graphically oriented. Highly recommended.

◆ **vi Editor Cheat Sheet** (University of the Virgin Islands, Center for Administrative Computing; http://cac.uvi.edu/miscfaq/vi-cheat.html). A text-based cheat sheet that covers many commands.

◆ **VI Cheat Sheet** (Tufts University, Computational Mechanics Studio; www.tufts.edu/as/medept/compstudio/vihelp.html). A short, text-based cheat sheet.

To include a / in either the target or replacement string:

◆ You use the backslash (\) to remove the special meaning (or separator) from the / character. This is similar to how you learned to use backslashes in Chapter 2, "Using the Command Line," to escape spaces in command-line arguments.

   If you wanted to replace every occurrence of /usr with /usr/local, you would use the following:

   `:1,$s/\/usr/\/usr\/local/g`

   There are only three un-escaped slashes in that command.

Vi has a great many more commands available. **Table 6.4** shows a few of the most useful ones, and the sidebar "Vi Cheat Sheets" tells you where to find some handy guides to keep near your keyboard.

✔ Tip

■ All of the above :set commands may be placed (without the :) in your ~/.exrc file to be executed every time you start vi. For example, you might have the following in your ~/.exrc file:

   `set ai`

   `set ruler`

   `set wm=7`

To repeat the last editing command:

◆ .

   The . command (that's just a period without pressing Return) repeats the last direct command (one that did not use the :) that changed text.

Vi Improved—the vim Editor

By now you are surely in love with vi. OK, maybe not. But it will grow on you. And there is an even better version, called vim. Vim includes multiple levels of undo, the ability to move the cursor with the arrows keys even in edit mode, and other features.

VIM—"Vi IMproved"! (www.vim.org) has information on how to obtain vim. If you don't see a Mac OS X version, then look for the FreeBSD version (remember, Mac OS X is based on Darwin, which is based on FreeBSD).

Unix Pioneer: Richard M. Stallman

Richard M. Stallman (known in the Unix community by his lowercase initials, rms) is a programmer with a major vision of programming as an art form that should share its fruits with all of society.

Rms' reputation in the Unix world is that of a passionate, dedicated, visionary and dogmatic advocate for free software ("free" as in freedom, not as in "free beer").

Rms's contributions to the Unix world have been crucial in making Unix as open and flexible as it is today. Rms is the principal author of some vital pieces of Unix software, and he is the founder of the Free Software movement. This is a worldwide effort to create and maintain software with which users have the freedom to examine and change its inner workings and to share their changes with anyone they wish.

One key piece of software that rms is responsible for is the GNU C compiler (gcc). Gcc is the most widely available compiler in the world.

Besides creating a number of important pieces of software, rms also created the basic license agreement under which most open-source Unix software is distributed. The GNU GPL (General Public License) gives permission to use a piece of software, to examine and alter its source code, and to redistribute the altered version of the software, but only if the altered source code is also distributed under the same GNU GPL license. The Linux operating system is the most well-known collection of GNU GPL software.

Richard M. Stallman's personal Web site is www.stallman.org, and the Free Software Foundation's is www.fsf.org or www.gnu.org.

Emacs—an Editor Without Modes

The emacs editor was invented by Richard M. Stallman, who is better known today as the founder of the Free Software Foundation and the GNU project.

Emacs is what's known as a *modeless* editor—you don't have to switch back and forth between command mode and edit mode. Emacs is not quite as widely used as vi, but it is very popular, and even though it's a large application with many features, its basics are actually easier than vi's.

To start emacs:

◆ emacs *filename*

Emacs will start up. Like vi, emacs is a full-screen editor that will fill your Terminal window. **Figure 6.19** shows a Terminal window after starting emacs.

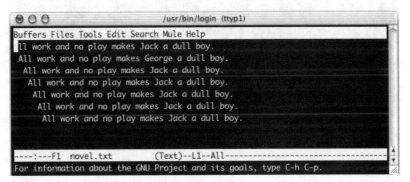

Figure 6.19 Emacs is another full-screen editor.

To move around in the file:

◆ Use the arrow keys.

To change text:

◆ Type to insert text; press [Delete] to remove text. Emacs automatically wraps lines for you.

To save changes:

1. [Control][x]

Emacs commands use the [Control] key. Most commands consist of two (or more) control characters. The save command is [Control][x], followed immediately by [Control][s].

2. [Control][s]

The file is saved.

To quit:

1. [Control][x]

Like the save command, the quit command is a pair of [Control] combinations: [Control][x] followed by [Control][c].

2. [Control][c]

If there are unsaved changes, emacs asks if you want to save (**Figure 6.20**).

To save changes, type y; to abandon changes, type n.

You can find more information about emacs on the man page (man emacs), which includes instruction on running an interactive tutorial feature from within the emacs program.

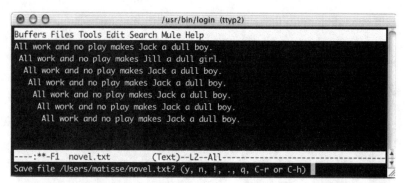

Figure 6.20 If you attempt to quit from emacs with unsaved changes, you will be asked if you want to save.

Printing Files

Now that you are creating files from the command line, you will undoubtedly want to print them. Of course, you can open the files in a GUI text editor or word processor and print using the standard Mac print dialog box, or simply select text in your Terminal window and choose Print from the Shell menu. But once you start using the command line, you will often want to stay there and not switch to a GUI application unless you absolutely have to. That means you'll want to print from the command line.

Also, you may want to create a script that sends information to a printer, so you will need a command line you can put in the script.

Here's the very short version (see the rest of this section for more gory details):

`lp filename`

You can print only certain types of files from the command line. Generally, you can print files in standard file formats such as PDF, JPEG, and plain text, but you cannot print proprietary file formats from the command line—for example, files in the native format of the applications that created them. That means no AppleWorks or PowerPoint files. Those need to be printed from within the applications that created them.

How printing works on a Macintosh

Starting in version 10.2, all printing is handled using the Common Unix Printing System, or CUPS (see the sidebar).

It is important to understand that printers generally can only print documents that are sent to them already converted into a format the printer can understand. For example, printers are not able to understand a Microsoft Excel spreadsheet, or a JPEG image.

When you print from within a conventional Macintosh application such as Adobe Photoshop, AppleWorks, or Excel, the application converts the document from the application's native format to a format called PICT, which is the native Macintosh graphics format (in some cases the application will convert to PostScript instead of PICT). It then hands the converted file to the Macintosh printing system, which converts the PICT image to the appropriate format for your printer.

Some printers expect documents to be sent to them as PostScript files, and other printers expect documents to be formatted using a proprietary page-description language like Hewlett-Packard's PCL (Printer Control Language). This is why each printer needs software specifically designed for that printer. In Mac OS X Classic mode (and Mac OS 9 and earlier), the printer-specific software shows up in the Chooser. In Mac OS X, the software that converts files to the format used by each supported printer (called a *filter*) is preinstalled by Apple, although you can install new filters.

CUPS—The Common Unix Printing System

CUPS is an open-source printing system for Unix. It uses its own Web server (listening on port 631) to receive printing requests. In Mac OS X, this is limited to your own machine unless you allow outside access.

The CUPS software attempts to determine what kind of file you are printing and passes it to the appropriate CUPS *filter* for conversion into the format used by your printer. You can add filters as they become available.

CUPS comes with extensive documentation and a very nice Web interface for managing print jobs. You can see the CUPS documentation and management system on your computer at http://localhost:631/; the CUPS home page is www.cups.org. A basic overview of the CUPS system is available at http://localhost:631/, while the CUPS users manual is at http://localhost:631/overview.html.

Two Ways to Print: lp vs. lpr

The lp ("line printer") and lpr ("line printer request") commands are the two most common Unix commands for printing. In Mac OS X, both commands have been configured to use CUPS.

The lp command was originally developed as part of BSD Unix, and the lpr command comes from AT&T System V version of Unix.

In Mac OS X you will see no practical difference between the commands.

The two commands do have different options, as comparing the man pages will show. However, most of the options (especially for the lpr command) are disabled, such as the option that allows printing of multiple copies.

Printing PostScript

If you have a PostScript printer, then you can print PostScript files from the command line with no problem.

If you are using a non-PostScript printer, such as most inkjet printers, then you should be aware that the version of CUPS installed with Mac OS X version 10.2.1 will *not* convert PostScript files for printing on a non-PostScript printer. However, you can install additional software that supports this, enabling you to print PostScript files to non-PostScript printers.

Printing from the command line

You print documents from the Mac OS X command line using the lp or lpr command (see the sidebar "Two Ways to Print: lp vs. lpr"). Wherever we refer to the lp command in a task, you can substitute the lpr command if you like. In either case, the file(s) you print will be passed through CUPS, and CUPS will use a filter to convert the file(s) into a format that your printer can understand.

Both lp and lpr take filenames as arguments, passing the files to CUPS for processing. You can also pipe the output of any command line into lp or lpr. As long as the command output is a format that CUPS supports, it prints properly.

The CUPS software recognizes most standard file types, such as plain text and GIF, JPEG, PNG, and TIFF images, as well as PDF and PostScript files. (But see the sidebar "Printing PostScript.")

CUPS converts the file to the format your printer uses, assuming that your printer is one of the many supported by CUPS.

Note that HTML files print as plain text, not as you see them in a Web browser.

Support for additional printers is added either through software updates from Apple (see the Software Update tool in System Preferences) or by downloading new filters and installing them (see the sidebar "Support for More Printers and File Formats").

To print a single file from the command line:

◆ `lp` *filename*

Here the `lp` command sends the file named *filename* to your default printer. For example, you can print the Software Users Manual for CUPS with

`lp /usr/share/doc/cups/sum.pdf`

(It's about 44 pages long.)

To print multiple files:

◆ `lp` *file1 file2...*

Just supply all the filenames as arguments on the command line. For example,

`lp hello.pdf flower.jpg`
`→smiles.tiff`

prints all three files.

To print the output from a command:

◆ *command line* `| lp`

For example,

`find /Users/vanilla -name "*.png"`
`→| lp`

prints a list of all the .png files in vanilla's home directory. The output of the command line is sent to `lp`.

As long as the output is a format recognized by CUPS, it prints properly, so commands that produce output in the form of image files, PDF, and PostScript can all be sent directly to a printer. For example,

`man -t ssh | lp`

sends the PostScript output of the `man` command (because of the `-t` option) to the printer.

To see information about printers:

◆ `lpstat -p`

The `lpstat` command is used to obtain information about CUPS. The `-p` option displays the list of available printers (**Figure 6.21**)

There are several more useful options to `lpstat`; for example, the `-d` option shows the current default printer (**Figure 6.22**), the `-R` option shows all jobs waiting to print, and the `-t` option shows all available information. See `man lpstat` for a list of all options.

```
[localhost:~] vanilla% lpstat -p
printer HP_Color_LaserJet_4500 is idle.  enabled since Jan 01 00:00
printer SC_860hUSBi is idle.  enabled since Jan 01 00:00
[localhost:~] vanilla%
```

Figure 6.21 Using `lpstat -p` to see a list of available printers.

```
[localhost:~] vanilla% lpstat -d
system default destination: SC_860hUSBi
[localhost:~] vanilla%
```

Figure 6.22 Using `lpstat -d` to see the system default printer.

Support for More Printers and File Formats

Apple adds support for additional printers every so often, and these are available to you via the online Software Update system (see Software Update in System Preferences).

Support for additional printers and file formats (as when printing PostScript files to non-PostScript printers) is also available through the hard work of many open-source programmers. An excellent resource for upgrading your CUPS system is the Gimp-Print project:

http://gimp-print.sourceforge.net/

Look for the Mac OS X link.

Gimp-Print is a source of high-quality open-source print drivers, and you will almost certainly see improved print quality using its software.

Gimp-Print, in combination with the ESP-Ghostscript software (both available at the Gimp-Print Web site), enables you to print PostScript files to non-PostScript printers such as the USB inkjet printers that are common for home and small-office use.

To set the default printer:

◆ sudo `lpadmin -d` *destination*

The sudo command attempts to run the rest of the command line as root—that is, with the maximum privileges possible on a Unix system. The sudo command is covered in detail in Chapter 11, "Introduction to System Administration," but for now you can just enter the command line as shown above. Trust me.

If you haven't used the sudo command within the previous few minutes, you will be asked for your password; enter it.

The command you are using to actually set the default printer is the `lpadmin` command.

The *destination* is a printer name from the list supplied by the `lpstat -p` command (described above). For example,

sudo `lpadmin -d` sudo `lpadmin -d`
→`SC_860hUSBi`

To print to a nondefault printer:

◆ `lp -d` *destination* *filename*

Use the `-d` option to specify a printer name (as reported by `lpstat -p`)—for example,

`lp -d HP_Color_LaserJet_4500`
→`bigfile.ps`

Note: If you are using the `lpr` command, use the -P option instead of `-d`

Printing to AppleTalk printers

This is actually pretty easy. You can print files on AppleTalk printers using the `atprint` command. First you have to select the printer from the command line, but only once—after that your selection is remembered.

To select an AppleTalk printer with at_cho_prn:

1. `sudo at_cho_prn`

   `at_cho_prn` means "AppleTalk choose printer." The `sudo` command attempts to run the rest of the command line as root; that is, with the maximum privileges possible on a Unix system. The `sudo` command is covered in detail in Chapter 11, "Introduction to System Administration," but for now you can just enter the command line as shown above. Trust me.

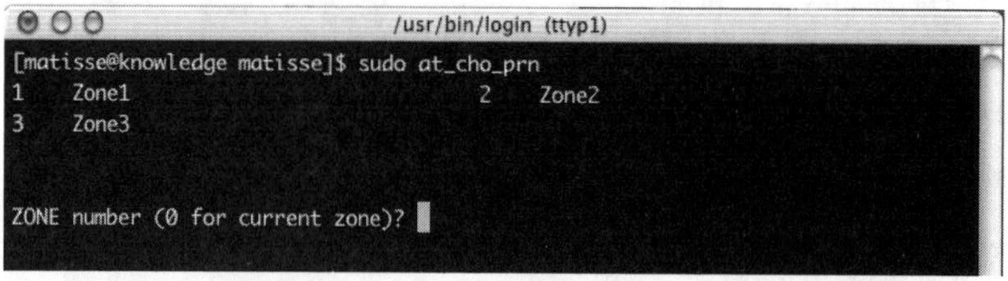

Figure 6.23 The `at_cho_prn` command shows you a list of available AppleTalk zones.

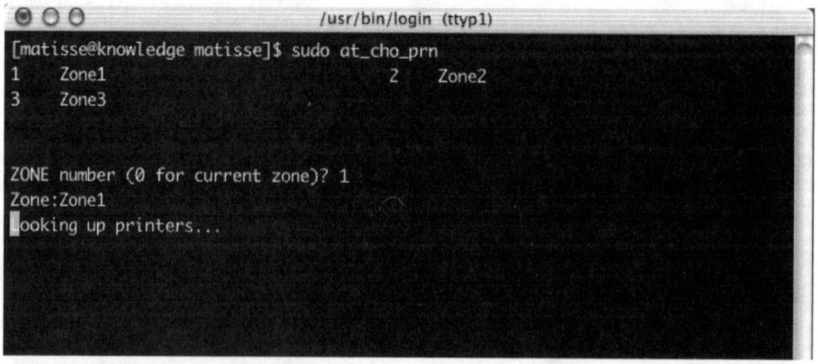

Figure 6.24 Once you select a zone, `at_cho_prn` will search for printers in that zone.

If you haven't used the sudo command within the previous few minutes, you will be asked for your password—enter it.

When the at_cho_prn command runs, it will show you a list of the AppleTalk zones your machine can see (**Figure 6.23**).

2. Enter the zone number to search, and then press Return.

Once you enter a zone number, at_cho_prn searches the zone for printers (**Figure 6.24**) and displays a numbered list of all the printers found.

3. Enter the printer number from the list.

You select a printer by typing its number and pressing Return (**Figure 6.25**).

4. You're done.

The selected printer will now be used for command-line printing with the atprint command.

```
                    /usr/bin/login (ttyp1)
0321.8f.e7 spool-ultra-HPColorProGA1_cmyk:LaserWriter
0321.8f.eb spool-ultra-rip3000_Gls_cmyk:LaserWriter
0321.8f.ef 4mv:LaserWriter
0321.8f.ed spool-ultra-rip2500_Ctd_cmyk:LaserWriter
0321.8f.f3 spool-ultra-HPColorProGA2:LaserWriter
0321.8f.f1 PDF-Maker:LaserWriter
0321.8f.f5 spool-ultra-rip3000_Gloss:LaserWriter
0348.b4.82 HP ColorPro GA - 2:LaserWriter
035d.d8.81 HP ColorPro GA:LaserWriter
0321.8f.f7 spool-ultra-rip3000_Coated:LaserWriter
0359.84.f3 HP 2500 Gloss CMYK:LaserWriter
0359.84.f6 HP 3000 Gloss CMYK:LaserWriter
0359.84.f5 HP 3000 Coated CMYK:LaserWriter
0359.84.f4 HP 2500 Coated CMYK:LaserWriter
0321.07.9e HP CLJ 8500:LaserWriter
0321.04.9e HP CLJ 8550:LaserWriter
0321.06.9d HP LaserJet 4050 Series :LaserWriter
0321.08.9d HP LaserJet 5000 Series:LaserWriter
0321.09.9d HP Color LaserJet 4500:LaserWriter
0321.82.9d LaserJet 4 Plus:LaserWriter
0321.84.9d Jack's Laserjet 5:LaserWriter
0321.83.9c HP DesignJet 2500CP:LaserWriter

number (0 to make no selection)?25
```

Figure 6.25 You select a printer in at_cho_prn

PRINTING FILES

To print to an AppleTalk printer:

◆ `atprint < filename`

For example,

`atprint < myfile.ps`

The **atprint** command sends its input to an AppleTalk printer (the last printer selected using `at_cho_prn`, described above).

You do not supply the filename to print as an argument to **atprint**. Rather, you must supply the file contents as input to the command, using the < input redirection operator (see Chapter 2, "Using the Command Line") or piping the output of a command to **atprint**. For example,

`last -25 vanilla | atprint`

sends the output of the last command to the default AppleTalk printer.

✔ Tip

■ You can override the default printer and specify the printer you want use as an argument to **atprint**—for example,

`atprint "HP Color LaserJet 4500:`
`→ LaserWriter@Zone1" < myfile.pdf`

See the man page for a more detailed description of available options.

Sharing printers with Windows users

The command-line utility **cupsaddsmb** is used to share printers with Windows users via the Samba system (see Chapter 14, "Installing and Configuring Servers" for more on Samba). Read the man page for **cupsaddsmb** and the CUPS documentation at http://localhost:631/sam.html#8_6.

Table 6.5

CUPS Printing Utilities

Goal	Command and Help
Get status information	lpstat
Export printer for Windows	cupsaddsmb
Manage printers	lpadmin or http://localhost:631/printers/

More about CUPS

The CUPS software has a great many options and possible configurations. One place to start learning about CUPS is with the documentation available using your Web browser at http://localhost:631/documentation.html. In particular we suggest reading the CUPS Software Users manual at http://localhost:631/sum.html.

CONFIGURING YOUR UNIX ENVIRONMENT

Many user-configurable Unix programs (such as your shell) read configuration files when they start up. These configuration files contain settings and commands that determine how the programs will behave—for instance, the files can modify the list of places your shell looks for the commands you enter (that list is called your PATH).

You change your Unix environment to have it more closely match your personal preferences and to shape it more closely to the way you work.

Examples of configuring your Unix environment include:

◆ Customizing your shell prompt so that it displays information you want to see.

◆ Creating shortcuts for commonly used command/option combinations (these can be "aliases," but they are distinct from the aliases you create in the Finder, and from the *shell functions,* which are short scripts that are part of your private configuration).

◆ Making it easier to use additional software you install; for example, if you add /Developer/Tools to your PATH, then you can use the commands in the /Developer/Tools directory without typing their full pathnames.

◆ Configuring specific programs such as vi to turn on various options whenever you use them, much the same way that traditional Mac programs often have a preferences dialogue box.

The first program to configure is your shell, since your shell is the primary program you use to interact with Unix. We will also show you how to configure the vi editor by editing a configuration file it uses (see Chapter 6, "Editing and Printing Files," to learn how to use vi).

It should come as no surprise by now that you configure your shell by editing text files.

Finding Configuration Files

User-configurable Unix programs (including your shell, the vi editor, and others) look for configuration files in your home directory when they start up. Most of the commands you have learned so far are not user-configurable; neither the `ls` nor the `cd` command uses configuration files, for example. They do accept options on the command line but do not read any configuration files when you run them.

Many configuration filenames begin with a dot (.), so they are called *dot files* (use `ls -a` to see them). Often the filenames end in "rc" (for *resource*). For example, the main configuration file for the `tcsh` shell is `~/.tcshrc`, a configuration file for the bash shell is `~/.bash_profile`, and the configuration file for the vi editor is called `~/.exrc` (ex is an older editor, and vi provides a "visual interface" for it). There are actually several configuration files available for each shell, and **Table 7.1** lists the more common ones. In this chapter, we will concentrate on the ones you would change in the course of normal use. These files each have settings and commands for the particular program being configured. (Remember that ~ [the tilde] is a synonym for your home directory.)

Configuration files for shells are actually scripts. This means they are a series of commands written in the scripting language for the corresponding shell. They make use of variables, if-then conditions, and other scripting elements such as loops. (See Chapter 9, "Creating and Using Scripts," for more on scripts.)

Am I Configuring the Terminal Application or My Shell?

There's an important distinction to understand here.

The Terminal application you are using to access the command line in Mac OS X is not the same as your shell.

Terminal is a regular Mac OS X graphical application, like your Web browser or word processor. When you open a new window in Terminal, the application runs the appropriate Unix shell (determined by the Terminal application's preferences). Terminal is the program that is handling the screen display and keyboard input for the shell. When you type something in Terminal, the Terminal application passes that to the shell, and when the shell produces output, Terminal draws it on your screen.

The subtle point here is that there are actually other ways besides Terminal in which you can use your shell. One example: You can connect to your Mac using the command line over a network from another machine, which we'll cover in Chapter 10, "Interacting with Other Unix Machines." So when we tell you in this chapter that a change you make will take effect "in the next Terminal window you open," that is really a shorthand way of saying that the change will take effect in the next instance of your shell that you run, and that the easiest way to see it is to open a new Terminal window.

Table 7.1

A Summary of Common Shells	
SHELL	NAME AND DESCRIPTION
sh	**Bourne shell**. The oldest and most standardized shell. Widely used for system startup files (scripts run during system startup). Installed in Mac OS X.
bash	**Bash** (Bourne Again SHell) is an improved version of sh. Combines features from csh, sh, and ksh. Very widely used, especially on Linux systems. See the Bash Reference Manual online (www.gnu.org/manual/bash/). Installed in Mac OS X.
csh	**C shell**. Provides scripting features that have a syntax similar to that of the C programming language (originally written by Bill Joy). Installed in Mac OS X.
ksh	**Korn shell**. Developed at AT&T by David Korn in the early 1980s. Ksh is widely used for programming. It is now open-source software, although you must agree to AT&T's license to install it. See the KornShell Web site (www.kornshell.com).
tcsh	An improved version of csh. The *t* in tcsh comes from the TENEX and TOPS-20 operating systems, which provided a command-completion feature that the creator (Ken Greer) of tcsh included in his new shell. Wilfredo Sanchez, formerly lead engineer on Mac OS X for Apple, worked on tcsh in the early 1990s at the Massachusetts Institute of Technology.
zsh	**Z shell**. Created in 1990, zsh combines features from tcsh, bash, and ksh, and adds many of its own. Installed in Mac OS X. The Web site for Z shell is http://zsh.sourceforge.net.

Configuring Your Shell

The first thing you need to know is which shell you are using. The default shell on Mac OS X is tcsh. Many experienced Unix users prefer the bash shell (see Chapter 15, "More Open-Source Software" at www.peachpit.com/vqp/ umox, to learn how to install bash).

It's very easy to find out which shell you are using. One simple command line will show you.

To determine which shell you are using:

◆ echo $SHELL

$SHELL is an *environment variable* (more about these in the "Environment Variables" section below) that contains the full path of the shell you are using. Unless you have changed from the Mac OS X default, you will see /bin/tcsh (**Figure 7.1**).

✔ Tips

■ You can change the shell that the Terminal program uses by selecting Preferences from the Terminal menu. If you want to change your default login shell (so that the new shell is used no matter how you get to the command line), then see "Changing a User's Login Shell" in Chapter 11.

■ See Chapter 11, "Introduction to System Administration," for instructions on changing your log-in shell not only within the Terminal application but also for when you connect to your Mac from another machine over a network using a command-line interface.

To configure your shell, edit the appropriate configuration file(s). **Table 7.2** lists the configuration files for the most common shells.

Unless you have changed the default Mac OS X setup, you configure your shell by editing your ~/.tcshrc file.

Note that some of the files are the systemwide defaults (those located in the /etc directory), and some are user files (located in each user's home directory). Also, some configuration files are only executed for *interactive* shells— these are shells that give you a command-line prompt (as opposed to a shell program started by a script or other process).

Table 7.2

Common Configuration Files

SHELLS AND CONFIGURATION FILES IN ORDER OF EXECUTION. REMEMBER THAT THE ~ CHARACTER IS SHORTHAND FOR "YOUR HOME DIRECTORY."

TCSH

/etc/csh.cshrc	Systemwide configuration file for the tcsh and csh shells. This is the first file that tcsh executes when it starts up (**Figure 7.2**).
/etc/csh.login	Systemwide configuration for tcsh and csh, executed only for interactive shells.
~/.tcshrc	The main personal configuration file for your tcsh shell. If tcsh doesn't find this, it looks for a .cshrc file.
~/.login	This file is executed after the .tcshrc file, but only if the shell is an interactive log-in shell. It won't be used if some other process is starting the shell.
~/.logout	Tcsh executes this file when you log out of an interactive shell.

BASH

/etc/profile	Systemwide configuration file for the bash and sh shells.
~/.bash_profile	The first personal configuration file that bash looks for.
~/.bashrc	This file is executed for interactive shells but not for your log-in shell (the shell that starts up when you open each Terminal window).
~/.bash_logout	Executed when you log out from a bash log-in shell.

```
[localhost:~] vanilla% echo $SHELL
/bin/tcsh
[localhost:~] vanilla%
```

Figure 7.1 Displaying the $SHELL environment variable.

```
# System-wide .cshrc file for csh(1).

if ($?prompt) then
        set promptchars = "%#"
        if ($?tcsh) then
                set prompt = "[%m:%c3] %n%# "
        else
                set prompt = "[%m:%c3] `id -nu`%# "
        endif
endif
```

Figure 7.2 /usr/share/init/tcsh/rc is the main tcsh configuration file. This is a shell script written in tcsh.

Environment Variables

In the configuration files for your shell, you will most commonly change the contents of various *environment variables*.

A *variable* is simply a piece of memory with a name. When the variable is used, the contents stored in memory are substituted for the name.

Usually when a program stores something in a variable, the stored information is not available to any other program. Environment variables are an exception to this.

Environment variables in Unix not only are available to the process that set them, but are also passed to any child processes at the moment the child process is created. (Review Chapter 2, "Using the Command Line," for an explanation of processes.) So if you set an environment variable in your shell, then any command you run from that shell will be

able to read the contents of that variable. And any processes created by the child will also "inherit" all the environment variables that were set when it was created (**Figure 7.3**). Note that shell variables, such as the prompt (which determines your shell prompt), are not passed to children.

Many programs use this ability to read information provided by their parents and to configure their behavior—think of it as programs adapting to their environment.

When your shell starts up, it automatically sets a number of environment variables. You can create more and alter the ones that have already been set. By convention, the names of environment variables are capitalized, as in PATH. When you want to obtain the value that is stored in a variable, you add a $ to it. Adding the $ to the variable name tells the shell that the value stored in the PATH variable should be substituted at that point, as in $PATH.

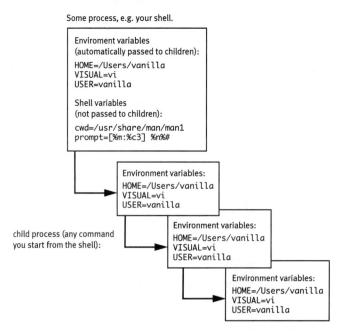

Figure 7.3 Illustration of how environment variables set by parent processes are passed to child processes.

Table 7.3

Common Environment Variables	
VARIABLE	**MEANING**
HOME	Full path of home directory.
SHELL	Full path of log-in shell.
USER	User name (a.k.a. "short name" in Mac OS X).
PATH	List of directories containing commands.
LOGNAME	Same as USER.
PWD	Full path of present working directory.
MANPATH	List of directories containing man pages.
VISUAL	Name of editor (such as vi , emacs) to be used when another program wants you to edit a file.

To see all your environment variables:

◆ env

The env command will show you all of the environment variables that are currently set (**Figure 7.4**). For an explanation of common variables, see **Table 7.3**.

Some of the environment variables contain information that is very short and easy to read (such as SHELL, HOME, and USER), while others, like the TERMCAP variable, have long values filled with

continues on next page

```
[localhost:~] vanilla% env
HOME=/Users/vanilla
SHELL=/bin/tcsh
USER=vanilla
LANG=en_US
PATH=~/bin/powerpc-apple-
darwin:/Users/vanilla/bin:/usr/local/bin:/usr/bin:/bin:/usr/local/sbin:/usr/sbin:/sbin
__CF_USER_TEXT_ENCODING=0x1F6:0:0
TERM=vt100
TERMCAP=d0|vt100|vt100-am|vt100am|dec vt100:    :do=^J:co#80:li#24:cl=\E[;H\E[2J:sf=2*\ED:
:le=^H:bs:am:cm=5\E[%i%d;%dH:nd=2\E[C:up=2\E[A:
:ce=3\E[K:cd=50\E[J:so=2\E[7m:se=2\E[m:us=2\E[4m:ue=2\E[m:
:md=2\E[1m:mr=2\E[7m:mb=2\E[5m:me=2\E[m:      :rf=/usr/share/tabset/vt100:
:rs=\E>\E[?3l\E[?4l\E[?5l\E[?7h\E[?8h\E[;r\E[0m\E(B\E)B\E[2J:    :ks=\E[?1h\E=:ke=\E[?1l\E>:
:ku=\EOA:kd=\EOB:kr=\EOC:kl=\EOD:kb=^H: :ho=\E[H:k1=\EOP:k2=\EOQ:k3=\EOR:k4=\EOS:pt:sr=2*\EM:vt#3:xn:
:sc=\E7:rc=\E8:cs=\E[%i%d;%dr:
TERM_PROGRAM=Apple_Terminal
TERM_PROGRAM_VERSION=57
HOSTTYPE=macintosh
VENDOR=apple
OSTYPE=darwin
MACHTYPE=powerpc
SHLVL=1
PWD=/Users/vanilla
LOGNAME=vanilla
GROUP=staff
HOST=localhost
ENV_SET=
MANPATH=/Users/vanilla/man:/usr/local/share/man:/usr/share/man
[localhost:~] vanilla%
```

Figure 7.4 The command env shows all of the current environment variables.

complicated settings (TERMCAP is short for *terminal capabilities*; programs like the man command read it to determine how to handle various display tasks, such as showing bold or underlined characters).

The env command is actually a good example of a child's inheriting its environment from its parent. When you run the env command, your shell is the parent process that "spawns" a child process to run env. When env runs, it inherits its parent's environment and then reads and displays its own environment.

✔ Tip

- The tcsh shell also has the setenv command, which is normally used to set an environment variable (see next task). If used with no arguments, setenv produces a neatly formatted list of all your environment variables.

You should leave most environment variables alone—they are set automatically to their correct values. For example, the USER variable has your user name, and changing it will simply confuse any program that tries to use it to determine which user you are.

Sometimes you will want to change environment variables, though; for example, the crontab program (used to schedule automatic execution of commands, discussed in Chapter 11, "Introduction to System Administration") reads the VISUAL environment variable to decide which editor to launch.

Setting environment variables is simple.

To temporarily change or create an environment variable in tcsh (or csh):

1. setenv VISUAL vi

   This sets the environment variable named VISUAL to have the value vi.

2. Test that it worked:

   echo $VISUAL

   Figure 7.5 shows the result.

✔ Tips

- If the value contains spaces, make sure to enclose it in quotes:

  setenv ORGANIZATION "Tony's Pizza"

- To reset (or *unset,* in Unix terminology) an environment variable, simply leave off the value:

  setenv VISUAL

```
[localhost:~] vanilla% setenv VISUAL vi
[localhost:~] vanilla% echo $VISUAL
vi
[localhost:~] vanilla%
```

Figure 7.5 Setting an environment variable in the tcsh or csh shell.

Environment variables that are set at a shell prompt will last only for as long as you use the current shell in each session. That is, the setting disappears when you log out.

To make a durable change to an environment variable in the tcsh shell:

1. Edit your ~/.tcshrc file (or type ~/.cshrc for the csh shell).

2. Add this line to the end of the file:
   `setenv ORGANIZATION "Tony's Pizza"`

3. Save the file.

4. Quit the editor.
   The change will take effect with the next shell you start.

5. Open a new Terminal window.

6. Test that the variable is set:
   `echo $ORGANIZATION`

✔ Tips

- A faster way to add a single line to a file is to use the output redirection you learned in Chapter 2, "Using the Command Line." Replace steps 1–4 above with

  `echo setenv ORGANIZATION \"Tony\'s` `→Pizza\" >> ~/.tcshrc`

- Make sure to use >> and not a single > character. If you use only >, you will wipe out the current contents of your .tcshrc file.

- Notice how you have to escape the quotes by preceding them with backslashes so that the shell itself doesn't try to interpret them. You want the quotes to be part of the arguments to the echo command so that they end up in the ~/.tcshrc file.

Different shells use different syntax to set environment variables.

To change or create an environment variable in bash (or sh):

1. `export VISUAL=vi`

   Make sure there are no spaces on either side of the equal sign.

   The **export** command brings variables into the environment. The command line above actually combines two operations: the setting of the VISUAL variable (VISUAL=vi) and the *exporting* of that variable into the shell's list of environment variables. The same result could be achieved in two separate steps:

   `VISUAL=vi`

   `export VISUAL`

   Without the export step, the VISUAL variable would be set, but only as a *shell variable*, which is a variable that the shell can read but that will not be passed on to any child processes it creates.

2. Test the setting with `echo $VISUAL` (**Figure 7.6**).

✔ Tips

- If you want the setting to be made each time you start a shell, put the **export** command line in your `~/.profile` file.

- As with the **tcsh** shell, you use quotes if the value has spaces in it:

  `export ORGANIZATION="Tony's Pizza"`

```
[localhost:~] vanilla%  VISUAL=vi
[localhost:~] vanilla%  echo $VISUAL
vi
[localhost:~] vanilla%
```

Figure 7.6 Setting an environment variable in the bash or sh shell.

Changing your PATH

Every time you execute a command by using only the command's name (for example, ls or pwd), your shell looks for the command in a list of directories. That list is stored in the PATH environment variable. The PATH list provides a shortcut for finding commands.

If it weren't for the PATH list, you would have to type /bin/ls instead of ls, and /usr/bin /vi instead of vi. The command-line utilities supplied with the Mac OS X Developer Tools are located in /Developer/Tools (some of those utilities, such as CpMac and MvMac, are described in Chapter 2, "Using the Command Line"). The /Developer/Tools directory is not normally in your PATH, so if you use any of the commands in /Developer/Tools, you need to type their full pathnames, unless you add the directory /Developer/Tools to your PATH. Here's how to do that.

Adding a directory to your PATH in tcsh:

1. Start by editing your ~/.tcshrc file. (Review Chapter 5, "Using Files and Directories," about editing files from the command line.) If you are using vi, the command is

   vi ~/.tcshrc

2. Add a line that says

   set path = ($path /Developer/Tools)

   This may seem a little odd. After all, you are trying to set the PATH environment variable, not path. What's going on? Well, tcsh uses an unusual method to set the PATH variable.

   Tcsh requires that you set the shell variable path, and then tcsh sets the actual PATH environment variable. As discussed earlier, shell variables are variables created in your shell that are available only in the shell you are currently using. They

continues on next page

are not passed on to child processes as environment variables are.

Also notice how the command line includes the existing **$path** value in the new definition, thus adding the new directory to the list. Without **$path** in the command line, the result would be to replace the old **PATH** with the single new directory—not at all what you want.

3. Save your file (the command will depend on which editor you're using).

4. Quit the editor (this command will also depend on which editor you're using).

   The change will take effect in the next shell you start.

5. Open a new Terminal window to test the change.

6. echo $PATH

   You'll see the new directory at the end of the list.

7. Test using one of the developer tools without typing its full path—for example,

   GetFileInfo "/Applications (Mac OS
   → 9)/SimpleText"

   Figure 7.7 shows the output from the GetFileInfo command.

```
[localhost:~] vanilla% GetFileInfo "/Applications (Mac OS 9)/SimpleText"
file: "/Applications (Mac OS 9)/SimpleText"
type: "APPL"
creator: "ttxt"
attributes: avBstclInMed
created: 05/30/1997 19:00:00
modified: 05/30/1997 19:00:00
[localhost:~] vanilla%
```

Figure 7.7 Using the GetFileInfo command once it is in your PATH.

```
localhost% export PATH="$PATH:/Developer/Tools"
localhost% echo $PATH
/usr/bin:/bin:/Users/matisse:/Developer/Tools
localhost%
```

Figure 7.8 Changing your PATH in the bash or sh shell; the new directory is added to the end of the list.

If you are using the bash shell or the sh shell, then you add a directory to your PATH by directly setting the PATH environment variable. Putting this setting in your ~/.profile ensures that it takes effect each time you start a new shell.

Adding a directory to your PATH in bash or sh:

1. Edit your ~/.profile file.

   If you are using the vi editor, the command is

   `vi ~/.profile`

2. Add a line to the file that says

   `export PATH="$PATH:/Developer/Tools"`

   Notice how the new value includes the current value of $PATH, then a colon (no spaces!), and then the new directory.

3. Save the file.

4. Quit the editor.

   The change takes effect immediately.

5. You can check it with

   `echo $PATH`

   Figure 7.8 shows the result. The new directory is added to the end of the list.

Environment Variables

Shell Aliases

Shell aliases are shortcut names for commands. Each alias consists of one word (or even one letter) that you can use instead of a longer command line. For example, you may find yourself using the command ls -F a lot. You can easily make a shortcut for that command: lf, for example. So when you use lf where the shell expects a command, then the shell will substitute ls -F.

To see all your current aliases:

◆ alias

The alias command with no arguments displays all your current aliases. The first item on each line is the alias (which must always be a single string, with no spaces), and the rest of the line is the full com-

mand for which the alias is a shortcut. **Figure 7.9** shows the default aliases for the tcsh shell. You can see that the alias l is a shortcut for the command ls -lg.

The first word on each line is the name of the alias; the rest of the line is what gets executed when the alias is used.

Several of the aliases are more complicated. The aliases in Figure 7.9 are for the tcsh shell, and several of them make use of specific advanced features of that shell (see man tcsh for all of the available features).

For example, the alias in Figure 7.9 called line expects two arguments (indicated by !:1 and !:2), while the alias called ll takes all of its arguments (indicated by !*) and inserts them into the middle of a command line.

```
localhost% alias
.          pwd
..         cd ..
cd..       cd ..
cdwd       cd `pwd`
cwd        echo $cwd
ff         find . -name !:1 -print
files      find !:1 -type f -print
l          ls -lg
line       sed -n '!:1 p' !:2
list_all_hostnames      grep -v "^#" /etc/hosts
ll         ls -lag !* | more
term       set noglob; unsetenv TERMCAP; eval `tset -s -I -Q - !*`
word       grep !* /usr/share/dict/web2
wordcount        ((cat !* | tr -s '      .,;:?!()[]"' '\012' | cat -n | tail -1 | awk '{print $1}'))
[localhost%
```

Figure 7.9 Using the alias command to see all currently set aliases. Shown are the default aliases for the tcsh shell.

You can create aliases at the command line or by adding them to a configuration file.

Aliases created at the command line are only in effect for as long as you use that shell—that is, they disappear when you close that Terminal window. If you want an alias to always be available, you must put it in a configuration file.

To create an alias in tcsh or csh:

1. `alias lf 'ls -F'`

   This will create an alias called `lf`, which the shell will translate into `ls -F` whenever you use `lf` as a command. Make sure to enclose the last argument in quotes, either single or double, so that everything after the alias name is treated as a single entity.

2. Check to see that the alias is set:

   `alias`

   The line

   `lf ls -F`

   should be included in your aliases now.

✔ Tips

- If you want to have an alias use arguments from the command line inside the alias definition, you can use `!:1` for the first argument, `!:2` for the second, and so on. But you must escape the `!` in the alias definition. So to define an alias called `myword` that takes its first argument and searches for it inside the file `~/mydictionary`, you would use

  `alias myword 'grep \!:1 ~/`
  `→ mydictionary'`

- You could use that alias in this way:

  `myword banana`

  as a shortcut for

  `grep banana ~/mydictionary`

To create an alias in tcsh (or csh) that is set every time you start a shell:

1. Open your `~/.tcshrc` file (for the csh shell use `~/.cshrc`).

2. Add a line with the alias

   `alias lf 'ls -F'`

3. Save the file.

4. Quit the editor.

   The new alias will be set for the next shell you start.

5. Open a new Terminal window to check that the alias is set:

   `alias`

   You should see your new alias in the resulting list.

✔ Tip

- A set of example aliases for the `tcsh` shell are contained in the file `/usr/share/tcsh/examples/aliases`.

To create an alias in bash:

1. `alias lf='ls -F'`

   Note that there are no spaces before or after the equal sign.

2. `alias`

   The shell shows all your current aliases, including the one you just created.

   As with the `tcsh` shell, bash aliases created at the command line will disappear when you exit the shell.

To create an alias in bash that is set every time you start a shell:

1. Open your ~/.bash_profile file.

2. Add a line with the alias—for example,

   alias lf='ls -F'

3. Save the file.

4. Quit the editor.

   The new alias will be set for the next shell you start.

5. Open a new Terminal window to check that the alias is set:

   alias

   You should see your new alias in the list:

   alias lf='ls -F'

Shell functions

Unlike aliases in the tcsh shell, aliases in bash cannot have command-line arguments included in them. However, bash allows you to create shell functions, which can make use of their arguments.

The term *shell function* applies to series of shell command lines. This is similar to an alias, except that a shell function can be many lines long, and you may use the special variables $1 for the first argument, $2 for the second, and so on.

Shell functions should be defined in your ~/.bash_profile.

To create a shell function in bash:

1. Open your ~/.bash_profile.

   The entire function you will be entering is shown in **Figure 7.10**. This sample function looks up a word in two different files that make up a dictionary.

```
word () {
    grep $1 /usr/share/dict/web2
    grep $1 /usr/share/dict/web2a
}
```

Figure 7.10 Code listing of a bash shell function.

```
bash-2.05$ word auspic
auspicate
auspice
auspices
auspicial
auspicious
auspiciously
auspiciousness
auspicy
inauspicious
inauspiciously
inauspiciousness
unauspicious
unauspiciously
unauspiciousness
ultra-auspicious
bash-2.05$
```

Figure 7.11 Using the new shell function to look up "auspic" in the dictionary.

2. Enter the first line of the new function.

In this example you are creating a function called "word":

word () {

The parentheses tell bash that this is a function definition. The bracket ({) marks the beginning of the commands in the function.

3. Enter the body of the function:

grep $1 /usr/share/dict/web2

grep $1 /usr/share/dict/web2a

Notice that the function can have more than one line of commands.

The $1 is a variable that will be replaced with the first argument when you use the function in a command line. (Read the file /usr/share/dict/README for a description of the web2 and web2a files.)

4. Finish the function definition with a }.

Double-check that what you entered looks like Figure 7.10.

5. Save the file.

6. Quit the editor.

The new function will be in effect with the next Terminal window you open.

7. Open a new Terminal window.

8. Test the function by trying it on the command line. If you are using the example function from Figure 7.10, then the first argument you supply is used in the function. The function searches two different files for its first argument.

9. word auspic

You should get the output shown in **Figure 7.11**. Your new shell function, word, takes its first argument (the $1 in the function) and searches for it in the two files. The function is really a short shell script (see Chapter 9, "Creating and Using Scripts") but is part of your personal shell configuration.

SHELL ALIASES

Shell Settings

Your shell uses a variety of settings that you will want to change from time to time. You should read the man page for your shell to learn about dozens of possible settings.

You may want your shell prompt to be shorter, or to display the date, time, or some other specific piece of information. This is easy to do by adding a line to your shell configuration file.

Another setting you may want to change is umask, which controls the permissions given to any new file you create. (Chapter 8, "Working with Permissions and Ownership," goes into detail on permissions.)

Customizing your shell prompt

Both tcsh and bash provide ways to customize your shell prompt. The simplest customization would be to simply have your prompt be a word or phrase, such as "Type something:," but far more interesting is the ability to have the prompt include information about what is going on in your shell. For example, the default prompt for tcsh uses the formatting pattern

[%m:%c3] %n%#

Table 7.4 lists the common formatting patterns available for the tcsh shell prompt.

If your computer's name is violet, and your user name is vanilla, and your current directory is /usr/share.man/man1, then the prompt would be

[violet:share/man/man1] vanilla%

See how the %m gets replaced with violet, the %c3 gets replaced with share/man/man1, the %n gets replaces with vanilla, and the %# gets replaced with %.

Table 7.4

Some tcsh Prompt Macros	
FORMATTING SEQUENCE	**TURNS INTO THIS**
%/	Your current directory.
%~	Your current directory, but with your home directory shown as ~ and other home directories shown as ~user.
%c	The last part of the current directory. If followed by a number *n* (for example, %c3), then only the last *n* components (directories) are shown. Your home directory and other users' home directories are shown, as with %~ above.
%C	Same as %c but does not show home directories with a ~.
%M	Your computer's Internet host name.
%m	The host name up to the first ".".
%B (%b)	Start (stop) bold mode.
%U (%u)	Start (stop) underline mode.
%t	The time of day in 12-hour a.m./p.m. format.
%T	Like %t but in 24-hour format.
%%	A single %.
%n	Your user name.
%d	The weekday in Day format.
%D	The day in dd format.
%w	The month in Mon format.
%W	The month in mm format.
%y	The year in yy format.
%Y	The year in yyyy format.
%#	A % for normal users and a # for the root user (helps you know if you are logged in as root).

See man tcsh for the complete list.

```
[localhost:~] vanilla% set prompt='%t:%c3 %# '
11:32am:~ %
```

Figure 7.12 Changing your tcsh shell prompt on the command line.

The following tasks show you how to customize your shell prompt so that it shows the current time (in 12-hour a.m./p.m. format), followed by your current directory, followed by your user name.

Don't worry about making a mistake—the changes you make will only be in effect for the single Terminal window in which you perform this task. Once you are satisfied that you have it right, you can add the setting to your ~/.tcshrc file to have it take effect for all future shells you start up (that is, all future Terminal windows).

To temporarily customize your prompt in tcsh:

◆ `set prompt='%t:%c3 %# '`

Your prompt will immediately change, as shown in **Figure 7.12**. Note the space at the end of the prompt—right after the # and before the last `'`. That space is actually part of the prompt, so when you type a command, it is visually separated from the prompt.

To make a durable customization of your tcsh shell prompt:

1. Open your ~/.tcshrc file.

2. Add a line with the new setting.

3. Using the example from the previous task, add
    `set prompt='%t:%c3 %# '`

4. Save the file.

5. Quit the editor.
    The change will take effect with the next Terminal window you open.

6. Open a new Terminal window to see your new prompt.

continues on next page

SHELL SETTINGS

The procedure for customizing your bash shell prompt is similar to that for the tcsh shell. The bash shell also uses a set of special formatting codes to allow the inclusion of things like the current directory and date in the prompt.

The bash shell calls these *escape sequences* because they all start with the backslash character, which is frequently used in Unix to alter the meaning of the following character, usually by removing some special meaning ("escaping" the character). But in this case, the use of the backslash creates a special meaning for the following character, so \d becomes the date, and \u becomes your user name.

Table 7.5 shows the common escape sequences for the bash shell prompt.

The default bash shell prompt uses the format '\s-\v\$ '

and produces a prompt that looks like bash-2.05$

The \s becomes bash; the \v becomes 2.05.

In the tasks below you will set your prompt to show the current time in 12-hour a.m./p.m. format, a colon, and the current directory, followed by the > character and a space.

To temporarily customize your bash shell prompt:

◆ PS1='\t:\w > '

Make sure there are no spaces on either side of the equal sign. Your shell prompt will immediately change, as in **Figure 7.13**. Note that even though this looks as if you are setting an environment variable (because PS1 is capitalized), you aren't. You are setting a variable (the PS1 variable), but you are setting it for this shell only. Unlike environment variables, this variable will not be passed on to child processes of this shell.

Table 7.5

Some bash Prompt Escape Sequences	
ESCAPE SEQUENCE	**MEANING**
\d	The date in "weekday month date" format (for example, "Tue May 26").
\h	Your computer's Internet host name up to the first ".".
\H	Your computer's Internet host name.
\j	The number of jobs currently managed by the shell.
\s	The name of the shell program (for example, bash).
\t	Current time in 24-hour HH:MM:SS format.
\T	Current time in 12-hour HH:MM:SS format.
\@	Current time in 12-hour a.m./p.m. format.
\u	Your user name.
\v	The version of bash you are using— for example, 2.05.
\w	Your current directory.
\W	Base name (last part) of your current directory.
\\	A backslash.

See man bash for the complete list.

```
bash-2.05$ PS1='\t:\w > '
10:17:03:~ >
```

Figure 7.13 Changing your bash shell prompt on the command line.

```
[localhost:~] vanilla% umask 002
[localhost:~] vanilla% umask
002
[localhost:~] vanilla%
```

Figure 7.14 Changing your umask on the command line.

To make a durable customization of your bash shell prompt:

1. Open your `~/.bash_profile` file.

2. Add a line with the new setting.

   Using the example from the previous task, you would add

   `PS1='\t:\w > '`

3. Save the file.

4. Quit the editor.

   The change will take effect with the next Terminal window you open.

5. Open a new Terminal window.

   You will see your new prompt.

Changing your umask

When you create a new file or directory, the initial permissions are determined by the umask (*user mask*) setting of the shell that created the file. So the umask is a shell configuration that affects the permissions of any file you create. (See Chapter 8, "Working with Permissions and Ownership," for more on permissions.)

Your umask setting can be either temporary or durable, like your shell prompt, which you customized in the tasks above.

You use the umask command to set (and view) your umask. Used with no arguments, umask simply displays your current umask setting. To set your umask, you supply one argument, which is a three-digit octal (base eight) number. If you use fewer than three digits, zeros are added to the left to bring the total up to three digits—so 2 becomes 002, and 22 becomes 022, for example. See Chapter 8 for an explanation of how the umask is actually applied to determine file permissions, and of what those permissions mean.

Your default umask is 022, which means that any new files you create will be readable by every user of your Mac, but only writable by you. A common change is to set one's umask so that newly created files are writable not only by oneself but also by other users in the same "group" (see Chapter 8 for more on groups). The umask setting for this is 002 (which can be abbreviated as simply 2).

To temporarily change your umask:

1. `umask 002`

   The change takes effect at once and will last until you log out of the shell or change it again.

2. Verify that the change took effect:

   `umask`

   Figure 7.14 shows an example.

Changing your umask for all future shells is simply a matter of putting the same command in your shell configuration file.

To make a durable change to your umask:

1. Open the startup file for your shell.

   For `tcsh`, edit `~/.tcshrc`. For bash, edit `~/.bash_profile`.

2. Add a line with the umask command and the new umask.

   For example, to have your umask set to 002, add a line that says

   `umask 002`

3. Save the file.

4. Quit the editor.

   The change will take effect on the next shell you start.

5. Open a new Terminal window.

6. `umask`

   to confirm it's correct.

Configuring vi

In addition to reading configurations from your shell, the vi editor will also read configurations from a text file, and since we've already shown you how to use it (in Chapter 6, "Editing and Printing Files"), We'll show you some common configuration settings you may want to use.

To configure vi:

1. Open your ~/.exrc file (using vi, of course!).

2. Add the setting(s) you wish to use.

   For example, to display the current mode (command or insert) on the status line (very useful for beginners!):

   ```
   set showmode
   ```

3. To have word wrap (indicated by wm) always be on, and to set it to kick in within five characters of the right edge of the screen, add a line that says

   ```
   set wm=5
   ```

4. To set a tab stop every four spaces (instead of the default eight), add a line that says

   ```
   set tabstop=4
   ```

   Table 7.6 lists some common setting possibilities, and of course you should read the vi man page to see the full list.

5. Save the file.

6. Quit.

   The new settings will be in effect the next time you use vi.

Table 7.6

Common vi Configuration Settings	
SETTING	**MEANING**
set autoindent	Vi will insert tabs and spaces at the start of each line to make the first character you type line up with the first character of the line above.
set extended	Allows extended regular expressions to be used in searches. See Chapter 4, "Useful Unix Utilities," the section "Searching for Text," for a discussion of regular expressions.
set ruler	Causes vi to display the position of the cursor at the bottom of the window (as two numbers: line,column).
set showmode	Displays the current mode (command or insert) on the status line.
set tabstop=n	Tells vi how many spaces between each tab stop. If you set it to 4, then pressing (Tab) will advance the cursor only four spaces.
set wm=n	Turns on automatic word wrap. Vi will automatically insert a new-line character when you get within n columns of the right edge of the screen.

WORKING WITH PERMISSIONS AND OWNERSHIP

8

The dual concepts of "permissions" and "ownership" in Unix are not only an important part of Unix's high level of stability—they are also the foundation for its system security.

This chapter covers these two critical concepts, and from the very first we want to impress upon you the difference between them. Even Unix veterans are sometimes tripped up when they don't have the two concepts sufficiently separated in their thinking.

It's really quite simple. *Ownership* in Unix deals with *who* controls something. *Permissions* deals with *what* the owners (and others) can do with something. Every file is "owned" by one user and one group. Every file has a set of "permissions" that define what the owning user, group, and all others may do with it.

This chapter shows you what users and groups are, how to see who owns each file, and how to understand and set the permissions on a file.

Because the setting of permissions in Unix involves so many possible combinations, we use several tables and examples to allow you to compare different permission settings and read an explanation for each one.

About Users and Groups

Because Unix is a multiuser system, it is quite normal to have many users (also called *user accounts*) on your computer. You could even have hundreds if your computer is being used as a server that many people can access, perhaps to retrieve their email.

To help manage system security, Unix uses *groups* to organize several users together so that you can grant file access to all of them. A user is always a member of at least one group, and may be a member of many groups. Think of how employees in a company might be organized—everyone has access to the email system, but only certain people in the accounting department have access to financial information. Thus, the people in accounting are members of two different groups for security purposes: They are members of group "staff" and also group "finance."

Every single file and directory on a Unix machine is owned by one user and one group. When a file is created, its ownership and permissions are based on the user who created it.

A file starts its existence under the ownership of the user who created it and within one of the groups that user belongs to (usually the user's *primary group*—for more on groups, see the following section, and the entries for 2775 and 2000 in tables 8.3 and 8.4, respectively). The file also has a set of permissions assigned to it, based on the *umask* of the user; the umask defines which permissions are *not* granted (or "masked out") for files you create (review "Changing your umask" in Chapter 7, "Configuring Your Unix Environment").

Every user account on a Unix system has a name and a number. The name is what Mac OS X calls your *short name*. In the Unix world, this short name is variously referred to as *log-in name, user name,* and frequently simply *user.* The number is referred to as the *user ID,* or *uid.*

Every user account on a Unix system belongs to at least one *group.* Like users, groups have both names and ID numbers. A Unix group contains a list of users. As we mentioned, users are frequently members of more than one group. The group's ID number is often referred to as the *gid.* See Chapter 11, "Introduction to System Administration," to learn how to add users to a group.

Seeing all the users and groups on your system

Even if you only created one account when you installed Mac OS X, you still have more than a dozen "users" on your system. This is because Unix uses a number of special user accounts that are never intended to be directly used by any human. These other "users" exist so that system files and processes may be owned and operated with differing sets of privileges. There are also a number of groups that exist for the same purpose.

To see a list of all the users on your system:

- `nidump passwd .`

  The `nidump` command (*NetInfo dump*) is a Mac OS X–specific command (actually derived from the NeXT operating system) that displays information from a database called NetInfo (**Figure 8.1**).

  Each line of output from `nidump` is a colon-separated series of entries for one user. **Figure 8.2** shows the meanings of the most important entries. Notice the primary group ID entry. Every user is a member of at least one group, called his or her *primary group.*

✔ Tips

- Although the passwords shown in Figure 8.2 are encrypted, if naughty people were to obtain the encrypted passwords from your system, they could also possibly obtain the unencrypted passwords as well—*if* the latter passwords are not well-crafted (for an explanation of how this is done, see "Choosing Good Passwords" in Chapter 12, "Security"). The short version: "Every password must contain letters, numbers, and punctuation marks."

■ **Ni dump** reads from a database that contains a variety of system information. The database is a series of files in */var/db/netinfo*. If you are experienced with other Unix systems, then nidump is one big difference with Mac OS X. The output from nidump looks like the */etc/passwd* file that other Unix systems use. See also the sidebar "Creating Users and Groups."

```
[localhost:~] vanilla% nidump passwd .
nobody:*:-2:-2::0:0:Unprivileged User:/dev/null:/dev/null
root:Nic5tRyw1Ll1s:0:0::0:0:System Administrator:/var/root:/bin/tcsh
daemon:*:1:1::0:0:System Services:/var/root:/dev/null
unknown:*:99:99::0:0:Unknown User:/dev/null:/dev/null
www:*:70:70::0:0:World Wide Web Server:/Library/WebServer:/dev/null
matisse:er5tFr4SiyT6gg:501:20::0:0:J Matisse Enzer:/Users/matisse:/bin/tcsh
vanilla:4ewuyTffdggP8X:502:20::0:0:Sample User:/Users/vanilla:/bin/tcsh
howard:eR5uYTT65Em07:503:20::::Howard Baldwin:/Users/howard:/bin/tcsh
noway:IjJJ63/t6Qwsd:504:20::0:0:Jose Marquez:/Users/noway:/bin/tcsh
news:*:250:250::0:0:News Server:/:/dev/null
mysql:*:251:251::0:0:MySQL Database Server:/:/dev/null
pgsql:*:252:252::0:0:PostgreSQL Database Server:/:/dev/null
games:*:253:253::0:0:Game Files Owner:/:/dev/null
canna:*:254:254::0:0:Canna Japanese Input Server:/:/dev/null
postfix:*:255:255::0:0:Postfix Mail Transfer Agent:/sw/var/spool/postfix:/dev/null
smmsp:*:25:25::0:0:Sendmail User:/private/etc/mail:/dev/null
[localhost:~] vanilla%
```

Figure 8.1 Using nidump to see a list of all the user accounts on the system. Your list will differ.

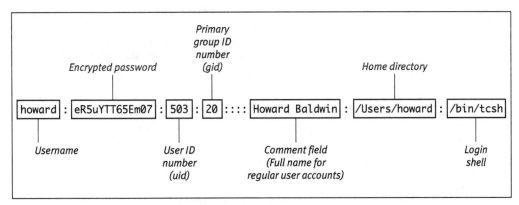

Figure 8.2 Diagram showing the important parts of each line in the output from nidump passwd.

To see a list of all the groups on your system:

◆ nidump group .

Figure 8.3 shows the output of this command, and **Figure 8.4** is a diagram showing what the parts of each line mean. Note that several users shown in Figure 8.1 have group 20 as their primary group. In Figure 8.3 we see that group 20 is called "staff."

✔ Tip

■ Even though no users are listed in the entry for group staff, there are still users who are members of it—they are those users who have group 20 listed as their primary group in Figure 8.1. So to see all the users who are a member of a group, you have to look in two places: the output of both

nidump passwd .

and

nidump group .

```
[localhost:~] vanilla% nidump group .
nobody:*:-2:
nogroup:*:-1:
wheel:*:0:matisse
daemon:*:1:root
kmem:*:2:root
sys:*:3:root
tty:*:4:root
operator:*:5:root
mail:*:6:
bin:*:7:
staff:*:20:root
guest:*:31:root
utmp:*:45:
uucp:*:66:
dialer:*:68:
network:*:69:
www:*:70:
admin:*:80:matisse
unknown:*:99:
peachpit:*:1000:matisse,howard
news:*:250:
mysql:*:251:
pgsql:*:252:
games:*:253:
canna:*:254:
postfix:*:255:
maildrop:*:256:
smmsp:*:25:
[localhost:~] vanilla%
```

Figure 8.3 Using nidump to get a list of all the groups on the system. Your results will differ.

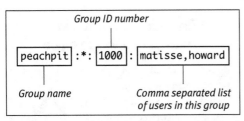

Figure 8.4 Diagram showing the important parts of each entry in the list of groups.

```
[localhost:~] vanilla% groups
staff
[localhost:~] vanilla%
```

Figure 8.5 Using the groups command to see which groups you belong to. Your results will differ.

```
[localhost:~] vanilla% groups matisse
staff wheel admin peachpit
[localhost:~] vanilla%
```

Figure 8.6 Using the groups command to see the groups another user belongs to. Again, your results will differ.

It is very easy to see which groups a particular user belongs to.

To see which groups you belong to:

◆ groups

The groups commands displays a list of all the groups you are a member of (**Figure 8.5**).

To see which groups another user belongs to:

◆ groups *username*

You use the same groups command to see which groups a user other than yourself belongs to. For example, to see which groups the user vanilla belongs to, type

groups vanilla

Figure 8.6 shows the result using users and groups from Figures 8.1 and 8.3.

✔ Tip

■ Membership in groups is not secret information. Any user on the system can see which groups other users are members of.

Creating Users and Groups

The Mac OS X methods for adding, modifying, and deleting users and groups are different from those used by all other Unix systems, possibly reflecting Apple's desire to use software it obtained in the acquisition of NeXT. Users may be added or deleted, and their passwords may be changed, from the Accounts tool in System Preferences. See Chapter 11, "Introduction to System Administration," for more.

Users may also be created with the more complex NetInfo Manager utility. NetInfo Manager allows an administrative user to make more detailed changes to a user's profile than with the Users tool in Preferences, but you should use it with caution.

You can also create and modify groups using the NetInfo Manager. Again, this is something you should do with great care, and only after having studied the documentation for NetInfo manager: www.opensource.apple.com/projects/documentation/howto/html/netinfo.html.

The Root User— Permission to Do Anything

There is one very special user on every Unix system: the one with the user name *root*. This individual is also called the *superuser*, because he or she has the power to override every safeguard on the system.

The root user on a Unix system has full control over every file on the system.

On most Unix systems, you use the root account to perform system-administration tasks. In practice, this means that on those Unix systems you either log in as the root user or use the **su** (*switch user*) command to assume the role of the root user after having logged in with your regular account.

Mac OS X uses a slightly different approach, in which you never actually log in as root but instead use a command called **sudo** (*superuser do*) to perform specific commands with the power of root (see the sidebar "Why Mac OS X Uses **sudo** Instead of a Root Log-In" for a discussion of why Mac OS X does this differently). Using the **sudo** command is covered in Chapter 11, "Introduction to System Administration," but you need to be aware at this point that there is a way to override any of the permission restrictions described in this chapter.

Why Mac OS X Uses sudo Instead of a Root Log-In

By requiring the use of the **sudo** command, Apple made it slightly less convenient for users to perform commands as root. Its goal: discouraging average Mac OS X users from working as root because of the danger that they could irreparably damage their systems, requiring a reinstall of the operating system. Apple probably thought it was making this more inconvenient than it actually did. Its intent, though—that naive users be protected from accidentally messing up their systems—is a good idea.

Understanding Permissions and Ownership

As we noted in the introduction, permissions and ownership in Unix are two tightly related but different concepts. While each file (and each process) is owned by one user and one group, each file also has a set of permissions that define what can be done with that file by the user who owns it, by the group that owns it, and by everyone else (all users who are neither the owning user nor members of the owning group).

The first step to understanding permissions and ownership is to learn how to determine the permissions and ownership of a file. If you have worked through Chapter 5, "Using Files and Directories," you have already learned to use the `ls` command with the `-l` option to get the long-format listing of files in a directory. Now you will learn exactly what the permission and ownership portions of those listings mean. (Review Chapter 2, "Using the Command Line," and Chapter 5 if the commands below are unfamiliar to you.)

To create a file and a directory to use as examples:

1. `cd`

   This ensures that you are in your home directory.

2. `mkdir examples`

   This creates a new directory called examples.

3. `cd examples`

   This changes your working directory so that your current directory is now `~/examples`.

   Create a directory and file inside the examples directory.

4. `mkdir testdir`

   This creates a new directory called testdir.

5. `date > testfile`

   Creates a new file called testfile containing the current date and time.

The following task assumes that you have created the directories and files in the task above, and that your current directory is ~/examples.

To view the permissions and ownership of all files in the current directory:

◆ ls -l

This shows the long-form listing of all the files in the current directory (**Figure 8.7**).

Figure 8.8 shows what the different parts of the listing mean. Notice that there is a part of the listing that shows the permissions and a part that shows the ownership, and that ownership has two parts: user and group. We'll go into more detail about the permissions part a little later on (just a preview: *r* stands for "read," *w* stands for "write," *x* stands for "execute," and - means "no permission," in sets of three characters for each of these—user, group, and all others.

```
[localhost:~] vanilla% ls -l
drwxr-xr-x   2 vanilla  staff     24 Jan 24 11:30 testdir
-rw-r-r-    1 vanilla  staff     29 Jan 24 11:30 testfile
[localhost:~] vanilla%
```

Figure 8.7 Using ls -l to view the permissions and ownership of all the files in the current directory.

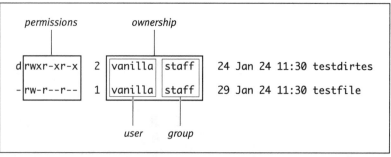

Figure 8.8 Diagram showing which parts of the listing are the permissions and which parts are the ownership information.

To list permissions for specific files:

◆ Supply the filenames as arguments to
   ls -l.

   For example,

   ls -l testfile

   shows the permissions and ownership for
   only the file testfile. You may supply multiple arguments.

   If any of the arguments are directory
   names, then the *contents* of the directory
   are listed.

To see the permissions for a directory:

◆ Add the -d option to ls -l:

   ls -ld testdir

   Figure 8.9 compares the output of

   ls -l ~/examples

   with

   ls -ld ~/examples

   In the first case the directory's contents
   are listed. The addition of the -d option
   shows the permissions for the directory
   itself instead of its contents.

```
[localhost:~] vanilla% ls -l ~/examples
total 8
drwxr-xr-x   2 vanilla  staff     24 Jan 24 11:30 testdir
-rw-r-r-   1 vanilla  staff     29 Jan 24 11:30 testfile
[localhost:~] vanilla% ls -ld ~/examples
drwxr-xr-x   2 vanilla  staff     92 Jan 24 11:29 /Users/vanilla/examples
[localhost:~] vanilla%
```

Figure 8.9 Comparing the output of ls -l and ls -ld when a directory is an argument.

Compare with Aqua

In Aqua you can view (and set) some of the
permissions for files by selecting a file (or
directory) in the Finder and choosing Get
Info from the File menu. Then click on the
Ownership and Permissions triangle. In
Figure 8.10, you see the Get Info window
displaying the permissions of the ~/examples
directory used in Figure 8.8.

The Aqua interface does not provide a way to
list the permissions for several files together
in one window, nor does it display the execute
permission (described in the next section).

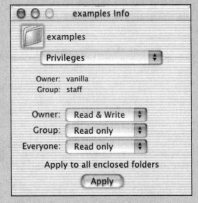

Figure 8.10 The Show Info window
displaying the permissions of the
~/examples directory used in Figure 8.8.

The types of permission

The permissions settings for a file in Unix pack a lot of information into only nine characters. **Figure 8.11** shows how the permissions listing of nine characters is divided into three groups of three characters each for the owning user, group, and all others.

There are three kinds of file permission in Unix, and each kind may be different for each of the three categories of owners (owning user, owning group, and all others).

The three main kinds of permission, for both files and directories, are

◆ Read permission

◆ Write permission

◆ Execute permission

In the nine characters of a permission listing, each set of three shows the read, write, and execute permission for the user, group, and others, respectively. **Figure 8.12** shows how letters indicate that permission is granted and a dash (–) signifies that permission is not granted.

Each type of permission (read, write, execute) has a different meaning for files than for directories.

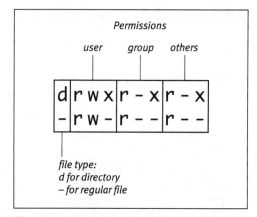

Figure 8.12 Diagram showing which parts of the permission listing are for read, write, and execute permission.

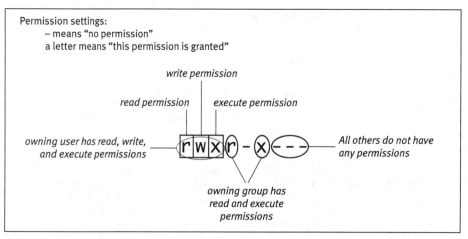

Figure 8.11 Examples of five files and three directories with different permissions.

What permissions mean for files

Read permission means that you can read the file. If you have read permission on a file, then you can see its contents with commands like `cat` and `less`, copy it with `cp`, and so on. You can view the file with an editor like `vi` but you can't alter the file unless you also have write permission.

Write permission means that you can change the file. You need write permission to edit the file or rename it. Note that if you have read permission but not write permission, you can make a copy of the file, and because you own the copy, you can alter it.

Execute permission means that if a file is a script, or program, you need to have execute permission to actually run, or *execute,* the program. Type `ls -l /bin` and see how the user, group, and others all have execute permission on all of the programs in that directory (you'll see the `ls` program itself in there, too).

What Permissions Mean for Directories

Read permission means that you can list the directory contents. It is often helpful to remember that a directory is actually a special kind of file whose contents are a list of file and directory names.

Write permission means that you can change the directory name, and create and delete files inside the directory and you can also change the permissions of files that you own inside the directory. Since a directory is really a special kind of file that contains a list of names, having permission to write to the directory means that you have permission to change the list, which includes changing filenames, and adding and removing files. See the sidebar "Deleting Files."

Execute permission means that you may `cd` into or through the directory. If you have read permission on a directory but not execute permission, then you can use `ls` to see the contents of the directory but cannot use `cd` to go into the directory.

Deleting Files

You do not actually need write permission to delete files.

To create or delete a file, you need only have write permission for the directory containing the file. This is because when you delete a file, you are really deleting its name from the list of items in a directory, and that means you are altering (writing) the *directory*. Review the section "Using hard links" at the end of Chapter 5, "Using Files and Directories," for more on how filenames are actually entries in directories.

If you try to delete a file for which you do not have write permission but where you do have write permission on the directory, you get a warning, but you are allowed to delete the file.

Looked at another way, if a user has write permission on a directory, he or she can delete every file inside that directory.

UNDERSTANDING PERMISSIONS AND OWNERSHIP

Examples of permissions

Using a set of examples is a good way to exercise your understanding of ownership and permissions.

Figure 8.13 shows a sample listing of eight files (three of which are directories). The explanations below all refer to Figure 8.13.

In each of the examples below, we tell you what the permission "mode" is on the file. The permission mode is a numerical representation of the permission settings on the file, for example 644 or 755. We explain these numerical modes in great detail later in this chapter's section, "Changing permissions with absolute modes."

File1 is the most common case. The user who owns the file (vanilla) has permission to read the file and write (or modify) it. Everyone else has permission to read it. The permission mode on this file is 644.

File2 is readable and writable by the owner, and readable by anyone in group staff. No one else can read or write to the file. The mode on this one is 640.

File3 has the standard permissions for an executable program or script. The owner has read, write, and execute permissions; everyone else has read and execute permissions. Only the execute permission is needed to

```
-rw-r--r--  1 vanilla  staff  21 Jan 24 15:21 file1
-rw-r-----  1 vanilla  staff  21 Jan 24 15:22 file2
-rwxr-xr-x  1 vanilla  staff  21 Jan 24 15:22 file3
-rw---r--  1 vanilla  losers 21 Jan 24 15:22 file4
-rw-rw-r--  1 vanilla  team1  21 Jan 24 15:22 file5
drwxr-xr-x  1 vanilla  staff  21 Jan 24 15:22 directory1
drwxrwxr-x  1 vanilla  staff  21 Jan 24 15:22 directory2
drwx------  1 vanilla  staff  21 Jan 24 15:22 directory3
```

Figure 8.13 Diagram showing which parts of the permission listing apply to the owning user, the owning group, and all others.

Be Careful with the Execute Bit

Be sure not to turn on execute permission for files that are not actually intended to be run as commands. Executing a file that was not created as a command file could cause undesirable results as the operating system attempts to read the file's contents as executable. Usually you simply get an error message, but if the file's contents happen to contain something that the system thinks is actually executable, you could lock up your Terminal window or lose data.

actually run the program/script; the read permission allows making copies of the file. The mode is 755.

File4 is an interesting case. The owner, vanilla, has read and write permission. Members of group staff have no permissions, and everyone else has read permission. What's going on here? When you try to use a file, the operating system checks permissions in this order: user, group, other. So if you are the user who owns the file, then the user permissions are used. If not, then the system checks to see if you are in the group that owns the file. If so, the group permissions are used, and if you are not the owner or in the group, then the "other" permissions apply. Only one set of permissions is applied. So in the case of *file4*, everybody has read permission *except* people in group losers. The mode is 604.

File5 has the standard permissions for a file that is part of a group project. The owner and any user in group *team1* have read and write permission; everyone else has read-only permission. The mode is 664.

Directory1 has the standard permissions for nonprivate directories. The owner has read, write, and execute permissions; everybody else has read and execute permissions. Everyone except the owner can list the contents of the directory and can **cd** into it, but cannot create files inside it. The mode is 755.

Directory2 has the standard permissions for a directory used in a group project. Permissions are the same as with *directory1* except that any member of group staff also has write permission on the directory. The mode is 775.

Directory3 has the standard permissions for a private directory. The owner has read, write, and execute permissions; everybody else has no permissions—they cannot see anything in the directory or even **cd** into or through it. The mode is 700.

Setting and Changing Permissions

Although "permissions" means different things for files than for directories, you use the same command to set permissions for both files and directories.

Only the user who owns a file may change its permissions (but see the "Using sudo" section in Chapter 11, "Introduction to System Administration," on how to use the sudo command to override this limitation).

You use the chmod (*change mode*) command to set the permissions of files.

The general form of a command line for chmod is

```
chmod mode file
```

where mode is the permission setting, and file is a filename or even multiple filenames.

The mode argument is in one of two forms: *symbolic* or *absolute*.

Symbolic modes are best used to make changes to permissions on a file when you want to alter some of its permissions but leave others unchanged.

Absolute modes are used to set all of the permissions for a file at once.

So if you want to add read permission to a file without disturbing any of the other permissions on the file, you use a symbolic mode. An example of this would be adding read permission to a file for the owning group without changing the permissions for the user or others.

On the other hand, if you want a file to have a specific set of permissions for the user, the group, and others all at once, then you should use an absolute mode. An example of this would be if you wanted to set a file to be readable and writable by the owning user, and only readable by the owning group and others.

Changing permissions with symbolic modes

The basic syntax of a symbolic mode is

who operator what

For example,

```
ug+w
```

would appear in a command line as

```
chmod ug+w file
```

The ug are the "who" (user and group), the + is the "operator" (add), and the w is the "what" (write permission). Many combinations are possible. **Table 8.1** shows the meaning of each of the characters.

Table 8.1

Symbolic Mode Changes	
SYMBOLS FOR THE "WHO" PART	
SYMBOL	MEANING
u	Applies change to the owning user.
g	Applies change to the owning group.
o	Applies change to all others.
a	Applies change to all (user, group, and others).
SYMBOLS FOR THE "OPERATOR" PART	
SYMBOL	MEANING
+	Adds the following permissions.
-	Removes the following permissions.
SYMBOLS FOR THE "WHO" PART	
SYMBOL	MEANING
r	Read permission.
w	Write permission.
x	Execute permission.

218

Here are a few tasks that use symbolic modes to change permissions.

To add read permission to a file for the owning group:

◆ chmod g+r *file*

For example,

chmod g+r myfile.txt

Figure 8.14 shows the permissions before and after using this command line.

To remove read permission to a file for the owning group:

◆ chmod g-r *file*

For example,

chmod g-r myfile.txt

Figure 8.15 shows the before and after for this command line.

```
[localhost:~] vanilla% ls -l myfile.txt
-rw----    1 vanilla  staff     29 Jan 24 11:30 myfile.txt
[localhost:~] vanilla% chmod g+r myfile.txt
[localhost:~] vanilla% ls -l myfile.txt
-rw-r---   1 vanilla  staff     29 Jan 24 11:30 myfile.txt
[localhost:~] vanilla%
```

Figure 8.14 Comparing permissions before and after adding read permission for the group with chmod g+r.

```
[localhost:~] vanilla% ls -l myfile.txt
-rw-r---   1 vanilla  staff     29 Jan 24 11:30 myfile.txt
[localhost:~] vanilla% chmod g-r myfile.txt
[localhost:~] vanilla% ls -l myfile.txt
-rw----    1 vanilla  staff     29 Jan 24 11:30 myfile.txt
[localhost:~] vanilla%
```

Figure 8.15 Comparing permissions before and after removing read permission for the group with chmod g-r.

SETTING AND CHANGING PERMISSIONS

To add read permission for the group and others:

◆ chmod go+r `file`

For example:

chmod go+r myfile.txt

Figure 8.16 shows the before and after for this command line.

To add write permission for the group and others:

◆ chmod go+w `file`

For example,

chmod go+w myfile.txt

Figure 8.17 shows the before and after for this command line.

To remove write permission for the group and others:

◆ chmod go-w `file`

For example,

chmod go-w myfile.txt

Figure 8.18 shows the before and after for this command line.

Notice how changing the permissions does not change the file's modification time.

```
[localhost:~] vanilla% ls -l myfile.txt
-rw----   1 vanilla  staff    29 Jan 24 11:30 myfile.txt
[localhost:~] vanilla% chmod go+r myfile.txt
[localhost:~] vanilla% ls -l myfile.txt
-rw-r-r-   1 vanilla  staff    29 Jan 24 11:30 myfile.txt
[localhost:~] vanilla%
```

Figure 8.16 Comparing permissions before and after adding read permission for the group and others with chmod go+r.

```
[localhost:~] vanilla% ls -l myfile.txt
-rw-r-r-   1 vanilla  staff    29 Jan 24 11:30 myfile.txt
[localhost:~] vanilla% chmod go+w myfile.txt
[localhost:~] vanilla% ls -l myfile.txt
-rw-rw-rw-   1 vanilla  staff    29 Jan 24 11:30 myfile.txt
[localhost:~] vanilla%
```

Figure 8.17 Comparing permissions before and after adding write permission for the group and others with chmod go+w.

```
[localhost:~] vanilla% ls -l myfile.txt
-rw-rw-rw-   1 vanilla  staff    29 Jan 24 11:30 myfile.txt
[localhost:~] vanilla% chmod go-w myfile.txt
[localhost:~] vanilla% ls -l myfile.txt
-rw-r-r-   1 vanilla  staff    29 Jan 24 11:30 myfile.txt
[localhost:~] vanilla%
```

Figure 8.18 Comparing permissions before and after removing write permission for the group and others with chmod go-w.

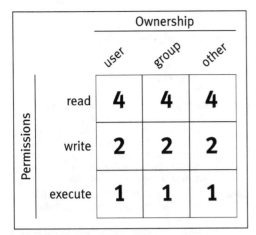

Figure 8.19 Diagram showing the values for the absolute modes for each type of permission.

Table 8.2

Value of Each Digit in a Three-Digit Absolute Mode	
VALUE	MEANING
0	No permission granted to this owner.
1	Execute permission only.
2	Write permission only.
3	Execute permission and write permission (1 + 2 = 3).
4	Read permission only.
5	Execute and read permission (1 + 4 = 5).
6	Write permission and read permission (2 + 4 = 6).
7	Execute, read, and write permission (1 + 2 + 4 = 7).

Changing permissions with absolute modes

An absolute mode consists of a three- or four-digit number such as 644 or 2775.

In practice you use these modes in this fashion:

```
chmod 644 file
```

That would set the permissions on file to be read and write (6) for the user, and read-only (4) for the group and others.

Most of the time you use three-digit numbers for absolute modes, so we address those first.

Each digit in a three-digit absolute mode represents the permissions for the user, the group, and others, in that order. The value of each digit is based on adding up the values of the kinds of permissions being assigned.

◆ Read permission has a value of 4.

◆ Write permission has a value of 2.

◆ Execute permission has a value of 1.

Figure 8.19 is a diagram showing the values for the absolute modes for each type of permission.

Table 8.2 shows the meanings of each of the eight possible mode values (0–7) for each digit in an absolute mode. Some of you might be thinking this looks like a base-8 (octal) numbering system. You would be correct.

To set a file's permissions using absolute mode:

◆ chmod *mode* `file`

For example,

`chmod 644 myfile.txt`

sets myfile.txt to be readable and writable by the owning user (4 + 2 = 6), and readable by the group and others.

`chmod 755 myscript.sh`

makes myscript.sh readable, writable, and executable (4 + 2 + 1 = 7) by the user, and readable and executable (4 + 1 = 5) by the group and others. These same permissions (755) are the standard permissions for nonprivate scripts and programs, as well as nonprivate directories (see **Table 8.3**).

Table 8.3 shows the most common permission settings using absolute mode. This table includes some four-digit modes. When a four-digit mode is used, the first digit has a different set of meanings from the other three. **Table 8.4** and **Table 8.5** show the meanings of the values for all the positions in three- or four-digit modes for files (Table 8.4) and for directories (Table 8.5). **Table 8.6** shows the options for the chmod command.

✔ Tip

■ The most useful option for the chmod command is -R, which allows you to change the permissions on a directory and everything inside it all at once. For example,

`chmod -R go-rwx private_dir`

removes read, write, and execute permissions for group and others from the directory private_dir and everything inside it. But be careful. It would probably be a mistake to do something like

`chmod -R g+x mydirectory`

because that adds group execute permission to the directory and everything

inside it. If the directory contains any files that are not actually scripts of programs, they would end up appearing as executable, and if someone tried to run one of them as a command, it could cause unpredictable results.

Table 8.3

Common Permission Modes	
MODE	COMMON USE
644	For files. Readable and writable by owning user, readable by everyone else.
755	For directories and programs (commands, scripts, and so on). For directories, this mode allows owning user to create and delete files in the directory, allows everyone to list directory contents and cd into or through the directory. For files allows owning user to alter the file, allows everyone to read and to execute the program.
664	Same as 644 but also allows owning group to alter the file. Used for files that are part of a group project.
775	For program files (scripts, commands, and so on). Same as 755 but also gives write permission to the owning group so that anyone in that group may alter the file.
2775	For directories only. Same as 755 but also gives the owning group write permission on the program or directory. In addition, the 2 at the beginning means that any file or directory created inside this directory is owned by the same group that owns this directory.
600	For private files. The owning user has read and write permission. No one else has any permissions.
700	For private directories or private executable files. The owning user has read, write, and execute permission. No one else has any permissions.

SETTING AND CHANGING PERMISSIONS

Table 8.4

Mode Values for File Permissions

PERMISSION	MODE	WHY AND WHEN
user read	0400	So the owning user may read it.
user write	0200	So the owning user may change it.
user execute	0100	So the owning user may execute it.
group read	0040	So the owning group may read it.
group write	0020	So the owning group may change it.
group execute	0010	So the owning group may execute it.
others read	0004	So all others may read it.
others write	0002	So all others may change it.
others execute	0001	So all others may execute it.
setuid	4000	Execute file as owning user ("Set user id on execution"). This property is removed and must be reset each time the file is changed (edited).
setgid	2000	Execute file as owning group ("Set group id on execution"). This property is removed and must be reset each time the file is changed (edited).
sticky bit	1000	A directory whose "sticky bit" is set has special restrictions on file deletion. In order to delete or rename a file inside a sticky directory, a user must have write permission on the directory or own the directory, and must also own the file. The root user is not restricted by sticky directories. The /private/tmp directory in Mac OS X is a sticky directory (and /tmp is a symbolic link to it). See man sticky for more on the sticky bit.

Table 8.5

Mode Values for Directory Permissions

PERMISSION	MODE	WHY AND WHEN
user read	0400	So the owning user may list contents.
user write	0200	So the owning user may create and delete files inside it.
user execute	0100	So the owning user may cd into or through it.
group read	0040	So the owning group may list contents.
group write	0020	So the owning group may create and delete files inside it.
group execute	0010	So the owning user may cd into or through it.
others read	0004	So all others may list contents.
others write	0002	So all others may create and delete files inside it.
others execute	0001	So all others may cd into or through it.
setuid	4000	No effect.
setgid	2000	Any files or directories created inside this directory is owned by the same group that owns this directory.

Table 8.6

Options for the chmod Command

OPTION	MEANING
-R	Makes changes recursively. Used when changing permissions on a directory and everything it contains.
	The next three options only work in combination with the -R option. Only one of the following may be used. If more than one is used, the last one on the command line takes precedence.
-H	If the -R option is specified, symbolic links on the command line are followed. (Symbolic links encountered in the directory traversal are not followed.) See Chapter 5, "Using Files and Directories," for more on symbolic links.
-L	If the -R option is specified, all symbolic links are followed.
-P	If the -R option is specified, no symbolic links are followed.

SETTING AND CHANGING PERMISSIONS

Changing Ownership

Files have two kinds of owners—the user owner and the group owner.

Only root can change a file's user ownership. You cannot "give away" a file.

In order to change a file's group ownership, you must be both the file's user owner and a member of the new group, or you must perform the change as root. Furthermore, when a file's group ownership is changed, the setuid and setgid properties are removed unless the change was made by root. This avoids some potential security problems (see the sidebar "Why setuid and setgid Are Cleared When a File Changes Groups" for more on this).

Group ownership can be changed using either the chgrp (*change group*) or chown (*change owner)* command.

To change the group ownership using chgrp:

◆ chgrp *newgroup file*

For example,

chgrp www index.html

changes the group ownership of file index.html to www. You must be the file's owner and a member of the new group to perform this. **Figure 8.20** shows an example of changing the group ownership of a file using chgrp. **Table 8.7** shows the options for chgrp.

✔ Tip

■ It is often useful to use the -R option to change the group ownership of an entire directory. For example,

chgrp -R www webteam

changes the directory webteam and all it contains so that it is owned by group www.

```
[localhost:~/Sites] vanilla% groups
staff www
[localhost:~/Sites] vanilla% ls -l index.html
-rw-r-r-  1 vanilla  staff  6186 Apr 30  2001 index.html
[localhost:~/Sites] vanilla% chgrp www index.html
[localhost:~/Sites] vanilla% ls -l index.html
-rw-r-r-  1 vanilla  www    6186 Apr 30  2001 index.html
 [localhost:~/Sites] vanilla%
```

Figure 8.20 Using chgrp to change the group ownership of a file.

Table 8.7

Options for the chgrp and chown Commands	
OPTION	**MEANING**
-R	Makes changes recursively. Used when changing permissions on a directory and everything it contains.
	The next three options only work in combination with the -R option. Only one of the following may be used. If more than one is used, the last one on the command line takes precedence.
-H	If the -R option is specified, symbolic links on the command line are followed. (Symbolic links encountered in the directory traversal are not followed.) See Chapter 5, "Using Files and Directories," for more on symbolic links.
-L	If the -R option is specified, all symbolic links are followed.
-P	If the -R option is specified, no symbolic links are followed.
-f	Ignore errors (force silence). This option squelches error messages resulting from inadequate permissions—for example, if you try to change the group ownership to a group to which you do not belong.

To change the group ownership:

◆ chgrp :*newgroup file*

For example,

chgrp:web index.html

The only difference between using this and using **chgrp** is the addition of the colon before the group name. The reason for this funny syntax is that the **chown** command is designed to change the user ownership and/or the group ownership of a file, and the first argument to **chown** is in the form

user:*group*

However, you can leave out the user or group portion to change only one or the other. If you leave out the user portion, you must still use the colon. See the next task for how to use **chown** to change the user ownership (which may be done only by root).

Why setuid and setgid Are Cleared When a File Changes Groups

If an executable file such as a script has the **setuid** property turned on, and if the file is executable by users other than the owning user (group or other executable), then when the program is run by someone other than the owning user, the process has the same permission as the owning user. This means you can create a script that alters files on which only you normally have write permission, and you can allow other people to run that script. Obviously this can be both useful and dangerous, like giving out the keys to your house. A similar situation occurs

with **setgid** permission—the process runs with the permission of the owning group.

When a user (other than root) changes the group that a file belongs to and **setuid** and **setgid** properties are removed, the properties must be reset as a security precaution. This helps avoid accidentally giving too much power to other users. If you truly want the file to have **setuid** or **setgid** permission, after changing its group you must reset the **setuid** and/or **setgid** permission.

As we've mentioned above, a file's user ownership can only be changed by the root user. On Mac OS X the standard way to perform a command as root is to use the sudo command. The following task shows how to change a file's user ownership using sudo and chown. (See Chapter 11, "Introduction to System Administration," for more on sudo.)

To change the user ownership using chown:

1. sudo chown *newuser file*

For example,

sudo chown howard index.html

changes the user ownership of the file index.html to howard.

The sudo command requires that you enter your password if you haven't used it within the last 5 minutes.

2. Enter your password if asked.

The command is executed after you enter your password and press (Return).

Figure 8.21 shows before-and-after views of using this command line.

```
[localhost:~vanilla/Sites] matisse% ls -l index.html
-rw-r-r-  1 vanilla  staff  6186 Apr 30 2001 index.html
[localhost:~vanilla/Sites] matisse% sudo chown howard index.html
Password:
[localhost:~vanilla/Sites] matisse% ls -l index.html
-rw-r-r-  1 howard  staff  6186 Apr 30  2001 index.html
[localhost:~vanilla/Sites] matisse%
```

Figure 8.21 Using chown to change a file's user ownership.

To change the user and group ownership simultaneously:

1. `sudo` *newuser*`:`*newgroup file*

   For example,

   `sudo chown vanilla:www index.html`

2. Enter your password if asked.

   The command is executed when you enter your password and press Return.

   Figure 8.22 shows the before-and-after of this command line.

✔ Tip

- The `chown` command uses the same options as the `chgrp` command. It is often useful to change an entire directory full of files at once:

  `sudo chown -R howard:www web_images`

  changes the directory web_images and all it contains to be owned by the user howard and the group www.

```
[localhost:~vanilla/Sites] matisse% ls -l index.html
-rw-r-r-  1 howard  staff  6186 Apr 30  2001 index.html
[localhost:~vanilla/Sites] matisse% sudo chown vanilla:www index.html
Password:
[localhost:~vanilla/Sites] matisse% ls -l index.html
-rw-r-r-  1 vanilla  www  6186 Apr 30  2001 index.html
[localhost:~vanilla/Sites] matisse%
```

Figure 8.22 Using chown to simultaneously change the user and group ownership.

Default Permissions for File Creation

When a file or directory is created, its initial permissions are determined by a setting called umask. A umask is a value similar to an absolute mode that is subtracted from full permissions to determine the permissions. A typical umask would be 022 or 002. Chapter 7, "Configuring Your Unix Environment," explains how to see, and change, your umask. You may see umasks displayed as one- or two-digit numbers; in those cases, assume that zeros are added to the left, so a umask of 2 is really 002.

"Full permissions" for files are considered to be 666 (readable and writable by everyone) and for directories to be 777 (readable, writable, and executable by everyone). You always have to explicitly change a file's permission to make a non-directory file (such as a script) executable.

The net result is that if you have a umask of 022, for example, and create a new directory, the permissions on the directory is 755 (777 – 022), and if you create a new file, the permissions is 644 (666 – 022).

Table 8.8 shows the effect of various umasks on the creation of new files and directories.

Table 8.8

Effect of umask on New File Permissions

UMASK	FOR FILE	FOR DIRECTORY
022	644 (rw-r--r--)	755 (rwxr-xr-x)
002	664 (rw-rw-r--)	775 (rwxrwxr-x)
077	600 (rw------)	700 (rwx------)
066	622 (rw------)	733 (rwx-x-x)

Recognizing Permission Problems

Ninety percent of day-to-day problems in running Unix systems are permissions-related. Most often, some process tries to write to a file or directory that it doesn't have permission to write to. Maybe it did yesterday, but someone accidentally or carelessly changed it, and then something stopped working.

Permission problems show up in so many ways that it is not reasonable to try to list them here, but there are a few rules you can follow to spot permission problems.

Often the first sign is an error message containing the words "Permission denied." Sometimes it is accompanied by more information—for example,

```
/usr/local/bin/script.sh: permission
denied: /etc/foo [3]
```

This is telling you that line 3 of the script /usr/local/bin/script.sh failed because it did not have enough permission to do something with /etc/foo. You have to look inside the script to see what exactly was going on, but you have a good place to start.

Some things to keep in mind:

1. To create a new file, rename a file, delete a file, or change a file's permissions, the process must have write permission in the directory where the file is being created.

2. To change an existing file, you must have write permission on the file.

3. To cd into a directory, the process must have execute permission on the *full path* of the directory. So to cd into /Users /vanilla/Sites/images/big_images, the processes doing the cd must have execute permission on the following:

    /

    /Users

    /Users/vanilla

    /Users/vanilla/Sites

    /Users/vanilla/Sites/images

    /Users/vanilla/Sites/images/big_images

4. To list the contents of a sub-directory, you must have read permission for it, as well as permission to cd into the directory where it's stored. So to list the contents of /Users/vanilla/Sites/images/big_images, you must be able to cd into /Users/vanilla/ Sites/images and have read permission on big_images. You do not need to be able to cd into a directory to list its contents.

To correct a permissions problem:

1. Write down the permissions of the files or directories you think should change.

    You might try redirecting the output of ls -l into a file, for example:

    ```
    ls -l bad_file > permission_save
    ```

2. Change the permissions to what you think will fix the problem.

3. Test the fix.

    If the fix doesn't work, change the permissions back to what they started as, and think through the problem again. Go back to step 2. Lather, rinse, repeat.

CREATING AND USING SCRIPTS

9

A script is simply a text file that contains a series of commands. By definition, a script must be read and executed by a program called an *interpreter*, a separate program that understands the commands in the script.

You may already be familiar with scripts written in AppleScript or JavaScript. In the Unix world, we often speak of *shell scripts*—scripts that are written to be interpreted by one of the Unix shells, such as sh, bash, and tcsh. These scripts use exactly the same commands you would type at the command line using the corresponding shell. Indeed, one of the reasons for using a script is to reduce the chance of mistyping a complicated command line. So when you see the term "Bourne shell script," you know it's referring to a script that is written to be interpreted by the Bourne shell (/bin/sh). See man sh for the online manual for the Bourne shell.

Think of a shell script as a small computer program. The languages available for writing shell scripts are numerous, but by far the most commonly used is the Bourne shell. This is because the Bourne shell has been around so long, it has become the de facto standard for programming system-configuration files and for system administration. A script written for the Bourne shell is likely to run properly on the widest variety of Unix systems. So in this chapter we will show you the basics of Bourne shell scripts.

In Chapter 2, "Using the Command Line," you created a simple shell script. Now you will delve more deeply into scripting, learning the basic tools through which all shell scripts are made: commands, operators, variables, conditionals, loops, and functions. Sound like computer programming? It is, but don't worry—you don't have to become a programmer to benefit from understanding and using scripts, and if you do want to get further into programming, then shell scripts are a good place to start.

Here are the most common uses of shell scripts:

System startup configuration files.
Mac OS X keeps its system startup files in /System/Library/StartupItems (virtually every other version of Unix keeps similar scripts in /etc/rc.d or /etc/init.d).

Automating common tasks. One example is the Bourne shell script /etc/weekly, which is run once each week by a scheduling program called cron. (See Chapter 11, "Introduction to System Administration," to learn about the cron command.) The /etc/weekly script rebuilds a couple of databases and compresses a few system log files. You can open it using vi if you like—it won't hurt anything to read it.

Creating new utilities for your personal use. In Chapter 2 you created a simple script to show a system status report. As you become more comfortable with Unix, you will undoubtedly create several small scripts to automate tasks, provide new commands, and in general handle problems that the existing set of commands doesn't quite cover. One example might be a shell script that allows you to use the Macintosh Trash from the command line.

CREATING AND USING SCRIPTS

Creating a Shell Script

Shell scripts are text files, so you create them the same way as any other text file. At the command line, that typically means using an editor like vi or emacs, but you can also use a GUI text editor or even a word processor. Just be sure to save the file as a plain-text file (often called "Text Only" in save-file dialog boxes), which means no font information, no boldface or underlining, just plain text. (Review Chapter 5, "Using Files and Directories," for details on editing files from the command line.)

The first task below simply takes you through the steps of creating an extremely minimal script. Subsequent tasks add features to the script covering the basic elements of scripting:

◆ Using variables

◆ Using arguments

◆ Using expressions

◆ Using control structures

◆ Getting user input

◆ Creating and using functions

To create a simple shell script:

1. Create a new file called myscript.sh in your text editor.

   The filename can actually be anything you like. The .sh extension indicates that the file is a Bourne shell script; however, this is simply a file-naming convention and is not required. It is the first line of the file itself that determines the kind of script.

2. Enter the first line of the script:

   `#!/bin/sh`

   Make sure there are no spaces before the #.

   This script is a Bourne shell script. The commands in it are read and executed by the program /bin/sh.

3. Enter a comment to describe what the script does.

   Lines that begin with just a # are comments and are ignored when the script is executed, as are blank lines. (Exception: See the sidebar, "The All-Important Shebang Line of a Script.")

   `# This script just says hello.`

4. Enter the first actual command line in the script:

   `echo "Hello, I am a script."`

   Notice that this line would work perfectly well if you entered it at the command line, even if you are using the tcsh shell. That's because the lines in shell scripts are simply Unix command lines. Even though this script uses the Bourne shell, many command lines are identical in both the Bourne and tcsh shells. The echo command in this example is a separate program (/bin/echo), executed by the Bourne shell when it gets to this line in the script.

5. Save the file.

   Use the appropriate command for your editor to save the file.

6. Quit the editor.

   You should be back at a shell prompt.

   Now you must make the script executable.

7. `chmod 755 myscript.sh`

   Changing the mode to 755 (review modes in Chapter 8, "Working with Permissions and Ownership") gives anyone the ability to read and execute the script file, while giving you (the owner) the additional permission to edit it.

   continues on next page

8. You can now execute the script with the command line

`./myscript.sh`

Figure 9.1 shows a code listing of the script and **Figure 9.2** shows the result of running it from the command line.

You need to use the `./` to specify a path to the script because the script is not in the list of places where your shell looks for commands. But see the next task to learn how to have the script be available just like any other command—that is, without having to type the path to it but simply by typing the script name.

Running a script without using a path

You can run a shell script simply by typing its name on the command line, just as if it were any other Unix command. In order for this to work, you must do a few things with the script, described in the following task.

To create a shell script that can be used like a command:

1. Make sure the script is executable.

2. Make sure the script is in a directory listed in your PATH environment variable.

For most scripts you create for your own personal use, the best place to put them is in your ~/bin directory—that is, the `bin` directory inside your home directory. (Remember: the ~ character is a shortcut for specifying your home directory.)

If you have not already done so, you should add your ~/bin directory to your PATH environment variable (instructions for doing this are in the "Changing Your PATH" section of Chapter 7 "Configuring Your Unix Environment"). Scripts intended

for systemwide use should go in `/usr/local/bin`.

You can either create the script in the appropriate place to begin with, or use the `cp` or `mv` command to copy or move the script into place—for example,

`mv myscript.sh ~/bin/`

If ~/bin does not exist, then create it with

`mkdir ~/bin`

3. Run the `rehash` command for any shell that is already running.

Any new shells (Terminal windows) you open read the PATH list when they start up. This step actually applies only to the `tcsh` shell which scans the directories listed in your PATH only when it starts up.

4. You can now run the script by simply typing its name.

✔ Tip

■ Be careful about creating scripts that have the same name as existing commands.

The standard date command is `/bin/date`. If you use `date` on a command line without specifying a path, then a `date` script in either ~/bin or /usr/local/bin is executed instead of the standard `/bin/date` command. This is because the shell looks in the directories in your PATH in order, and your ~/bin directory and /usr/local/bin are listed earlier than /bin in your PATH.

```
#!/bin/sh
# This script just says hello.
echo "Hello, I am a script."
```

Figure 9.1 Code listing of a simple script. It has only one line of executable code.

```
[localhost:~] vanilla% ./myscript.sh
Hello, I am a script.
[localhost:~] vanilla%
```

Figure 9.2 Running the new script from the command line.

The All-Important Shebang Line of a Script

In a shell script, the # character at the start of a line marks that line as a comment—to be ignored when the script is executed. But when the # is the first character in the whole file, it takes on a different and very special meaning.

Each time you execute a command, the operating system looks at the first two characters of the file for that command. If the first two characters are #!, then the rest of the first line is assumed to be a path to a program that knows how to execute the rest of the file (an *interpreter*). The operating system executes the interpreter and hands it the script file as input. If the first two characters are not #!, then the operating system assumes that the file consists of compiled machine-readable binary code and will try to execute it directly.

The # character is often called a *sharp* (as it is in musical notation), and the ! character in Unix is pronounced "bang" (the literal sense of an exclamation point), hence *shebang*.

This trick of looking at the first two bytes of a file has been part of Unix for more than 20 years, starting in an early version of BSD Unix version 4, around early 1980. The shebang line is one of the mechanisms that make shell scripts so common in Unix.

You can see a copy of an email from Dennis M. Ritchie describing the "new" feature at www.uni-ulm.de/~s_smasch/various/shebang/sys1.c.html.

You can still run a shell script without the shebang line by supplying the script filename as an argument to the shell program itself—for example,

`sh myscript`

So if the first line of the file contains

`#!/bin/sh`

then the operating system will execute the program located at `/bin/sh` and feed it the whole file as input.

If the first line of a script is

`#!bin/sh`

when you run it you will probably get the error message "Command not found." Why? Because when you run the script, the operating system looks for `bin/sh` and doesn't find it. The line is missing the / before `bin`. A simple typographical error like that can lead to a lot of frustration. (Extra credit: Can you think of a situation in which that typo would not cause an error message? Hint: What if your working directory is /?)

Using Variables

Can you think back on all that stuff you learned in high school algebra? Things like

$a2 - b2 = (a - b)*(a + b)$

or

$E = MC2$

Those letters are variables, essentially storage containers with names. Any time you see a variable, you are supposed to replace it with whatever is in the container. If you store the number 23 in a variable called X, for example, then when you *access* the contents of X you will get 23.

Commonly in programming you want to use the contents of a variable inside a string of text; for example, if you have:

`"Hello $name"`

you probably want to replace the variable $name with its contents to create a new string of text. In computer programming, the act of replacing a variable with its contents to create a new string of text is called *interpolating* (which is not at all the same as turning someone over to the international police organization Interpol).

All computer programming makes heavy use of variables. There are two major things you do with variables: *assign* something to them (store information in the container) and interpolate them (replace them with the contents of the container).

In a shell script, you assign a value to a variable using the = operator. It copies the value on the right side into the variable on the left side. For example:

`greeting="Top of the morning to you."`

or

`maximum_length=25`

Variables are replaced with their contents any time they appear in a command line with a $ in front of their name:

`echo "Then he said: $greeting"`

The following task creates a script that assigns a value to a variable and then interpolates it in a command line. This is commonly done to store an error or warning message in a variable so that it may be used in several places in the script. That way, if you want to change the message, you only have to change it in one place.

To assign a value to a variable and then interpolate it:

1. Edit a new script file. For example,

   `vi newscript.sh`

2. The first line is the same as before:

   `#!/bin/sh`

3. Enter some comments to explain what the script does:

   `# This script assigns values to`
   `→variables`

   `# and then interpolates them.`

4. `line1="The queen, my lord, is dead."`

5. `line2="She should have died hereafter."`

   Assigning a value to a variable in a Bourne shell script is very simple. You start the line with the variable name. This can be any combination of letters, numbers, and the underscore character _ (for example, a variable named `item_23_01` is fine). However, variable names may not begin with a number.

   Right after the variable name you put an equal sign (=). Do *not* put any spaces before or after the = sign.

   After the = sign comes the value that is stored in the variable. The value can be a number or text. If the value has spaces inside it, then enclose the value in quotes.

```
#!/bin/sh
# This script assigns values to variables
# and then interpolates them.

line1="The queen, my lord, is dead."
line2="She should have died hereafter."

# Now interpolate the variables.
echo "SEYTON: $seyton"
echo "MACBETH: $macbeth"
```

Figure 9.3 Code listing of a script that assigns values to two variables and then interpolates them.

```
[localhost:~] vanilla% ./myscript.sh
SEYTON: The queen, my lord, is dead.
MACBETH: She should have died hereafter.
[localhost:~] vanilla%
```

Figure 9.4 Running the script that uses variables.

About Those Algebraic Equations

The first one we listed shows how to calculate the difference between two squared numbers. So the difference between 9^2 and 4^2 is $(9 - 4)$ times $(9 + 4)$. That is, 81 – 16 equals 5 times 13. Check it out. Works every time. Pretty cool, huh? For more, see www.mste.uiuc.edu/users/dildine/sketches/Diff2sq.htm.

The second equation is Einstein's famous formula expression of his special theory of relativity, that energy (E) is equal to mass (M) multiplied by the square of the velocity of light (C). That formula plus a lot of technology can get you global thermonuclear war if you are not careful. For more, see www.aip.org/history/einstein/voice1.htm.

6. Add another comment:

Now interpolate the variables.

7. echo "SEYTON: $line1"

8. echo "MACBETH: $line2"

Interpolating a variable is simply a matter of using the variable name in a command line with **$** added to the beginning of the variable name.

When the shell reads any command line, either one entered at a shell prompt or one found in a script, the first thing the shell does is replace variables that start with **$** with their contents.

Figure 9.3 is a code listing of a script that assigns a value to a variable and then interpolates it, and **Figure 9.4** shows the result of running the script.

✔ Tip

■ If you want to include quotes in the value, then you escape the quotes with backslashes:

response="MACBETH: \"Liar and
→slave!\""

It is quite common to use the value of a variable inside the assignment of another variable. This is easy to do because the shell performs *variable interpolation* on all the variables in a line before actually executing the command at the start of a line.

To use a variable inside another variable:

◆ Simply use a variable with the $ inside the value of a new variable.

For example,

```
first_name="Alexis"
last_name="Pushkin"
full_name="$first_name $last_name"
```

Figure 9.5 is a code listing of a complete script that uses a variable inside the value assigned to another. **Figure 9.6** shows the output of the script.

The first line of output comes from line 8 of the script. Notice how the contents of $message are what were assigned to it on line 6. The assignment of a new value to $directory on line 7 does not change what was already assigned to $message. On line 9, there is a new assignment using $directory, which has a new value. The second line of output (which comes from line 10 of the script) shows this.

Using a command inside a variable

It is very common in shell scripts to store the name of a command in a variable and then use the variable in a command line later in the script. This is commonly done to allow the same command to be used in many places in the script, but to have only one place where it needs to be changed if you decide to use a different command later.

To use a command inside a variable:

1. Assign the command name to a variable. For example,

```
command="ls"
```

```
1    #!/bin/sh
2    # Example of using a variable inside the value
3    # assigned to another variable.
4
5    directory="/Applications (Mac OS 9)"
6    message="OS 9 applications are in \"$directory\""
7    directory="/Applications"
8    echo "$message"
9    message="OS X applications are in \"$directory\""
10   echo "$message"
```

Figure 9.5 Code listing of a script that uses variables inside the values assigned to other variables.

```
[localhost:~] vanilla% ./newscript.sh
OS 9 applications are in "/Applications (Mac OS 9)"
OS X applications are in "/Applications"
[localhost:~] vanilla%
```

Figure 9.6 Output of the script in Figure 9.5.

2. Use the variable (with $) anywhere you want to use the command.

For example,

`$command /usr`

Figure 9.7 is a code listing of a script that uses a command in a variable, and **Figure 9.8** shows the output of the script.

✔ Tips

■ Use variables in scripts whenever you want the same thing to appear in more than one place. This minimizes the number of places where you need to make changes.

■ Try creating the script in the task above and changing the command to `ls` and `options1` and `options2` to different options for the `ls` command—for example `-ld` and `-F`.

```
#!/bin/sh
# This script uses a command in a variable

# The du command shows disk usage
command="du"
# The -s option means "summary". The -k means "in kilobytes"
options1="-sk"
options2="-s"

# NOTE: This next variable shold be set to the path to
# your Mac OS 9 Applications directory. If you have installed Mac OS 9
# on a separate partition then the path will differ from what is shown here.
directory="/Applications (Mac OS 9)/"

echo "Trying $command with options $options1 on $directory"
# Note the use of quotes around $directory since it contains spaces.
$command $options1 "$directory"

echo "Trying $command with options $options2 on $directory"
$command $options2 "$directory"
```

Figure 9.7 Code listing of a script that uses a command name in a variable. (Note that if you have installed Mac OS 9 on a separate partition from Mac OS X, then the setting of the "directory" variable must be changed.)

```
[localhost:~] vanilla% ./diskuse.sh
Trying du with options -sk on /Applications (Mac OS 9)/
771156  /Applications (Mac OS 9)/
Trying du with options -s on /Applications (Mac OS 9)/
1542312 /Applications (Mac OS 9)/
[localhost:~] vanilla%
```

Figure 9.8 Output from the script in Figure 9.7.

USING VARIABLES

Using environment variables in a script

In previous chapters (especially Chapter 7, "Configuring Your Unix Environment"), you learned about a special kind of variable called an *environment variable*. When you execute a script, you are creating a child process of your shell, and so the script's processes inherit your shell's environment. As a result, you can use all of your shell's environment variables in your scripts. Note that assigning anything into an environment variable in a script does not change the contents of that variable for the parent process (your shell), but sets it for any child processes the script creates.

To use an environment variable in a script:

◆ Use the environment variable as you would any other variable.

For example,

```
echo "Hello $USER"
echo "Your home directory is $HOME"
```

Figure 9.9 is a code listing of a script that uses environment variables, and **Figure 9.10** shows the output from the script.

```
#!/bin/sh
# This script uses environment variables

command="du"
options="-sk"
command_line="$command $options $HOME"

echo "User is:                $USER"
echo "Home directory is:      $HOME"
echo "Command line will be:   $command_line"
echo "Disk space usage in kilobytes:"
$command_line
```

Figure 9.9 Code listing of a script that uses environment variables.

```
[localhost:~] vanilla% ./envscript.sh
User is:               vanilla
Home directory is:     /Users/vanilla
Command line will be:  du -sk /Users/vanilla
Disk space usage in kilobytes:
2160    /Users/vanilla
[localhost:~] vanilla%
```

Figure 9.10 Output from the script in Figure 9.9.

Table 9.1

Special Variables

VARIABLE	USE / MEANING
$0	The name with which the script was called on the command line.
$1	The first command-line argument.
$2	The second command-line argument, and so on, up to $9.
$@	A list of all the command-line arguments.
$#	The number of command-line arguments.
$?	The exit status of the most recent command. (0 means success; other numbers mean some kind of error.)

Using Arguments

You can pass arguments to scripts just as with any other command. The arguments to a script are accessed inside the script using a series of special variables. (**Table 9.1**)

The variable **$0** contains the name of the script itself; the first argument to a script can be obtained from **$1**, the second argument from **$2**, and so on. Arguments with more than one digit must be written with braces around the number—for example, **${10}**, **${25}**.

An important difference between a script and a regular command is that if you supply options to a script, such as **-A** or **-r**, the script thinks of them as simply arguments. So in the command line

```
myscript.sh -A foo
```

$0 contains **myscript.sh**, **$1** contains **-A**, and **$2** contains **foo**. **$3** contains nothing (because there were only two arguments).

Compare with Aqua: Using the Trash from the Command Line

The script in Figure 9.13 allows you to move files to the Trash instead of using the Unix **rm** command, but there are some important differences between the behavior of this script and the way the Finder uses the Trash.

When you drag a file to the Trash, a check is performed in the Finder to see if a file with the same name already exists in the Trash. If so, the new file is renamed by adding a 1 at the end of its name, or a 2 if this is the second duplicate, and so on. There can be only one file with any particular name

inside a folder (or directory). The Finder won't simply replace the older file, since the whole point of the Trash is that using it is not the same as actually deleting a file.

The script shown in Figure 9.13 is not as sophisticated as the Finder. If a file with the same name as an argument has already been moved to the Trash, this script will overwrite the older file.

Later in this chapter we will show you how to improve the script to make its behavior more like the Finder's use of the Trash.

To use command-line arguments in your script:

◆ You simply use the special variables as you would any other variable. For example,

echo "The first argument was $1"

Figure 9.11 is a code listing that shows the use of the special variables for command-line arguments, and **Figure 9.12** shows the output of the script. Notice how the second and third arguments in Figure 9.12 are enclosed in quotes. Without the quotes, only the first three words would have been printed out ("What," "a," and "long").

There are a couple of ways to handle large numbers of arguments. The first is to use the shift command. The shift command (which typically appears on a line all by itself) moves all of the arguments "down" one step. That is, after you use shift, $1 contains what used to be in $2, $2 contains what used to be in $3, and so on.

One good reason to use shift is if your script has an optional first argument that could be followed by more arguments. You write most of the script to use $1, $2, and so on, but at an earlier point in the script you check to see what the first argument ($1) is. If it matches something in particular, you have the script do something special and then use shift so that the rest of the arguments are in the same places ($1, $2, and so on) as they would be if the first argument did not contain the special value.

The second way is to use the special variable $@, which contains a list of all the arguments. By using $@ in combination with a *loop* (see "Using loops," below), it is possible to *iterate over* (a programming term for "running through") all of the script's arguments, regardless of how many there are.

We cover loops later in this chapter.

```
#!/bin/sh
# This script uses the special variables for
# command line arguments.

echo "Hey $USER called me:   $0"
echo "First argument: $1"
echo "Second argument: $2"
echo "Third argument: $3"
```

Figure 9.11 Code listing of a script that uses special variables to access command-line arguments.

```
[localhost:~] vanilla% ./args.sh What "a long strange trip" "it's been"
Hey vanilla called me:   ./args.sh
First argument: What
Second argument: a long strange trip
Third argument: it's been
[localhost:~] vanilla%
```

Figure 9.12 Output from the script shown in Figure 9.11.

To use shift to access arguments:

1. Put the shift command on a line by itself. For example,

```
echo "First argument was: $1"
echo "Ninth argument was: $9"
shift
```

2. Use any of the special variables, such as $1 or $2. For example,

```
echo "Here's one: $1"
echo "And here's nine: $9"
```

After shift is used, all the arguments are "shifted" over, so if you think of the list of arguments as something like $1, $2, $3, $4, $5, $6, $7, $8, $9, you can picture using shift to move all the arguments one place to the left.

The contents of $1 disappear (they do not go into $0), and whatever was in ${10} goes into $9.

You can use shift as many times as you like in your script.

To use more than nine arguments:

◆ Use the special variable $@.

The special variable $@ contains all of the command-line arguments (only the arguments—it does not contain $0). You can use it to pass all the arguments your script received to a command inside your script. For example,

```
ls "$@"
```

Figure 9.13 is a code listing of a script that is a simple replacement for the rm command. Instead of deleting the files named in its arguments, this script moves them all into the user's Trash (the .Trash directory in the user's home directory). See the sidebar "Compare with Aqua: Using the Trash from the Command Line" for some important differences between moving files with this script and actually dragging a file to the

continues on next line

```
#!/bin/sh
# trash - script for moving files to the Trash
# from the command line.


# Each users' Trash is a directory called .trash in their
# home directory
trash_directory="$HOME/.Trash/"


# We use MvMac and not mv so this will work properly
# even on old-style Mac files with resource forks.
# We use $@ to pass all the arguments
/Developer/Tools/MvMac "$@" "$trash_directory"
```

Figure 9.13 Code listing of a script that moves files to the Trash from the command line, using $@ to pass all the command-line arguments.

Trash in the Finder. **Figure 9.14** shows an example of using this script, including how to see the contents of the Trash from the command line. Notice how you can use command-line wildcards with the script. The argument badfile* in Figure 9.14 ended up matching two files: bad-file1 and badfile2, and all four arguments were captured in $@ and passed to the MvMac command in the script.

Figure 9.15 shows the Finder view of the Trash folder after using the script.

✔ Tip

- Create this script with the name "trash," and follow the instruction in "Running a script without using a path" at the beginning of this chapter. This script is one you could use every day.

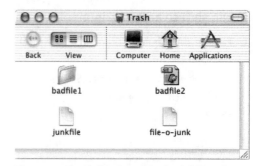

Figure 9.15 The Finder view of the Trash folder after using the script for moving files to the Trash.

```
[localhost:~] vanilla% ./trash junkfile file-o-junk badfile*
[localhost:~] vanilla% ls .Trash
badfile1     badfile2     file-o-junk   junkfile
[localhost:~]
```

Figure 9.14 Example of using the script in Figure 9.13.

Using Commands Within Commands

Now that you have used variables and arguments, you are probably wondering how to have your scripts do something simple like add two numbers together and store the results in a variable. The answer to this lies in using a powerful feature of Unix shells called *backquoted commands*. Backquoted commands enable you to incorporate one command line within another command line. The backquote is the ` character, usually found in the upper-left corner of your keyboard.

You use backquoted commands in scripts any time you want to store the output of a command line in a variable. You also use them when you want to create a command line in which part of the command line comes from the output of some other command.

We mentioned the use of backquotes (also called *backticks*) briefly in Chapter 2, "Using the Command Line," and now we will go into more detail about them.

To use backquotes in a command line:

◆ Enclose part of a command line in backquotes. The part of the command line you enclose in backquotes must itself be a valid command line:

```
file `which \ls`
```

Any time the shell sees a part of a command line that is enclosed in backquotes (`which \ls` in the example above), it executes the enclosed commands first, just as if they were a complete command line of their own. In this case, it will return the full path of the `ls` command.

The shell takes the output (`/bin/ls`, in the case of the example) and replaces the backquoted portion of the original command line with the output from the backquoted command. So the command line would then read:

```
file /bin/ls
```

The shell then executes this final command line, which in this case gives the output

```
/bin/ls: Mach-0 executable ppc
```

This tells you that the actual executable file for the `ls` command is a "Mach-0 executable ppc," which means that it is a binary file, not a text file, compiled for the PowerPC chip.

To save the output of a command in a variable:

◆ Start a command line as you would for a normal variable assignment. For example,

today=

◆ Put the backquoted command right after the = sign. For example,

today=`date`

When the line is executed, the shell first executes the backquoted portion, and then stores the output of that portion in the variable. **Figure 9.16** is a code listing of a script that stores the output of a backquoted command in a variable. The +%A, %B %d is a formatting argument for the date command. %A is the full weekday name, %B is the full month name, and %d is the two-digit day of the month. See man date and man strftime for details on the available formatting options. Notice that the backquoted command may include arguments (in this case a formatting string for the date command). **Figure 9.17** shows the output from the script in Figure 9.16.

✔ Tip

■ You can (and should) test whatever you put in backquotes by typing it at a shell prompt first.

```
#!/bin/sh
# This script uses a backquoted command.

today=`date "+%A, %B %d"`
echo "Hello $USER, today is $today"
```

Figure 9.16 Code listing of a script that stores the output of a backquoted command in a variable.

```
[localhost:~] vanilla% ./script.sh
Hello vanilla, today is Monday, June 17
[localhost:~]
```

Figure 9.17 Output from the script in Figure 9.16.

Table 9.2

Math Operators for Use with expr

All numerical values must be integers. See the expr body page for other operators.

EXPRESSION	MEANING
$a + $b	Returns the sum of $a and $b.
$a - $b	Subtracts $b from $a.
$a * $b	Returns the product of $a times $b. (You must escape the * with a backslash.)
$a / $b	Divides $a by $b.
$a % $b	Returns the remainder after dividing $a by $b.

Floating-Point Math

Two Unix commands do floating-point arithmetic at the command line or in a shell script: dc and bc. Both are fairly complex programs. Dc uses "reverse Polish notation" (developed in 1920 by Jan Lukasiewicz; see the RPN page on MoHPC, www.hpmuseum.org/rpn.htm), in which you enter numbers and operators and then ask for a result. For example, to use dc to divide 23 by 5 with a precision of four decimal places, you would enter

```
echo "4 k 23 5 / p" | dc
```

This is not pretty. The equivalent command line for bc is only slightly better:

```
echo "scale=4; 23 / 5" | bc
```

Read the man pages for these commands for the full details.

Doing Arithmetic and Using Expressions

It is frequently useful to have a script add two numbers together, or perform multiplication, division, or other arithmetic. The Bourne shell itself does not provide built-in arithmetic functions. Instead, it uses the standard Unix expr command to evaluate *expressions*.

The expr command sees expressions as a set of three arguments consisting of two arguments with an *operator* in between them, such as

```
3 + 4
```

or

```
$x - $y
```

Table 9.2 lists the operators you are most likely to use with expr. Read the man page (man expr) for the complete list. The math operators supported by expr only work on integers and only give integers as results— no decimal places. See the sidebar "Floating-Point Math" for notes about doing this type of calculation.

Try the following task at a shell prompt before you try it in a script.

To evaluate an expression:

◆ `expr 3 + 4`

This should give you a result of 7. The spaces before and after the + are required, as expr needs to see each item as a separate argument (3, +, and 4).

Figure 9.18 is a code listing that shows a script using the expr command in backquotes to perform integer arithmetic, and **Figure 9.19** shows the output of the script.

To add something to an existing variable:

◆ Simply use the variable as one of the arguments to expr.

Let's say you want to add 1 to whatever is stored in $count. You could use this:

`count=`expr $count + 1``

This construct is often used inside loops to count the number of times a loop was executed. See "Using loops," later in this chapter.

```
#!/bin/sh
# This script uses expr to perform integer arithmetic.

total=`expr $1 + $2`
difference=`expr $1 - $2`
product=`expr $1 \* $2`
fraction=`expr $1 / $2`
remainder=`expr $1 % $2`

echo "$total is the sum of $1 and $2"
echo "$difference is the difference between $1 and $2"
echo "$product is the product of $1 and $2"
echo "$fraction is  $1 divided by $2"
echo "$remainder is the remainder of dividing $1 by $2"
```

Figure 9.18 Code listing of a script that uses the expr command in backquotes to perform integer arithmetic.

```
[localhost:~] vanilla% ./math.sh 517 23
540 is the sum of 517 and 23
494 is the difference between 517 and 23
11891 is the product of 517 and 23
22 is  517 divided by 23
11 is the remainder of dividing 517 by 23
[localhost:~]
```

Figure 9.19 Output from the script in Figure 9.18.

Using Control Structures

There are times when you want to control which commands in your script actually get executed, in what order, and how many times. In those instances, you use tools called *control structures*. Without control structures, your script is executed line by line, from start to finish. Often this is just fine. The simple trash script you created earlier in this chapter is an example of this, but the trash script would be better if it could change its behavior—such as pausing—if it finds that it is about to overwrite a file.

In scripting (and in computer programming in general), there are two basic kinds of control structures: *conditionals* and *loops*.

Conditionals are the familiar "If ... then" construct we use in everyday life—for example, "If you are going to call me after 5 p.m., then use my home number."

We also use loops in everyday language, but less consciously. For example, we say, "Put the dishes on the table" instead of saying, "Put the first dish on the table. Put the second dish on the table. Put the third dish on the table." A loop involves a command or set of commands that are to be repeated.

Using conditionals

In shell scripts, you use conditionals so that your script performs different actions based on questions like "Did the user supply enough arguments to the script?," "Does this file exist?," "Do we have permission to create a file in this directory?," "Is $a greater than $b?," and so on.

Fundamental to the use of conditionals is the idea of something being "true" or "false." In a shell script, 0 (zero) is true, and any other value is false.

Using the if ... then conditional

The most basic conditional is the *if state-ment*. When an if statement is used, a command or set of commands is executed only if something is true.

While reading through the next task, refer to **Figure 9.20**. It is a code listing of a script that uses an if statement, while **Figure 9.21** shows the output from two executions of the script. In the first case, the if statement finds a false when comparing $1 to see if it is equal to (-eq) $magic_number, and in the second case the if statement find a true result.

```
#!/bin/sh
# This script uses an if statement


magic_number=17


echo "Checking to see if your guess ($1) is the magic number...."


if [ $1 -eq $magic_number ]
then
    echo "You got it!"
fi


echo "Thanks for playing!"
```

Figure 9.20 Code listing of a script using an if statement.

```
[localhost:~] vanilla% ./if.sh 5
Checking to see if your guess (5) is the magic number....
Thanks for playing!
[localhost:~] vanilla% ./if.sh 17
Checking to see if your guess (17) is the magic number....
You got it!
Thanks for playing!
[localhost:~] vanilla%
```

Figure 9.21 Output from two uses of the script in Figure 9.20 showing the text expression being false and then true.

To use an if ... then structure:

1. `if [ expression ]`

   An `if` statement begins with the word `if` and is followed by a test expression enclosed in square brackets. There must be a space after the `[` and before the `]`.

   There are two main types of test expressions: *comparisons* and *file tests*.

   Comparison expressions are similar to the expressions used with `expr`, in that they consist of two arguments separated by an operator. Examples of `if` statements using comparison tests are

```
if [ $count -eq 1 ]
```
```
if [ $a -gt $b ]
```
```
if [ $word1 > $word2 ]
```

File-test expressions use one operator and a filename or path. Examples include

```
if [ -f "$filename" ]
```
```
if [ -d "$filename" ]
```

Table 9.3 lists the most common text expressions. See `man test` for the complete list.

continues on next page

Table 9.3

Test Expressions for Use in [ ]

Expression	Meaning
INTEGER COMPARISONS	
n1 -eq n2	Integer comparison. True if n1 equals n2. Example: [$a -eq $b].
n1 -ne n2	True if n1 is not equal to n2.
n1 -lt n2	True if n1 is less than n2.
n1 -gt n2	True if n1 is greater than n2.
n1 -le n2	True if n1 is less than or equal to n2.
n1 -ge n2	True if n1 is greater than or equal to n2.
STRING (TEXT) COMPARISONS USING ASCII VALUES OF TEXT	
str1 = str2	True if str1 is identical to str2. Example: [$guess = $password].
str1 != str2	True if str1 is not identical to str2.
str1 < str2	True if str1 is alphabetically lower than str2.
str1 > str2	True if str1 is alphabetically higher than str2.
-z string	True if string is not empty. Example: [-z $word].
FILE-TEST EXPRESSIONS	
-e filename	True if filename exists.
-f filename	True if filename exists and is a regular file.
-d filename	True if filename exists and is a directory.
-r filename	True if filename exists and is readable.
-w filename	True if filename exists and is writable.
-x filename	True if filename exists and is executable.
-L filename	True if filename exists and is a symbolic link.
file1 -nt file2	True if f1 exists and is newer than f2 (has a more recent modification time).
file1 -ot file2	True if file1 exists and is older than file2.
file1 -ef file2	True if file1 exists and refers to the same file as file2.

2. `then`

The next line after you start the `if` statement is simply the word **then**. All the lines between the **then** line and the end of the `if` statement will be executed if the test expression is true.

3. Enter one or more command lines.

This is where you enter the commands that are executed if the test expression is true.

It is customary (and makes for more readable scripts) to indent every line between the "then" and the end of the `if` statement. For example,

```
echo "If you see this the test
returned true"
```

You can have as many lines as you want after the **then** line.

4. The `if` statement is closed off (ended) with a line that says simply

```
fi
```

That's "`if`" backward. Have a look at Figure 9.20 for a complete example.

✔ Tip

■ You can make your scripts a bit easier to read by putting the **then** part of an `if` statement on the same line as the test by using a semicolon after the test:

```
if [ $number -le $guess ] ; then
  echo "$a is less than or
  equal to $b"
fi
```

You can reverse the meaning of any test expression by adding a !, which you can think of as "not."

To reverse the meaning of any test expression:

◆ Add a ! to the expression:

```
[ ! -f "$filename" ]
```

will be true if the file *does* exist and false if the file does not. The spaces around the ! are required.

The `if` statement is very useful, but what about when you want to do one thing if the test is true and another if it is false? In that case, you add an "else" clause to your if statement. Refer to **Figure 9.22** for a code listing of a script that uses an if...then...else structure, and **Figure 9.23** for sample output from the script.

To create an if...then...else structure:

1. `if [ testexpression ]`

Create the first part of the `if` statement, including the part that gets executed if true.

For example, from Figure 9.22:

```
if [ $1 -eq $magic_number ]
```

2. `then`

This line simply begins the block of code that will be executed if the condition is true.

3. Enter the commands for the true part.

Remember to indent these commands to make the script more readable.

From 9.21:

```
echo "You got it!"
```

Now, instead of finishing the `if` statement, add a line (not indented) that says simply:

4. else

The commands that follow the else line will be executed if the test is false.

5. Enter the commands for the false part.

As with the commands for the true part, you may enter as many command lines here as you like.

Using Figure 9.21 again as an example:

echo "Oh no! You didn't get it."

Finally, you still end the entire if statement with the backward if:

```
#!/bin/sh
# This script uses an if...then...else structure

magic_number=17

echo "Checking to see if your guess ($1) is the magic number...."

if [ $1 -eq $magic_number ]
then
    echo "You got it!"
else
    echo "Oh no! You didn't get it."
fi

echo "Thanks for playing!"
```

Figure 9.22 Code listing of a script using an if...then...else structure.

```
[localhost:~] vanilla% ./else.sh 5
Checking to see if your guess (5) is the magic number....
Oh no! You didn't get it.
Thanks for playing!
[localhost:~] vanilla% ./else.sh 17
Checking to see if your guess (17) is the magic number....
You got it!
Thanks for playing!
[localhost:~] vanilla%
```

Figure 9.23 Output from two tries on the script in Figure 9.22; on the second try, the "if" clause is fulfilled, so the "then" clause is executed.

USING CONTROL STRUCTURES

253

6. `fi`

Sometimes `if...then...else` is not enough.
You'd like to try one test, and then if that
fails, try another. You could do this by nest-
ing one or more `if` statements inside one
another as in **Figure 9.24**, but a better way
is to use `elif` clauses, as shown in **Figure
9.25**. **Figure 9.26** shows the output that
would result from either script. They both do
the same thing in different ways.

`elif` means "else if" and is a way of having
multiple tests in the same `if` statement.
Only the first true `elif` is used.

```
#!/bin/sh
# This script uses nested if statements.

magic_number=17

echo "Checking to see if your guess ($1) is the magic number...."

if [ $1 -eq $magic_number ]
then
    echo "You got it!"
else
    if [ $1 -gt $magic_number ]
    then
        echo "Your guess ($1) is greater than the magic number."
    fi

    if [ $1 -lt $magic_number ]
    then
        echo "Your guess ($1) is less than the magic number."
    fi
fi

echo "Thanks for playing!"
```

Figure 9.24 Code listing of a script that uses nested `if` statements.

```
#!/bin/sh
# This script uses elif clauses in an if statement.


magic_number=17


echo "Checking to see if your guess ($1) is the magic number...."


if [ $1 -eq $magic_number ]
then
    echo "You got it!"
elif [ $1 -gt $magic_number ]
then
    echo "Your guess ($1) is greater than the magic number."
elif [ $1 -lt $magic_number ]
then
    echo "Your guess ($1) is less than the magic number."
fi


echo "Thanks for playing!"
```

Figure 9.25 Code listing of a script that does the same thing as Figure 9.24 but uses the elif clause instead.

```
[localhost:~] vanilla% ./guess.sh 100
Checking to see if your guess (100) is the magic number....
Your guess (100) is greater than the magic number.
Thanks for playing!
[localhost:~] vanilla% ./guess.sh 5
Checking to see if your guess (5) is the magic number....
Your guess (5) is less than the magic number.
Thanks for playing!
[localhost:~] vanilla% ./guess.sh 17
Checking to see if your guess (17) is the magic number....
You got it!
Thanks for playing!
[localhost:~] vanilla%
```

Figure 9.26 Output from either of the scripts in Figures 9.24 and 9.25.

USING CONTROL STRUCTURES

Using the case conditional

You might be tempted to use a series of `elif` clauses where you have a variable that is storing one item from a list of possibilities such as `start`, `stop`, or `restart`, and you want to execute a different set of commands based on which one of the words the variable actually has. You could use a series of `elif` clauses in an `if` statement to do this, but because this is such a common occurrence, the Bourne shell provides a conditional structure called `case` exactly for this purpose.

Using a `case` structure involves setting up a series of *cases*, which are each associated with a pattern that is checked against a single variable. The first case whose pattern matches is executed, while the rest are ignored.

Refer to **Figure 9.27** while reading the following task. Figure 9.27 is a code listing of a script using a case structure. **Figure 9.28** shows the output of the script with four different arguments, each one triggering a different case.

```sh
#!/bin/sh
# This script uses a case structure.

# We will do different things based on
# the first argument to this script.

time=`date`

case "$1" in
    start)
        echo "Received start command at $time"
    ;;

    stop)
        echo "Received stop command at $time"
    ;;

    restart)
        # To restart we execute this same script twice, supplying
        # arguments of stop and start
        "$0" stop
        "$0" start
    ;;

    *)
        # The * will always match, so this is the default
        # section. Do this if nothing above matched.
        echo "Usage: $0 (start|stop|restart)"
    ;;

esac
```

Figure 9.27 Code listing of a script that uses case structure to perform one of four different cases, depending on the script's first argument.

To use a case structure:

1. `case $variable in`

   The variable can be anything, such as one of the special variables for command-line arguments, like **$1** or **$USER**, or any variable you have assigned earlier in your script.

   Using Figure 9.27 as an example:

   `case "$1" in`

   The contents of the variable will be matched against a series of patterns.

2. `pattern)`

   This is the pattern that the variable must match to activate this case. The pattern can be a literal string of text, as it is in the first three patterns in Figure 9.27, or it can use the same wildcards available on the command line. For example, ***** will match anything.

   `file*)`

   matches `file`, `files`, `file system`, and so on.

The pipe character (|) can be used to specify alternatives:

`start|go)`

matches either **start** or **go**.

Only the first matching case will be executed (or no cases if none of the patterns match).

In Figure 9.27 the first pattern is

`start)`

After you declare a pattern, enter a series of command lines to be executed for that case.

3. Enter one or more command lines.

   This is just like the lines that follow the then part of an `if` statement.

   Each case is terminated with a double semicolon. See Figure 9.27 for four examples. The first one is

   `echo "Received start command at $time"`

```
[localhost:~] vanilla% ./case.sh start
Received start command at Mon Jun 17 22:49:15 PDT 2002
[localhost:~] vanilla% ./case.sh stop
Received stop command at Mon Jun 17 22:49:21 PDT 2002
[localhost:~] vanilla% ./case.sh restart
Received stop command at Mon Jun 17 22:49:26 PDT 2002
Received start command at Mon Jun 17 22:49:26 PDT 2002
[localhost:~] vanilla% ./case.sh go
Usage: ./case.sh (start|stop|restart)
[localhost:~] vanilla%
```

Figure 9.28 Output from the script in Figure 9.27 showing the effect of using different arguments. Notice how the usage message comes up.

USING CONTROL STRUCTURES

4. ;;

You may have as many cases as you like.

5. Repeat steps 2–4 for each pattern you wish to match.

Usually the last case uses the pattern

```
*)
```

which matches anything. You use this case to handle the possibility that none of the prior cases matched. You do not need to do this, but it is usually a good idea. Figure 9.27 uses this case to provide a *usage message* stating the allowable arguments for the script.

6. Finally, you terminate the entire **case** structure:

```
esac
```

That's **case** spelled backward. The Bourne shell seems to like this backward stuff.

✔ Tip

■ Notice how the script in Figure 9.27 uses the **$0** variable as a command name to execute itself again in the **restart** case. That's worth remembering.

Using loops

Use a loop when you want a command line or lines to be repeated over and over.

Loops are most commonly used in shell scripts to process each element of a list. These are called *for loops* and can easily be used to iterate over every argument in $@.

Another common use of a loop is to keep performing a series of commands as long as some test keeps returning a true result. These are called `while` *loops,* and we'll show you how to improve the trash script using this technique.

We'll start with a for loop. Refer to **Figure 9.29** while reading the following task. Figure 9.29 is a code listing of a simple script that tells you the largest number of all its arguments (it only works with integer arguments). **Figure 9.30** shows a couple of examples of output from the script with different arguments.

```
#!/bin/sh
# This script uses a for loop to find the biggest of its arguments.

# Start by saving the first argument in $biggest
biggest=$1

# Now loop over all the arguments, one at a time
for arg in "$@"
do
    if [ $arg -gt $biggest ] ; then
        biggest=$arg
    fi
done

echo "The biggest number is $biggest"
```

Figure 9.29 Code listing of a script using a for loop to find the largest of its arguments.

```
[localhost:~] vanilla% ./biggest 3 8 9 101 78 344 5 7 8
The biggest number is 344
[localhost:~] vanilla% ./biggest -6 -20 -41 -1 -17
The biggest number is -1
[localhost:~] vanilla%
```

Figure 9.30 Output from the script in Figure 9.29.

To use a for loop:

1. `for loop_variable in list`

The *loop_variable* will have a different value each time through the loop. The first time, it will hold the first item from list, then the second item, and so on.

In Figure 9.29 the special variable $@ is used to create the list. This is the only variable that will be treated as a list of items when enclosed in quotes. In all other cases, enclosing a variable in double quotes causes its contents to be treated as a single item.

The list can be a series of values like

`for fate in Clotho Lachesis Atropos`

The first time through the loop, `$fate` will hold `Clotho`, `Lachesis` on the second go-round, and `Atropos` on the third.

It can come from a variable:

`winds="Boreas Eurus Notus Zephyrus"`

`for wind in $winds`

Notice that `$winds` is not enclosed in quotes—the shell splits it into separate items based on the spaces, resulting in four winds.

The list can come from more than one variable:

`muses="Calliope Clio Erato Euterpe"`

`muses2="Melpomene Thalia Polyhymnia"`

`muses3="Terpsichore Urania"`

`for muse in $muses $muses2 $muses3`

2. `do`

The next line is simply the word **do** by itself.

You can put the **do** on the first line if you use a semicolon:

`for bird in $flight ; do`

3. Enter a series of one or more command lines.

This marks the top of the loop body. The command lines in the loop body repeat for each item in the list, with the loop variable having a different value each time through.

4. `done`

This terminates the loop body.

The for loop is an excellent way to process each element in a list (similar loops in other programming languages are sometimes called *foreach* loops, as in "For each item in the list, do something"). There are times when you don't have a list but still want to repeat a series of commands. Usually the while loop will do what you want.

A while loop combines a conditional test (like an if statement) with a loop body. The test is performed, and if true, the loop body is executed. Then the test is performed again. Lather, rinse, repeat. Unless something happens to alter the outcome of the test, the loop can run forever. Of course, usually you put something in the loop body that alters at least one of the variables in the test. Sometimes the test is checking something happening outside the script, perhaps to see if a file still exists.

```
#!/bin/sh
# This script uses a while loop to count to 10


count=0
while [ $count -le 10 ] ; do
    echo $count
    count=`expr $count + 1`
done
```

Figure 9.31 Code listing of a script using a while loop to count to 10.

```
[localhost:~] vanilla% ./count.sh
0
1
2
3
4
5
6
7
8
9
10
[localhost:~]
```

Figure 9.32 Output from the counting script. Pretty much what you would expect.

Refer to **Figure 9.31** while reading the following task. Figure 9.31 is a code listing of a script that uses a while loop to count from 0 to 10. Notice how the contents of a variable in the test are altered each time through the loop. **Figure 9.32** shows a run of the script.

To use a while loop:

1. `while [ test_expression ] ; do`

   The test expression is the same thing you used for the if statement earlier in this chapter. See Table 9.3 for a list of common test expressions, or man test for the complete list.

   The do command can go on the next line, but by now we think you want to do it like the pros and use a semicolon to put it on the same line as the test.

2. Enter the commands for the loop body.

   As with the for loop, these commands will be executed each time through the loop, as long as the test is true.

   In Figure 9.31 the script adds 1 to the value of $count on each pass though the loop. Eventually the test is false (when $count is 11, it is no longer "less than or equal to" 10). The script exits the loop and continues with the next line after the loop.

3. done

   That's the line that marks the end of the loop, the same as with the for loop.

Earlier we promised you an improved version of the trash script. **Figure 9.33** is a code listing of a script that lets you use the Macintosh Trash from the command line, and checks to see if the file(s) you are trashing might overwrite other files in the Trash. The script mimics the behavior of the Finder by renaming the trashed file if a conflict is found. Notice that the script uses a `while` loop to keep checking to see if a file exists, and if it does, it adds 1 to `$count` and uses the new value in the filename it checks for. Eventually a filename that is not already in the Trash is found, and the trashed file gets moved to the Trash with the new name (actually copied, then deleted).

```
#!/bin/sh
# Better trash - script for moving files to the Trash
# from the command line.

# Each users' Trash is a directory called .trash in their
# home directory
trash_directory="$HOME/.Trash"

if [ ! -d "$trash_directory" ] ; then
    echo "Whoa! $trash_directory doesn't exist."
    exit ; # The exit command quits the script immeadiatly
fi

# We want to use MvMac in case the file we are trashing is
# an old-style Macinstosh file, but MvMac won't rename a
# file the way the standard mv does so instead we will copy
# the file to the trash using CpMac, then delete the original.
cp="/Developer/Tools/CpMac"
rm="/bin/rm"

# loop over each command line argument
for file in "$@" ; do
    if [ -e "$file" ] ; then
        count=0
        filename="$file"
        trashname="$trash_directory/$filename"

        # If there is no file with this name in the Trash
        # then the while loop won't execute even once, which is OK.
        #
        while [ -e "$trashname" ] ; do
            count=`expr $count + 1`
            trashname="$trash_directory/$filename $count"
        done

        # We now have a $trashname that is not in use
        # Here's where we actually move the file into the Trash
        #
        "$cp" "$file" "$trashname"
        "$rm" "$file"
    fi
done
```

Figure 9.33 Code listing of a better trash script. This one uses file tests, a `for` loop, and a `while` loop.

Getting User Input

You've seen one way to get user input into your scripts—by using the command-line arguments and then accessing them with $1, $2, and so on, or $@. But what if you want your script to ask the user for input while it is running? No problem—you use the read command.

Refer to **Figure 9.34** while reading the following task. Figure 9.34 is a code listing of a script that asks the user for input and stores the input in a variable. **Figure 9.35** shows the script being used.

```
#!/bin/sh
# This script asks the user for input and stores it in a variable.

echo "Hello $USER, we just want ask you a few questions."

# Use the -n option to echo to supress the newline
echo -n "Enter an integer: "
read number

square=`expr $number \* $number`

echo "The  square of $number is $square"
```

Figure 9.34 Code listing of a script using the read command to get user input.

```
[localhost:~] vanilla% ./read.sh
Hello vanilla, we just want ask you a few questions.
Enter an integer: 7
The  square of 7 is 49
[localhost:~] ./read.sh
Hello vanilla, we just want ask you a few questions.
Enter an integer: 17
The  square of 17 is 289
[localhost:~]
```

Figure 9.35 Output from the script in Figure 9.34.

To read user input into a variable:

◆ read *variable*

The **read** command takes one or more arguments that are the names of variables—for example,

read var1 var2 var3

When executed, **read** waits for user input and reads a line of input from the keyboard (actually from standard input; see Chapter 2, "Using the Command Line," for more on standard input).

Read splits the input into pieces, based on the spaces between words, and stores each piece in one of the variables.

If there are more pieces (input) than variables, the extras go in the last variable. This means that if you use **read** with a single variable name, you get an entire line of user input in that one variable. If there are more variables than input, the extra variables are left empty. If the script has

read var1 var2 var3

and the user types

good morning

then var1 will contain good, var2 will contain morning, and var3 will be empty.

Creating and Using Functions

Functions are series of commands that have a name. They are very much like miniature scripts that can be stored inside another script.

The main reason you use functions is to make your code easier to understand and maintain. If you have a series of commands that you use more than once in your script, or that you want to use in more than one script, then consider putting it in a function. You give the set of commands a name, and then in your script you use the name instead of repeating all of the command lines the name refers to. You can pass arguments to functions in a manner similar to passing arguments to commands.

Refer to **Figure 9.36** while reading the following task. Figure 9.36 is a code listing of a script that uses a function, and **Figure 9.37** shows output from the script.

```
#!/bin/sh
# The script uses a function

magic=77
guess=0

# define a function called "ask"
ask () {
    echo -n "Pick a number between 1 and 100: "
    read guess
}

while [ $guess -ne $magic ] ; do
    ask
    if [ $guess -lt $magic ] ; then
        echo "Try a higher number."
    elif [ $guess -gt $magic ] ; then
        echo "Try a lower number"
    else
        echo "Hey! You got it!"
    fi
done
```

Figure 9.36 Code listing of a script that uses a function.

```
[localhost:~] vanilla% ./function.sh
Pick a number between 1 and 100: 13
Try a higher number.
Pick a number between 1 and 100: 50
Try a higher number.
Pick a number between 1 and 100: 75
Try a higher number.
Pick a number between 1 and 100: 88
Try a lower number
Pick a number between 1 and 100: 80
Try a lower number
Pick a number between 1 and 100: 79
Try a lower number
Pick a number between 1 and 100: 78
Try a lower number
Pick a number between 1 and 100: 77
Hey! You got it!
[localhost:~] vanilla%
```

Figure 9.37 Output from the script in Figure 9.36.

Where to Learn More

Of course the Bourne shell man page, man sh, will at least give you a good overview of what else there is to learn, although it may not be the best guide for a beginner to actually work from.

Here are two online tutorials:

◆ Unix Bourne Shell Scripting (http://unix.about.com/library/course/blshscript-outline.htm)

◆ Steve Parker's Web site: steve-parker.org/sh/sh.shtml

If you use the bash shell, you should read "Learning the bash Shell," 2nd Edition, by Cameron Newham and Bill Rosenblatt (O'Reilly; www.oreilly.com/catalog/bash2/).

To create a function:

1. name () {

The function name can be any combination of letters, numbers, dashes, and underscore characters as long as it isn't the same as a shell command, such as if, while, and so forth.

2. Enter a series of command lines.

The body of the function is a series of command lines. Indent the commands in the function to make the script easier to read.

3. }

The } ends the function. Now you can use the function at any point farther on in your script, as if you have added a new command to the Bourne shell language. (You cannot use a function in a script at a point earlier than where the function is defined.)

Functions can take arguments just like a script or command does.

To use arguments in a function:

◆ Use the special variables for arguments in the function.

The special variables you have used for script arguments all work inside a function. When used inside a function, they refer to the arguments used with the function, not the script around the function. So the $3 inside a function is the third argument to the function, not the third argument to the script.

Figure 9.38 is a code listing of a script using a function that takes arguments, and **Figure 9.39** is output from that script.

```
#!/bin/sh
# The script uses a function that takes arguments

magic=63
a=0
b=0
sum=0

ask () {
    echo -n "Enter two integers: "
    read a b
}

add () {
    sum=`expr $1 + $2`
}


while [ $magic -ne $sum ] ; do
    ask
    add $a $b
    if [ $sum -lt $magic ] ; then
        echo "Try HIGHER."
    elif [ $sum -gt $magic ] ; then
        echo "Try lower."
    else
        echo "Very good. $a + $b = $magic which is the magic number."
    fi
done
```

Figure 9.38 Code listing of a script using a function that takes arguments.

```
[localhost:~] vanilla% ./function.sh
Enter two integers: 23 37
Try HIGHER.
Enter two integers: 30 40
Try lower.
Enter two integers: 29 40
Try lower.
Enter two integers: 27 37
Try lower.
Enter two integers: 25 37
Try HIGHER.
Enter two integers: 26 37
Very good. 26 + 37 = 63 which is the magic number.
[localhost:~] vanilla%
```

Figure 9.39 Output of the script in Figure 9.38.

✔ Tip

■ If you have a function or functions that you want to use in more than one script, you should put the function(s) in a separate file and read that file into your script(s) using the . command:

`. file`

File must be a path to the file you want to read. If it is simply a filename, then the file must be in your current directory when you execute the script. The script will read the named file and execute its contents as if they were typed into the script at this point.

CONNECTING OVER THE INTERNET

Using Unix means being part of a global system for collaborative computing. The ability to connect with and perform interactive tasks on other Unix machines is built into Mac OS X and every other version of Unix in use today.

Most of the interactions you have with other Unix machines will fall into one of two categories: logging in to another machine to get a command-line interface on the remote machine, or copying files between your machine and a remote machine.

Technically speaking, the programs we describe in this chapter are not limited to interacting with Unix machines; the underlying requirement is simply that they understand the lingua franca of the Internet, TCP/IP. However, Unix is so prevalent that chances are, the system you connect to will be Unix-based. The basics of interaction with non-Unix machines, as well as more advanced forms of interaction, such as setting up virtual private networks and automated (unattended) file transfers, are beyond the scope of this book. We will, however, guide you to places where you can learn more about what is possible and how to do it.

About Hostnames

Connecting to another machine over a network requires that you have some way of identifying the remote machine.

All of the tools covered in this chapter use the TCP/IP (Transmission Control Protocol/Internet Protocol) suite of protocols to communicate across networks, and thus we refer to them generally as *Internet tools*.

When you use the Internet, there are two ways to identify another machine. One is to use an IP (Internet Protocol) address, and the other is to use a *hostname*. Data sent over the Internet always uses IP addresses, but IP addresses are hard for humans to remember. This is where hostnames and domain names come in.

An IP address looks like this: 192.168.23.45. Every computer's numbers are different, but IP addresses always have four parts separated by dots. Each part is a value between 0 and 255. In fact, each part is actually an 8-bit binary number, from 00000000 (0 in base 10) to 11111111 (255 in base 10). Every machine on the Internet must have at least one unique IP address—it's like its telephone number. You can always use an IP address to connect to another machine over the Internet, but usually you will want to use a more user-friendly text-based domain name.

The familiar format of "www.something.com" is called a *fully qualified domain name* (FQDN). Your computer translates FQDNs into IP addresses through a process of asking other computers on the Internet for the translation, sort of like using directory assistance for telephone numbers. FQDNs consist of a *top-level domain* (.com, .edu, .int, .us, and so on) on the right end, then any number of sub-domains on the left, with the leftmost item being the name of one specific computer inside the preceding sub-domain. So in this example,

www.yahoo.com

.com is the top-level domain, *yahoo* is a sub-domain (a sub-domain of .com), and *www* is a hostname. The whole thing, www.yahoo.com, is a fully qualified domain name and can be translated by your computer into an IP address. Because "fully qualified domain name" or even "FQDN" is such a mouthful, it is common practice to say "domain name" or "hostname" when what is really meant is "fully qualified domain name." Technically, domain names and the hostname are just parts of an FQDN, but people are sloppy, what can we say?

The next version of IP addresses

The IP addresses described in this book meet a standard called Internet Protocol version 4 or IPv4. The next version of the standard for IP addresses is Internet Protocol Version 6 or IPv6 and allows for much longer addresses. (IPv4 addresses are 32 bits long. IPv6 addresses are four times that size—128 bits long.) See www.ipv6.org for more information.

When you use SSH to connect to another machine, the SSH software on your end (the "client" software) and the sshd daemon on the other end (the "server") exchange information about each other.

One of the things the client asks for is the "identity" of the remote host. If you already have the remote machine's encrypted identity stored in your ~/.ssh/known_hosts or ~/.ssh/known_hosts2 file (depending on which version of the SSH protocol the client and server have agreed to use), the client trusts the server's identity; otherwise, you get the prompt shown in Figure 10.1. If you say "yes" to the prompt, then the client adds the encrypted identity supplied by the server to your ~/.ssh/known_ hosts or known_hosts2 file.

The most secure way of establishing the identity of the remote host is to obtain the remote host's identity file from that machine and manually add it to your ~/.ssh/known_hosts or known_hosts2 file. One way of doing this is to have the remote machine's administrator email the file to you. Because there are variations in how different versions of the SSH software work, you need to get help from the remote machine's administrator to make sure you add the host identity information in the proper format.

In practice this is rarely done, and people simply answer "yes" to the prompt shown in Figure 10.1 the first time they connect to a machine using SSH.

Logging In to Another Unix Machine

The most basic and common way you interact with other Unix machines is to log in to them using a command-line interface from your own machine.

Once you log in to another Unix machine using a command-line interface, you can use that machine in the same way as you use your own machine from the command line. Of course, you may not have the same level of permissions that you have on your own machine, and if the remote machine is running a different version of Unix, there will be some differences in availability of commands and variations in how some commands work. Overall, however, you will find yourself in an environment very much like the command-line environment on your own machine.

In this section we describe two ways of getting to a command-line prompt on remote machines. The first (and preferred) method uses SSH to establish an encrypted connection to the remote machine, while the second method uses an older program called Telnet to establish an unencrypted connection. Both SSH and Telnet are useful for more than simply logging in to another machine, but connecting via SSH is not always supported, so sometimes you have to use Telnet.

Secure connections using SSH

SSH stands for "secure shell" and is the name of both a protocol and a command.

The SSH protocol sets up an encrypted connection between two machines over a network such as the Internet. The primary tool for using the SSH protocol is the ssh command. This means that if you are communicating with a remote host using SSH and someone is able to tap into the connection, it is extremely difficult or impossible for him or her to read the data flowing between the two machines. For this reason, SSH is the preferred method for logging in to other machines over the Internet.

To do this, you need to have an account on the remote machine. That means having a user name and password. You also need to know the network address of the remote machine—either its IP address or a hostname that your machine can translate into an IP address. As complicated as that sounds, it is actually simple in practice: If you are supposed to be connecting to a remote machine, you will have been given the address to use.

Refer to **Figure 10.1** for the following task. The figure shows the process of logging in to a remote machine using the **ssh** command.

To log in using ssh:

1. ssh *username@hostname*

   Username is your user name on the remote system. *Hostname* is either the typical text-based domain name or an IP address of the remote machine. For example, the following will connect to the machine well.com with the user name puffball:

   ssh puffball@well.com

Logging into your own machine via SSH

Your Mac OS X machine comes with SSH server software installed, but you have to turn it on before you can login to your machine from another Internet host using ssh. It's pretty easy though: Open the Sharing pane of System Preferences, go to the Application tab, and check the "Allow remote login" checkbox. That's it.

This text is from your own computer.
The text you enter is **highlighted.**

Your password is not displayed when you type it.

```
[localhost:~] vanilla% ssh puffball@well.com
The authenticity of host 'well.com (206.14.209.5)' can't be established.
RSA key fingerprint is cc:91:d8:9a:c5:29:c1:80:72:80:bd:3a:9a:88:dc:e7.
Are you sure you want to continue connecting (yes/no)? yes
Warning: Permanently added 'well.com,206.14.209.5' (RSA) to the list of known hosts.
puffball@well.com's password: [        ]
```

```
    You own your own words. This means that you are responsible for
    the words that you post on the WELL and that reproduction of those
    words without your permission in any medium outside of the WELL's
    conferencing system may be challenged by you, the author.

        *** Support is in the wellcome conference or (415) 645-9300;
        at www.well.com/tools.html or mail helpdesk@well.com ***
```

```
OK (Return for menu):
```

This text is from the remote computer.
There may be messages about the remote
system, but often you will see only the
remote systems' shell prompt.

A shell prompt from the remote computer. Remember
that your shell on the remote system may be different
from the shell you use on your local machine.

Figure 10.1 Diagram showing the use of SSH to connect to a remote machine.

If your user name is the same on both the local and remote machines, you may omit the *username*@ portion of the command line:

```
ssh well.com
```

Sometimes you get an IP address to use instead of a name. You can experiment on your own machine using the special IP address 127.0.0.1, which always means "this machine right here," or use the hostname "localhost," which is a Unix standard name for the local machine.

```
ssh username@127.0.0.1
```

or

```
ssh 127.0.0.1
```

or

```
ssh localhost
```

If this is the first time you have used **ssh** to connect to a particular hostname or IP address, you see a prompt as shown in Figure 10.1. Despite the apparent security warning, you should answer "yes" to the question. See the sidebar, "Authenticity of Hosts and SSH."

The next thing you see is the prompt for your password:

```
puffball@well.com's password:
```

2. Enter your password.

Your typing is not displayed, to prevent your password from being visible.

You are then logged in to the remote machine. The remote machine may display an informational message about itself, perhaps telling you the last time you logged in or giving you a telephone number for the system support staff. Often you will get only a prompt from that machine. You can now start entering command lines to the remote machine.

When you want to log out of the remote machine, type

```
logout
```

and you return to a shell prompt on your own machine.

✔ Tips

- It is a good idea to open a new Terminal window for each connection to a remote machine (you can have many open at the same time).

- Consider changing the Terminal window title and/or text color for each window in which you are connected to a remote machine. This will help you remember which machine you are "on" in each window. You can make these changes in the Terminal application's Shell menu, by choosing Inspector.

- If you are having trouble on the remote machine while connected via **ssh** you can terminate the connection (without closing the Terminal window) by using a special sequence of keys:

  Return ~ .

  That's the Return key, followed by the ~ character, followed by a period. You can get a list of the available "escape" commands with:

  Return ~ ?

- Bear in mind that your shell may not be the same on the remote machine as on your local machine. For example, your account on your own machine might be set to use the **tcsh** shell, while on the remote machine your account might use the **bash** shell, so you can expect some slight differences in how the command-line environment behaves. One way to see which shell you are using is

  ```
  echo $SHELL
  ```

Using SSH to run a command on another machine:

One of the nifty things about SSH is that you can use it to run commands on another machine without actually logging in to the remote machine.

For example, the who command shows a list of users logged in to a machine. If you want to check who is logged in to a remote machine on which you have an account, you can use SSH to run the who command on the remote machine and see its output on your machine.

To run a single command line on a remote machine:

◆ ssh *user@host commandline*

For example,

ssh puffball@well.com who

runs the who command as the user puffball on the remote machine well.com (**Figure 10.2**).

The command line you run on the remote machine may be a full command line, including options and arguments. For example, to see a list of the files in the remote system's /etc directory, you could use

ssh puffball@well.com ls -l /etc

More About SSH

SSH is both the name of a protocol and the name of a widely used Unix command (ssh).

As with many facets of Unix, there is more than one variety of the SSH software. Mac OS X comes with OpenSSH, an open-source implementation of the SSH protocol that combines the work of several prior implementations. You can read a brief history at OpenSSH Project History and Credits (www.openssh.org/history.html).

The OpenSSH tool set includes several commands that are installed on your Mac OS X machine, including ssh, sshd, scp, and sftp.

```
[localhost:~] vanilla% ssh puffball@well.com who
puffball@well.com's password:
geffrey     pts/1       Jun 25 10:30    (12.112.115.3)
mikkee      pts/7       Jun 25 10:32    (14-226-92-54.clients.attbit.com)
lalla       pts/2       Jun 25 09:21    (werks.kinemia.com)
jmassoun    pts/53      Jun 25 11:10    (huffman.wunterk.com)
rpdoctor    pts/12      Jun 25 06:59    (63.113.8.116)
jperk       pts/26      Jun 25 06:14    (fl-boca-cuda1-c2a-132.pbc.adelphia.net)
fanson      pts/56      Jun 25 10:44    (119-176-36-34-cdsl-rb1:S.0)
```

Figure 10.2 Using SSH to run a command on the remote machine without logging in.

to produce output like that shown in **Figure 10.3**.

Some programs don't simply spit out their output and quit, though—they expect to take over your whole screen and interact with you. For example, the vi editor is a *full-screen* program. It takes over the whole Terminal window and allows you to move around inside that window entering and editing text (review Chapter 6, "Editing and Printing Files," for more on vi). To run these kinds of programs via SSH, add the -t option, which makes SSH pretend you are on a terminal on the remote machine. For example:

```
ssh -t puffball@playroom.matisse.net
→vi myfile
```

runs the vi editor on the remote machine. When you quit from vi, the SSH connection closes, but the file you edited is still on the remote machine.

```
[localhost:~] vanilla% ssh puffball@playroom.matisse.net ls -l /etc
puffball@playroom.matisse.net's password:
total 1292
drwxr-xr-x   3 root     root        4096 Feb  4  2001 CORBA
-rw-r-r-    1 root     root        2045 Sep 24  1999 DIR_COLORS
-rw-r-r-    1 root     root           9 Sep 14  2001 HOSTNAME
-rw-r-r-    1 root     root        5421 Sep 25  1999 Muttrc
drwxr-xr-x  12 root     root        4096 Jul 24  2001 X11
-rw-r-r-    1 root     root          38 Apr 28  2001 adjtime
-rw-r-r-    1 root     root         947 Sep 27  2001 aliases
-rw-r-r-    1 root     root       20480 May  2 08:53 aliases.db
-rw-r-r-    1 root     root         276 Apr  6  1999 bashrc
drwxr-xr-x   2 root     root        4096 Feb  4  2001 charsets
drwxr-xr-x   3 root     root        4096 Feb  4  2001 codepages
-rw----     1 root     root         331 Apr 27  2001 conf.linuxconf
drwxr-xr-x   2 root     root        4096 Feb  4  2001 cron.d

(Partial Output)
```

Figure 10.3 You can supply options and arguments to commands run on a remote machine with SSH.

Connecting using Telnet

Before there was SSH there was Telnet. The `telnet` command is the lowest-common-denominator method of logging in to a remote Unix machine. These days it is deprecated in favor of SSH because all of the data in a Telnet connection (including your user name and password) is sent over the network unencrypted. Still, some systems don't support SSH, and there are things you can do with Telnet besides logging in to another machine.

When using Telnet, you need the same things as you do for SSH—that is, the remote machine's address (either a hostname or an IP address) and an account on the remote machine (user name and password).

To log in using Telnet:

1. `telnet` *hostname*

As with SSH, *hostname* can be either a text-based network address, such as well.com, or an IP address, such as 206.14.209.5. If you use a hostname, the Telnet program asks the operating system to translate the hostname into an IP address. That's why you see an IP address in this line:

`Trying 206.14.209.5...`

When you use `telnet`, your machine tells you it is trying to connect to the remote machine. Once it connects, you see text from the remote machine identifying itself, followed by a "login:" prompt from the remote machine (**Figure 10.4**).

This text is from your own computer.

```
[localhost:~] vanilla% telnet well.com
Trying 206.14.209.5...
Connected to well.com.
Escape character is '^]'.
```

```
SunOS 5.6

This is the WELL

Type    newuser    to learn how to sign up (password:  newuser)
Type    trouble    if you are having trouble logging in (password: trouble)

If you already have a WELL account, type your username.

login:
```

This text is from the remote computer.

Figure 10.4 Using Telnet to log in to a remote machine.

2. Enter your user name.

Once you enter your user name, you should see a password prompt from the remote machine.

3. Enter your password.

You are now logged in. Some systems will show you a short message about themselves (called "the message of the day"). In any case, you get a prompt from the remote machine, and you can now type commands to it.

✔ Tip

■ If you are having trouble on the remote machine while using `telnet`, you can quit the Telnet program by typing a special keyboard combination that gets you a prompt from the Telnet program itself.

Notice in Figure 10.4 the line that says

```
Escape character is '^]'
```

This is part of the text that comes from your own computer before you get the login: prompt from the remote machine. The Telnet program is telling you that if you press (Control)(]), you'll get a prompt from the Telnet client on your own machine:

```
telnet>
```

and you can then exit the Telnet program (and kill the connection to the remote machine) by typing

```
quit
```

Using Telnet to test other systems

Besides using Telnet to log in to a remote machine, you can also use it to test services running on other machines.

You do this by using Telnet to connect to a remote machine but to a different *port number* than the one normally used for logging in with `telnet`.

When one machine connects to another over the Internet, it always uses a combination of an IP address and a port number. The IP address identifies the particular machine, while the port number leads to one of the (possibly many) pieces of software that are "listening" for incoming connections. Each Internet service has a standard port number that it listens on; the server software for `telnet` login, for example, normally listens on port 23. We provide a more extensive discussion of ports in Chapter 12, "Security," and **Table 12.1** lists the most commonly used port numbers.

When you use `telnet` to log in, you are using the Telnet client program (also called Telnet) to connect to a Telnet server program (called `telnetd`) on the remote machine. Server programs like `telnetd` (and `sshd` mentioned earlier in this chapter) are said to "listen" on specific port numbers. The `telnet` command normally connects to port 23 on the remote machine.

On the Internet there are standard port numbers for all the comsmon Internet services, so the `telnetd` server listens on port 23, Web servers normally listen on port 80, email servers listen on port 25, the `sshd` server listens on port 22, and so on. This allows all of those services to be running on the same machine and sharing the same IP address. It is their port numbers that distinguish them.

You can use the `telnet` command to connect to a remote machine on a port other than the standard Telnet port (23). If the connection itself is successful, you at least know that something is listening on that port on the remote machine. If you are familiar with the protocol that the remote service uses, you may be able to try a test interaction with the remote service.

Refer to **Figure 10.5** while working through the following task.

To connect to a remote Web server to test it:

1. `telnet www.peachpit.com 80`

   The only new thing about that command line is that you are specifying that Telnet connect to port 80 on the remote machine instead of the default (port 23).

   If there is anything listening on port 80 on the remote machine, we should connect to it.

   In Figure 10.5 you see that something is in fact listening—that's why you get the line

   `Connected to www.peachpit.com.`

   Even though the Web server on the remote machine is waiting for input from you, there will be no prompt.

2. Now type a few lines to request some information from the Web server:

   `HEAD / HTTP/1.1`

   You are asking for the summary information (the "head") about the main page on this Web server (/) Use GET instead of HEAD to request the full page instead of only the summary information. You are also telling the server that you are using HTTP version 1.1.

3. `Host: www.peachpit.com`

   This line specifies which domain name you are requesting information about, in case the server software is configured to respond to requests for more than one domain name.

```
[localhost:~] vanilla% telnet www.peachpit.com 80
Trying 165.193.123.104...
Connected to www.peachpit.com.
Escape character is '^]'.
HEAD / HTTP/1.1
Host: www.peachpit.com
Connection: close

HTTP/1.1 200 OK
Server: Microsoft-IIS/5.0
Date: Tue, 25 Jun 2002 20:44:05 GMT
Connection: close
Content-Length: 31269
Content-Type: text/html
Expires: Tue, 25 Jun 2002 20:43:05 GMT
Set-Cookie: session%5Fid=%7B028A7168%2D023C%2D41C8%2DAAFA%2D53C6BDF961ED%7D; path=/
Cache-control: private

Connection closed by foreign host.
[localhost:~] vanilla%
```

Figure 10.5 Using Telnet to test a remote Web server.

More About HTTP

If you want to learn more about HTTP, you'll find a nice online tutorial and reference in HTTP Made Really Easy (www.jmarshall.com/easy/http/), or check out the *HTTP Pocket Reference,* by Clinton Wong (O'Reilly; www.oreilly.com/catalog/httppr/).

4. Connection: close

Here you are telling the Web server that after it sends you the information, you are requesting that it close the connection.

5. Press `Return`.

Adding a blank line tells the server that you are finished creating your request. If the Web server and network connection are functioning properly, you will immediately see a response like that in Figure 10.5.

In the response shown in the figure, you see several lines of information, including one that tells you the Web server is running the Microsoft IIS software and that the Web page we asked about is 31269 bytes long.

Copying Files Between Unix Machines

There are many reasons to copy files from one machine to another. The most common: downloading software so that you can install it, uploading Web pages you have created to the machine that will serve them, and copying files from one machine to another as a way of backing them up.

The most widely available method for copying files between Unix machines is *FTP* (File Transfer Protocol). FTP software (both client and server) is available for virtually every type of operating system, not only Unix. So you might find yourself using FTP from your Unix machine to transfer files to or from a Windows NT machine that is running an FTP server. The big advantage to FTP software is its widespread availability. The biggest downside is that, like Telnet, it transfers everything "in the clear" (that is, unencrypted), including your user name and password.

If security is a concern, you should always use one of the secure methods of file transfer, either **scp** (described next) or **sftp** (described in the sidebar "Other Command-Line FTP Clients," below).

About transferring Macintosh files

All of the command-line file-transfer tools described in this chapter have one weakness: They will not properly handle certain older Macintosh files. This is the same issue described in Chapter 5, "Using Files and Directories," in the section "Copying files and preserving the Mac metadata."

In almost all cases, this won't be a problem if you are only transferring Mac OS X files, which are not affected, but if you are transferring files created with Mac OS 9 or earlier applications, those files *may* be at risk. In those cases, the safe thing to do is to use Aladdin Systems' StuffIt application to compress the file, and then transfer the compressed file. The compressed file is not affected, and when the file is uncompressed by the recipient, the file's resource fork and other Mac metadata are preserved.

This is also *not* an issue for plain-text files and for many documents created with recent versions of Macintosh applications.

Using scp

The **scp** (*secure copy*) command works very much like the **cp** command (review Chapter 5, "Using Files and Directories"). The basic syntax is

`scp existingfile newfile`

The key difference between **scp** and **cp** is that any of the files specified can be on another machine, so the proper syntax for **scp** is

`scp user@host:file user@host:file`

Furthermore, **scp** automatically uses SSH to make the connection to the remote machine, so the entire transaction is encrypted, including the file(s) being copied across the network.

To send a file using scp:

◆ `scp localfile user@host:newfile`

where *localfile* is a file pathname on the local machine, *user* is your user name on the remote machine, *host* is the domain name or IP address of the remote machine, and *newfile* is a file pathname on the remote machine. If the *newfile* path does not begin with a /, then it is a path relative to the home directory for *user* on the remote machine.

Here are some examples:

`scp Report.doc files.mycompany.com:`

copies the local file Report.doc to your home directory on the remote machine `files.mycompany.com`. The file has the same name on the remote machine.

`scp Report.doc puffball@host.com:`
`↪NewReport.doc`

copies the local file `Report.doc` to puffball's home directory on the remote machine and renames the copy `NewReport.doc`.

`scp /etc/rc.boot puffball@host.com:`
`↪files/`

copies the local file `/etc/rc.boot` into a directory called `files` in the home directory of user puffball on the remote machine.

`scp /etc/rc.boot host.com:/etc/`
`↪rc.boot.net`

copies the local file `/etc/rc.boot` to `/etc/rc.boot.net` on the remote machine. This assumes your user name is the same on both machines.

To copy a file from a remote machine using scp:

1. `scp` *user@hostname:path path*
   Examples:
   `scp well.com:myfile.txt .`
   `scp puffball@well.com:myfile.txt`
   `↪myfile_copy.txt`

2. Enter your password.
   See **Figure 10.6**, and notice how scp provides a progress indicator. The series of asterisks fills up as the file is copied over the network.

Copying a file *to* a remote machine is the same as copying *from* a remote machine. All you have to do is put the remote file description second instead of first.

To copy a file to a remote machine using scp:

1. `scp` *path user@hostname:path*
   The command line is the same as in the previous task, except that the first argument is a path to a file on your local machine, and the second argument is the one that includes the remote machine's name.

2. Enter your password.
   The file will be copied to the remote machine.

```
=[localhost:~] vanilla% scp puffball@well.com:myfile.txt copy.txt
puffball@well.com's password:
myfile.txt      100% |*****************************************|  9939      00:00
[localhost:~] vanilla%
```

Figure 10.6 Using scp to copy a file from a remote machine to your local machine.

COPYING FILES BETWEEN UNIX MACHINES

Sometimes you want to copy an entire directory from one machine to another. Scp handles this with the -r option (for *recursive* copy).

To copy an entire directory using scp:

◆ `scp -r original copy`

where either *original* or *copy* includes a remote-machine name. Examples:

`scp -r images puffball@well.com:`
`→new_images`

copies the local directory called images to the remote machine, while

`scp -r puffball@well.com:`
`→images new_images`

copies the remote directory ~puffball/ images to the local current directory and names the copy new_images. But be careful—if there is already a local directory named new_images, that command line would put the copy inside the existing directory. You can avoid this by adding a trailing / to any path that is supposed to be a directory:

`scp -r puffball@well.com:images`
`→new_images/`

There are a number of options for scp that you may find useful. You've seen one (the -r option) in the task above. **Table 10.1** lists the most common options for scp, and as always, you should read the man page for the complete list.

Table 10.1

Options for the scp Command	

OPTION	MEANING/USE
-r	Recursive copy. Used to copy entire directories.
-q	Disables the progress meter (or quiets it).
-p	Preserves permissions and modification times.
-v	Causes lots of debugging information to be displayed (verbose).
-C	Uses compression to speed up copying.

Table 10.2

FTP Commands	

COMMAND	MEANING/USE
ascii	Sets file-transfer type to plain text.
binary	Sets the file-transfer type to binary.
cd	`cd directory`
	Changes the current directory on the remote machine.
get	`get remotefile [localfile]`
hash	Toggles hash-mark printing (progress indicator during file transfer).
lcd	`lcd [directory]`
	Changes your current directory on the local machine. With no argument, it changes to your home directory. When you quit FTP, your current directory in the shell will be what it was when you started the FTP program.
ls	`ls [directory]`
	Like the regular ls command, lists the names of files and directories; usually uses the "long-form" listing.
mkdir	`mkdir directory`
	Creates a new directory on the remote machine.
mput	`mput file1 file2 ...`
	Uploads multiple files.
mget	`mget file1 file2 ...`
	Downloads multiple files.
put	`put localfile [remotefile]`
pwd	Prints your current directory on the remote machine.
quit	Quits the FTP program.

Arguments in square brackets ([]) are optional.

Using FTP

FTP is one of the oldest protocols on the Internet and is still widely used for downloading software as well as uploading and downloading files for Web sites and general file-transfer work.

As with virtually all Internet tools, you use FTP by running a client application on your machine that connects to a server application on the remote machine. Mac OS X comes with not one, not two, but three command-line FTP client applications. This chapter will focus on the most common FTP client application, which is called simply ftp. The other two are sftp and ncftp (see the sidebar "Other Command-Line FTP Clients," below).

Other Command-Line FTP Clients

sftp

Sftp is actually an FTP-like interface that uses SSH to create a secure connection to the remote machine and then allows you to use commands similar to those of the FTP program to transfer files. If it's available, you should use sftp instead of FTP. The commands are mostly the same, but read the man page to see a few differences. For example, sftp has an lpwd command to show your (local) current directory, and a rename command that lets you rename remote files.

Ncftp

Ncftp is a more user-friendly program than the old ftp command. Ncftp can be used to connect to any FTP server. Ncftp has a really good man page, and you should read that and try using ncftp instead of ftp when scp or sftp isn't an option.

We are showing you the older and more basic FTP program here because we want you to be able to use other Unix machines besides your Mac OS X machine. Still, ncftp is a nicer and easier program to use, so as long as you are using Mac OS X, you should read the man page for ncftp (the command itself is all lowercase) and try using that instead of ftp.

The ftp client application has its own command prompt, at which you enter commands that are specific to the FTP program itself. You can think of it as a miniature shell that has several dozen of its own commands. **Table 10.2** shows the most common FTP commands; see man ftp for the complete list.

Using the FTP program generally involves the following steps:

- Connecting to the remote machine.
- Logging in with a user name and password.
- Navigating around the directories on the remote machine and/or your local machine.
- Specifying options about how file transfers will be made—for example, specifying that transferred files should be treated as plain text as opposed to binary, or requesting that a progress indicator be displayed during file transfer.
- Giving the actual command to upload or download one or more files.
- Quitting the FTP program to get back to your shell prompt.

The following task assumes that you want to upload a file called poetry.html from the current directory on your local machine to a remote machine called webhost.somewhere. sf.ca.us, and that you want the file to end up in the directory /usr/local/apache/htdocs/ written_work on the remote machine.

A key thing to keep in mind when using FTP is that you are using two machines simultaneously: your own machine (the "local" machine) and the remote machine.

Refer to **Figure 10.7** throughout the following task.

To upload a file using ftp:

1. ftp *hostname*

In Figure 10.7, the hostname is webhost. somewhere.us, so the command line is

ftp webhost.somewhere.us

Throughout this process, the FTP remote server will send you messages about each action you take. When your client software first connects to the server, you get the message

220 FTP Service

The remote machine's FTP server then prompts you for a user name.

Your shell prompt and the command line that starts the ftp client application.

Your password is not displayed when you type it.

```
[localhost:~] vanilla% ftp sbgnews.snapbevgrp.com
Connected to webhost.somewhere.us.
220 FTP Service
Name (webhost.somewhere.us:vanilla): puffball
331 Password required for puffball.
Password:
230 User puffball logged in.
Remote system type is UNIX.
Using binary mode to transfer files.
ftp> cd /usr/local/apache/htdocs/written_work
250 CWD command successful.
ftp> ascii
200 Type set to A.
ftp> put poetry.html
local: poetry.html remote: poetry.html
200 PORT command successful.
150 Opening ASCII mode data connection for poetry.html.
226 Transfer complete.
4691 bytes sent in 0.00882 seconds (531678 bytes/s)
ftp> ls
200 PORT command successful.
150 Opening ASCII mode data connection for file list.
drwxr-xr-x   3 puffball    client         59 Jun 27 11:34 .
drwx--xr-x  10 puffball    client       2048 Jun 27 11:29 ..
-rwxr-xr-x   1 puffball    client       4505 Jun 27 11:34 poetry.html
-rwxr-xr-x   1 puffball    client       4605 Jun 19 21:42 prose.html
226 Transfer complete.
ftp> quit
221 Goodbye.
[localhost:~] vanilla%
```

A prompt from the ftp client program.

Everything in this box is from the ftp client application.

Your shell prompt after you quit the ftp client application.

Figure 10.7 Using FTP to upload a file.

2. Enter a username.

You can simply press [Return] if the user name of your account on the remote machine is the same as your user name on the local machine. In the example, the user name entered is puffball.

The server gives you a status message:

`331 Password required for puffball.`

and prompts you for a password.

3. Enter a password.

The password is not displayed as you type it.

You are now logged in to the remote machine.

The server responds with a series of messages:

`230 User puffball logged in.`

`Remote system type is UNIX.`

`Using binary mode to transfer files.`

The last message tells you the default setting for file transfers assumes that any file you send (or receive) is a binary file (as opposed to a plain-text file).

The next thing you see is a prompt from the `ftp` client—this is like a shell prompt in that the client waits for you to enter commands:

`ftp>`

While you are logged in using FTP, you have two current directories: one on the local machine and one on the remote machine.

The FTP server on the remote machine keeps track of your current directory on the remote machine, and the FTP client software keeps track of which directory you are in on your local machine.

When you first log in using FTP, your current directory on the remote machine is determined by how the remote FTP server is configured, and your local current directory starts off being whatever it was when you typed the `ftp` command to log in.

In the example here, you are changing directories on the remote machine so that you may upload a file into a specific directory on the remote machine.

4. `cd directory`

The FTP program has a `cd` command that changes your current directory *on the remote machine.*

In Figure 10.7 the example is

`cd /usr/local/apache/htdocs/written_`
`→work`

There is a different command to change your current directory on the local machine:

`lcd` (*local change directory*)

The server responds with a status message:

`250 CWD command successful.`

5. `ascii`

In this example, the file being uploaded is a plain-text file, so you must tell the FTP server to change the file-transfer type from binary to ASCII (American Standard Code for Information Interchange, a long way of saying plain text). If you transfer a plain-text file as binary, the file may not have the correct end-of-line characters, and if you transfer a binary file (such as an image or compressed file archive) as plain text, it will almost certainly be damaged and unusable.

The server responds with

`200 Type set to A.`

and you are now ready to actually upload the file.

6. `put poetry.html`

This example assumes that the file you are uploading (`poetry.html`) is in your local directory.

The server responds with a series of messages as shown in Figure 10.7. In particular, the line

`local: poetry.html remote:poetry.html`

tells you that the file will be copied to the remote machine and have the same name on the remote machine. You could upload the file and give the copy a different name:

`put poetry.html lyrics.html`

7. You can also list the contents of a directory on the remote machine:

`ls`

Just like the regular Unix `ls` command, the `ftp ls` command lists file and directory names. Most FTP servers use the long-style listing shown in Figure 10.7.

The file was copied successfully. If you have more files to transfer, do so.

8. `quit`

This quits the FTP program, and you get a shell prompt from your local machine.

Compare with Aqua

♦ There are quite a few graphical interfaces for FTP and a few that handle secure transfers using SSH as well.

♦ Any Web browser is able to use FTP to download files—when you see a URL that begins with *ftp://*, that instructs the browser to use FTP (instead of the more common HTTP).

♦ A number of full-fledged FTP client applications provide a GUI for both uploading and downloading.

♦ RBrowser (www.rbrowser.com) comes in a shareware version that handles both FTP and secure transfers, and a freeware version that handles only FTP. You can download demo versions.

♦ There used to be several Mac FTP clients that were totally free of charge, but this no longer seems to be true. The Mac OS X version of the venerable Dartmouth University Fetch program is now $25 from Fetch Softworks (www.fetchsoftworks.com).

The FTP program has more than five dozen commands, all of which are described in the man page, and the more common ones are described in Table 10.2. Still, it is useful to get help while you are actually using the FTP program at the ftp> prompt.

To get help inside FTP:

1. ?

The ftp command ? (just a question mark), typed at the ftp> prompt, lists all the available FTP commands, as shown in **Figure 10.8**.

The message "Commands may be abbreviated" means that you only need to type enough of each command name to make it unique. So you can type

as

instead of

ascii

```
ftp> ?
Commands may be abbreviated.   Commands are:

!               debug           mget            put             size
$               dir             mkdir           pwd             status
account         disconnect      mls             quit            struct
append          form            mode            quote           system
ascii           get             modtime         recv            sunique
bell            glob            mput            reget           tenex
binary          hash            newer           rstatus         trace
bye             help            nmap            rhelp           type
case            idle            nlist           rename          user
cd              image           ntrans          reset           umask
cdup            lcd             open            restart         verbose
chmod           ls              passive         rmdir           ?
close           macdef          prompt          runique
cr              mdelete         proxy           send
delete          mdir            sendport        site
ftp>
```

Figure 10.8 Using the ? command to get a list of all the available FTP commands.

2. You can also get a one-line description of any individual command:

? *command*

For example,

? ascii

Figure 10.9 shows several examples.

Besides uploading files, you will of course use FTP to download files.

You may be working on a Web site on a remote machine and need to download copies of HTML pages and graphics from that machine. Another common situation would be to use FTP to download the source code for software you want to install (see Chapter 13, "Installing Software from Source Code").

Software is available for download from many publicly accessible FTP servers. Public FTP servers differ from servers on which you have an account (with a user name and password) in that they allow you to log in using the special user name "anonymous" and to use your email address as a password. Generally speaking, you cannot upload files to these "anonymous FTP servers," but you can download files from them.

Often the easiest way to download files from anonymous FTP servers is to use a GUI tool such as a Web browser or the `curl` or `wget` command (covered later in this chapter). But it is also useful to know how to do it the "old-school" way with a command-line FTP client. You will often be given the location of a file to download as an FTP URL—that is, a URL that starts with ftp://. **Figure 10.10** shows how to extract the hostname, directory, and filename from an FTP URL like this:

```
ftp://ftp.gnu.org/gnu/hello/hello-2.1.
→1.tar.gz
```

Refer to **Figure 10.11** throughout the following task. The steps are almost identical to those in the task of uploading a file.

```
ftp> ? ascii
ascii          set ascii transfer type
ftp> ? as
ascii          set ascii transfer type
ftp> ? lcd
lcd            change local working directory
ftp> ? pwd
pwd            print working directory on remote machine
ftp> ? umask
umask          get (set) umask on remote side
ftp>
```

Figure 10.9 Getting one-line descriptions of individual FTP commands.

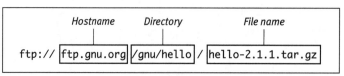

Figure 10.10 Extracting the hostname, directory, and filename from an FTP URL.

```
[localhost:~] vanilla% ftp ftp.gnu.org
Connected to ftp.gnu.org.
220 GNU FTP server ready.
Name (ftp.gnu.org:vanilla): anonymous
331 Please specify the password.
Password:
230-If you have any problems with the GNU software or its downloading,
230-please refer your questions to <gnu@gnu.org>.
230-
((output abbreviated))
230-The FSF provides this archive as a service to GNU users.  Please
230-consider donating to the FSF at http://donate.fsf.org/.
230 Login successful. Have fun.
Remote system type is UNIX.
Using binary mode to transfer files.
ftp> cd /gnu/hello
250 Directory successfully changed.
ftp> ls
200 PORT command successful. Consider using PASV.
150 Here comes the directory listing.
-rw-r-r-    1 0        0            16452 Sep 17  1992 hello-1.0-1.1.diff.gz
-rw-r-r-    1 0        0            25676 May 22  1993 hello-1.1-1.2.diff.gz
-rw-r-r-    1 0        0             2919 May 23  1993 hello-1.2-1.3.diff.gz
-rw-r-r-    1 0        0            87942 May 23  1993 hello-1.3.tar.gz
-rw-r-r-    1 0        0             2020 Jun 09 06:31 hello-2.1.0-2.1.1.diff.gz
-rw-r-r-    1 0        0           389049 Jun 09 07:54 hello-2.1.0.tar.gz
-rw-r-r-    1 0        0           389363 Jun 09 06:33 hello-2.1.1.tar.gz
-rw-r-r-    1 0        0             1936 Jun 09 07:55 index.html
226 Directory send OK.
ftp> hash
Hash mark printing on (1024 bytes/hash mark).
ftp> get hello-2.1.1.tar.gz
local: hello-2.1.1.tar.gz remote: hello-2.1.1.tar.gz
200 PORT command successful. Consider using PASV.
150 Opening BINARY mode data connection for hello-2.1.1.tar.gz (389363 bytes).
################################################################################
################################################################################
################################################################################
#######################################################################
226 File send OK.
389363 bytes received in 5.65 seconds (68935 bytes/s)
ftp> quit
221 Goodbye.
[localhost:~] vanilla%
```

Figure 10.11 Downloading a file with FTP.

To download a file using FTP:

1. `ftp hostname`

   This step is exactly the same as in uploading. You are simply connecting to the remote machine.

2. Enter a user name.

   If you have an account on the remote machine, then use it. If your remote user name is the same as your local user name, just press Return; otherwise, type in your remote user name.

   If you are logging in to an anonymous FTP server, use the special user name "anonymous."

   The server prompts you for a password.

3. Enter your password.

   If you are logging in to a machine on which you have an account, enter the password. If you are logging in to an anonymous FTP server, enter your email address.

   The server shows a status message (which has been abbreviated in Figure 10.11) and then an `ftp>` prompt.

4. You now change the directory to find the file you want to download:

   `cd directory`

   Using the example from Figures 10.10 and 10.11, the command would be

   `cd /gnu/hello`

   The server gives you a status message and another prompt.

5. `ls`

   Listing the contents of the current directory (on the remote machine) verifies that the file you want is really there (Figure 10.11).

6. You are now ready to download the file, but first you can tell the server to create a progress indicator during file transfers so

that you can see something happening while transferring a large file:

`hash`

The `hash` command toggles the file-transfer progress indicator, which means that if it was off (the default), it is turned on, and if it was on, it is turned off.

7. Now you give the command to copy the file to your machine:

   `get filename`

   In the example, the filename is `hello-2.1.1.tar.gz`, so the command is

   `get hello-2.1.1.tar.gz`

   This copies the file to the current directory on the local machine and gives it the same name. If for some reason you want the copy to have a different name, you can type

   `get currentname newname`

   The file transfer takes place, and because you turned on the `hash` command earlier, you see a series of hash marks (#), one for each 1024 bytes transferred. When the transfer is complete, the server gives you a status message and the total number of bytes copied. You then get another prompt.

   If you have more files to transfer, you can do that, and when you are done, you quit the FTP program.

8. `quit`

   This quits the FTP program and takes you back to your shell.

✔ Tips

- Many anonymous FTP servers permit the shorter user name "ftp" instead of "anonymous."

- You don't really need to enter your email address—the server doesn't check it. But it is a courtesy to let the administrators know who is using the resources they are providing free of charge to the world.

Retrieving files using curl

Mac OS X includes the curl command which allows you to retrieve (and in some cases send) files from servers using several of the common Internet protocols (for example HTTP and FTP).

To retrieve a web page using curl:

◆ curl *url*

For example:

curl http://www.matisse.net/files/
→glossary.html

fetches the page and puts the result on the screen.

✔ Tips:

■ To save the output of curl to a file, use redirection:

curl *url* > *file*

■ The curl command has many options. It is designed to be used in scripts without any live human interaction. All of these capabilities make it a bit complex, but powerful. See man curl for the Unix man page.

Retrieving files using wget

Yet another useful command-line tool for retrieving files is the wget command. In our opinion, wget is much easier to use than the curl command described above, especially for retrieving Web pages complete with images and other pages linked into the page.

Wget takes a URL as an argument and acts like a Web browser. It fetches the file indicated by the URL and saves it to disk. In addition, if the file is an HTML page with links, wget is smart enough to fetch all the associated pages and images and save them to disk as well, giving you a complete local copy of the Web site.

Wget does not come with Mac OS X. It is pretty easy to install, though, using the Fink program described in Chapter 13, "Installing Software from Source Code."

To fetch a file using wget:

◆ wget *url*

where *url* is any valid URL using the HTTP or FTP. (The wget-ssl program supports HTTPS as well.) For example, the following are all valid command lines:

wget http://www.matisse.net/files/
→glossary.html

wget ftp://ftp.gnu.org/gnu/hello/
→hello-2.1.1.tar.gz

Either of those command lines saves the requested file in the current directory on your machine. The file will have the same name as the remote version (glossary. html or hello-2.1.1.tar.gz in the examples above). **Figure 10.12** shows an example of retrieving an HTML page using wget.

✔ Tip

■ Be very careful using the –recursive option (see **Table 10.3**), because you can end up downloading hundreds of files.

Table 10.3

Options for the wget Command

There are many more options. These are just a few to whet your appetite.

OPTION	MEANING
–recursive	Follows links in the URL and downloads the pages and images found. Wget normally follows links five levels deep. Wget creates a directory on your machine that has the same name as the domain name in the URL, and the saved files will all be inside that directory.
–level=depth	Used with –recursive. For example, –level=2 instructs wget to follow links for only two levels (the original page and its links), and links in the following pages).
–convert-links	After downloading, converts links in documents for local viewing. This will mean converting all the links in the pages so that they work properly when you view the pages in a browser from your disk (as opposed to viewing them from the remote site).

```
[localhost:~] vanilla% wget http://www.matisse.net/files/glossary.html
–15:47:20–  http://www.matisse.net/files/glossary.html
           => `glossary.html'
Resolving www.matisse.net... done.
Connecting to www.matisse.net[66.47.69.194]:80... connected.
HTTP request sent, awaiting response... 200 OK
Length: 77,217 [text/html]

100%[====================================================>] 77,217          9.20M/s    ETA 00:00

15:47:20 (9.20 MB/s) - `glossary.html' saved [77217/77217]
[localhost:~] vanilla%
```

Figure 10.12 Using wget to download an HTML page.

Synchronizing directories using rsync

The rsync command is used to make a directory on one machine identical to a directory on another machine. A very sweet feature of rsync is that it is fast—it only sends the differences between the directories across the network. So if you have already synchronized a directory and a few of the files have changed by the time you run rsync again on that directory, then only the new portions of the changed files get sent across the network. You can read about the algorithm used by rsync at http://rsync.samba.org.

Furthermore, rsync can use SSH to connect between machines, so the entire process uses an encrypted connection.

When you use rsync to synchronize directories, you give it a source directory and a destination directory. Rsync compares the source and destination directories file by file and sends the files required to make sure the destination has all the files that are in the source directory. The following tasks refers to **Figure 10.13**.

```
[localhost:~/Sites] vanilla% rsync -e ssh -avz images puffball@somewhere.us:webdocs
rsync: open connection using ssh -l puffball somewhere.us rsync —server -vlogDtprz . webdocs
puffball@somewhere.us password:
rsync: building file list...
rsync: 4 files to consider.
images/
images/apache_pb.gif
images/macosxlogo.gif
images/web_share.gif
images/
wrote 16210 bytes  read 64 bytes  10849.33 bytes/sec
total size is 18525  speedup is 1.14
[localhost:~/Sites] vanilla%
```

Figure 10.13 Using rsync with a local directory as the source directory.

To synchronize using a local directory as the source:

1. `rsync -e ssh -avz source_dir`
   `→user@host:remote_dir`

   For example,

   `rsync -e ssh -avz images puffball@`
   `→somewhere.us:webdocs`

   The `-e ssh` option tells `rsync` to use `-e ssh` to make an *encrypted* connection as user puffball to `somewhere.us`. The specification for the destination directory uses the same format as `scp` (described earlier in this chapter).

   You will be prompted for a password just as with SSH (because you are in fact using SSH).

2. Enter your password.

   Your password is not displayed.

   Table 10.4 explains the `-a`, `-v`, and `-z` options, and a few others.

   The source directory will be the directory called images. It is important that you understand the difference between

   `images`

   and

   `images/`

   "Images/" means "the contents of the images directory," while "`images`" means "the images directory itself." Usually you will *not* put the / at the end of the source directory.

Table 10.4

Some Options for rsync

As always, see the man page for the complete list.

OPTION	USE/MEANING
-a	Archive mode. This recursively copies subdirectories and will preserve permissions and file-modification times. Actually a shortcut for the seven options rlptgoD. See man rysnc for the meanings of all seven options.
-v	Verbose mode. Rsync gives more information during transfer.
-z	Uses compression. Makes transfer of most files faster.
-e ssh	Uses SSH to make an encrypted connection.
-n	Stands for not really. Rsync will show you what it would do, but will not actually transfer anything. Very useful for testing with the -delete option (below).
-delete	Deletes files on the destination side that do not exist on the source side. Be very careful with this one. Try it with the -n option first to see what would be deleted.
-u	Updates. Skips files that already exist on the destination side and have a date later then the source side. Only files on the source side that are newer than the destination side are sent.
-r	Recursive mode. Copies everything inside the source directory.
-l	Copies symbolic links as symbolic links (instead of the files they point to).
-p	Preserves permissions.
-t	Preserves modification times.

Rsync will use SSH to connect to the host somewhere.us as the user puffball.

The destination directory is the `webdocs` directory inside puffball's home directory. Rsync will copy the source directory into the destination directory.

Taking the example from Figure 10.13 further, if you were to add one image to the local directory, **Figure 10.14** shows what you would see at the command line.

If you were then to add a file to the local images directory (for example, adding a file called `dancer.jpg`) and make a change to one other file (for example, changing `web_share.gif`), and were to repeat the `rsync` command, you would get something like Figure 10.14, in which `rsync` only sends the changed files across the network.

```
[localhost:~/Sites] vanilla% rsync -e ssh -avz images puffball@somewhere.us:webdocs
rsync: open connection using ssh -l puffball somewhere.us rsync —server -vlogDtprz . webdocs
puffball@somewhere.us password:
rsync: building file list...
rsync: 5 files to consider.
images/
images/dancer.jpg
images/web_share.gif
images/
wrote 88304 bytes   read 168 bytes   58981.33 bytes/sec
total size is 94385   speedup is 1.70
[localhost:~/Sites] vanilla%
```

Figure 10.14 Re-synchronizing a directory with `rsync`. Note that only two files are updated.

The process of synchronizing works both ways—you can use a remote directory as the source.

To synchronize using a remote directory as the source:

1. `sync -e ssh -avz` *user@host:remote_dir*
   →*destination*

   You are prompted for a password.

2. Enter your password.

   The positions of the source and destination directories are simply reversed.

   For example,

   `rsync -e ssh -avz puffball@somewhere.`
   →`us:webdocs/images Sites`

   That source directory is the `webdocs/images` directory inside puffball's home directory on the host `somewhere.us`, and the destination directory is the Sites directory in your current directory.

   Figure 10.15 shows what this looks like at the command line.

   So the result transfers to `Sites/images` the same files as those in the remote `webdocs/images` directory.

✔ Tip

■ You can safely experiment with **rsync** by using the -n (*not really*) option. Rsync will show you what it would have done, but will not actually transfer, delete, or overwrite any files.

```
[localhost:~] vanilla% rsync -e ssh -avz puffball@somewhere.us:webdocs/images Sites
rsync: open connection using ssh -l pufball somw rsync —server —sender -vlogDtprz . webdocs/images
puffball@somewhere.us password:
receiving file list ... done
images/
images/flower.gif
wrote 32 bytes   read 3077 bytes   6218.00 bytes/sec
total size is 97294   speedup is 31.29
[localhost:~] vanilla%
```

Figure 10.15 Using `rsync` with a remote directory as the source directory.

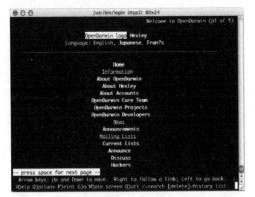

Figure 10.16 lynx display of www.opendarwin.org/

Using lynx—a text-based Web browser

Why use a text-based Web browser, you ask? Well, it is faster than a GUI Web browser (no pictures!), and it provides a convenient way to view and download files from other machines while staying at the command line.

The lynx Web browser handles HTTP, FTP, gopher, and other protocols. Lynx does not come with Mac OS X but is easily installed using the Fink program as described in Chapter 13, "Installing Software from Source Code."

Lynx is a full-screen command-line program, which means that like the vi editor, it takes over the whole Terminal window.

To start lynx:

◆ lynx *URL*

   For example:

   lynx http://www.opendarwin.org/

   Figure 10.16 is a screen shot showing the lynx display of www.opendarwin.org/.

To navigate in lynx:

1. Use the down arrow key to select the next link.

2. Use the up arrow key to select the previous link.

3. Press ⟨Return⟩ to follow the currently selected link.

4. Use the left arrow key to go back to a previous page (like the Back button in a GUI Web browser).

5. Use the right arrow key to go forward after having used the left arrow key to go back to a previous page (like the Forward button in a GUI Web browser).

6. Press the [Spacebar] to scroll down in the current page.

7. Use [-] (a hyphen) to scroll back in the current page.

8. Use [H] to get the lynx help screen.

   Remember that you can use the left arrow key to go back to previously viewed pages.

9. Use [Esc] to quit lynx.

To use lynx to fetch a URL and save the result to a file:

◆ lynx -dump *url* > *file*

   For example,

   lynx -dump ftp://ftp.gnu.org/gnu/
   →hello/hello-2.1.1.tar.gz > hello.
   →tar.gz

   fetches the file hello-2.1.1.tar.gz and saves it as hello.tar.gz.

   lynx -dump http://www.matisse.net/
   →files/glossary.html > glossary

   fetches the file glossary.html and saves it as glossary. Note that the HTML file is saved as a plain-text file, with the HTML formatting already processed by lynx, so that the resulting file can be read by humans. If you want to preserve the raw HTML codes, add the -source option:

   lynx -dump -source
   http://www.matisse.net/files/
   →glossary.html > glossary

More Advanced Interactions

As you probably have guessed, this chapter has only covered the most common ways of interacting with other machines over networks.

As you become more proficient using Unix, you may wish to tackle more advanced forms of interaction with other machines—for example, creating scripts to perform unattended copying of files, or setting up virtual private networks.

In this section we'll give you some pointers about where you can find information to take you further along the Unix path.

Automated (unattended) file transfers

To perform unattended file transfers, you need to learn about creating scripts (review Chapter 9, "Creating and Using Scripts") and to become familiar with one or more of the file cross-network copying tools, such as scp or rsync. Because you are likely to do your file transfer using an encrypted connection, you will also want to learn more about SSH.

Here are some resources to use in building up your knowledge and skills:

◆ Chapter 9, "Creating and Using Scripts."

◆ For more on scripts, try these two books:

Learn the bash Shell, 2nd Edition, by Cameron Newham and Bill Rosenblatt (O'Reilly; www.oreilly.com/catalog/bash2/).

and

Using csh & tcsh, by Paul DuBois (O'Reilly; www.oreilly.com/catalog/tcsh/).

◆ The man pages for rsync, scp, sftp, and SSH.

◆ To learn more about SSH, we recommend OpenSSH (www.openssh.org), which has the addresses of email discussion lists (www.openssh.org/list.html). Start by subscribing to the general list, and read it for a while before asking questions.

Virtual private networks

If you have a private network you wish to connect to another private network (perhaps you have a company with offices in two or more cities), you can lease private lines connecting the offices to create one larger network (or *internetwork*). You can also connect the separate private networks through the public Internet using encrypted connections, creating a virtual private network (VPN).

Here are some resources to use in learning more about VPNs and how to set them up:

◆ vpnd—The Virtual Private Network Daemon (http://sunsite.dk/vpnd/).

◆ The Internet Connect application included with Mac OS X allows you to connect to a VPN.

Sharing disks with other Unix machines

The Network File System (NFS) protocol is the Unix way of doing what AppleShare does in the traditional Macintosh world—it allows machines to mount disks on other machines over networks.

The Webmin system, which we'll describe in Chapter 11, "Introduction to System Administration," may be used to configure NFS. You can find a shareware GUI tool designed to configure NFS on Mac OS X at MBS's NFS-Manager page (www.bresink.de/osx/NFSManager.html).

INTRODUCTION TO SYSTEM ADMINISTRATION

System administration is the job of keeping a system up and running, and providing a suitable environment for whatever work the system is doing—whether it's serving Web pages, being used for software development, or acting as a workgroup file server.

Most Mac OS X users are working on single-user desktop machines, but some of you are stepping out into the strange new world of running a multiuser system. Perhaps you're giving friends accounts on your machine so they can ssh in and edit Web pages, or running a mail server with accounts for dozens of colleagues. If this is the case, you have fallen into what may seem like the rabbit hole of system administration, where everything appears strange. This chapter will help you transcend that complexity and become the author of your own Wonderland, where in our world—the Unix world—you will be known as a *sysadmin*.

You are starting to be concerned about backing up your users' data (at least you should be concerned about it!), managing users' accounts and permissions on the system, and troubleshooting problems for other people.

In this chapter we will give you a whirlwind tour of the basic elements of system administration. We're sure the information here will provide a good basis for learning even more as your skills and interest grow.

Almost all of the tasks in this chapter require that you log in as an admin user. Admin users are specific to Mac OS X and are accounts that have been set to "allow user to administer this computer" when the account was created (see "Adding and deleting users with the System Preferences application" later in this chapter). Mac OS X admin users have a very powerful capacity—a capacity known in the wider Unix world as "having root." That is, they have the ability to execute any command on the system with the privileges of the all-powerful root account. The first thing a system administrator needs to learn about is the power of root.

About root

The traditional Unix approach to system administration makes heavy use of one highly privileged account: root. Every Unix system has a root account.

The root account is not limited by the permissions or ownership settings of any file on the system, so root can edit, delete, rename, move, and otherwise mess with every file on the system. Most basic system processes run as the root user so that they can access any part of the disk and so other users cannot interfere with them.

Protection of the root password is critical to system security. The root account is all-powerful. There is no way to stop the root account from altering anything on the system.

To maintain the highest level of system security, access to root must be limited to the smallest possible number of people, and the power of root should be used only when strictly necessary.

The root account is often referred to as the *super user,* and Unix veterans have been known to refer to all non-root accounts as "mere mortals." Determining whether the seemingly all-powerful root is God or the Devil, and how they differ, is left as a theological exercise for the reader.

Because the directories and files that contain system software and configuration settings can only be changed by the root user, most system-administration tasks must be performed by the root account.

On most Unix systems, an administrator uses the root account in one of two ways:

◆ By logging in as the root user. This method is often disabled, however, in which case the next method is required.

◆ By logging in as a "regular" user and then switching to the root account with the **su** command (su stands for *substitute user identity* and is described later in this chapter).

Many systems do not allow the root account to log in directly; those systems require that an administrator use the second method. That way only someone who knows the password to a regular account as well as the root password is able to run commands as root.

The Mac OS X approach to root

Mac OS X is designed to reduce to an absolute minimum the situations in which users execute commands as root, while still giving users full control over their machines and allowing them to perform any needed system-administration tasks.

As long as you stick to the Aqua GUI, you never come across "root." Instead, a part of the operating system called the Authentication Manager occasionally prompts you to enter the name and password of an admin user before completing a task that modifies a part of the file system outside your home directory, such as installing software.

But if you use the command line, the situation is different. Unlike Mac OS X, command-line programs that require root privileges almost never prompt you for a password—they simply fail if they are not executed by root. So at the command line you must know in advance that what you are about to do requires root, and take some action to "become root" before executing certain commands, such as changing a user's password or installing software.

Sudo—the Mac OS X way of using root

Mac OS X ships with the root account disabled, and unless you enable it (see "To run any command line as root," below), you can neither log in as root nor use the **su** command to assume the root identity. Instead, Mac OS X uses the **sudo** command (for *super-user do*) to provide root access at the command line.

Every time someone uses **sudo**, a record of what that user did is added to the system log file, /var/log/system.log.

The **sudo** command itself is not unique to Mac OS X—it is used on many Unix systems. But in Mac OS X, it is normally the *only* way to use root from the command line. In this system, no one has the root password, but instead anyone who is an admin user is a member of the admin group, and anyone in group admin can use **sudo** to execute any

Problems with the Mac OS X Approach to root

The way Mac OS X allows root access is fine if your Mac OS X machine is being used only by you and perhaps a couple of trusted family members and friends, and if it's not on a publicly accessible network.

On the other hand, if your machine is used by many people, especially by people you don't know, or if it's connected to the Internet on a full-time basis, then Apple's approach to root access could be considered problematic.

On most modern Unix systems, in order for users to operate as root, they have to have two passwords: their own (that is, the one they log in with) and the root password (the one they can only use after having logged in as themselves).

The Mac OS X approach requires only that a user know his or her own password to gain root privileges. As long as that user is an admin user, his or her account can perform any command as root without having to know any other password.

Compounding the problem (only needing one password instead of two) is the fact

that the **nidump** command can be used by any user to reveal the encrypted passwords of all users. The encryption used is fairly weak, and poor passwords (those based on words or that use simple patterns) can be cracked in a matter of days or hours on modern machines. (Apple knows this is a problem and is planning to fix it.)

The Mac OS X approach is easier on the user—there's only one password to remember, and for people using their Mac OS X machine as an isolated desktop machine, this is probably fine. However, if the computer is a true multiuser machine in a networked environment—used the way Unix was intended—the wisdom of this approach is debatable.

One measure you should take is to ensure that the password for any admin user is a good one (see the sidebar "Choosing a Safer Password").

Perhaps in future versions of Mac OS X, admin users will be divided into groups with different levels of access to root, but at present (version 10.2), any admin user is essentially equivalent to root.

command as root. (Review Chapter 8, "Working with Permissions and Ownership," to learn about groups.)

The sudo command is supposed to allow specific users or groups of users to execute specific commands with the power of root. The sudo command has a configuration file (see man sudoers) that lists who can perform which commands as root.

The idea behind sudo is that a trusted user or group of users can be given the ability to run specific commands, such as restarting a Web server if it crashes.

In Mac OS X, sudo is configured so that any user in group admin can execute *any* command with the power of root. The first account you created (perhaps it is the only account you created) on your Mac OS X system is always in group admin. If you are using a Mac OS X system set up by someone else, then your account may not be in group admin. In order to perform the tasks in this chapter, you need to ask whomever administers your system (that would be the system administrator!) to allow you to be an admin user. Only admin users are supposed to perform system-administration tasks on Mac OS X.

The most common way you use the sudo command is to run a command line as root.

To run any command line as root:

1. sudo *commandline*

   commandline can be any command line. For example,

   sudo du -sk /Users/*

   runs the du command (for *disk usage*) and shows a summary (-s) of how much disk space is being used (in kilobytes because of the k option) by each directory in the /Users directory, effectively showing every user's disk usage. You could not do this without being root, because many of the files in each user's directory are not readable by other regular users. When the command is run by the root user, it can read the size of every file and produce a complete report (**Figure 11.1**).

   As you can see, the first time you use sudo, unusual messages appear. You receive a little lecture on the use of root, and then sudo prompts you for your password.

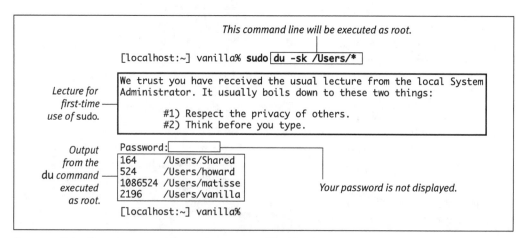

Figure 11.1 Using the sudo command to execute a command line as root.

Table 11.1

Common Options for sudo

Remember to see the man page for the complete list.

Option	Meaning/Use
-l	Lists the allowed and forbidden commands for the current user. This is a good way of seeing what you can (and can't) do with sudo.
-k	Kills the 5-minute grace period. Sudo requires a password on the next use, no matter how soon it is.
-K	Removes the time-stamp directory entirely. Next time you use sudo, you get the lecture again.
-u *user*	Runs the command line as user instead of as root.
-s	Gives you a root shell. Very dangerous. *Every* command you enter until you exit the new shell is run as root. Uses the shell in the SHELL environment variable if it is set; otherwise, uses the user's default shell.
-H	Sets the HOME environment variable to the home directory of the user whose identity sudo takes on (default is root). Normally sudo does not change the HOME variable.

More About sudo

The sudo command has an entire Web site devoted to it: Sudo Main Page (www.sudo.ws). There you can learn the whole story of how it can be used, find security alerts, peruse a troubleshooting FAQ list, and more.

2. Enter your password.

If this is the first time you have used sudo, then sudo creates a directory named after your user name in /var/run/sudo/ (for example, /var/run/sudo/vanilla).

Each time you use sudo, it checks the modification time on that directory. If the modification time is more than 5 minutes old, you are prompted for your password again to make sure that you haven't walked away from your keyboard, allowing someone else to try to use sudo.

Your password is not displayed as you type it.

Once sudo accepts your password, it executes the command line you gave it and updates the modification time on your directory in /var/run/sudo.

✔ Tips

- You can force sudo to ask for a password (overriding the 5-minute time period) with

  sudo -k

- The 5-minute grace period can be modified with the visudo command (see "Configuring sudo," below). See **Table 11.1** for a summary of the options for sudo.

Configuring sudo

To configure sudo, you need to edit a configuration file named /etc/sudoers.

Apple provides a special command, visudo, for editing the sudoers file. Visudo not only invokes the vi editor (hence the vi in the command name), it also makes sure that you are the only one editing the file and performs a syntax check on the file before saving it. This last feature is invaluable and prevents you from accidentally disabling the sudo system with a mistake in the configuration file.

Before proceeding, make sure you are comfortable editing files. (If necessary, review Chapter 6, "Editing and Printing Files," to learn how to use the vi editor.)

To edit the sudo configuration with visudo:

1. `sudo visudo`

   If you are prompted for your password, enter it. You then find yourself in the vi editor.

2. Make changes to the configuration.

   Figure 11.2 lists a few common configuration entries for the sudoers file. The man page for the sudoers file (`man sudoers`) lists all the possibilities, which are quite extensive.

   For example, to change the grace period for not having to reenter your password for multiple uses of sudo from 5 minutes to 7 minutes, add this line:

   `Defaults  timestamp_timeout = 7`

   After making your changes, save your work.

3. `Esc`

   gets you back to command mode.

continues on page 310

Compare with Aqua

In its graphical interface, Mac OS X uses an approach very much like the one used with sudo. Whenever you use Aqua to attempt a change that requires root access (for example, installing system software using the Software Update command), the GUI prompts you for an administrator name and password.

There is a big difference between the GUI and the command line in this case, however: The GUI "knows" when something must be done by root and prompts you, and it does not provide a way to run arbitrary programs as root. The command line, on the other hand, leaves it all up to you—if you try to perform an action with insufficient privileges, you get an error, and by using sudo you can run any command as root. This is very much in the Unix spirit of not trying (or bothering) to protect you from yourself. Unix expects you to avoid doing foolish things because you know you haven't learned how yet, not because it prevents you from trying.

How sudo Makes Command Names Case-Insensitive

When you execute a command using sudo, the command name is not case-sensitive. So,

`sudo DATE`

and

`sudo date`

do the same thing. This has to do with a combination of how sudo looks up command names and the peculiarities of the Mac file system.

As we discussed in Chapter 5, "Using Files and Directories," the standard Mac file system is a "case-preserving, case-insensitive"

file system. In some cases in Mac OS X, then, you can ignore case when specifying file and command names. But do not rely upon it. The default shell tcsh is case-sensitive in the way it looks up command and filenames, while the bash and Bourne shells are not. The sudo command, however, uses a way of finding command names that isn't case-sensitive. So if you are using tcsh, then

`sudo DATE`

works, but

`SUDO date`

does not.

```
# Lines beginning with # are comments
# Examples of valid entries for the sudoers file.
# ALWAYS use the visudo command to edit the file.

# You can change the default for a number of things

# Change the timeout period for entering a password
#
Defaults  timestamp_timeout = 7

# Cause all uses of sudo to be logged to a file
#
Defaults  logfile = /var/log/sudo.log

# Specify address to send error and warning email to. Default is root.
# Address should be enclosed in "quotes"
#
Defaults  mailto = "somebody@somehost.com"



# The message displayed if a user enters the wrong password.
# Default is "Sorry, try again."
#
Defaults badpass_message = "Bad password. Check CAPS LOCK key and try again."

# User privilege specification. Format is:
#    user HOST=(RUN AS USER) command
# The host part is there to allow the same configuration file to
# be used on many machines. In your case this should be (ALL)

# user root on any machine can run as (any user), any coomand
#
root    ALL=(ALL) ALL

# Users in group admin on any machine can run as any user, any command
#
%admin  ALL=(ALL) ALL

# User vanilla on any machine can run only the du command.
# The default is to run the command as root when using sudo.
#
vanilla ALL=/usr/bin/du

# User vanilla can run any command located in /Users/puffball/bin/
# and when they do it will be run as user puffball.
vanilla ALL=(puffball) /Users/puffball/bin/
```

Figure 11.2 Examples of sudo configuration entries. Always use the visudo command to enter or change these.

4. `:w`

saves your changes. Then quit from `vi`.

5. `:q`

`Visudo` checks that your changes do not have any syntax errors. If all is well, you are returned to a shell prompt.

If you mess up, `visudo` gives you a warning as shown in **Figure 11.3**.

Pressing (Return) gives you a list of choices as shown in **Figure 11.4**.

Type either *e* to edit the file again or *x* to exit without saving changes. *Do not ever* select Q unless you are absolutely positive you know what you are doing. These options only appear when errors occur, so you don't want to save them.

✔ Tips

- If you would like to use a more restrictive policy than allowing any admin user to use `sudo`, then "comment out" the

  `%admin ALL=(ALL) ALL`

  line. (To "comment out" a chunk of code means to turn it into a comment; in this case it means adding the # character to the beginning of the line. That way, the commented-out code remains available for inspection or reactivation, but it is not executed.) If you do this, you should *first* enable the root account (see the next section) and learn how to use the `su` command to become root (see "Becoming Another User," below) You can also enable only specific users to use `sudo`.

- If you want to use a different editor (for example, `emacs`), you can set your `EDITOR` environment variable accordingly. For example, if your `EDITOR` environment variable is set to `emacs`, then `visudo` uses `emacs` instead of `vi`. (Review Chapter 7, "Configuring Your Unix Environment," to learn how to set environment variables.)

Other ways of becoming root

Although using `sudo` will probably handle all the things you need to do as root from the command line, this wouldn't be Unix if there weren't other ways to do it. Besides, you may come across a situation in which using `sudo` doesn't achieve what you need. So here are a couple of more ways to become root. We're not including these so much for you to use them as for you to know what is possible.

The default configuration for Mac OS X has the root account disabled—you cannot use the `su` command to assume the root account's identity, nor can you log in to Aqua as root, nor can you log in to the machine over the Internet as root (using `ssh`, for example; see Chapter 10, "Interacting with Other Unix Machines"). Once you enable the root account, you can do all of these.

Darwin and thus Mac OS X use a database of user and system information called NetInfo, derived from the NeXT operating system. You'll be using the NetInfo Manager application to enable the root account.

```
>>> sudoers file: syntax error, line 9 <<<
What now?
```

Figure 11.3 Output from `visudo` asking you how to proceed after it has detected a syntax error in the file you edited.

```
Options are:
  (e)dit sudoers file again
  e(x)it without saving changes to sudoers file
  (Q)uit and save changes to sudoers file
(DANGER!)

What now?
```

Figure 11.4 Output from `visudo` listing the options available after it has detected a syntax error.

All Unix machines have ways of keeping track of the users and system resources (such as printers). Darwin uses a different approach than most other varieties of Unix. The Darwin method uses a software system called NetInfo. NetInfo works like a database that other programs on your machine use to get information about users and system resources.

Darwin includes a collection of command-line tools for using the NetInfo database; Mac OS X also provides a GUI application (NetInfo Manager) for working with NetInfo.

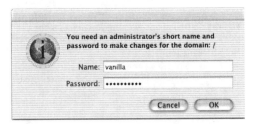

Figure 11.5 Dialog box in NetInfo Manager asking you to authenticate as an administrative user.

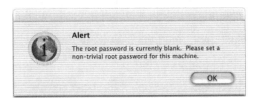

Figure 11.6 Pop-up window warning you that the root password is blank.

Figure 11.7 Dialog box for setting the root password in NetInfo Manager.

To enable the root account:

1. Launch NetInfo Manager by opening Utilities > Applications.

   (You could open it from the command line with

   ```
   open "/Applications/Utilities
   →/NetInfoManager.app/Contents/MacOS/
   →NetInfo Manager"
   ```

   but that's an awfully long path to type.)

2. Authenticate as an Admin user.

   Either click on the lock icon at the bottom left of the window or select "Authenticate..." from the Security menu.

   A dialog box pops up with your short user name filled in (**Figure 11.5**).

3. Enter your password.

   You have now been authenticated to NetInfo Manager as an admin user. This is akin to authenticating with **sudo**. When using Aqua, it is the one case where you initiate the authentication process instead of being prompted by the system when it thinks you need administrative (root) privileges to proceed.

   Now you can go ahead and enable the root account.

4. From the Security menu, choose the Enable Root Account option.

   Another window appears (**Figure 11.6**). The root account doesn't have a password yet.

5. Click OK.

   A dialog box where you can set the root password appears (**Figure 11.7**).

6. Enter a password for the root account.

   Excellent passwords are critical to system security. Just as your own password could be used (via the **sudo** command) to gain control of the system, the root password

   continues on next page

ABOUT ROOT

is a key to the palace. See the sidebar "Choosing a Safer Password."

The password is not displayed as you type it (a series of bullets is displayed instead).

7. Click OK.

To confirm what you typed, a dialog box appears, asking you to reenter the new root password (**Figure 11.8**).

8. Enter the root password again, and click Verify.

The root account is now enabled. NetInfo Manager removes your authentication privileges to prevent you from accidentally making other changes. A warning dialog box telling you this appears (**Figure 11.9**).

9. Click OK.

10. Quit NetInfo Manager.

You can now log in to your machine as root either over the network or in Aqua.

One other way to become root in Mac OS X is to boot the machine in single-user mode. Most Unix systems have a way of allowing you to start up in a manner that prevents any other user from logging in, and that logs you in automatically as root.

Figure 11.8 Dialog box for confirming the root password in NetInfo Manager.

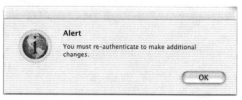

Figure 11.9 Dialog box warning you that you must reauthenticate if you wish to make further changes in NetInfo Manager.

Choosing a Safer Password

Choosing a password means choosing a mixture of letters, numbers, and punctuation marks that do not include a dictionary word. For example, *secret23* would be a terrible password, far too easy for a computerized guessing program to figure out.

One way to make a good password is to use the first letter from each word in a song lyric or poem, and change some of the characters to numbers and punctuation. For example, the lyric "Sporting 50-dollar sneakers and all

the money's spent" (from Grandmaster Flash's "All Wrapped Up") might become the password *S50$s&atm*.

In addition to the root password, all user passwords, especially those for admin users, must also be excellent in order for your system to have good security. In Mac OS X, having an admin user's password is equivalent to having the root password. (We'll go into more security for choosing good passwords in Chapter 12, "Security.")

ABOUT ROOT

Using the System in Single-User Mode

If you want to use the system in this state, you run the command line

```
/sbin/mount -uw /
```

This mounts the system disk in read/write mode. And then enter

```
/sbin/SystemStarter
```

To learn more about SystemStarter, which handles startup items, see the Boot Sequence section of Apple's Mac OS X Developer Documentation (http://developer.apple.com/techpubs/macosx/Essentials/SystemOverview/Booting Login/The_Boot_Sequence.html).

Typically, the operating system is only partly operational at this point. For example, networking has not been initiated, so you cannot yet interact with other machines. You are in a text-only environment—no GUI, no mouse, only white text on a black background. This is really a tool that enables advanced users to tackle troubleshooting and advanced system maintenance. But in the spirit of telling you the whole story, and trusting that you won't try this on a machine you depend on, here's how to boot into single-user mode.

To boot into single-user mode:

◆ Hold down ⟨Cmd⟩ and ⟨S⟩ while the machine is starting up. This can be during a restart or a start from a complete shutdown.

After 5 to 15 seconds, the screen should turn black, and white text should start to appear. You can release the keys at this point.

Diagnostic information appears on the screen, eventually ending with a prompt that says simply

```
localhost #
```

You are now logged in as root, and the machine is in single-user mode.

Most of the command-line tools are available at this point.

You should *not* do this on a machine that has critical data or applications. Experiment, by all means, but only on a machine whose operating system you don't mind reinstalling if things go wrong.

◆ To reboot into normal, multiuser mode, type

```
reboot
```

ABOUT ROOT

Becoming Another User

As we mentioned above, on most Unix systems, a system administrator uses the root account by invoking the **su** command to *substitute* the root account's identity for his or her own.

If you have enabled the root account on Mac OS X, then admin users may use the **su** command to assume the root account's identity. (Technically, any user with group permissions may use **su** to assume the root identity. Making someone an admin user puts him or her in the admin group as well.)

The **su** command allows you to temporarily assume the identity of another user on the system. Therefore, administrators can log in to the system as themselves, "su to root," perform whatever tasks need to be done as root, and then exit from the **su** session and reassume their own identities.

You can also use the **su** command to switch to users other than root, which is useful if you want to test a configuration for another user, or run a particular command as another user without bothering to actually log in as that user.

Refer to **Figure 11.10** through the following task.

To switch to another user:

1. `su -l username`

   The -l option (in some versions of **su** it's abbreviated as simply a hyphen: -) tells **su** that the new shell should be a *log-in* shell. The current directory for the new shell is the home directory of the target user.

   Username is the target user; that is, the user you want to switch to. If you omit *username*, then the target user is root.

   For example, to assume the identity of user puffball:

   `su -l puffball`

   To assume the identity of root:

   `su -l`

   You are then prompted for the user's password.

2. Enter the user's password.

   Su starts a new shell as the target user. If you used the -l option, then the new shell is a log-in shell that causes the target user's personal configuration files (.tcshrc, and so on) to be read. (Review Chapter 7, "Configuring Your Unix Environment.")

   continues on next page

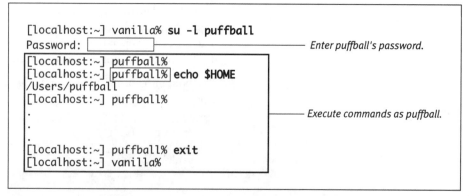

```
[localhost:~] vanilla% su -l puffball
Password: [        ]                    ———— Enter puffball's password.
[localhost:~] puffball%
[localhost:~] puffball% echo $HOME
/Users/puffball
[localhost:~] puffball%
.
.
.
[localhost:~] puffball% exit
[localhost:~] vanilla%
```
———— Execute commands as puffball.

Figure 11.10 Using su to assume the identity of another user.

If you omitted the -l option—for example,

`su puffball`

or

`su`

—then only the environment variables USER, HOME, and SHELL are set to the values appropriate for the target user, unless the target user is root, in which case the USER variable is left unchanged. All other environment variables for the new shell are inherited from your environment.

3. Run commands as the target user.

Every command you run in the new shell is executed with the permission of the target user.

4. If you used su to become root with

`su -l`

then when you have finished performing tasks as the target user, exit the shell to go back to being yourself, at your own shell prompt:

`exit`

✔ Tips

■ Once you have a root shell, you can su to another user *without* having his or her password.

■ You can specify which shell you want su to start up for the target user by giving it as an additional argument. For example,

`su puffball /bin/sh`

■ Once again, be aware of the power of root. From the su man page: "By default (unless the prompt is reset by a startup file) the super-user prompt is set to '#' to remind one of its awesome power."

Backups

Keeping a good set of backup files is one of the primary responsibilities of a system administrator. Even if you're the only person on the system, you still want to have backups!

An ideal backup system

◆ Makes copies that are easy to recover.

◆ Preserves all file attributes, including ownership, permissions, and creation/ modification date. This is an important difference between a backup copy and a copy made with the cp command.

◆ Only backs up files that have changed since a particular prior backup. This is called an *incremental* backup.

There are a number of venerable Unix tools for creating backups that are all designed to preserve the ownership, permissions, and modification dates of files when used by root, and are commonly used in scripts that automate the backup process. The most common of these tools are the tar *(tape archive)* command and the dump and restore commands.

The dump command is designed to make backups and includes the ability to make incremental backups. Another frequently overlooked tool is pax—so named because it combines can handle files created by tar and another program, cpio, allowing them to peacefully coexist. One valuable feature of pax: it allows you to specify files to copy based on their modification date. See man pax for details.

Unfortunately, dump and restore do not work at all on the Macintosh's standard HFS+ file-system format. And neither tar nor pax nor any of the standard Unix tools for copying files properly handle so-called complex files created by older Mac applications. These files have multiple *data streams* or *forks*. (Review the sidebar "Old Mac Files in an OS X World" in Chapter 5, "Using Files and Directories.")

As of this writing (fall 2002), Apple had no plans to create new versions of the standard Unix backup tools that handle HFS+ file systems or complex files. There are, however, third-party efforts underway to create an HFS+-compatible versions of Unix backup tools, including pax, rsync, and tar. See the sidebar "Unix Backup Tools for HFS+" for more information.

Unix Backup Tools for HFS+

We are aware of several projects underway to create HFS+ compatible versions of standard Unix tools.

One such project is a new version of the `tar` command that works properly with the HFS+ file system and with older Mac files. We tested it successfully but not extensively as this book went to press. The new tar, `hfstar`, can be obtained from www.metaobject.com in the Community section of the Web site.

Two new HFS-compatible tools are available, though we have not tested them. `Hfspax` is intended to replace the `pax` program that comes with Mac OS X. You can get `hfspax` from its creator at http://homepage.mac.com/howardoakley/. A version of the `rsync` command is available from www.macosxlabs.org/rsyncx/rsyncx.html.

For an excellent technical discussion of the issues, see "The Challenges of Integrating the Unix and Mac OS Environments" (www.mit.edu/people/wsanchez/papers/USENIX_2000/)

So you cannot reliably use the standard Unix tools to perform backups of every file on your Mac OS X system. However, you can use standard Unix tools to copy and back up files and directories that do not contain complex files. This includes all the critical system-configuration files in /etc.

The `CpMac` command (covered in Chapter 5, "Using Files and Directories") properly handles old-style Mac files, so it can be used to copy entire directories such as your home directory (using the -r option), but it does not preserve the ownership, permissions, or modification times of copied files. (We have reported this to Apple as a bug, so perhaps it will be changed in the future.) To make a real backup copy, you want to preserve everything about a file—ownership, permissions, and creation and modification dates.

BACKUPS

Full backups cannot be done from the command line

What is really unfortunate is that Mac OS X currently (fall 2002) provides no way to perform a full backup of your entire system from the command line. The `ditto` command (covered in the next section) backs up entire directories, preserving (in most cases) all the file attributes such as permission, ownership, and dates, and handles complex files. For a variety of reasons, however, it is not a practical tool for creating a full backup. See the sidebar "Full Backups from the Command Line."

Using ditto

The `ditto` command comes with Mac OS X and properly handles both standard Unix files and older complex files.

From the `ditto` man page: "Ditto copies one or more source directories to a destination directory. If the destination directory does not exist it will be created before the first source directory is copied."

`Ditto` preserves the ownership, permissions ("mode"), and modification times of all the files it copies, but will not alter the ownership, mode, or times on any directories that already exist in the destination. Thus, if you change the permissions (or ownership) of a directory you have already copied with `ditto`, and then copy it again to the same destination, the copy will not pick up the new ownership or mode.

The `ditto` command must be run as root (this is listed as a bug in the `ditto` man page, since you should be able to run it as a regular user and preserve everything except user ownership).

Compare with Aqua

The simplest way to make backups in Aqua is to have a second disk drive—such as an external FireWire drive—and simply copy files using the Finder.

Automated backup software for Mac OS X includes the minimalist PocketBackup from Pocket Software (www.pocketsw. com) or the industry-standard Retrospect from Dantz (www.dantz.com).

PocketBackup (as of version 1.0.1) is most useful for backing up files in your own home directory. In order to use it to properly back up files for multiple users and all system files, you would have to log in to Aqua as root, which is generally a bad idea.

Full Backups from the Command Line

As of Mac OS X version 10.2, it isn't possible to do a proper full backup from the command line. None of the standard Unix tools for full backups work under Mac OS X (`dump`, `tar`, `cpio`, `pax`) because of problems these tools have, either with the HFS+ file system or with the complex files created by older Mac applications, or both.

The one tool Apple provides for command-line backups, `ditto`, cannot be used for full backups because of some bugs (see the sidebar "Bugs in `ditto`"). `Ditto` is a very useful tool for making backups in Mac OS X, but it just isn't quite capable of backing up an entire system in the way a professional system administrator requires.

In the following tasks we assume you have an additional disk for backups, perhaps an external FireWire disk. All disks and partitions besides the boot partition are mounted as subdirectories of /Volumes, so if you had an external FireWire hard drive named "big disk," for example, it would show up in the file system as /Volumes/big_disk (review Figure 5.1 for a schematic diagram of a typical Mac OS X file system).

There are subtle differences in how you use ditto when copying directories as opposed to copying individual files. We'll show you directories first.

To back up a directory with ditto:

◆ sudo ditto -rsrc *source destination*

The -rsrc option (it is one option, not four) tells ditto to preserve the extra data in old-style complex files.

◆ Enter your password if sudo prompts you for it.

In this task we assume that *source* is a directory. You can specify more than one source. The *destination* must be a directory, not a file.

Ditto will copy the contents of the *source* directory (or directories) into the *destination* directory.

Bugs in ditto

There are a few bugs in ditto as of Mac OS X version 10.2.

◆ Ditto fails on locked files. If a file has been set to "locked" (typically in the Finder via the Get Info window), ditto stops working when it encounters that file, even though it actually *does* copy the file. We have reported this bug to Apple (bug ID# 2979202). When ditto encounters a locked file, it stops and gives an error message consisting of the path to the locked file and "Operation not permitted." You must then unlock the file, either from the Finder (select the file, choose Show Info from the File menu, and deselect the "locked" box), or with

SetFile -l *path_to_file*

Then unlock the backup copy that ditto made (the copy it made is locked, so ditto fails again if it tries to overwrite the locked copy; review Chapter 5, "Using Files and Directories," for more on SetFile).

◆ Ditto doesn't use correct mode, owner, or dates when creating directories specified in the destination path. If ditto creates

AAAA/BBBB

then the permissions, ownership, and dates on BBBB will be correct, but on AAAA/ they will be wrong. (Reported to Apple, this bug has ID# 2984815.3). If the source argument to ditto is a symlink, ditto follows the link instead of copying it (ditto does properly copy symlinks that are *inside* directories it is copying).

So ditto behaves like cp -RH without any option to have it behave like

cp -RP

(The -P option means "Do not follow symlinks.") This is not exactly a bug, but it is a serious software problem nonetheless. (Reported to Apple, this bug has ID# 2984824.)

For example, to back up all your users' home directories to an external disk mounted on /Volumes/big_disk:

```
ditto -rsrc /Users/Volumes/big_disk
→/backups/Users
```

That command line will copy the contents of /Users into /Volumes/big_disk →/backups/Users.

It is very important to note that ditto will not copy the source directory itself, just its contents. So in the example above, ditto does not copy the /Users directory, but instead copies everything *inside* /Users into /Volumes/big_disk/backups →/Users.

✔ Tip

- Use the -v option to ditto to have it print out the name of every source directory, or use the -V option to see the name of every file it copies.

Backups are only good if you can use them to recover files. When you are recovering files from backups (which is, essentially, copying them back), you have one of two common situations: Either you want to recover one or more specific files, or you want to recover entire directories. If you want to recover a directory, you can use ditto as described in the task above. If you want to recover specific files, then you need to use ditto in a subtly different way.

To use ditto to copy or recover individual files:

- ◆ `sudo ditto -rsrc source destination`

  If that command-line pattern looks the same as the one in the previous task, you are right, it is the same. The difference here is that if the *source* is a file (as opposed to a directory) then the *destination* may be either a file or a directory. If the *destination* is a directory, then the

source file(s) are copied into the directory. If the *destination* is a file, then it is overwritten. If the *destination* does not exist, then it is created as a file. For example,

```
sudo
ditto -rsrc /Volumes/big_disk/
→backups/Users/vanilla/Documents/
→Contract.doc /Users/vanilla/
→Documents/Contract_recovered.doc
```

copies the file Contract.doc and calls the copy Contract_recovered.doc.

As with all uses of sudo, you may be prompted for your password if you haven't used sudo in the last 5 minutes. If you are prompted, then enter your password.

Compare with Aqua

Restoring files from backup copies in Aqua can be as simple as copying them from the backup media using the Finder.

Copying files in the Finder works fine for files that are supposed to be owned by the user doing the copying, but it is not a good idea for system files or files belonging to multiple users, because the ownership and permissions on the files will be wrong (the files will end up being owned by the user who performs the copy, and in some cases you won't even have permission to make another copy). In those cases, you should either use the GUI application that created the backups in the first place (such as Retrospect) or use the command-line ditto program.

BACKUPS

Managing User Accounts and Groups

The system administrator's job includes adding new users to the system and managing the ability of various groups to access different parts of the file system (review Chapter 8, "Working with Permissions and Ownership").

The best way to add a user in Mac OS X is with the User panel in System Preferences. This not only adds the user, but it also creates his or her home directory and several files that each user needs. It *is* possible to add a user to your system using the command line, but the process is rather complex and is beyond the scope of this book. (If you really *must* know how, see the sidebar "Adding a User from the Command Line.")

Adding and Deleting Users with the System Preferences Application

The Mac OS X System Preferences is a GUI interface for many basic administrative tasks. If you have used earlier versions of the Mac OS, you will recognize that many of the tasks were previously handled by control panels. As you did with the control panels of yesteryear, you access System Preferences from the Apple menu (**Figure 11.11**).

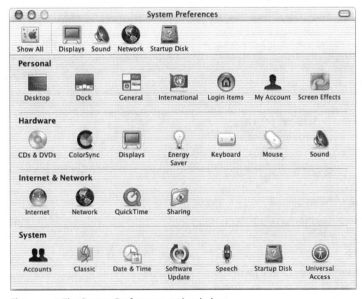

Figure 11.11 The System Preferences main window.

To create a new user:

1. Choose System Preferences from the Apple menu. The main System Preferences window opens.

2. Click the Accounts icon.

   The Accounts window opens showing the Users pane (**Figure 11.12**).

   All the current regular users are shown (not shown are special system accounts, including the root account).

3. Click on the New User button.

   This drops a window shade with fields for the new user's information (**Figure 11.13**).

4. Fill in the Name and Short Name fields for the new user.

   Mac OS X uses the term *short name* for what all Unix systems call the "user name" or "login name." The short name must be eight characters or less and should consist only of lowercase letters and numbers.

5. Fill in the user's new password.

   You type the password twice, and it is displayed as a series of bullets (so someone looking over your shoulder won't see it).

   Passwords are the backbone of system security. If a malicious person obtains a user's password, he or she could cause serious harm to that person's system: disabling it altogether, obtaining root privileges, or copying any information on the system.

   As we mentioned earlier, good passwords always have a combination of numbers, punctuation marks and symbols (!@#$%^&*_+-=":;'><,.?/\|), and letters, and never contain a dictionary word.

   You can fill in a "password hint" for the user. This will show up in the Aqua Login Window if he or she fails three log in

Figure 11.12 The Users window from System Preferences.

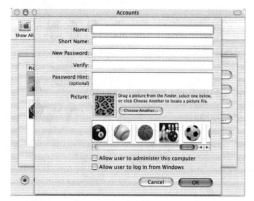

Figure 11.13 The windows shade that appears when you click "New User…"

Figure 11.14 The New User window shade all filled in and ready to save.

Figure 11.15 The Accounts window, showing the new user added to the list.

Bug in New-User Creation

If /Users is a symbolic link, the System Preferences tool will not create a new user's home directory as it is supposed to.

The reason /Users might be a symbolic link is that you might want all your users' home directories to be on a different disk or partition from the boot partition. So you might have /Users be a symbolic link to /Volumes/partition2/Users.

attempts in a row. (The hint option must also set in the "Login Options" pane of the Accounts Preferences tool.)

If you want to choose a "log-in picture" for the user, you may do that here. The Login Picture appears in the Aqua log-in screen if you have "Display Login Window:" set to "List of users" in the Login Options pane.

6. If you want the new user to have root access on the machine, then select the checkbox next to "Allow user to administer this computer."

If you want the user to be able to mount his or her home directory as a file share from a Windows machine, then select the checkbox for "Allow user to log in from Windows." **Figure 11.14** shows an example of the new user window shade filled in and ready to save.

7. Click Save.

At this point the new user has been added to the system, and that person can log in.

The Accounts window reappears, with the new user's name in the list (**Figure 11.15**).

The new user's home directory has been created, along with various subdirectories such as his or her Documents folder. (But be sure to see the sidebar "Bug in New-User Creation.") Also, a configuration file for the Apache Web server is created for the new user in /etc/httpd/users/.

Add more users if you like.

8. Quit System Preferences.

✔ Tip

■ Be very careful about giving users the ability to "administer this computer," since that essentially gives them root access. Users with this ability (or anyone who gets their password) can take complete control of the machine.

Occasionally you'll need to remove a user, and you can use the System Preferences tool to do that as well. The tool does not actually delete the user's home directory; it transfers the directory's ownership to the account you are logged in as (this task, like all the others in this chapter, assumes that you are logged in as an admin user). You must then delete the home directory manually to completely remove the user.

To remove a user:

1. Open the System Preferences window.

2. Click the Accounts icon.

3. Select the user from the list.

4. Click the Delete User button.

   The user's home directory will be moved into the "/Users/Deleted Users" directory. You can delete it manually from there.

5. Quit System Preferences.

6. Remove the user's home directory.

✔ Tip

■ There may be files outside the user's home directory that were owned by that user. For example, if you are running a Web server, you may have allowed many users to put HTML files in /Library /WebServer/Documents. You can create a list of all the files in a directory that are owned by unknown users with the -nouser option to the find command:

   sudo find /Library/WebServer/
   →Documents -nouser > orphanlist.txt

   You can then look at the resulting list and decide which files to delete and which to change the ownership of (so that they are owned by a user still on the system).

Perhaps the most common task for a system administrator is to help users who have forgotten their password.

Adding a User from the Command Line

OK, you want to be a hotshot Unix sysadmin. Here's the list of things you'd have to do to add a user from the command line the same way as the System Preferences does it. Each of these steps actually has several substeps. You'll want to study the man pages for niutil and nidump before trying this—and please, experiment on a noncritical machine.

1. Use niutil to add the user. Apple has some documentation for how to do this at http://developer.apple.com/ techpubs/macosx/Darwin/ PortingUNIX/additionalfeatures/ Example_Add_Command_Line.html.

2. Set the entries for the user's home directory, full name, password, and log-in shell.

   (You can use

   sudo nidump -r /users /

   to see all the fields you need to fill in for a user.)

3. Create the user's home directory.

4. Populate the home directory with the standard files (create a user with the System Preferences to see what files are created).

5. Change the ownership on the user's home directory and its contents so that the user owns all the files.

6. Create
   /etc/httpd/users/*newuser*.conf

Copy one of the other files in the /etc /httpd/users directory and edit the copy to make it appropriate for the new user.

While there is no easy way to find a user's current password, it can be changed easily. You can use the System Preferences tool, but you can also do this easily from the command line.

Refer to **Figure 11.16** throughout the following task.

To change a user's password:

1. `sudo passwd username`

   The *username* argument is the same as the short name that was entered when the user's account was created. For example,

   `sudo passwd sarafina`

   If you haven't used `sudo` in the last 5 minutes, you are prompted for *your* password, with just

   `Password:`

   After you enter your password, or if you have recently used `sudo`, you will see a prompt from the `passwd` command.

2. Enter the user's new password.

3. Reenter the new password.

   Because the passwords are not displayed, you have to enter them twice to make sure you have it right. If the entries don't match, you'll be prompted to enter them again.

   Use a secure method to tell the user his or her new password—that is, in person or on a phone line you trust. *Never* send an (unencrypted) password over email or leave it on a voice-mail system.

Changing a user's log-in shell

Although it's not as common an activity as changing passwords, system administrators occasionally are asked (or decide) to change a user's login shell. For example, a user might want to use the bash shell as their login shell instead of the Mac OS X default (which is tcsh).

The command-line tool for changing a user's shell in Darwin and Mac OS X is quite different from that used in other versions of Unix (in which you would probably use either usermod or chsh). As we mentioned earlier, Darwin and thus Mac OS X use a database of user and system information called NetInfo, derived from the NeXT operating system. You've already seen the GUI application for viewing and manipulating the NetInfo database (NetInfo Manager, which we showed you in "To enable the root account," at the start of the chapter). There is also a set of command-line tools for working with the NetInfo database, and you use a good example of one of them to change a user's log-in shell: the niu-til command. (See the sidebar "Deeper into NetInfo" for a list of the other tools.)

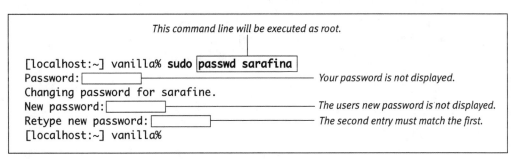

```
                        This command line will be executed as root.
                                        |
[localhost:~] vanilla% sudo passwd sarafina
Password:[          ]——————————————————— Your password is not displayed.
Changing password for sarafine.
New password:[          ]—————————————— The users new password is not displayed.
Retype new password: [          ]——————— The second entry must match the first.
[localhost:~] vanilla%
```

Figure 11.16 Changing a user's password with the passwd command.

MANAGING USER ACCOUNTS AND GROUPS

Figure 11.17 shows all the steps in the following task.

To change a user's log-in shell:

1. `niutil -read . /users/name=username`

   This shows you all the information in the NetInfo database about the user.

   For example:

   `niutil -read . /users/name=puffball`

   shows several items, including

   `shell: /bin/tcsh`

   (See Figure 11.17 for the full list.)

2. `sudo niutil -appendprop . /users/name=username shell newshell`

   For example, if you are changing the user's shell to be **/bin/bash** (after having installed **bash**, per Chapter 15, "More Open-Source Software" at www.peachpit.com/vqp/umox), the command line would be

   `sudo niutil -appendprop . /users/name=puffball shell /bin/bash`

   The database now has two entries for the user's shell.

   You can check this, if you like, with

   `niutil -read . /users/name=puffball`

   The shell entry now has

   `shell: /bin/tcsh bin/bash`

   A user can have only one shell, though, so now you have to remove the old shell from the database.

3. `sudo niutil -destroyval . /users/name=username shell oldshell`

   For example,

   `sudo niutil -destroyval . /users/name=puffball shell /bin/tcsh`

   That removes the /bin/tcsh shell entry for puffball.

4. You can check it with `niutil` and can ask to see only the shell entry:

   `niutil -readprop . /users/name=username shell`

   For example,

   `niutil -readprop . /users/name=puffball shell`

   shows the shell entry just for the user puffball, which should now be
   `/bin/bash`

Table 11.2

Files Used to Track User Log-Ins

FILE	PURPOSE AND COMMANDS
var/run/utmp	Shows who is logged in right now (tmp stands for *temporary*). Used by the users, w, and who commands.
/var/log/wtmp	Records each log-in and log-out. Used by the last and ac commands. This file is "rolled over" every month by the script /etc/monthly. See "Running Regularly Scheduled Commands," later in this chapter.
/var/log/lastlog	Records the date and time of each user's last log-in. The date of the last log-in is displayed when logging in via a command-line interface (for example, when you open a new Terminal window).

Tracking who uses the system

Every time a user logs in, entries are made in three log files. These files enable you to see who is currently using the system and a history of log-ins to the system.

Table 11.2 lists these files and the commands used to view them.

Using the commands listed in Table 11.2, you can see a good deal of information about who was and is using your system.

To see a list of users logged in right now:

◆ users

The users command simply lists the user name of anyone who is currently logged in. The output looks like this:

```
vanilla matisse puffball
```

```
[localhost:~] vanilla% niutil -read . /users/name=puffball
picture: /Library/User Pictures/Flowers/Dahlia.tif
_shadow_passwd:
hint: blah blah
realname: Power Puff Person
_writers_passwd: puffball
uid: 502
_writers_hint: puffball
gid: 20
name: puffball
passwd: 1Re49x66qkGNQ
_writers_picture: puffball
home: /Users/ puffball
sharedDir: Public
shell: /bin/tcsh
[localhost:~] vanilla% sudo niutil -appendprop . /users/name=puffball shell /bin/bash
Password:
[localhost:~] vanilla% sudo niutil -destroyval . /users/name=puffball shell /bin/tcsh
[localhost:~] vanilla% niutil -readprop . /users/name=puffball shell
/bin/bash
[localhost:~] vanilla%
```

Figure 11.17 Using niutil to change a user's log-in shell.

327

To see a list of users and where they logged in from:

◆ who

The who command shows you one line for each log-in shell each user is running. So if you had three Terminal windows open and another user was logged in over the Internet, who would show *five* entries (**Figure 11.18**).

That's one entry for your Aqua log-in (the "console" entry), the three Terminal windows (the **ttyp1**, **ttyp3**, and **ttyp4** entries), and an entry for a user logged in over the Internet. The entry for the remote user shows where he or she is logged in from (the host well.com).

Ttyp means *teletypewriter, pseudo.* In the old days, people used electromechanical teletypewriters to log in to computers; now those ttys are emulated in software, hence the "pseudo."

Using the -H option adds a line of headings to the output.

The -u option adds the idle time for each entry (in hours:minutes).

Figure 11.19 shows the output with the -Hu options.

```
[localhost:~] vanilla% who -Hu
USER     LINE     WHEN          IDLE    FROM
vanilla  console  Jul  6 08:32 21:19
vanilla  ttyp1    Jul  9 10:31   .
matisse  ttyp2    Jul  9 10:36   .      (well.com)
vanilla  ttyp3    Jul  6 12:39 00:09
vanilla  ttyp4    Jul  9 10:37 00:09
[localhost:~] vanilla%
```

Figure 11.19 Output from the who command with -Hu options.

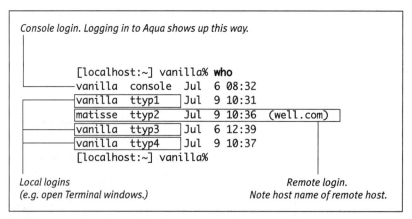

```
Console login. Logging in to Aqua shows up this way.

         [localhost:~] vanilla% who
        ─vanilla   console  Jul  6 08:32
         ┌vanilla   ttyp1  │ Jul  9 10:31
         │matisse   ttyp2  │ Jul  9 10:36  (well.com)
         │vanilla   ttyp3  │ Jul  6 12:39
         │vanilla   ttyp4  │ Jul  9 10:37
         [localhost:~] vanilla%

Local logins                          Remote login.
(e.g. open Terminal windows.)      Note host name of remote host.
```

Figure 11.18 Annotated output from the who command.

Deeper into NetInfo

The NetInfo system used by Darwin is intended to be a database of system information that is or can be shared across multiple machines. For exam- ple, NetInfo makes it possible to have a single list of users who have accounts on many machines, and to change a user's password in one place for all those machines. The data stored in NetInfo is mostly data that is stored on other Unix systems in plain text files: The file /etc/passwd has the list of all users, their home directories, and log-in shells. In Darwin, /etc/passwd is used only when the machine is in single-user mode, but on most Unix systems, /etc/passwd is the only database of users.

There are several command-line tools for working with NetInfo, each with its own man page:

- Niutil for manipulating data in the NetInfo database.

- Nidump for dumping data from NetInfo in the format used by traditional Unix tools.

- Nireport for dumping data from NetInfo in a different format from nidump. Can also dump more kinds of data than nidump.

- Niload for loading data from traditional Unix-format text files into NetInfo.

- Nifind for searching the NetInfo database.

The official Apple document giving an overview of the NetInfo system is available online at http://developer.apple.com/techpubs/macosx/Darwin/howto/netinfo/netinfo.html.

To see who is logged in and what they are doing:

◆ w

The w command shows output similar to who -Hu but adds a line of information reporting system uptime and load (actually, it is the output from the uptime command; see "Monitoring System Usage," later in this chapter). It also tries to show the last command that each user exe-

cuted. This last feature isn't working in Mac OS X 10.2, but it works on many Unix systems and may work on Mac OS X in the future. **Figure 11.20** shows output from w on a Mac OS X system, and **Figure 11.21** shows partial output from w on another Unix system (running Sun's Solaris 2.6 operating system). Notice that that system had 152 users logged in at the time the command was run.

```
[localhost:~] vanilla% w
11:15AM  up 3 days, 11:53, 5 users, load averages: 0.39, 0.48, 0.60
USER    TTY FROM            LOGIN@  IDLE WHAT
vanilla  co -              Sat08AM 21:38 -
vanilla  p1 -              10:31AM     0 -
matisse  p2 well.com       10:36AM     0 -
vanilla  p3 -              Sat12PM     0 -
vanilla  p4 -              10:37AM     0 -
[localhost:~] vanilla%
```

Figure 11.20 Output of w on Mac OS X. The last column is not reporting what it should.

```
Love ya babe 34: w
11:20am  up 20 day(s),  5:08,  152 users,  load average: 5.98, 6.62, 6.74
User    tty        login@ idle  JCPU  PCPU  what
java    pts/3      5:49am   41    22    16  -bash
swede   pts/8     10:49am    5     5     4  /usr/local/lib/mailwrapper/pine
fluffer pts/15    11:04am          4     4  more
maxie   pts/35     6:14am        1:32    55  -picospan
flute   pts/58    11:06am    7     2     2  extract -g -f weblog -J -k web /
bottle  pts/44    10:36am          2        ped -t -z /home/b/o/bottle/.muse
risc    pts/19    11:11am    3                more
artgrrl pts/41     8:35am    1     1     1  ssh -l artgrrl artgrrl.net
omni23  pts/100   11:14am                  lynx villagevoice
starboy pts/13    11:14am          2        -bash
bunch   pts/60    10:26am   39     8     5  -picospan
bloomsb pts/162   10:07am        1:08    38  irc NihiAtWrk irc.wagill.com
libre   pts/134   10:48am    2     2     2  /usr/bin/vi /home/l/i/libre/cf.buf
pwolf   pts/90     9:53am  1:28             /usr/bin/ksh
....output abbreviated....
```

Figure 11.21 Abbreviated output from w on a machine running Sun's Solaris 2.6 version of Unix.

To see a history of log-ins for all users:

◆ last

The last command shows a history of all sessions (log-in/log-out pairs) for the current month (**Figure 11.22**).

Besides showing user sessions, the last log also shows entries for shutdowns, reboots, and crashes.

The information is taken from the /var/log/wtmp file, which is emptied out and started again each month by the /etc/month script. Last month's file is /var/log/wtmp.0.gz, the prior month is wtmp.1.gz, and so on up to wtmp.4.gz. You can uncompress the older files and supply the filename as an argument with

continues on next page

```
[localhost:~] vanilla% last
vanilla    ttyp4                      Tue Jul  9 10:37    still logged in
matisse    ttyp2      well.com        Tue Jul  9 10:36 - 11:20  (00:43)
vanilla    ttyp1                      Tue Jul  9 10:31    still logged in
vanilla    ttyp2                      Tue Jul  9 10:31 - 10:36  (00:05)
vanilla    ttyp3                      Sat Jul  6 12:39    still logged in
vanilla    ttyp2                      Sat Jul  6 10:29 - 10:31 (3+00:02)
puffball   ttyp2                      Sat Jul  6 08:43 - 10:29  (01:45)
vanilla    ttyp1                      Sat Jul  6 08:34 - 10:09  (01:35)
matisse    console    user-112uhed.biz Sat Jul  6 08:32    still logged in
root       console                    Fri Jul  5 12:30 - 12:32  (00:01)
vanilla    console    user-112uhed.biz Fri Jul  5 12:29 - 12:30  (00:00)
puffball   ttyp1      playroom.matisse Thu Jul  4 11:00 - 12:36 (1+01:35)
vanilla    ttyp2                      Tue Jul  2 16:45 - 14:21 (2+21:36)
vanilla    ttyp1                      Tue Jul  2 16:35 - 11:00 (1+18:24)
vanilla    console    user-112uhed.biz Tue Jul  2 16:23 - 12:29 (2+20:05)
reboot     ~                          Tue Jul  2 16:20
shutdown   ~                          Tue Jul  2 16:14
root       console    user-112uhed.biz Tue Jul  2 16:14 - 16:14  (00:00)
vanilla    ttyp2                      Tue Jul  2 15:06 - shutdown  (01:08)
puffball   ttyp1                      Tue Jul  2 15:04 - shutdown  (01:09)
vanilla    ttyp1                      Tue Jul  2 15:04 - 15:04  (00:00)
vanilla    ttyp3                      Tue Jul  2 11:53 - shutdown  (04:20)
matisse    ttyp1                      Tue Jul  2 10:10 - 15:04  (04:53)
vanilla    ttyp2                      Mon Jul  1 21:43 - 15:06  (17:22)
vanilla    ttyp1                      Mon Jul  1 21:42 - 10:10  (12:27)

wtmp begins Mon Jul  1 09:18
[localhost:~] vanilla%
```

Figure 11.22 Output from the last command showing all log-in sessions, reboots, shutdowns and crashes for the current month.

the -f option to last to look at the previous month's data:

```
cd /var/log
sudo gunzip wtmp.2.gz
last -f wtmp.2
```

To see a history of all log-ins for one user:

◆ last *username*

If you supply a user name as an argument to last, it limits the output to the sessions for that user. For example,

```
last puffball
```

gives output like that in **Figure 11.23**.

✔ Tip

■ You can use last with the pseudo-user names reboot, shutdown, and crash to see all the corresponding entries in the last log. For example,

```
last reboot
```

shows all the reboots this month.

To see a summary of log-in times:

◆ ac

Short for *connect time accounting*, this shows the total of all sessions since the start of this month (the data comes from /var/log/wtmp).

For example,

```
total    197.15
```

You can supply a list of one or more user names to get a total for the selected users only. For example,

```
ac puffball
```

shows a total (in hours:minutes) of all of puffball's sessions for the current month, and

```
ac puffball vanilla
```

shows the total for the two users.

You may use the -p option to get a per-user breakdown of the time, or the -d option to get a daily subtotal, but not both.

Figure 11.24 shows several different results for the ac command with different arguments and options.

```
[localhost:~] vanilla% last puffball
puffball   ttyp2                    Sat Jul  6 08:43 - 10:29  (01:45)
puffball   ttyp1     playroom.matisse Thu Jul  4 11:00 - 12:36 (1+01:35)
puffball   ttyp1                    Tue Jul  2 15:04 - shutdown  (01:09)

wtmp begins Mon Jul  1 09:18
[localhost:~] vanilla%
```

Figure 11.23 Output from last showing only one user.

```
[localhost:~] vanilla% ac
        total      197.22
[localhost:~] vanilla% ac -p
        vanilla    196.20
        root         0.29
        puffball     0.73
        total      197.22
[localhost:~] vanilla% ac -d
Jul  3  total       62.19
Jul  4  total       24.00
Jul  5  total       23.97
Jul  8  total       72.00
Jul  9  total       15.06
[localhost:~] vanilla% ac vanilla
        total      196.20
[localhost:~] vanilla% ac puffball vanilla
        total      196.94
[localhost:~] vanilla% ac -p puffball vanilla
        vanilla    196.21
        puffball     0.73
        total      196.94
[localhost:~] vanilla% ac -d vanilla
Jul  1  total       14.35
Jul  3  total       47.84
Jul  4  total       24.00
Jul  5  total       23.69
Jul  8  total       72.00
Jul  9  total       14.34
[localhost:~] vanilla%
```

Figure 11.24 Output from using the ac command with a variety of arguments and options.

✔ Tip

- You can use the -w option for ac to have it read a different file from the default. For example,

  ```
  cd /var/log
  sudo gunzip wtmp.0.gz
  ac -w wtmp.0 -p
  ```

  shows a per-day summary for the month whose data is in the file.

Managing groups

Mac OS X/Darwin uses the NetInfo database described earlier for managing groups as well as users.

In Chapter 8, "Working with Permissions and Ownership," you learned about how Unix uses groups to grant permission for various file operations (read, write, execute) to groups of users. And earlier in this chapter, you learned that Mac OS X allows any user in the admin group to use **sudo** to execute commands as root.

In this section we're going to show you how to change a user's group assignment, and how to add and remove groups.

A common reason to create a new group is if you have several people using your computer and want to allow some of them to have write permission in a directory where the other users do not. You would create a new group and put each of the team members into that group. Users can be members of many groups.

To see a list of all the groups:

◆ `nireport . /groups name gid`

This shows a list of all the groups on your system. Each line has the group name and its group ID number (`gid`), as shown in **Figure 11.25**.

✔ Tips

■ Another way to list the groups:

`niutil -list . /groups`

This gives the list of the groups along with their NetInfo ID numbers. These numbers are used internally by NetInfo and are different from (and not to be confused with) the group IDs.

■ `Nireport` can be used to produce reports for many things from the NetInfo database. See `man nireport` for more.

To see all the groups a user belongs to:

◆ `groups username`

For example,

`groups puffball`

lists all the groups that puffball is a member of—for example,

`staff www`

✔ Tip

■ Supposedly, the `groups` command is being made obsolete by the `id` command, which has several options and can show more information about a user. Unfortunately, the `id` command is quite different on different Unix systems. In Mac OS X,

`id -Gn username`

behaves the same as

`groups username`

See `man id` for more.

```
[localhost:~] vanilla% nireport . /groups name gid
nobody   -2
nogroup  -1
wheel     0
daemon    1
kmem      2
sys       3
tty       4
operator          5
mail      6
bin       7
staff    20
guest    31
utmp     45
uucp     66
dialer   68
network  69
www      70
admin    80
unknown  99
news     250
mysql    251
pgsql    252
games    253
canna    254
postfix 255
maildrop          256
smmsp    25
[localhost:~] vanilla%
```

Figure 11.25 Using `nireport` to see a list of all the groups.

To see all the users who belong to a group:

◆ There isn't any easy way to do this. Yes, we know it seems strange, but it's true.

The problem is that there are two different places where a user can be included in a group. One is the NetInfo database for groups, in which each group has a list of users that belong to it. But ... when a user is created, he or she is assigned one group as his or her "primary" group, and that information is stored in the NetInfo database record for the user. In Mac OS X, all new users have group "staff" as their primary group, yet their user names do not appear in the NetInfo database record for group staff.

In order to really find out who all the members of a group are, you would have to examine every user on the system, as well as the group entry in NetInfo. You could write a script to do this, but there's no single command to do it. Sorry.

Compare with Aqua

You can use the GUI application NetInfo Manager to see who is a member of a group, as well as to add and remove groups.

Even though NetInfo Manager is a GUI application, it is far less easy to use than most Mac applications. This is one case where the command-line tools are probably easier than the GUI equivalent.

To create a new group:

1. First get the list of all groups as described above:

   `nireport . /groups name gid`

2. Choose a group name and `gid` that are not in use.

   Group names should be all lowercase and eight characters or less. The `gid` you choose should be a higher number than any of the existing ones. It's probably a good idea to give groups you add yourself a `gid` of 500 or higher.

3. `sudo niutil -create / /groups/` ↪`groupname`

   You must be root to modify the NetInfo database, hence the use of `sudo`.

   You are creating a new entry in the NetInfo database, in the `groups` "directory."

   For example, to create a group called dancers:

   `niutil -create / /groups/dancers`

   Enter your password if `sudo` prompts you for it.

4. `sudo niutil -createprop / /groups/` ↪`name=dancers passwd \*`

   This adds a password property (that is, a requirement to be fulfilled) to the `dancers` group and sets its value to `*`. The `\` is needed to prevent the shell from interpreting the `*` as a wildcard. Groups can in theory have passwords, but they are virtually never used. Instead, a `*` is placed where the encrypted password would be.

5. `sudo niutil -createprop / /groups/` ↪`name=dancers gid 501`

   That adds a `gid` property to the group and sets its value to 501.

   The last step is to add a `users` property.

continues on next page

6. `sudo niutil -createprop / /groups/`
`→name=dancers users`

This adds the users property and leaves it empty.

✔ Tip

- If you know a user you want to add to the group right away, you can add his or her user name as the last argument:

  `sudo niutil -createprop / /groups/`
  `→name=dancers users puffball`

  This adds the user's property and puts puffball in the group.

  If you add a user to a group while the user is logged in, the user's current shells won't know that he or she is in the new group. The user has to log in again (or open a new Terminal window).

To add a user to an existing group:

- `sudo niutil -appendprop / /groups/name=`*groupname*` users `*username*

  This adds the user *username* to the group *groupname*. For example,

  `sudo niutil -appendprop / /groups/name=dancers users fireboy`

  adds user `fireboy` to group `dancers`. The change takes effect the next time `fireboy` logs in.

To remove a user from a group:

- `sudo niutil -destroyval / /groups/name=`*groupname*` users `*username*

  This removes the user *username* from group *groupname*. For example,

  `sudo niutil -destroyval / /groups/name=dancers users fireboy`

  removes the user `fireboy` from group `dancers`.

To remove a group:

- `sudo niutil -destroy / /groups/`*groupname*

  For example,

  `sudo niutil -destroy / /groups/dancers`

  removes the group `dancers`.

  ⚠ Be very careful!! If you leave off the group name, you could remove every group.

Monitoring System Usage

Staying aware of what's happening on your machine is a big part of system administration. The two most important things to watch on a day-to-day basis are (1) disk space and (2) load on the processor(s). Run out of disk space, and many processes stop working because they have no place to create temporary data. Let a runaway program consume too much processor time, and everything else slows down.

Monitoring disk space

Anticipating the need to add disk space before you run out is an important system-administration function.

You can view both available and used space for the entire system or for any directory in the file system.

To see a summary of disk usage for the entire system:

◆ df -lk

The df command *(display free disk space)* displays information about all the disks

mounted on your system. The -l option tells df to display only locally mounted file systems (omitting network drives and some special entries that are not really disks), while the -k option tells df to show disk space in kilobytes, instead of the default half-kilobyte (512-byte) units (**Figure 11.26**).

✔ Tip

■ If you supply a directory as an argument to df, it shows a listing for only the file system containing the directory, so

df -k .

shows a listing only for the file system containing the current directory (which is also a tricky way of finding out which file system the current directory is located in).

df -k /Users

shows a listing only for the file system containing /Users. If the directory is a symlink, then df reports on the file system containing the directory that the link points to, not the link itself.

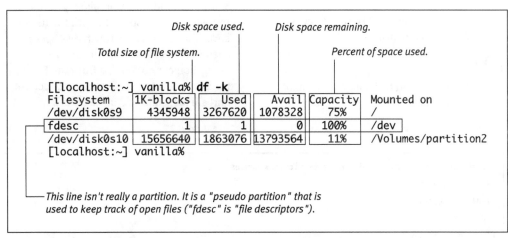

Figure 11.26 Annotated output from df -k displaying free space (in kilobytes) on the system disks.

To see disk usage for a particular directory:

◆ `du -sk directory`

The `-s` asks for a summary of the target directory, and the `-k` says to show sizes in kilobytes. **Table 11.3** shows all the options for the du command.

To see a summary of the disk space used by puffball's home directory:

`sudo du -sk /Users/puffball`

The `sudo` is needed in this case because you might not have read permission on everything in the directory.

To see disk usage for several directories:

◆ `du -sk dir1 dir2 dir3 ...`

Simply list as many directories as you like on the command line. The `-s` option generates a subtotal for each one. For example, if you type

`du -sk Documents Pictures Movies`

you get the output shown in **Figure 11.27**. You can see how much each user is using with

`du -sk /Users/*`

The shell expands the `*` so that du gets a list of several directories.

✔ Tip

■ Add the `-c` option to get a grand total of disk space used.

Table 11.3

Options for the du Command	
OPTION	MEANING/USE
-H	Follows symbolic links in the command-line arguments. (Symbolic links encountered inside directories are not followed.)
-L	Follows all symbolic links.
-P	Does not follow symbolic links.
-a	Displays something for every file counted.
-k	Displays sizes in kilobytes instead of the system default for measuring files (usually 512 bytes).
-c	Displays a grand total at the end.
-s	Displays a subtotal for each directory on the command line.
-x	Does not follow symbolic links that point to directories on other partitions.

Compare with Aqua

In the Finder you can see how much space is available on each disk by selecting it and choosing Show Info from the File menu. And you can see how much disk space specific folders are using, *if* you have read permission for them.

The command-line tools allow you much more flexibility, especially with the use of sudo. You can see how much disk space each folder in a user's home directory is using. You cannot do this from the Finder (unless you have enabled the root account and are logged in to Aqua as root).

```
[localhost:~] vanilla% du -sk Documents Pictures Movies
82740    Documents
71204    Pictures
320      Movies
[localhost:~] vanilla%
```

Figure 11.27 Using du -sk to get disk-use subtotals for several directories.

Monitoring processes and load on your machine

If you have read Chapter 2, "Using the Command Line," then you already have seen two of the best tools for monitoring running processes: ps and top. (See "About Commands, Processes, and Jobs" in Chapter 2).

Reading the man pages for ps and top yields a great deal of information about the kinds of things you can monitor on your system. Here are some highlights for the top command, which shows a wealth of information in real time.

More about top

Figure 11.28 is an annotated example of output from top, showing the most significant indicators of system use.

Note how the ID of each process is displayed. If a process gets out of control, you can use the kill command (described in Chapter 2, "Using the Command Line") to terminate it. You need to use sudo to kill processes you didn't start yourself. Be very careful, since you could crash the machine by killing a system process such as process 2 (mach_init).

continues on next page

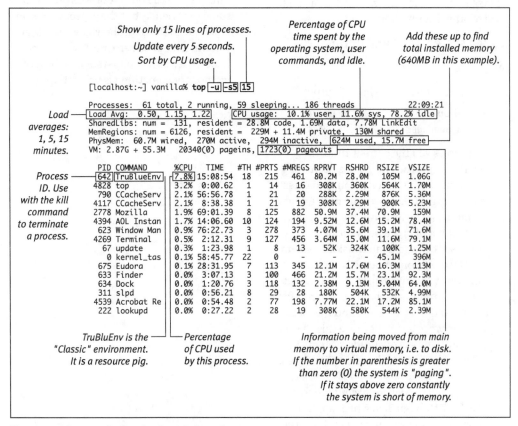

Figure 11.28 Annotated example of output from the top command.

If you use **top** frequently, you will quickly notice that your system spends a great deal of the time doing very little. It is quite common for computers, especially desktop machines used by only one or a few people, to run at 90 percent idle most of the time. Most of the computing power in the world is wasted, just generating heat and performing no useful work (see http://sctiathome.ssl.berkeley.edu and www.distributed.net for ways to put those spare CPU cycles to work in a good cause).

Another noteworthy command is **uptime**, which shows the same thing as the first line of output from the **w** command. The **top** command also displays the information from **uptime** in its first few lines, as well as a great deal of other information.

To see system load and uptime:

◆ uptime

This gives you a single line of output,

```
9:42PM up 3 days, 22:20, 6 users,
→load averages: 0.42, 0.89, 0.85
```

that shows you the current time, the length of time the system has been up, the number of users logged in, and three *load averages* taken over the past 1, 5, and 15 minutes. The load average is the average number of processes waiting for processor time. In a multitasking system like Unix, only one process is actually running at any given instant. The operating system allows each process to run for a tiny fraction of a second and then lets another process run. Because this sharing is enforced by the operating system, it is called *preemptive multitasking* and is one of the major reasons for Unix's stability (as opposed to *cooperative multitasking* in Mac OS 7 through 9, in which applications were supposed to play well together without supervision).

A Tool for Monitoring Memory Usage

Another command worth knowing about is **vm_stat** *(virtual memory statistics)*, often called **vmstat** on other Unix systems. **Vm_stat** reports on several aspects of memory usage, in real time.

Vm_stat is normally executed as

```
vm_stat 5
```

which gives a summary since startup and then a new line every 5 seconds. It keeps running until you type Ctrl C.

Interpreting the output of **vm_stat** takes some experience, but the **pageout** column is similar to the data shown by **top**—that column should be zero most of the time. Otherwise, either your system is short of memory or something is using it up.

Running Regularly Scheduled Commands

Remember the `locate` command mentioned in Chapter 2, "Using the Command Line"? We told you that the database `locate` uses is rebuilt every week. But how? By a standard Unix tool called `cron` (as in *chronological*).

The `cron` daemon executes programs according to a schedule. (*Daemons* are programs that run in the background, waiting to be needed for various system tasks. Most server software such as Web servers run as daemons, as do many pieces of the operating system that are constantly running, waiting to do some particular kind of work.) Every minute, the `cron` daemon checks the directory `/var/cron/tabs` for files whose names match user names—for example, root—and reads any new or changed files into memory. The `cron` daemon also checks the system administration file `/etc/crontab`. These files, called *crontabs* (for *chronological tables*), are in a special format (described below) that tells `cron` what commands to execute and when. Commands in a crontab file are executed as the user who owns the crontab file (except for the special `/etc/crontab` file; see "About `/etc/crontab`," below).

When a command from a crontab file is executed, any output from the command is emailed to the user owning the crontab file.

Users' crontab files are created and edited with the `crontab` command, which uses the `vi` editor (or the editor specified in your `VISUAL` environment variable) and performs a syntax check on the file before installing it. (This is similar to the working of the `visudo` command covered earlier in this chapter.) The system administration crontab file, `/etc/crontab`, must be edited directly using an editor such as `vi`. Unfortunately, the `crontab` command cannot be used to perform a syntax check on `/etc/crontab`.

You can view the man page for the `crontab` command with `man crontab`, and the man page for what goes inside crontab files with `man 5 crontab`. (To see why you need to add the "5," review the `man` command in Chapter 3, "Getting Help and Using the Unix Manual.")

Make certain your are familiar with the vi editor before editing your crontab file.

To run a command every day:

1. crontab -e

   The -e option says, "I want to *edit* my crontab file."

2. Add the crontab command line.

   Let's say you want a summary of your disk-space usage to be added to a file every day at 10:23 p.m.

   The basic command you want to run is

   /usr/bin/du -skc /Users/vanilla >> →/Users/vanilla/disk_use.log

   You should always use full paths for commands in crontab files because cron runs them with a very limited environment (you can find the path to a command with which command).

   You add a series of five items to the crontab file, specifying when you want the command to run, and then the command line goes after the fifth item. It must be one long line.

   Figure 11.29 shows the meaning of each of the time fields and the entry to run the above command every day at 10:23 p.m.

3. Save the file and quit the editor.

   If you are using vi, the command is

   (Esc) :wq

✔ Tip

■ When redirecting the output of a command line in your crontab, as in the example above, you can't have multiple commands on the command line. So if you want to run a series of commands from cron, you must create a shell script and run that from your crontab.

   For example, you might have a script like this:

   #!/bin/sh

   /bin/date

   /usr/bin/du -skc /Users/vanilla

   You could then run the script with cron and redirect the output of the script (which includes the date) into a log file.

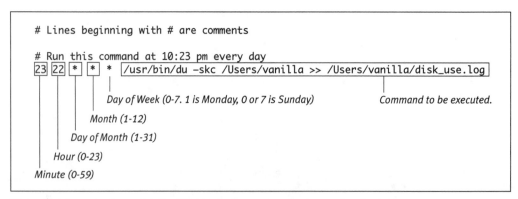

Figure 11.29 Example of a crontab file with an entry to run a command every day at 10:23 p.m.

Figure 11.30 show a series of examples of crontab entries. Man 5 crontab gives the full, detailed specification for what is possible.

Controlling who uses cron:

You don't have to allow every user on the system to use cron. If you have a large number of users, there might be some you want to bar from using cron, or you might want to restrict the use of cron to a few users. This is easy to do.

If the file /var/cron/allow exists, then only users who are listed in that file may use cron.

If the file /var/cron/deny exists, then any user listed in that file may not use cron.

```
# This is a comment. I love comments.


# Set the SHELL to use for running cron commands, overrides whatever
# the system default is.
SHELL=/bin/sh


# Mail any output to 'puffball', regardless of whose crontab this is.
MAILTO=puffball



# You can use ranges, e.g. 1-5 means 1,2,3,4,5
# Run at 9:00am every Monday, Wednesday and Friday
0 9 * * 1,3,5 mail -s "bring me flowers" spouse@work.com


# run five minutes after midnight, every day.
# Also redirects stderr to stdout so errors get emailed.
5 0 * * *        $HOME/bin/daily.job >> $HOME/tmp/out 2>&1


# run at 2:15pm on the first of every month
15 14 1 * *        $HOME/bin/monthly



# run at 10 pm on weekdays, annoy Joe
# You can use % to include a <return> in an argument.
0 22 * * 1-5    mail -s "It's 10pm" joe%Joe,%%Where are your kids?%"


23 0-23/2 * * * echo "run 23 minutes after midn, 2am, 4am ..., everyday"


5 4 * * sun      echo "run at 5 after 4 every sunday"
```

Figure 11.30 Examples of several crontab entries.

To restrict cron use to a list of specific users:

1. Edit the file /var/cron/allow.

   This must be done by root, so if you are using the vi editor, the command would be

   `sudo vi /var/cron/allow`

   Enter your password if prompted for it.

   If the file already exists, make a copy of it first, in case you mess it up and need to go back to the original version.

2. Add the user names of those who are allowed to use cron.

   These should appear one per line—for example,

   `vanilla`

   `puffball`

3. Save the file and exit the editor.

   If you are using vi, the commands would be

   Esc :wq.

To create a list of users who are not allowed to use cron:

1. Edit the file /var/cron/deny.

   This must be done by root, so if you are using the vi editor, the command would be

   `sudo vi /var/cron/deny`

   Enter your password if prompted for it.

   If the file already exists, make a copy of it first, in case you mess it up and need to go back to the original version.

2. Add user names to the file.

   Enter one user name per line—for example,

   `jackie`

   `wesley`

3. Save the file and quit the editor.

   If you are using vi, the commands would be

   Esc :wq

   Any user listed in the file is unable to use cron.

About /etc/crontab

There is one special crontab file, /etc/crontab, already on your computer for system administration purposes.

Because the /etc/crontab file is run by root, it uses a format a little different than the crontab files for users. The command entries in /etc/crontab have an extra field (the sixth field) that specifies which user the command will run as. So instead of the actual command line being everything after the first five fields, the command in an /etc/crontab entry is everything after the first *six* fields. This allows root to schedule commands to be run by a less-privileged user.

The crontab file /etc/crontab is shown in **Figure 11.31**. The first few lines are comments.

The last three lines are the most interesting.

The commands run by the last three lines are:

periodic daily

periodic weekly

periodic monthly

Each of the three command lines runs the periodic command with an argument of daily, weekly, or monthly.

The periodic command is designed specifically to be run from a crontab file. The argument to the periodic command is the name of a directory inside the /etc/periodic directory; for example, the argument daily means that the periodic command will look inside /etc/periodic/daily/, and execute every executable file in that directory in alphabetical order.

In Mac OS X 10.2.1 there are two files inside /etc/periodic/daily, and one each in the weekly and monthly directories.

The periodic command itself has a number of configuration options, which are set in the file /etc/defaults/periodic.conf and can be overidden by settings in other files (again, see man periodic). The default settings in /etc/defaults/periodic.conf are set to get output from the daily scripts put in the log file /var/log/daily.out, the weekly scripts in /var/log/weekly.out, and the monthly scripts in /var/log/monthly.out.

RUNNING REGULARLY SCHEDULED COMMANDS

```
# /etc/crontab
SHELL=/bin/sh
PATH=/etc:/bin:/sbin:/usr/bin:/usr/sbin
HOME=/var/log
#
#minute hour    mday    month   wday    who     command
#
#*/5     *       *       *       *       root    /usr/libexec/atrun
#
# Run daily/weekly/monthly jobs.
15      3       *       *       *       root    periodic daily
30      4       *       *       6       root    periodic weekly
30      5       1       *       *       root    periodic monthly
```

Figure 11.31 The contents of the sytem's crontab file.

System Log Files

Unix systems keep quite a few log files. Entries in the system logs record a variety of events, such as system startups, email being sent, people logging in, and each use of sudo.

Mac OS X keeps most log files in /var/log, which is the same place as on many versions of Unix. **Figure 11.32** shows a typical listing for that directory. You'll notice that most of the filenames end in .gz, indicating they have been compressed using the gzip program (and can be viewed with zcat; see the man pages). The log files in /var/log are "rolled over" by the script /etc/daily, which is run from root's crontab. (See "Running Regularly Scheduled Commands," earlier in this chapter.)

```
[localhost:~] vanilla% ls /var/log
CDIS.custom          lookupd.log.2.gz     mail.log.4.gz        system.log.3.gz
OSInstall.custom     lookupd.log.3.gz     monthly.out          system.log.4.gz
daily.out            lookupd.log.4.gz     netinfo.log          system.log.5.gz
ftp.log              lpr.log              netinfo.log.0.gz     system.log.6.gz
ftp.log.0.gz         lpr.log.0.gz         netinfo.log.1.gz     system.log.7.gz
ftp.log.1.gz         lpr.log.1.gz         netinfo.log.2.gz     weekly.out
ftp.log.2.gz         lpr.log.2.gz         netinfo.log.3.gz     wtmp
ftp.log.3.gz         lpr.log.3.gz         netinfo.log.4.gz     wtmp.0.gz
ftp.log.4.gz         lpr.log.4.gz         secure.log           wtmp.1.gz
httpd                mail.log             statistics           wtmp.2.gz
lastlog              mail.log.0.gz        system.log           wtmp.3.gz
lookupd.log          mail.log.1.gz        system.log.0.gz      wtmp.4.gz
lookupd.log.0.gz     mail.log.2.gz        system.log.1.gz
lookupd.log.1.gz     mail.log.3.gz        system.log.2.gz
[localhost:~] vanilla%
```

Figure 11.32 Listing of the /var/log directory showing the system log files.

Table 11.4

Commands for Looking at Files	
COMMAND	WHAT IT DOES
less	Views the file one screen at a time.
grep	Searches for text patterns.
tail	Views the end of a file. The -f *(follow)* option is especially useful for log files.

If you have Web sharing turned on (in the Sharing section of System Preferences, in the Finder), then the Apache Web-server logs are of interest. These are /var/log/httpd/access_log and /var/log/httpd/error_log. Every request handled by the Web server is logged in access_log, and errors are logged (surprise!) in error_log.

If you suspect that something is going wrong with your system, especially if something is happening over and over, looking through the system log files can reveal the cause of the problem.

There isn't any special command needed for most of the logs; they are simply text files, and you can use the tools described in earlier chapters to look at them (see especially Chapter 5, "Using Files and Directories"). **Table 11.4** lists the most useful tools for looking through log files.

One particularly common situation involves watching a log file to see what is being added to it. See "To view the end of a file while it is growing" in Chapter 5, "Using Files and Directories."

One other important log file is the console log, which is located at /var/tmp/console.log.

The console log is where most error messages go during regular operations. It can be viewed from Aqua using the Console utilities (under Applications, look for Console in the Utilities>Console folder).

The console log is created each time you log in to Aqua, and it is owned and readable only by the user logged in to Aqua (of course, root can also read it). Everything in /var/tmp is removed when the system boots up.

The Boot Sequence

As anyone who's turned on a computer knows, a computer has to go through a series of steps before it becomes generally available for use. This process is called *booting*, which is short for *bootstrapping*—itself an abbreviation of "pulling itself up by its own bootstraps." Booting involves an iterative sequence of software starting up that in turn launches other software, and so on, until eventually the entire operating system is loaded.

Though you may not have cared about this sequence before, it's useful to know what the steps are when you're administering a machine. We'll give you an overview of the fundamental layers of software involved, and of the various places where something can go awry.

Every type of operating system has a somewhat different boot process. The official Apple documentation of the Mac OS X boot sequence is at http://gemma.apple.com/ techpubs/macosx/Essentials/SystemOverview /BootingLogin/The_Boot_Sequence.html.

Here's an abbreviated version:

1. When the power comes on, a part of the hardware called the BootROM performs a test of the hardware (Power On Self Test, or POST) and runs a piece of software called Open Firmware. This is the software that selects which operating system to use. Open Firmware is the same on Mac OS 9 and Mac OS X.

2. Once BootROM or the user has selected Mac OS X, the next piece of software to take over is the BootX booter (this is getting silly, right?), located in `/System /Library/CoreServices`. The system is now using software from the disk. BootX searches `/System/Library/ Extensions` for software drivers needed

to communicate with various hardware devices. BootX then runs the kernel of the operating system: `/mach_kernel.`

3. The kernel performs more initialization procedures and then runs `/mach_init`, which handles communication to and from the kernel.

4. The `mach_init` command starts a process called `init`. Init has a process ID of 1 and is the mother of all other processes on the machine.

5. The `init` command runs the system-initialization scripts, which are shell scripts you can look at.

6. The first script to run is `/etc/rc.boot`, followed by `/etc/rc`, which in turn runs the SystemStarter program.

7. SystemStarter runs a series of scripts found in `/System/Library/StartupItems` and `/Library/StartupItems`. (The scripts in `/System/Library/StartupItems` are supplied by Apple and you should not change them. The `/Library/StartupItems` directory is where you should install any new startup scripts of your own. See "Creating a New StartupItem," later in this chapter.) Inside the StartupItems directories you'll find a series of directories, each of which contains at least two files:

   ◆ A program (which is usually a shell script) that has the same name as the directory—for example, the program that starts up AppleTalk services is

   `/System/Library/StartupItems/ →AppleTalk/AppleTalk`

   ◆ A configuration file called a property list.

   Figure 11.33 shows the AppleTalk startup script, and **Figure 11.34** shows the AppleTalk properties file.

```
#!/bin/sh

##
# AppleTalk
##

. /etc/rc.common

StartService ()
{
    if [ "${APPLETALK:=-NO-}" != "-NO-" ] &&
       [ "$(uname -p)" = "powerpc" ]; then

        ConsoleMessage "Starting AppleTalk"

        helper=/System/Library/SystemConfiguration/Kicker.bundle/Resources/restart-AppleTalk
        if [ -x "${helper}" ]; then
            ##
            # if "configd" is managing the network configuration then we
            # should use the restart script to start AppleTalk and update
            # the configuration cache.
            ##
            ${helper}
            exit
        fi

        ATO=""
        if [ "${APPLETALK_HOSTNAME:=-AUTOMATIC-}" != "-AUTOMATIC-" ]; then
            ATO="-C ${APPLETALK_HOSTNAME}"
        fi

        case "${APPLETALK}" in
          -ROUTER-)
            # Router mode
            appletalk ${ATO} -r -q
            ;;
          -MULTIHOME-)
            # Multihome non-routing mode
            appletalk ${ATO} -x -q
            ;;
          *)
            # Single port on specified interface, non-routing
            appletalk ${ATO} -u ${APPLETALK} -q
            ;;
        esac
    fi
}
```

(continues on next page)

Figure 11.33 Startup script for AppleTalk: /System/Library/StartupItems/AppleTalk/AppleTalk

The startup scripts are all designed to start a service when executed with an argument of **start**, and should also be designed to stop the service when executed with an argument of **stop**. The startup scripts also restart a service (that is, stop it and start it again) when executed with an argument of **restart**. This approach is standard practice for system startup scripts on many Unix systems. The big difference with Mac OS X and Darwin is the location of the system startup scripts and how the arguments to the startup scripts are processed. The actual result is the same as on other Unix systems.

Most of the scripts define functions called StartService, StopService, and RestartService (see Chapter 9, "Creating and Using Shell Scripts" for more on

function in scripts). At the end of the script (see the last line of **Figure 11.33**) there is a line that says:

RunService "$1"

RunService is another function, defined in /etc/rc.common (which the startup scripts read in; see top of Figure 11.33) and the RunService function translates "start" into StartService, "stop" into StopService (and "restart" into RestartService). Why did Apple add the extra layer of functions and files? We think it was to allow greater flexibility in the startup process of future versions of Mac OS X and Darwin.

The system startup scripts all start their eponymous service when executed with a **start** argument but do not properly handle a **stop** argument. (OK, "eponymous" was a big word—it means they launch the

Figure 11.33 (continued)

```
StopService ()
{
    ConsoleMessage "Stopping AppleTalk"
    appletalk -d
}

RestartService () { StopService; StartService; }

RunService "$1"
```

```
{
    Description     = "AppleTalk networking";
    Provides        = ("AppleTalk");
    Requires        = ("Network", "Network Configuration");
    OrderPreference = "None";
}
```

Figure 11.34 Properties list for AppleTalk StartupItems: /System/Library/StartupItems/AppleTalk/
StartupParameters.plist

```
##
# /etc/hostconfig
##
# This file is maintained by the system
↪control panels
##


# Network configuration
HOSTNAME=-AUTOMATIC-
ROUTER=-AUTOMATIC-



# Services
AFPSERVER=-YES-
APPLETALK=en0
AUTHSERVER=-NO-
AUTOMOUNT=-YES-
CONFIGSERVER=-NO-
CUPS=-YES-
IPFORWARDING=-NO-
IPV6=-YES-
MAILSERVER=-YES-
NETBOOTSERVER=-NO-
NETINFOSERVER=-AUTOMATIC-
NISDOMAIN=-NO-
RPCSERVER=-AUTOMATIC-
TIMESYNC=-YES-
QTSSERVER=-NO-
SSHSERVER=-YES-
WEBSERVER=-YES-
SMBSERVER=-NO-
DNSSERVER=-NO-
CRASHREPORTER=-YES-


APPLETALK_HOSTNAME=*52d57320436f0456e7a6570757
↪4a204d6174697726d373646572*
```

Figure 11.35 A typical /etc/hostconfig file. Yours will
look different.

service using the same name as the
script, so the Sendmail script starts the
Sendmail server, for example.)

Most of the startup scripts run the script
/etc/rc.common, which in turn reads the
file /etc/hostconfig (**Figure 11.35**).

The /etc/hostconfig file sets a number of
variables that control which StartupItems
actually start something. The file is mostly
maintained by the System Preferences
tools. For instance, if you activate Personal
Web Sharing in the Sharing tool, then the
WEBSERVER variable in /etc/hostconfig is
changed from -NO- to -YES-. The script
/System/Library/StartupItems/Apache/
Apache checks that variable setting during
boot-up.

If you want to activate the mail server
(Sendmail), you change the SENDMAIL setting to -YES- and run the StartupItems
script for Sendmail with an argument
of start:

sudo /System/Library/StartupItems
↪/Sendmail/Sendmail start

(Be sure to read "Configuring Sendmail—
Internet Email Server" in Chapter 14,
"Installing and Configuring Servers,"
before starting Sendmail.)

After all of the StartupItems have been
run, the system should be fully operational and available for multiuser use.

Setting the Hostname

If your machine is being used as a server on the Internet, you usually want it to be identified by a kind of name called a *fully qualified domain name*, or FQDN. You've already seen FQDNs, although you might not have known that's what they are called. The URL www.peachpit.com is an FQDN, as is mail.yahoo.com. If your machine has been assigned an FQDN, it may be able to figure that out by itself, but it may not. The `hostname` command shows what your machine thinks its FQDN or hostname is. If you want to set the name to something else, see the first task in Chapter 14, "Installing and Configuring Servers," for a more detailed discussion of FQDNs and instructions on telling your machine what hostname (or FQDN) to use.

Creating a New StartupItem

A StartupItem consists of at least two files: the actual system startup script which should handle arguments of "start" and "stop" and a `StartupParameters.plist` file.

Any new StartupItems you create should go below the `/Library/StartupItems` directory. Do not add StartupItems inside `/System/Library/StartupItems`, as it is reserved for StartupItems that are part of the base operating system (that is, the one distributed by Apple).

Apple's official documentation for creating new StartupItems is athttp://developer.apple.com/techpubs/macosx/Darwin/howto/system_starter_howto/system_starter_howto.html (that's one long URL!).

Apple has said (as of fall 2002) that the technology of StartupItems is still in flux, so expect changes in how they are created and used. You must be logged in as an Admin user or root to create a new StartupItem.

More About StartupParameter.plist Files

The GUI tool is at `/Developer/Applications/Property List Editor`.

There are actually two allowed formats for these files. The example uses the XML *(eXtensible Markup Language)* format described in `/System/Library/DTDs/PropertyList.dtd`.

For more on XML, see *XML for the World Wide Web: Visual QuickStart Guide*, by Elizabeth Castro (Peachpit Press; www.peachpit.com).

For more on plist files, see Apple's documentation at http://developer.apple.com/techpubs/macosx/Darwin/howto/system_starter_howto/system_starter_howto.html#plist.

To create a new StartupItem:

1. Create a new directory inside /Library/StartupItems

   The new directory should have the same name as the service you are installing. For example, if you are installing the MySQL database engine (which we'll do in Chapter 15, "More Open-Source Software," on the Web at www.peachpit.com/vqp/umox), then you would call the directory MySQL:

   ```
   mkdir -p /Library/StartupItems/MySQL
   ```

   The -p option is necessary because the directory /Library/StartupItems may not already exist, and adding the -p tells mkdir to create the entire path.

2. Create a StartupParameters.plist file (for *property list*) in the new directory.

   It's a good idea to copy an existing file and modify it to suit your needs. For example, you might copy the StartupParameters.plist file that already exists for AppleTalk and then edit it:

   ```
   cd /Library/StartupItems/MySQL
   cp /System/Library/StartupItems/
   →AppleTalk/StartupParameters.plist .
   vi StartupParameters.plist
   ```

   That would copy the StartupParameters.plist file for AppleTalk into the current directory and then load it into the vi editor.

   Figure 11.36 shows an annotated version of the AppleTalk StartupParameters.plist file. You would make a few changes to that file, such as changing "AppleTalk" to "MySQL."

3. Create the startup script itself.

   The best way to learn how to do this is to copy an existing script and modify it. For example, you might start by copying the startup script for AppleTalk (shown in Figure 11.33).

   continues on next page

CREATING A NEW STARTUPITEM

Figure 11.36 An annotated copy of the AppleTalk Properties file. You can use this as a template when creating new StartupItems.

Figure 11.37 is a code listing of a sample startup script for the MySQL database engine, but it could be adapted for many purposes. (Review Chapter 9, "Creating and Using Scripts.")

4. Test the script from the command line to see that AppleTalk starts up.

5. Reboot the machine for further confirmation.

✔ **Tip**

■ You'll need to decide what should go in the "Requires" entry of the `StartupParameters.plist`. Have a look at the different `StartupParameters.plist` files in each of the subdirectories of `/System/Library/StartupItems/` and see what is in the "Provides" entry for each item. You could see all the "Provides" entries with the following command line:

```
grep Provides /System/Library
→/StartupItems/*/*.plist
```

```
#!/bin/sh
# Darwin/Mac OS X StartupItem script for MySQL
# This script should be saved as /Library/StartupItems/MySQl/MySQL


# Read in common system configuration stuff
# Among other things this will cause /etc/hostconfig to be read
#
. /etc/rc.common


# /etc/hostconfig should have    MYSQL=-YES-
# If $MYSQL has not been set then we set it to -NO-
# If   $MYSQL is not -YES- then we exit and skip everything else.
if [ "${MYSQL:=-NO-}" != "-YES-" ] ; then
    exit
fi


# If we get here then /etc/hostconfig has MYSQL=-YES-

# Set the path to the directory where we installed MySQL
# Depending on how you installed it this could be /sw, /usr/local
# of perhaps something else.
BASE_DIR="/sw"

# Command to start MySQL
MYSQL_START="$BASE_DIR/bin/safe_mysqld"
```

Figure 11.37 Code listing of a sample startup script for the MySQL database engine.

Figure 11.37 (continued)

```
# Location of MySQL process ID file
hostname=`hostname`
PID_FILE="$BASE_DIR/var/mysql/$hostname.pid"

if [ ! $# -gt 0 ] ; then
    1='no arguments!'
fi

case "$1" in
    start)
        ConsoleMessage "Starting MySQL"
        cd "$BASE_DIR"
        $MYSQL_START &
    ;;

    stop)
        # As of MySQL version 3.23.49 there is no clean way to
        # shutdown the MySQL server without using the msqladmin
        # tool, which requires the MySQL root password.
        # If you decide to use this part, make this file readable
        # ONLY by root (chmod 700 MySQL) then uncomment the next two lines
        # and fill in your MySQL root password where the XXXXXXXX is.
        # There must not be any spaces between the -p and the password.
        # ConsoleMessage "Stopping MySQL"
        # /sw/bin/mysqladmin -u root -pXXXXXXXX shutdown
    ;;

    restart)
        $0 stop
        # wait 3 seconds
        sleep 3
        $0 start
    ;;
    *)
        ConsoleMessage "Usage: $0 start|stop|restart"
    ;;
esac
```

Webmin—A GUI Tool for System Administration

Webmin is a Web-based interface for Unix system administration that allows you to use a Web browser to perform a large variety of tasks, such as managing users and groups, managing servers such as database servers, setting up cron jobs, and much more.

Webmin installs its own tiny Web server that uses the HTTPS protocol if possible. HTTPS is the HTTP protocol plus Secure Socket Layer; it causes all data sent to or from the Web server to be encrypted. This greatly reduces the risk of a packet-sniffing attack, which could intercept the Webmin user name and password, giving the attacker the equivalent of root access. In order for Webmin to use SSL, you must install the Perl Net::SSLeay module. Chapter 13, "Installing Software from Source Code," describes how to do this. If you do not install Net::SSLeay, you may still use Webmin, but any use of it when the Web browser is on another machine is vulnerable to packet-sniffing attacks.

The following instructions are based on Webmin version 0.99 but should be the same for later versions. Webmin versions before 0.99 do not properly handle directory names that contain spaces.

Before proceeding with the installation of Webmin, read Chapter 13, in particular the section "Manually Installing from Source Code," which goes into more detail about the procedures you should use.

To install Webmin:

1. Check out the Webmin documentation.

   Webmin (www.webmin.com) has a collection of documentation and links; particularly useful is Joe Cooper's Webmin Users Guide (www.swelltech.com/support/webminguide/).

   We suggest you bookmark it or download and save it.

2. Become root:

   `sudo -s`

   You'll need to be root for the remaining steps.

   Enter your password if prompted.

3. `mkdir /usr/local/webmin`

   This is the directory into which you download the compressed archive file containing all of Webmin's files.

4. `cd /usr/local/webmin`

5. Download the Webmin source code in `tar.gz` format from the Webmin site.

6. Move the downloaded source archive file into the directory created in step 3.

   For example, you might have downloaded the archive to the Desktop for the user vanilla using a GUI Web browser. You could then use this command at the command line

   `mv ~vanilla/Desktop/webmin-0.990.`
   `↪tar.gz .`

   which moves the file to the current directory.

7. Unpack the tarball.

Assuming the archive file is named `webmin-0.990.tar.gz`, the command is

`tar xfvz webmin-0.990.tar.gz`

Webmin contains a *lot* of files, so this may take a minute. The process creates a new directory called `webmin-0.990`

Do *not* remove the compressed tar file.

8. `Cd` into the new directory:

`cd webmin-0.990`

9. Read the read-me file:

`less README`

This is where the latest installation and other news is found. The README file may direct you to read other files for more information.

10. Run the install script:

`./setup.sh`

You are asked a series of questions. We suggest you accept the default answers to all of them, with the possible exception of the question about the Web-server host name.

- If the default shown does not look right, then enter an FQDN that points to your machine's IP address, or enter your machine's IP address. If you have not installed the

Net::SSLeay module, then we suggest you use a hostname of "localhost," which means that you can only access Webmin from the same machine it is running on.

- If you have already installed the Perl Net::SSLeay module *(very highly recommended)*, answer "y" when asked if you want to use SSL. This makes Webmin much more secure.

- If you want Webmin to start when the machine is booted up, answer "y" to the question "Start Webmin at boot time?" That causes the install script to create the appropriate StartupItems directory and files. In version 0.99 (but not later versions), Webmin creates the StartupItems directory in `/System/Library/StartupItems/`, which is supposed to be reserved for Apple-installed items. Later versions of Webmin use `/Library/StartupItems/`, which is the correct place for user-installed StartupItems.

11. Stop being root:

`exit`

That should bring you back to your regular shell prompt.

12. Test the installation.

Use a Web browser on your machine to look at https://localhost:10000/ (or *http* instead of *https* if you are not using SSL).

That should bring up the Webmin log-in screen.

- If you are using SSL, you get a warning from your browser about Webmin's Certificate—it is OK to accept the certificate Webmin is using. **Figure 11.38** shows a typical Web-browser warning message (this one is from Mozilla).

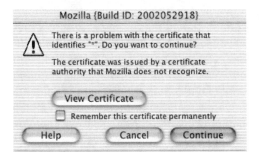

Figure 11.38 A warning message from a Web browser (Mozilla in this case) indicating a Secure Server certificate signed by an unknown party.

13. Try making some changes to your system. Make gentle ones at first—things you know how to reverse from the command line. For example, try changing a user's real name or shell. **Figure 11.39** shows a screen shot of the Webmin interface for managing a single user's information.

Webmin installs parts of itself in a variety of places on your hard drive, but it is very easy to remove (we wish more Unix software worked like this).

To remove Webmin:

◆ `sudo /etc/webmin/uninstall.sh`

If prompted for your password, enter it.

Executing this script removes all the files Webmin installed, as well as the directory created in step 3 of the previous task.

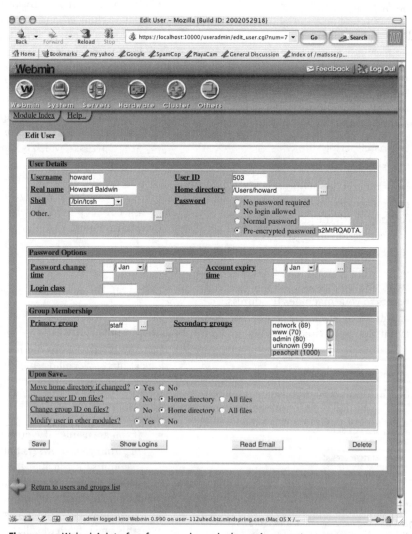

Figure 11.39 Webmin's interface for managing a single user's account.

Troubleshooting Tips

Not that *anything ever* goes wrong with your system, but when something *does* go wrong, there are some things you can try in order to figure out what has happened.

Troubleshooting problems in a Unix system is similar in many ways to troubleshooting on any system: You start by comparing the symptoms of the problem with the patient's medical history. When did the problem start? Oh, right after you installed the system-configuration files you were up all night editing? Hmmm. Maybe that's a clue to the problem ...

Using the system log files

The system log files (described earlier in this chapter) often have an error message related to the problem you are experiencing. Usually you won't understand the error message, but don't stop there. You can search the Web for information regarding the exact error message you are seeing.

To search the Web for an error message:

1. Copy whatever seems to be the most descriptive part of the error message.

2. Use your favorite Web search engine to search for the error message.

   This usually means enclosing all the words in quotes—for example, "DNSAgent: dns_send_query_server - timeout"

3. Consider adding "Mac OS X" or "Darwin" as a separate search string.

   For example, using the Google search engine,

   "DNSAgent: dns_send_query_server - timeout" + "Mac OS X"

   limits the search to pages that contain both of the phrases enclosed in quotes. (We found five pages with that search.)

Permission problems

If you are getting an error that includes the words "Permission denied" or something similar, it's a sign that you have a permission problem somewhere—a common problem in Unix. Permission problems crop up because a program might not be able to write to a directory or file it expects to, or because it might not be able to read a file and thus is missing some configuration information.

Tracking down permissions problems, like much computer troubleshooting, requires that you think like the machine. Remember that in order to create a file, a process must have write permission for the *directory* containing the file (because the filename is an entry in the directory), while in order to change a file, you must have write permission on the *file* itself.

Review Chapter 8, "Working with Permissions and Ownership," for details on permissions.

Dealing with "device full" problems

Another problem you are likely to run into sooner or later is when a disk fills up.

If you see an error message that says, "Write Error: No space left on device," you've filled up a disk partition; that is, you've used up all the available storage space.

Although this doesn't happen every day (hopefully!), the consequences can be pretty harsh: Some programs may simply stop working. For example, a mail server cannot save incoming mail if there is no disk space left.

You can quickly see if you are running out of disk space by using the df command (described in "To see a summary of disk usage for the entire system," earlier in this chapter).

If you see that any of the regular partitions are at or near 100 percent capacity, it's time to start worrying. By "regular partitions," we mean the ones where the filesystem column in df starts with /dev/disk. Remember that df displays information about various pseudo-partitions that always show up at 100 percent capacity—for example, the fdesc (*file descriptor*) filesystem, which is used to keep track of open files.

This is possible because the operating system keeps a small amount of disk space in reserve to reduce the chance of a partition's filling up. If you see that a disk partition is at 101 percent capacity, then you have a problem *now*.

Basic steps to free up space on a disk partition:

◆ Delete unneeded files on the critical partition. Remember that using the Trash does not actually delete files—it moves them. To actually delete the files, use rm and/or empty the Trash. See "To clear out users' trash for them," below.

◆ Move one or more directories to a different partition and put a symbolic link where the directory used to be. See "To move directories from one disk to another," below.

◆ Add more disks, and then move directories to the new disk. In Mac OS X, this is as easy as it has always been on the Mac. With external FireWire and USB hard drives, you don't even need to shut down.

Note that Mac OS X automatically makes any disks you add show up in /Volumes. On almost all other Unix systems, adding a disk is more complicated, but you can mount new disks on any directory. For example, you could mount a new disk on /Users (though you would still have to copy the old contents onto the new disk).

To clear out users' trash for them:

1. Find each user's Trash directory.

Each user has a .Trash directory in his or her home directory.

If the partition that's filling up is the one that holds users' home directories, go into each user's home directory and delete his or her .Trash directory (it is re-created when the user needs it).

You'll need to do the next step for each user.

2. sudo rm -rf ~*username*/.Trash

That removes an entire .Trash directory.

Also, if you use the Finder to trash a file that is on a different partition than your home directory, then instead of going into ~/.Trash, that file goes into a different trash directory.

Going over 100 Percent

On some Unix systems, df may show you that a filesystem (as it does with a partition) is *over* 100 percent capacity.

On those systems, the "used" and "available" columns in df add up to something less than the column showing the total capacity. On Mac OS X the numbers add up exactly.

There are directories at the root level of the directory on which each partition is mounted. Huh, you say? Here is an example:

Let's say you have three disk partitions. Perhaps you have two disks, and one of them has two partitions. Your df output might look like that shown in **Figure 11.40**. Note the use of the -lk options to show only local partitions, and the sizes in kilobytes. Note too that df will only show partitions, not the trash files themselves.)

In that case, there are three directories, each called .Trashes:

/.Trashes

/Volumes/partition2/.Trashes

/Volumes/flamepit/.Trashes

Each of the directories has subdirectories for each user ID that has trashed file from that partition. So if user puffball has uid 502, then there might be

/Users/puffball/.Trash

/Volumes/partition2/.Trashes/502
→/puffball

/Volumes/flamepit/.Trashes/502
→/puffball

You want to remove the .Trashes directory from the critical partition (don't worry, it will be re-created when needed).

3. `sudo rm -rf /partition-in-trouble`
   `→/.Trashes`

   To remove the .Trashes directory for the partition mounted on /Volumes /partition2:

   `sudo rm -rf /Volumes/partition2`
   `→/.Trashes`

If you have one partition that is filling up and another with more space (perhaps you've added a second disk), you can move directories from the full partition to the spacious one, and replace the original directory with a symbolic link.

To move directories from one disk to another:

1. Use ditto to copy the directory.

   For example, if you want to move the /Users directory to the partition mounted on /Volumes/partition2, you can use

   `sudo ditto -rsrc /Users`
   `/Volumes/partition2/Users`

continues on next page

TROUBLESHOOTING TIPS

```
These two partitions are on the same disk.
All partitons except the first are mounted in /Volumes.              Uh oh! About to fill up.

       [localhost:~] vanilla% df -lk
       Filesystem     1K-blocks      Used     Avail Capacity | Mounted on
   ┌──/dev/disk0s9     4345948    4345925        23     99% │ /
   │   fdesc                 1          1         0    100%   /dev
   └──/dev/disk0s10   15656640    1701424  13955216     10%   /Volumes/partition2
   ┌──/dev/disk2s9    97845880    8040888  89804992      8%   /Volumes/flamepit
   │   [localhost:~] vanilla%
   │
   This partition is on the second disk.
```

Figure 11.40 Example of output from df -lk showing two disks with a total of three partitions.

2. `mv ` *`olddir`* ` olddir.save`

For example,

`mv /Users /Users.save`

You'll delete it later after making sure that everything is OK.

3. Create a symbolic link where the old directory was, pointing to the new directory.

For example,

`ln -s /Volumes/partition2/Users`
`→/Users`

So anything that accesses `/Users` still works.

⚠ As of Mac OS X 10.1.5, there is a bug that causes home directories not to be created for new users added through the Users panel in System Preferences when `/Users` has been moved. Apple knows about this (bug #2984838) and is working on it.

4. When everything seems OK, delete the old directory.

For example,

`rm -rf /Users.save`

Getting More Help

There are plenty of places to get deeper into Unix system administration. Here are a few:

The official Apple documentation for the Darwin layer of Mac OS X can be found by starting http://developer.apple.com/darwin/.

Another useful set of documentation from Apple is oriented toward developers (programmers) but contains much information of interest to anyone wanting to dig deeper into Mac OS X: http://developer.apple.com/techpubs/macosx/Essentials/SystemOverview/.

The Mac OS X Hints Web site (www.macosxhints.com) is a wonderful user-supported site run by Rob Griffiths. The site is basically a big bulletin board for Mac OS X information. It's free, but you can make a donation to support it.

Two valuable books in the Unix systems-administration world are

Essential System Administration, 3rd Edition, by Æleen Frisch (O'Reilly; www.oreilly.com/catalog/esa3/)

and

UNIX System Administration Handbook, 3rd Edition, by Evi Nemeth, Garth Snyder, Scott Seebass, and Trent R. Hein (Admin.com; www.admin.com).

TROUBLESHOOTING TIPS

If the machine won't fully boot up

In the unlikely and scary event that your machine won't completely boot up, you may still be able to get things working again—assuming that the machine can at least begin the boot process.

If you are able to boot into single-user mode, then you can attempt to repair filesystem damage using the `fsck` *(file system check)* command.

To watch all the system-startup messages:

◆ Hold down [Cmd] and [V] while booting. In a normal, healthy boot-up, you see a great deal of text messages scrolling across the screen as the system goes through the boot-up process. It won't hurt anything to do this even when the system is working fine, so try it a couple of times and watch what a normal startup looks like.

Booting in verbose mode won't directly fix anything, but you may be able to see what's going wrong, or at least copy a message off the screen to give to someone else to assist in troubleshooting.

To check and repair the filesystem with fsck:

1. Boot into single-user mode.

   You do this by holding down [Cmd] and [S] while the machine starts up (covered in "To boot into single-user mode," at the beginning of this chapter).

   If the system isn't too badly messed up, you end up at a prompt like this:

   `localhost#`

   Your next move is to try to check and repair the filesystem.

2. `/sbin/fsck -y`

   This is basically the command-line version of the repair feature in Disk Utility.

   When you get back to the prompt, run it again to make sure that the repairs were effective.

3. `/sbin/fsck -y`

   If you get a message saying that your disk "appears to be OK," then `fsck` worked.

   If it didn't work, you are going to need to find an experienced Unix administrator to help, or contact Apple for assistance.

   If it worked (or even if it didn't), go ahead and reboot the machine.

4. `reboot`

   Hopefully, the machine starts up and all is well.

TROUBLESHOOTING TIPS

SECURITY

Security, like freedom, is a goal and an ideal, not an absolute condition.

As shipped, Mac OS X is fairly secure. If you use your machine only as a personal computer and do not install any new server software on it, then your only security assignment is to regularly use the Apple Software Update tool (see "Keeping Up-to-Date," later in this chapter).

On the other hand, if you have multiple users or you install new Internet server software on your machine, then you are well advised to pay more attention to security.

Because Unix systems are inherently multiuser, they tend to have many people using them. This means there are likely to be a number of people who have various levels of access to a machine running Unix, and each of these users' accounts is a potential entry point for an attacker. Also, Unix's origin as a system created to foster collaborative work means that security settings default to letting all users on a system have at least read-only access. (In Mac OS X, users' home directories are set up with a higher level of security, but most system files are still readable by all users.)

You achieve security only by preventing unauthorized access to your system. It is also important to monitor your system to see if its security has been breached.

In this chapter we cover the basics of Unix system security, including physical security, choosing and protecting passwords, protecting against attacks over the Internet, and keeping up-to-date with the latest software and security-related announcements.

A note about terminology: Throughout this chapter we use the terms server and service, and you need to keep in mind their different meanings. Server can refer to either a physical machine, as in "That G4 in the corner is our Web-server box," or a piece of software that provides a service; for example, "That G4 in the corner is running the Apache Web server" or "Sendmail is the server software that provides email service on this box."

Physical Security

It might seem obvious, but we think it is worth pointing out that you should keep your computer as physically secure as you want its data to be.

If someone has physical access to your machine, she could boot it into single-user mode and then have the run of the system. (See Chapter 11, "Introduction to System Administration," for more on booting into single-user mode.)

And of course, if someone has physical access to the machine, he might be able to steal it, install malicious software on it, or even install a hardware keystroke-recording device (see Privacy.org; www.privacy.org/print.php?sid=990).

The main idea here is to remember that computers, hard drives, and wires all exist in the physical world, and that the same security precautions you apply to, say, your checkbook should be applied to your data.

Choosing Good Passwords

Passwords are the foundation of Unix security. All the other security measures are for naught if you have weak passwords (meaning that they're easy to guess or obtain) or if someone is able to obtain a user's password, no matter how good it is.

As we discussed in Chapter 11, a good password is one that is both easy to remember (so it doesn't get written on a note taped to the user's screen) and hard to guess. The latter means that the password should not be susceptible to a "dictionary attack" (described below).

How passwords are vulnerable

Unauthorized people obtain passwords in three ways. Think about whether you're vulnerable to any of these:

◆ **User error.** This includes writing the password on a note stuck to your screen, or sending a password via email or leaving it in voice mail.

◆ **Dictionary attacks.** Done by a software program that tries millions of guesses to figure out a password. These attacks start by obtaining the encrypted version of a password and comparing it with every possible encrypted version of a huge list of words and possible passwords (the *dictionary*). If they match, then the attacker knows what the password is.

◆ **Packet-sniffing attacks.** These occur when a monitoring device is illicitly used to examine all of the data flowing on a network. User names and passwords can be "sniffed" out of the data stream with ease, so any unencrypted traffic is completely vulnerable. These attacks are described in more detail below in "Protecting Yourself from Internet Attacks."

The first two vulnerabilities (user error and dictionary attacks) are fairly easy to reduce or eliminate, so we'll tackle those first. The third vulnerability, packet-sniffing attacks, comes from the vulnerability of unencrypted data traveling over a network. Reducing this vulnerability is more complex, and we tackle that in the section "Protecting Yourself from Internet Attacks."

You need to communicate to your users the potential consequences of their passwords' being obtained by an attacker: The system can be rendered unusable, data can be lost or altered, private information can be made public, and the system can be used as a staging area for further attacks.

Passwords are liable to be compromised when users do foolish things like writing them on notes left under their keyboard, letting someone watch them enter their password, or sending a password via email. Email messages are like postcards—they can be read at several places along their journey, and there is no way of knowing if the intended recipient is actually the person who reads the email. It is a very bad idea to send unencrypted passwords via email. Ultimately, you prevent the compromise of passwords through user error by educating your users.

Because computers are so fast these days, a dictionary attack using a very large dictionary of possible passwords can be completed in a matter of hours or days. This method includes adding numbers to the beginning and end of every word, so a dictionary attack can guess a password of sunny23 or 7times7.

A dictionary attack can only work if the encryption method used always produces the same encrypted text from the same input (such systems are said to be deterministic), and if the attacker's dictionary includes the plain-text password. Sadly, the

continues on next page

standard encryption method used to store passwords on Unix systems does indeed produce the same output whenever it is given the same input. (The encryption method used, known as *crypt*, is an advanced version of the World War II–era Enigma encryption system used by the German military and cracked by the Poles and later the British.)

Many modern Unix systems add a layer of defense against dictionary attacks by making the encrypted passwords available only to the root account. However, on Mac OS X (as of version 10.1.5), anyone can use the `nidump` command to reveal all of the encrypted passwords. Apple is aware of this weak point and intends to fix it.

It would be best if computer systems did not use authentication methods that are vulnerable to dictionary and packet-sniffing attacks (see the sidebar "S/Key and Kerberos: Better Authentication Systems" for two examples), but the crypt system of password encryption is so widely used in the Unix world that this will not happen soon (enough).

So, the best available defense against dictionary attacks is to use passwords that are not in anyone's dictionary. This means passwords that contain a combination of letters, numbers, and punctuation, and that do not contain a dictionary word.

S/Key and Kerberos: Better Authentication Systems

There are alternatives to the standard Unix password system, which uses passwords that are vulnerable to dictionary and packet-sniffing attacks.

These alternatives have been around for many years but are still far from being universally adopted:

S/Key. Secure Key is a onetime password (OTP) system—that is, a system that generates and uses passwords that are valid only once. S/Key is a registered trademark of Bell Communications Research (where it was developed), so the acronym OTP is often used instead.

When a user attempts to log in to an OTP-protected system, he gets a "challenge" (some numbers) from the server, which he enters into an OTP response generator on his end, along with his password. The response generator then creates a onetime password, which the user enters into the protected system to obtain access.

An OTP response generator for Mac OS X is SkeyCalc (www.orange-carb.org/ SkeyCalc/).

Kerberos. Developed at the Massachusetts Institute of Technology, Kerberos (http:// web.mit.edu/kerberos/www/) is an even more secure system. (Kerberos is the Greek name for the three-headed dog that guarded the entrance to Hades, better known by its Latin name, Cerberus.) Kerberos exchanges encrypted information between the client and server, and the server issues a temporary "ticket" to the client. Kerberos is designed to be invulnerable to packet sniffing and to situations in which an attacker is able to commandeer a machine between the user and the service she is trying to authenticate into (a "man in the middle" attack). We believe that Apple is considering adding increased support for Kerberos to future versions of Mac OS X.

CHOOSING GOOD PASSWORDS

To choose a good password:

1. Pick a song lyric, poem, or phrase from your favorite story—for example, "Can any human being ever reach that kind of light?" (from "Galileo," by Emily Saliers of the Indigo Girls).

2. Take the first letter of each word in the phrase, so here we have

   Cahbertkol

3. Change some of the letters to numbers. The changes should be ones that make sense to you. Perhaps the C becomes 100 because C is the Roman numeral for 100: 100ahbertkol.

4. Change the result to include some punctuation.

   Perhaps the k becomes a % because it sort of looks like a %, and perhaps you add a ? at the end because the phrase itself is a question. So you have 100ahbert%ol?

5. Make sure the remaining characters include both upper- and lowercase letters.

   Maybe you make the h and b uppercase because you like human beings: 100aHBert%ol?

6. You've got a great password.

   The result is very unlikely to be in anyone's dictionary of passwords and should be easy for you to remember because it is based on something that has personal meaning for you.

✔ Tip

- Many Unix password systems only pay attention to the first eight characters of the password, but there is no harm in using a longer one if it helps you remember.

Protecting Yourself from Internet Attacks

If your computer is connected to a network, then by definition, other computers on that network can communicate with your computer. If your network is connected to another network (that is, if it's part of an internetwork), then your exposure is potentially greater. If your computer is connected to the world's largest internetwork, the Internet, then your exposure to potentially naughty people is about as big as it gets.

The default configuration for Mac OS X is reasonably secure from Internet attacks. Nonetheless, it is helpful to have a basic understanding of the security risks of connecting to the Internet and of how to protect your machine from attack.

If your machine is connected to the Internet, it may be exposed to unauthorized and malicious people attempting to gain control of it or to harm it in some way. We say "may be" because some ways of connecting your machine to the Internet do not expose it to attack, and there are things you can do to configure your machine to reduce its exposure.

Every machine connected to the Internet has either a public or a private IP address.

Some IP addresses are actually not part of the public Internet. These addresses (known as private addresses) are used by networks that are, well, private, and not accessible to machines on the public Internet. Think of it this way: All machines that are connected to the Internet have an IP address, but not all machines that have an IP address are connected to the Internet. See the sidebar "Connecting to the Internet with a Private IP Address."

Connecting to the Internet with a Private IP Address

Private TCP/IP network addresses are those that begin with 10., 172.16., or 192.168. (for example, the following are all private addresses: 10.1.1.23, 172.16.20.35, 192.168.1.254).

If your machine has a private address, it can still use the public Internet via a process called Network Address Translation (NAT).

Private networks often have a NAT server that allows the machines on the local, private network to connect to the Internet.

A NAT server translates the return addresses of all outgoing data so that to the rest of the world, the data is coming from a nonprivate IP address. When responses come back in to the NAT server from the outside world, it again translates and forwards the data to the appropriate machine on the private network.

One effect of using NAT is that machines on the public Internet cannot initiate connections to machines behind the NAT server. The NAT server will only pass data to the local, private machines if it comes in response to a connection started from the local network.

The BrickHouse application (described below for its role as a security tool) includes an experimental feature that can be used to turn your Mac into a NAT server.

You can read more about private addresses at www.ietf.org/rfc/rfc1918.txt and about NAT at www.ietf.org/rfc/rfc1631.txt and www.ietf.org/rfc/rfc2766.txt.

On the other hand, if your machine has a publicly reachable IP address, then machines anywhere on the Internet can initiate connections to it. They only succeed in making a connection if your machine is "listening" for the type of connection being attempted. For example, if you have activated Web sharing, these machines can connect to your Web server.

Packet-sniffing attacks

Packet-sniffing attacks are the most insidious type of attack you are likely to deal with. In a packet-sniffing attack, a sniffer program running on a computer examines all of the data flowing on that machine's local network. This makes all the unencrypted data on that network easily available for examination: user names, passwords, credit card numbers, medical histories, you name it. Any data whatsoever that is traveling unencrypted on a network is open for examination via a packet sniffer.

There are legitimate uses of packet sniffers, primarily having to do with diagnosing networking problems, so the mere existence of a packet-sniffer program doesn't automatically mean that someone is attacking your system or network, but it is certainly something to be concerned about.

To run a packet sniffer, though, one must have full control over the machine on which it is run. For a Unix machine, that means having root access. But a user running a Mac OS 9 or Windows machine can also run packet sniffers. (The packet sniffer needs to be able to alter settings in the network interface card—the Ethernet adapter—to put it into promiscuous mode, in which it reads every packet of data passing by on the wire.)

Using easily available tools (see the sidebar "Packet Sniffers and Port Scanners"), it is possible to grab user names and passwords that are being sent over the local network between machines. **Figure 12.1** is a diagram of a typical local area network (LAN) connected to the Internet. The packet sniffer could be on your local network, or on a network where someone is connecting to a server on your network. In either case, the sniffer will be able to obtain unencrypted passwords that are being sent to your server. So if you are

continues on next page

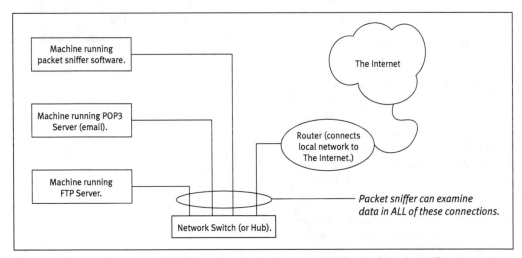

Figure 12.1 Diagram showing a typical LAN connected to the Internet and the reach of a packet sniffer.

running any services on your machine that use unencrypted passwords for access, it is possible that a user account on your machine will get sniffed, and then the attacker could log in to your machine and cause further mischief.

One defense against packet sniffing is to not run any services that allow log-in via unencrypted passwords (for example, not running a Telnet or FTP server). In the real world, however, you may need to run some services that use unencrypted passwords. Most email programs use either POP or IMAP protocols to collect a user's email from the mail server, and the passwords are sent over the network without encryption. If you find yourself running a POP or IMAP server, then you should consider setting each user's account so that he cannot log in and get a shell prompt from the machine. So you might set all the IMAP users to have a log-in shell of /usr/bin/false, which allows them to use IMAP to collect their email but not use the same user name and password to log in and get a shell prompt. That way, even if an IMAP user's password is sniffed, the attacker cannot use it to get a shell prompt and attempt further attacks from the "inside." (Review Chapter 11, "Introduction to System Administration," for more on how to change a user's log-in shell.)

Attacks on services

Most attacks against a machine via the Internet occur when an attacker connects to a service running on the target machine and exploits a security hole in that service. For example, there may be a security weakness in Sendmail, the program that provides email services. An attacker might connect to the email server on your machine and then attempt to exploit the security vulnerability.

The exact method of each attack is different, depending upon the exact security hole being exploited.

What an Attack on IIS Looks Like

If you turn on Web sharing (in the Sharing panel of System Preferences), and if your machine is connected to the Internet with a publicly accessible IP address, you can almost be certain to see entries in the server log file (/var/log/httpd/access_log) that reveal attacks directed at Microsoft's IIS server software.

A typical attack will show up in the Web-server log as

```
66.169.207.82 - - [13/Jul/
→2002:07:59:19 -0700] "GET
→/scripts/..%c0%2f../winnt/
→system32/cmd.exe?/c+dir HTTP/
→1.0" 404 319
```

That line shows an attack originating from the machine with the IP address 66.169.207.82 on July 13, 2002, at 7:59 GMT. The attack attempted to run a program called cmd.exe. The Web server returned a "Page Not Found" code (404), and the attack had no effect besides using up a bit of bandwidth and creating a log entry. On the other hand, had this machine been running Windows NT with an unsecure version of IIS, the attack might have succeeded in gaining control of the machine. Seeing a dozen or more of these attacks every day is quite common.

One common type of attack is called a buffer-overflow attack. In situations where software has a buffer-overflow vulnerability, that vulnerability can be exploited by an attacker who sends the target software more data than it was designed to handle. If the target software is vulnerable, a portion of memory the target is using gets overwritten by the excess data (perhaps a command of many kilobytes where the software expected only a few characters). The excess data now occupies a part of the target's memory where legitimate commands are supposed to be, only now those commands are ones that were supplied by the attacker. Of course, well-designed software doesn't allow this, but sometimes such vulnerabilities exist and are exploited.

Other attacks, known as denial-of-service (frequently abbreviated DoS) attacks, simply seek to overload a server with more requests than it can handle, causing the server to either crash or simply be unable to respond to normal requests—very much like keeping someone's fax machine constantly busy.

Denial-of-service attacks are very hard to defend against, since they often do not rely upon any weakness in your server software but instead simply keep it too busy to be useful. Thankfully, DoS attacks are not very common, because they require a sustained effort on the part of the attacker, often from multiple machines.

The most common attacks involve software that probes a network looking for server software that is known to have a particular weakness, and then attempts to exploit the weakness. Most commonly, this type of attack seeks servers running Microsoft's Internet Information Server (IIS)—its Web-server software—versions of which have been shipped with serious security flaws. Virtually every Web server on the Internet sees multiple daily attacks aimed at IIS software. Of course, since you are running Mac OS X, these attacks mean nothing to you. (See the sidebar "What an Attack on IIS Looks Like.")

An example of a problematic weakness in server software was discovered in late June 2002 with servers that handle SSH connections. The `sshd` server software, part of a package called OpenSSH (www.openssh.org), is not turned on in the default Mac OS X configuration. Many Internet-connected users do activate it to provide a secure (encrypted) form of command-line access to their machines (see Chapter 14, "Installing and Configuring Servers"). A little over a week after the problem was discovered, a security update was available for download from Apple. Notification and installation of the update were automatic for Mac OS X users who had Software Update turned on in the System Preferences.

You can read about the specific problem at Pine Internet (www.pine.nl/advisories/pine-cert-20020301.html). You can see a list of the frequent security updates Apple provides at www.info.apple.com/usen/security/security_updates.html. See "Keeping Up-to-Date," later in this chapter.

Limiting the number of services running on a machine limits both its exposure and the number of things you need to keep up-to-date. For this reason, it is a good idea not to run services you don't need.

Mac OS X comes with all Internet services turned off. If you take over maintenance of a machine that has been set up by someone else, you should read Chapter 14, "Installing and Configuring Servers," and consider deactivating servers you are not using. Look for active servers in the `/etc/hostconfig` file, in each file in the `/etc/xinetd.d` directory, and in the `/etc/inetd.conf` file (if it exists on your system). (For more about

continues on next page

inetd, see the sidebar "The Server of Servers: inetd.") Chapter 14 gives examples of editing these files to both enable and disable services, using actual servers as examples (remember, a server is a piece of software that provides a service).

Besides limiting the server software you run on a machine, you should also limit which ports are accessible.

About ports

Think of ports this way: If an IP address is your machine's Internet "telephone number," then ports are "extensions" on that number. Each Internet service running on a machine "listens" on a specific port number. For example, the default port for email servers is port 25, for an SSH server it is port 22, for Web servers it is port 80, and so on. **Table 12.1** describes the most commonly used ports.

When a client program connects to a remote machine, it needs not only the remote machine's IP address but also the port number of the service it is connecting to. (Review Chapter 10, "Interacting with Other Unix Machines.")

If outside access to a port is blocked, you are protected even if there is a server (perhaps inadvertently) listening on that port.

The primary type of traffic carried on the Internet uses TCP (Transmission Control Protocol). You can test whether a particular port is open or blocked to TCP traffic quite easily by using the telnet command, described in Chapter 10, "Interacting with Other Unix Machines." Review the section "Connecting using Telnet" in Chapter 10 before proceeding with this task.

Table 12.1

Commonly Used Ports	
PORT	**USE**
20 & 21	File Transfer Protocol (FTP) servers use both ports 20 and 21. FTP is turned off in the default Mac OS X configuration (it can be turned on in the Sharing panel of System Preferences). FTP passwords are sent over the wire unencrypted ("in the clear").
22	The Secure Shell (SSH) protocol. Part of the default Mac OS X configuration.
23	Telnet servers listen on port 23. Not used in the default Mac OS X configuration. Telnet passwords are sent in the clear.
25	The default port for email servers—the Simple Mail Transport Protocol (SMTP). Not turned on in the default Mac OS X configuration, but see Chapter 14, "Installing and Configuring Servers."
80	The default port for Hypertext Transfer Protocol (HTTP) used by Web browsers and servers. Not turned on in the default Mac OS X configuration, but see Chapter 14.
109	The Post Office Protocol (POP), version 2. POP servers provide remote access to your email box.
110	The POP protocol, version 3.
	Interim Mail Access Protocol (IMAP). A newer, better way of allowing users to pick up their email over networks. In particular, IMAP makes it easy to read your email from more than one computer.
	AppleTalk. This is the networking protocol used by AppleShare, Apple's system for allowing Macintoshes to share disks over networks.
443	HTTPS (HTTP plus Secure Socket Layer). Encrypted version of HTTP. Web sites whose URLs begin with *https* are normally on port 443.
	AppleShare over TCP/IP. The latest versions of AppleShare encrypt the password before sending it.
4000	ICQ. A popular live chat system.

How Do Services Get Assigned to Port Numbers?

The list of "well-known" and "registered" ports is maintained by IANA—the Internet Assigned Numbers Authority (www.iana.org).

The current official list of port numbers is at www.iana.org/assignments/port-numbers, and the standard Unix file `/etc/services` on your machine is simply a slightly reformatted version of that same information. (But see the note below about Darwin.) For many years the IANA was mainly one man: Jon Postel, a true hero of the Internet whose mantra was "Be liberal in what you accept, and conservative in what you send." He gave much good and shaped a world in which the contributions of others flourished. Postel's early death at age 55 was a great blow to the Internet community (see www.postel.org/jonpostel.html).

(However, Darwin/Mac OS X does not use the `/etc/services` file; instead, the same information is stored in the NetInfo database. The command

`nidump services .`

will show you the "services" part of the NetInfo database in the same format that is used in the `/etc/services` file. Changes must be made using either the NetInfo Manager GUI application or the `niutil` command-line tool. See the Darwin Network HOWTO page at www.opendarwin.org/documentation/).

To check if a particular port is blocked:

1. `telnet` *hostname* *port*

   Hostname can be either a name or an IP address, and *port* is the port number you are checking. For example,

   `telnet localhost 25`

   attempts to connect to your own machine on port 25.

   `telnet www.matisse.net 80`

   attempts to connect to port 80 on the machine www.matisse.net.

   Software that blocks ports often blocks access to some hosts (usually any host except itself) and allows access to others (usually just itself, or machines on the local network), so you should try checking from both your own machine and another machine outside your network (that means you will need a shell account on a Unix machine on another network).

   ◆ If you get a response that says

   `Trying 205.21.36.191...`
   `→Connected to localhost.`
   `→Escape character is '^]'.`

   (the IP address will be different), that means you have connected to server software on the target machine, and the port is not blocked for access from the machine you are testing from.

   You may get further output from the target machine, depending on what server software you have connected to.

   ◆ If you get a response that says

   `telnet: Unable to connect to`
   `→remote host: Connection refused`

   then the port is not blocked, but there is no server software listening on that port.

   continues on next page

◆ If you get a response that says

Trying 66.47.69.205...

(the IP address will be different) and then nothing, then the port probably is blocked. Eventually the Telnet program will give up, although this may take a few minutes.

2. Stop the connection.

You do this by pressing [Control][ ]. You get a prompt that says

telnet>

3. quit

This brings you back to your shell prompt.

Any server software can be configured to listen on a nonstandard port, but this is not common. The client software needs to know what port the server is on in order to contact it, so generally speaking, servers use "well-known ports"—numbers 0 through 1023.

These ports are also called privileged ports, and only root can bind a service to a privileged port. On the other hand, any user on the system can run server software that listens on port number 1024 and above.

The following task describes a simple Perl script that reproduces the port-scan feature of the GUI application Network Utility (located in Applications/Utilities). One advantage of a script is that you can easily save its output to a file, run it automatically as a **cron** job (see Chapter 11, "Introduction to System Administration"), or pipe it into email.

To see which ports are open:

1. Create a Perl script, using the code listing in **Figure 12.2**, in a file named scan.pl. (Review Chapter 9, "Creating and Using Scripts.")

2. Set the file permissions to make the script executable:

chmod 755 scan.pl

Packet Sniffers and Port Scanners

Besides simply checking for open ports, any machine on your local network can examine all of the data flowing on that network. This means that any machine on a local network is capable of obtaining any user names and passwords that flow across that network, unless they are encrypted before transport.

Nmap (www.insecure.org/nmap/) is an open-source network mapping tool that has many more features than the simple script in Figure 12.2. Nmap doesn't come with Mac OS X but can be easily installed with Fink (see Chapter 13, "Installing Software from Source Code").

Another newer, even more powerful tool is ettercap, which can also be installed using Fink (see the sidebar "Tools for Monitoring Your System"). Ettercap is primarily designed for analyzing machines on the same local network as your machine, and it allows you to do such naughty things as intercepting traffic and collecting passwords.

```perl
#!/usr/bin/perl
# scan.pl
# Simple port-scanning script
# Pointing this script at someone else's machine could be considered
# rude, like trying all the doorknobs on their house.
#####################################################################

use strict;
use IO::Socket::INET;
use Socket;

# The Well Known Ports are 1 through 1023.
# The Registered Ports are 1024 through 49151
# The Dynamic and/or Private Ports are 49152 through 65535
#
my $low_port = 1;   # lowest port number to check
my $high_port = 1023;  # Highest port number to check.

my $host = $ARGV[0];
 _usage() unless ($host);   # Gives usage message if no hostname supplied


my $ip_addr = gethostbyname( $host );
$ip_addr = inet_ntoa( $ip_addr );
print "Scanning $host ($ip_addr), ports $low_port through $high_port\n\n";

for my $port ( $low_port..$high_port ) {
    my $socket = IO::Socket::INET->new(PeerAddr => $host,
                        PeerPort => $port,
                        Proto    => 'tcp',
                        Timeout  => 1,
                        Type     => SOCK_STREAM);
  if ( $socket ) {
    close $socket;
    # Is there a standard name for this port?
    my($protocol,$service) = getservbyport($port,'tcp');
    my $description;
    if ( $protocol ) {
      $description = " ($protocol";
      if ( $service ) {
```

Figure 12.2 Code listing of a Perl script that scans a machine and tells which ports are open.

3. `./scan.pl localhost`

Figure 12.3 shows what the output would look like if you have activated Secure Login, AppleShare file sharing, Web file sharing, and an email server. (See Chapter 14, "Installing and Configuring Servers," for instructions on activating these servers.)

Figure 12.2 (continued)

```
        $description .= ", $service)";
      } else {
        $description .= ")";
      }
    }
  }
    print "Connected! Port $port is open.$description\n";
    }
  }
}

sub _usage {
    print STDERR <<"EOF";
Usage: $0 host

'host' may be a hostname or IP address.
Try 'localhost' to test this machine.

EOF
    exit 1;
}
```

```
[localhost:~] vanilla% ./scan.pl localhost
Scanning localhost, ports 1 through 1023

Connected! Port 22 is open ──────────── sshd (SSH server).
Connected! Port 25 is open ──────────── Mail server.
Connected! Port 80 is open ──────────── Web server.
Connected! Port 427 is open ─────────── Server Location Protocol.
Connected! Port 548 is open ──────      Used by AppleTalk.
Connected! Port 587 is open ──         AppleTalk over TCP/IP.
[localhost:~] vanilla%

None of these services are active          Email message submission.
in the default Mac OS X configuration.     Used by email server with
See Chapter 14 for instructions on activation.  Extended Simple Mail
                                           Transfer Protocol
                                           (ESMTP).
```

Figure 12.3 Annotated output of the scan.pl script.

Blocking access to ports

Mac OS X comes with two systems for blocking access to ports. One system is a graphical interface to a simple port-blocking firewall (/System/Library/CoreServices/SecuritySecurityServer to be precise). The other is the standard Unix tool `ipfw` *(Internet Protocol FireWall)* that allows you to block access to any or all of the ports on your machine but requires complex configuration.

We'll show you how to start and configure the simple graphical interface tool, and we'll also show you how to install and configure a shareware program called Brickhouse that provides a graphical interface to configuring the more advanced `ipfw` system.

To block ports using the GUI firewall tool:

1. Open the Sharing tool from System Preferences.

2. Choose the Firewall tab.

   This shows how to start, stop, and configure the built-in firewall (**Figure 12.4**).

3. Click the "Start" button.

   The built-in firewall software starts up and blocks access to every port on your machine, except for those explicitly listed and marked as "On" in the "Allow:" list in this same window.

The list of allowed ports in the GUI Firewall tool can be easily changed. Deleting an item from the list is a matter of selecting it and clicking the delete button. Here's how to add an item to the list (pretty obvious, but we figure we'll walk you through it for fun.)

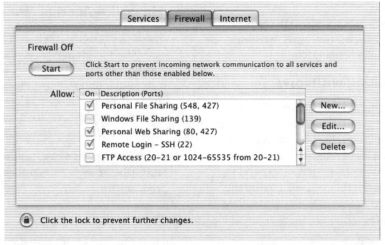

Figure 12.4 Partial screenshot showing the Firewall tab of the Sharing tool from System Preferences.

To add an entry to the GUI Firewall:

1. Open the Firewall tab in the Sharing tool.

2. Click the "New" button.

   A windowshade appears (**Figure 12.5**).

3. Choose an item from the "Port name" pull-down list.

   If you chose "Other," then you get a new windowshade (**Figure 12.6**), where you fill in two fields: "Port Number, Range, or Series," and "Description." The first is either a single port number such as 8000, a range such as 6000-6010, or a series such as 7000, 70023, 7034 (you can separate the items with commas, spaces, or both).

   If you chose one of the port names already in the list, then the port number will be filled in for you.

4. Click the "OK" button.

   The new entry is added to the list of ports and is checked as "on" (to allow access to that port.

   If you wish to block access to the port, then uncheck the entry and make sure the firewall is actually "On."

Port blocking with ipfw

The built-in firewall tool in Mac OS X is probably sufficient for most users. However, there may be cases where you want a more sophisticated set of rules, and want to see logs of the attempts to connect to ports you have blocked. For this, you want to use the more advanced capabilities of the standard Unix tool `ipfw`.

The `ipfw` program has been available on Unix systems for many years and is widely used. It is possible to construct quite complex sets of rules using `ipfw`.

Although the man page for `ipfw` is quite good `ipfw` is still is pretty complicated to configure.

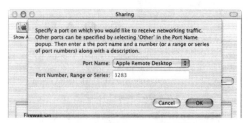

Figure 12.5 Partial screenshot showing the windowshade for creating a new entry in the built-in Firewall tool.

Figure 12.6 Partial screenshot showing the additional field that appears if you choose "Other" as the Port Name.

Firewalk—Another Firewall Tool

Besides BrickHouse, there is at least one other GUI application for configuring `ipfw` on Mac OS X. Firewalk X 2 has more features than BrickHouse, including the ability to set a time when rules expire and to have alerts pop up when a rule blocks incoming traffic.

Firewalk X 2 has a $39.95 license fee and is available at www.pliris-soft.com/products/firewalkx/.

So that you can better understand how `ipfw` works, we'll explain a bit about the configuration for `ipfw` before telling you how to install a graphical configuration tool for it.

Entries in the `ipfw` configuration file (`/etc/firewall.conf`, not installed by default) look like this:

```
add 2029 deny log tcp from any to
→66.47.69.205 31789,31791 in via en0
```

That line means "Add rule #2029. Deny all inbound TCP traffic from anywhere on the Internet to 66.47.69.205 on ports 31789 and 31791 that are coming in on Ethernet interface en0." A typical firewall.conf file may have dozens of such rules. Not only does each rule have to be correctly written, but the order of the rules in the file is important. Ipfw does have a lengthy man page, and it can be used for more than simply blocking access to your machine (for example, it can be used to forward incoming data to another machine), but for a beginning or even an intermediate Unix user, it is rather daunting. If you want to learn more about ipfw, check out the article "Building Your Own Personal Firewall," by Stefan Arentz (http://wopr.norad.org/articles/firewall/).

Luckily, there is a nice shareware utility called BrickHouse that makes it quite a bit easier to configure ipfw.

BrickHouse: GUI Firewall Configuration

BrickHouse is a "regular" Mac OS X application—that is, a GUI program that runs in Aqua. It is also shareware, which means that if you like it, you should send the author the $25 he requests.

The Server of Servers: inetd

Mac OS X (like virtually all versions of Unix) comes with a special server program called inetd (the *Internet Daemon*) as well as the more advanced xinetd. xinetd acts as a kind of dispatch office for several networked servers. It is configured using the file /etc/xinetd.conf, which typically lists one or more directories containing additional configuration files corresponding to a service handled by xinetd. The standard location (used in Mac OS X 10.2) for additional xinetd configuration files is the /etc/xinetd.d directory, where you find over a dozen small configuration files.

Mac OS X 10.1 and earlier had only the older inetd program (no "x"). In Mac OS X 10.2, Apple added xinetd, but the inetd program may still be running, depending on your system configuration. Inetd uses a single configuration file, /etc/inetd.conf, but we suggest you leave it alone.

The configuration files for xinetd tell it which services (such as remote-access services) it is responsible for. Xinetd can listen on multiple ports, and when it receives a connection, it starts up the appropriate software and hands off the connection to the software it started. Following the general rule of only running servers you actually need, Mac OS X comes with all the entries in /etc/xinetd.d/ disabled, because none of the services listed are required for normal operation (once again, keep in mind that a *service* is some useful function provided by a *server*). Both xinetd and inetd do start when your Mac boots up (by the /System/Library/StartupItems/IPServices /IPservices script).

If in the course of your work with Mac OS X, you are installing something that is supposed to be run from xinetd, you will find yourself adding or editing a file in the /etc/xinetd.d directory. But until that day comes, you can just be aware that it exists and leave it alone (and of course have a look at the file and the inetd man page).

The instructions in the following task are based on BrickHouse version 1.1b6. You need an administrative password to configure BrickHouse.

To install and configure BrickHouse:

1. Download the software.

   BrickHouse is available online from author Brian Hill's Web site (http://personalpages.tds.net/~brian_hill/.)

2. Read the "Read Me First!" file.

   This will contain the latest news about the version you have downloaded.

3. Read the BrickHouse FAQ file.

4. Install the software.

   As of BrickHouse's version 1.1b6, you install it by simply dragging it into the appropriate folder. We suggest the Utilities folder inside the Applications folder.

5. Run the application.

   All configuration of BrickHouse is performed from within the application.

6. Choose Setup Assistant from the Tools menu (**Figure 12.7**).

7. Click the lock icon to authenticate as an admin user.

   The Authenticate dialog box opens (**Figure 12.8**).

8. If you are logged in as an admin user, simply enter your password. If the account you are using is not an admin user, enter the name of an admin account in the Name field and the user's password in the "Password or phrase" field.

9. Click OK.

   The External Network screen appears (**Figure 12.9**).

10. From the pop-up menu, select the type of Internet connection you have.

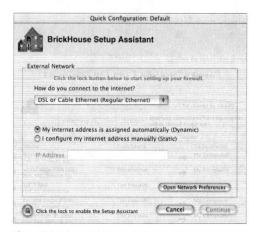

Figure 12.7 The BrickHouse Setup Assistant.

Figure 12.8 The standard Mac OS X Authenticate dialog box.

Figure 12.9 The External Network screen of the BrickHouse Setup Assistant, where you indicate the kind of Internet connection you have. This screen looks the same as in Figure 12.7 except that the lock in the lower-left corner is now open.

11. Select the appropriate radio button for the type of IP address you have: either automatically or manually assigned.

If you have a manually assigned (static) IP address, you can look it up quickly by clicking the Open Network Preferences button. You can copy your IP address from Network Preferences and paste it into BrickHouse.

Figure 12.10 The Public Services screen of the BrickHouse Setup Assistant, where you select which services (ports) will be open to the public.

Figure 12.11 The Blocked Services screen of the BrickHouse Setup Assistant, where you select services (ports) to block.

12. Click Continue.

The Public Services screen appears (**Figure 12.10**).

13. Scroll through the list, checking the boxes for the services you wish to be accessible. (You are actually selecting which ports will be accessible. BrickHouse shows you the names of services instead of the port numbers they each use.)

You will notice that some of the items mention either TCP or UDP; see the sidebar "TCP? UDP?" for an explanation.

When you click an item in the list (even if you do not select the check box), a brief description of it appears below the list.

Typical services to allow include World Wide Web, SMTP Mail, Remote Login (SSH), AppleShare IP/iDisk, Network Browser (SLP), AOL Instant Messenger, and various games.

14. Click Continue.

The Blocked Services screen appears (**Figure 12.11**).

This is where you select services (actually ports) to block from outside access.

We suggest that you leave the first two items unchecked (Standard Services [TCP] and Standard Services [UDP]) and select all the remaining items.

15. Click Continue.

The Firewall Setup Complete screen appears (**Figure 12.12**).

16. Click Apply Configuration.

This activates the rules you have chosen.

17. Click Install Startup Script.

This saves the rules to the file /etc /firewall and installs a StartupItem directory called /Library/StartupItems /Firewall. Now the firewall rules will

continues on next page

PROTECTING YOURSELF FROM INTERNET ATTACKS

take effect each time the machine boots up (review Chapter 11, "Introduction to System Administration," for more on StartupItems).

18. Click Done.

This closes the Firewall Setup Complete screen and brings you back to the main BrickHouse window (**Figure 12.13**).

BrickHouse does not need to be running for ipfw to work.

19. Quit BrickHouse.

✔ Tips

■ BrickHouse has very good built-in help (available from the Help menu). Use it to learn about monitoring the firewall and other features of BrickHouse, such as its IP Sharing/NAT feature (experimental as of version 1.1b6).

■ In the future, if you are having trouble getting some service to work, you should consider that BrickHouse might be blocking it. Go back into BrickHouse and try changing its configuration.

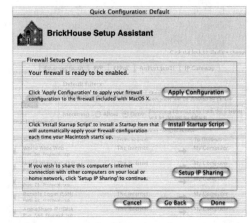

Figure 12.12 The BrickHouse Firewall Setup Complete screen.

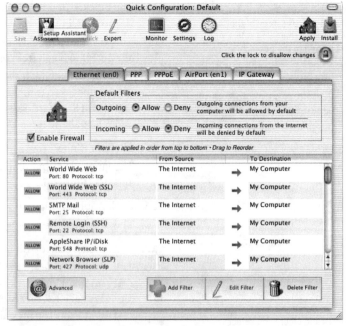

Figure 12.13 The main BrickHouse window after configuration is complete.

Searching for Files That Make You root

If root owns a file, and that file has the `setuid` bit set, then it executes with the power of root, regardless of who runs it (review Chapter 8, "Working with Permissions and Ownership"). If a `setuid` root file has its permissions set so that anyone can execute it (known to programmers as *world executable*), then anyone on the system can run the file and perhaps use it to obtain root access.

Some world-executable commands are intentionally "`setuid` root" because they need to access parts of the system normally available only to root. These programs are (hopefully) carefully written to prevent anyone from using them to create a new shell or to execute other commands.

You can use the `find` command to search your entire system for `setuid` root files.

As of Mac OS X version 10.2, there are dozens of world-executable `setuid` root programs on the system.

A good security practice would be to create a list of all the `setuid` root programs on your machine and save it somewhere safe (such as on a CD) and periodically compare the saved list with a newly generated version. If you find any new programs on the list, you would want to check with Apple to see if they are really supposed to be there.

This is obviously a time-consuming and annoying process, which is true of most security tasks.

TCP? UDP?

Some of the descriptions of services shown in BrickHouse include TCP (Transmission Control Protocol) or UDP (User Datagram Protocol).

TCP and UDP are two different kinds of data packets that are sent over the Internet. Both protocols are part of the TCP/IP suite of protocols (which also include Internet Control Message Protocol (ICMP) and Internet Protocol (IP).

The firewall software that BrickHouse configures (`ipfw`) is capable of blocking any of the four types of data (ICMP, IP TCP, UDP), and the menu choices include the most likely combinations of services and protocols. If and when you become familiar with the intricacies of different types of Internet traffic, you may wish to create custom filters in BrickHouse.

To learn more about filters, start by reading the `ipfw` man page, the `/etc/firewall.conf` file created by BrickHouse, and the FreeBSD documentation on firewalls (www.freebsd.org/doc/en_US.ISO8859-1/books/handbook/firewalls.html).

To search for setuid root files:

◆ sudo find / \(-type f -user root
→ -perm -4000 \)

The command must be run as root in order to read every file on the system, hence the sudo (see Chapter 11, "Introduction to System Administration," for more on sudo). The find command is being told to search starting at / for files (-type f) owned by root (-user root) that have the setuid bit set (-perm -4000).

✔ Tip

■ The command will take a while to finish, since it has to look at every file on your system. You might want to pipe the results into email and put it in the background by adding the following to the command line:

| mail *youremailaddress* &

Keeping Up-to-Date

Mac OS X comes with an application called Software Update that automatically contacts Apple over the Internet to check if there are new versions of any of the Apple-supplied software. These can be as minor as a new version of a program like iTunes, or as major as a new version of Mac OS X itself. One of Software Update's key uses is to maintain the security of your Mac. Apple has been very good about quickly getting new versions of software into its update system when a security problem is discovered.

Because Software Update only deals with Apple-supplied software, you must keep yourself informed of security issues with any other software you install, especially servers. See "Security news and announcements," below.

Software Update

If you are running an Internet-connected Mac, you should be using Software Update.

If your machine has an "always-on" connection to the Internet, you can have Software Update check for updates automatically. If you connect to the Internet intermittently, you can manually request an update check when you are connected.

To run softwareupdate from the command line:

1. softwareupdate

   You will see a list of packages available for update (**Figure 12.14**).

   continues on next page

```
[localhost:~] randall% softwareupdate
Software Update Tool
Copyright 2002 Apple Computer, Inc.


Software Update found the following new or updated software:

   - SecurityUpd2002-08-02
        Security Update 2002-08-02 (1.0), 5300K - restart required
   - iPod
        iPod Software Updater (1.1), 2140K

To install an update, run this tool with the item name as an argument.
        e.g. 'softwareupdate <item> ...'

[localhost:~] randall%
```

Figure 12.14 Output from sudo softwareupdate command showing a list of available updates.

2. Pick a package to install:

`sudo softwareupdate` *packagename*

Enter your password if prompted for it. For example,

`sudo softwareupdate XXXXXX`

as shown in **Figure 12.15**.

✔ Tip

■ You could create a cron job to run `soft-wareupdate` every day or so.

To configure automatic Software Update via the GUI:

1. Launch Software Update (found in the System Preferences).

2. Select the update frequency you desire (**Figure 12.16**).

It can check automatically on a daily, weekly, or monthly basis. You may also choose to perform only manual updates.

In either case, you may request an immediate check for available updates by clicking Update Now.

Figure 12.16 The Software Update window in System Preferences.

```
[localhost:~] randall% sudo softwareupdate SecurityUpd2002-08-02
Password:
Software Update Tool
Copyright 2002 Apple Computer, Inc.

Downloading "Security Update 2002-08-02"... 10% 20% 30% 40%
50%2002-08-06 22:59:07.143 softwareupdate[2185] File to verify:
/var/root/Library/Caches/a1028.g.akamai.net/5/1028/3093/1/1a1a1a88ff63d249b72392f35785e656c63297c5289
7043397067deb57c6278bfe2d82d504346a9bc8f8295a91c03867cb337bf3478cf055960b71c5fd74a51258c53f99/Securit
yUpd2002-08-02.tar
2002-08-06 22:59:09.583 softwareupdate[2185] File verification succeeded
2002-08-06 22:59:09.585 softwareupdate[2185] Verified file now to
install: /tmp/SecurityUpd2002-08-02.pkg.tar
2002-08-06 22:59:09.586 softwareupdate[2185] Returning 1 from VerifyFile

Unarchiving "Security Update 2002-08-02"... 50%
Installing "Security Update 2002-08-02"... 67% 71% 80% 90%
Installing "Security Update 2002-08-02"... 67% 71% 80% 90% 100% done.

You have installed one or more updates that requires that you restart your
computer.  Please restart immediately.
[localhost:~] randall%
```

Figure 12.15 Output from selecting a package to update using `softwareupdate` at the command line.

The actual download and installation process will take anywhere from a few minutes to over an hour depending on the size of the update and the speed of your connection.

When Software Update finds that a new version of software is available, it asks if you wish to install it. Sometimes (although infrequently) a restart will be required when installing new software.

Security news and announcements

Staying up-to-date on security matters involves more than simply running Software Update. It means keeping abreast of the latest news about Mac OS X security issues and the solutions available.

The following online resources are all good places to visit regularly for Mac OS X security news:

Books on Unix Security

These two books are intended for experienced Unix users. Both were written by people who have many years of experience in the Unix and Internet security fields. Their authors are well known in the Unix and Internet communities.

Practical UNIX & Internet Security, 2nd Edition, by Simson Garfinkel and Gene Spafford (O'Reilly; www.oreilly.com/catalog/puis/).

Building Internet Firewalls, 2nd Edition, by Elizabeth D. Zwicky, Simon Cooper, and D. Brent Chapman (O'Reilly; www.oreilly.com/catalog/fire2/).

- Apple Security Updates page (www.apple.com/support/security/security_updates.html).

  The official Apple source of security news for Mac OS X.

- The CERT® Advisory email list (www.cert.org/contact_cert/certmaillist.html).

  CERT (which originally stood for Computer Emergency Response Team) advisories are the primary central source of Internet security notifications. If you run a busy Internet site or are simply interested in seeing the latest internet security issues, then your should subscribe to the CERT Advisory list.

  CERT also maintains a Unix Security Checklist (www.cert.org/tech_tips/usc20_essentials.html).

- Mac-specific Security sites:

  SecureMac.com (www.securemac.com).

  MacSecurity.org (www.macsecurity.org).

- Apple security information for developers (http://developer.apple.com/internet/macosx/securityintro.html).

- The BugTraq mailing list (http://online.securityfocus.com/archive/1).

  "BugTraq is a full disclosure moderated mailing list for the detailed discussion and announcement of computer security vulnerabilities: what they are, how to exploit them, and how to fix them." (From the BugTraq Web site.)

- The Common Vulnerabilities and Exposures (CVE) list (http://cve.mitre.org/cve/).

  Maintained by Mitre (a nonprofit corporation that provides engineering support to the U.S. government), the CVE list is a dictionary of security issues that seeks to present standardized descriptions of security problems.

Monitoring Files for Changes

If an attacker gains root access to your system, one of the first things he is likely to do is alter or replace one or more programs with one of his own making to enable him to gain access again in the future, or to use for launching attacks against other systems.

There are commercial programs available to automate the process of checking files on your system to see if they have been changed, such as Tripwire (see the sidebar "Tools for Monitoring Your System"). You can perform this type of check yourself with the freely available md5sum program.

Using md5sum to check for file changes

Mac OS X doesn't come with md5sum, but md5sum does come with the Fink tool described in Chapter 13, "Installing Software from Source Code." If you have installed Fink, then you have md5sum installed (as /sw/bin/md5sum).

The md5sum program creates and reads something called a message digest or checksum. A message digest is a compact summary of a file that is guaranteed to be different for different files. It is sometimes called a fingerprint for a file. Although much smaller than the file it represents (only 32 characters long in the case of md5sum), an MD5 message digest for a file is different if even a single character in the file is changed.

You use md5sum to create MD5 message digests for files before an attack occurs, and then to save the digests on a read-only disk—for example, by putting the list of checksums on a CD.

You can then periodically use md5sum to compare the message digests with the actual files to see if any of the files have been changed since the checksums were created.

The following tasks assume that you have md5sum installed on your system and that it is in your PATH.

To create an MD5 checksum of a single file:

◆ md5sum *file*

For example,

md5sum /bin/ps

generates an MD5 checksum of the file /bin/ps (which is a **setuid** root program; finding programs that are **setuid** root is covered earlier in this chapter).

The output from md5sum is a single line showing the checksum and the file path it was generated from. For example,

aa37faf342591346cf6c7bd661bdc42c
→/bin/ps

✔ Tip

■ It is best to use a full path when creating an MD5 checksum if you are going to save the checksum for later use (see the next task). If you use a relative path, then you will need to have the same current directory when you check the file later as you did when you created the checksum.

To save MD5 checksums for every file in a directory:

◆ `sudo find -L /etc -type f | xargs`
`→sudo md5sum > checksums.txt`

This creates a file (checksums.txt) containing an MD5 checksum for every file inside the /etc directory. **Figure 12.17** shows a portion of that file.

Here we use the /etc directory as an example, but it should be clear that you can use the same technique for any directory on the system. Simply replace /etc with another directory name.

Review the `find` command in Chapter 4, "Useful Unix Utilities." We use the -L option to `find` (follow symbolic links) because the /etc directory is actually a symbolic link to /private/etc (a Mac OS X peculiarity).

✔ Tips

■ Remember that you can redirect output and add to an existing file by using the >> operator instead of the > operator. (Review Chapter 2, "Using the Command Line.") With this technique, you can create one big file of checksums from several directories.

■ Save the file containing the checksums on a CD-ROM (or other read-only media). Then once a month (or more often if you suspect mischief), insert the CD-ROM and use `md5sum` to check the files for changes. See the next task for instructions.

■ You should consider generating MD5 checksums for all the files in /etc and for every directory in your PATH (review Chapter 7, "Configuring Your Unix Environment," for more on your PATH) and also the /Applications directory.

```
e55afe6e88abb09f0bee39549f1dfbbd    /etc/afpovertcp.cfg
6d0bb903a21cb10ae7d4ea7480caf770    /etc/appletalk.cfg
bc318349980373649fd2e50960067d85    /etc/appletalk.nvram.en0
e4930a8941c566c713c3b2d2b33d354d    /etc/authorization
4502908de9ae68407ff1805b13567328    /etc/bootstrap.conf
81b0ceeba65a41331fb1ec56c25cceed    /etc/crontab
baefa93d0b4ca5620c88cfaf995fbe6f    /etc/csh.cshrc
3014ac4b1963ac9c330f27022f332609    /etc/csh.login
3492636224dac9d0591d01f6794b64ee    /etc/csh.logout
7892620baebb30b82a3777cf728879f4    /etc/daily
7cefd2323b6ce3160815c5258a94202f    /etc/daily.orig
d41d8cd98f00b204e9800998ecf8427e    /etc/dumpdates
d41d8cd98f00b204e9800998ecf8427e    /etc/find.codes
5c0ead44bd58b49f3b4c4cf0c45b7895    /etc/firewall.conf
```

Figure 12.17 Partial list of MD5 checksums generated with `sudo find -L /etc -type f | xargs sudo md5sum >` `checksums.txt`.

Once you have a file containing MD5 checksums, you can have md5sum use the file as a reference to see if any of the files in the list have changed.

Note that md5sum will only tell you if the file's contents have changed. It will not look for changes in permissions, ownership, or modification date (a file could have been edited and saved with no actual changes, which would have updated its modification time).

To use md5sum to check a list of files for changes:

1. Generate a file containing a list of MD5 checksums as described in the previous task.

For example, if you followed the instructions for the task above, you will have a file called checksums.txt, and will have saved it on a CD-ROM.

For this task, we assume that the file containing the checksums is on a CD-ROM called "checksums" and that you have inserted the CD-ROM into your machine. The full path to the checksums.txt file is

`/Volumes/checksums/checksums.txt`

2. `md5sum -c checksumfile`

The -c option runs md5sum in "check" mode. The *checksumfile* argument is the path to the file where you saved the checksum in step 1 (**Figure 12.18**).

```
[localhost:~] vanilla% md5sum -c checksum.txt
md5sum: MD5 check failed for '/Users/vanilla/Documents/Contract'
[localhost:~] vanilla%
```

Figure 12.18 Using md5sum with the -c option to check a file whose checksum was saved earlier.

Tools for Monitoring Your System

There are many tools for monitoring the your system's security. A good place to find a general round-up of available tools is SecureMac.com, a Web site devoted entirely to Mac security issues (www.securemac.com). It has news, security alerts, and software downloads, as well as tutorials and articles on Mac security.

Here are some useful tools :

Snort is an open-source intrusion-detection system. Documentation and source code are available at www.snort.org.

Ettercap is a packet-sniffer/logging program that can be installed using Fink (http://ettercap.sourceforge.net).

Swatch is a tool for automating the watching of system log files, written in Perl. You'll find downloads and mailing lists at www.stanford.edu/~atkins/swatch/.

Tripwire is a commercial security tool capable of monitoring hundreds (or even thousands) of servers. Although the current version (3.3) doesn't list Mac OS X as a supported platform, it does list FreeBSD 4.4. In any event, Tripwire is widely used in large Unix installations, so you should at least be aware of it (www.tripwire.com).

For example,

```
md5sum -c /Volumes/checksums/
→checksums.txt
```

Md5sum reads the checksum file (Figure 12.18 shows a sample of what the file would contain), and for each file listed, md5sum generates a new checksum and compares it with the one you saved.

If the checksums do not match or if the original file is not found, then md5sum issues a warning. If the checksums match, then md5sum produces no output for that line and moves on to the next line. So even if md5sum checks a thousand files, it will only produce output if a checksum doesn't match or if a file is missing. (This is an example of the Unix standard "Silence means success.")

Figure 12.19 shows an example in which md5sum finds that two files in the list have changed and one file from the list is missing.

✔ Tip

■ To be really useful for detecting security problems, MD5 checksums need to be saved somewhere they cannot be altered by an attacker. This means copying the file containing the checksum to a read-only media, such as a CD-ROM. See the next task for how to create a file containing checksums for many files.

```
[localhost:~] vanilla% sudo md5sum -c /Volumes/checksums/checksums.txt
Password:
md5sum: MD5 check failed for '/etc/firewall.conf'
md5sum: MD5 check failed for '/etc/firewall.conf.bak'
md5sum: can't open /etc/hostconfig.old
[localhost:~] vanilla%
```

This file is missing (either deleted, or moved).   *These files have changed.*

Figure 12.19 Using md5sum to examine a list of files. Three changes are found: Two files have changed, and one is missing.

Security Checklist

Here's a checklist to go though when you set up a new system, when you take responsibility for a system, and periodically after that:

1. Maintain good physical security.

2. Use only strong passwords, and change them regularly.

3. Give as few people admin (root) access as is practical.

4. Change all admin passwords at least once every three months.

5. If the machine provides any services (such as POP, IMAP, or FTP) that use unencrypted passwords, set up special shells for the users of those services so that they cannot log in to a standard shell. This defends against password-sniffing attacks by preventing a sniffed user name and password from being used to log in to a regular shell.

6. Do not allow Telnet access (it uses plain-text passwords to provide shell access).

7. Only run servers you actually need.

8. Keep your software (especially servers) up-to-date.

9. Configure the included firewall software (ipfw) to block access to all ports you are not using.

10. Periodically search your system for setuid root files.

11. Create MD5 checksums of all files in /etc and in each of the directories in your PATH. Save these on a CD-ROM, and run an md5sum check against the list every month.

Installing Software from Source Code

Thousands of software applications run on Mac OS X. These applications come in two forms: *precompiled* and *source code*. With precompiled software, all you have to do is install it and it is ready to run. Shrink-wrapped applications like Adobe Photoshop and Microsoft Excel are sold in precompiled form and are not available as source code. Unix software applications are sometimes available in both precompiled and source-code forms, but many applications are only available in the latter form.

Programmers create source code as text files that can be read by users. Except in the case of scripts (review Chapter 9, "Creating and Using Scripts"), source code must be converted into software the computer can understand; this is done by a process called *compiling*. The source code is fed through another piece of software (called a *compiler*), which produces a machine-readable file *(object code);* this is the actual software you run on your machine. The Mac OS X Developer Tools include the compiler you need to convert software from source code into machine-readable code (if you have not already installed the Developer Tools, see the sidebar "The Mac OS X Developer Tools"). The object code only works with a specific combination of hardware architecture and operating system. Just as shrink-wrapped Mac applications won't run on a PC, object code compiled for the G4 processor and Mac OS X will not run on a Pentium running Windows.

In order to take advantage of the full range of software available for Mac OS X, you need to learn how to install software from source code. It is actually fairly easy, and once you're done, you'll have access to an amazing variety of software.

In this chapter we will first explain the general process for installing from source code, and then will show you how to install the Fink tool, which automates the process for many software packages. We will also show you in detail how to install software manually without the aid of Fink.

You will need to have your computer connected to the Internet in order to download software.

Installing from Source Code — the Basics

Installing software from source code always involves the same basic steps: download the compressed source code, *unpack* (the term most frequently used in the Unix world for expanding code) it, move to the new directory using `cd`, compile, and install. The mantra that Unix veterans use is

```
./configure
make
make test
make install
```

Here's a more detailed look at the general steps involved.

To install software from source code:

1. Obtain the source code. Usually you do this by downloading a compressed `tar` file from a Web site. (Review Chapter 4, "Useful Unix Utilities.")

2. Uncompress the directory containing the source code (this automatically creates a directory). The most common way to do this at the command line is to use the `tar` command with `xfz` options.

3. `cd` into the newly created directory.

4. Read the README and INSTALL files (the filenames are in all caps so that they stand out clearly—you should always read them).

    These will tell you how to configure and install the software.

5. All the following steps need to be executed as root, so give yourself a root shell (review Chapter 7, "Configuring Your Unix Environment," for more on shells; see Chapter 11, "Introduction to System Administration," for more on **root** and **sudo**):

    ```
    sudo -s
    ```

The Mac OS X Developer Tools

The Developer Tools, which contain the compiler you need to install software from source code, come on a separate CD in the Mac OS X set. If you don't have the CD, you can find links to download the Developer Tools from http://developer.apple.com/tools/ or http://connect.apple.com.

6. Following the instructions in the INSTALL file, configure the source code so that it's ready for the compiler.

The most common configuration method is to run a script called `configure` that comes with the source code. Type

`./configure`

The configuration process sometimes asks you questions about your system, which directory you want to install the software in, and what options you want to include. In most cases, you can simply accept the default answers, because the configuration process automatically determines the information it needs (such as asking "Do you have multiple processors?") and creates one or more files (called *makefiles*) it uses to run the compiler process in the next step. The INSTALL file is your main reference for specific issues that arise, such as the meanings of available options and when to use them.

7. Compile the software.

This will almost certainly be a matter of simply running the `make` command, which reads the makefiles and runs the compiler. You will see quite a bit of output on your screen while `make` runs the compiler. We show examples of this later in this chapter.

8. Run any tests included with the source code.

Some packages include preinstallation tests that can be run with `make test`.

9. Perform the actual installation process.

Again, follow the instructions from the INSTALL file—usually a matter of running `make install`.

10. You're done.

Using Fink to Install Software

Fink is an open-source program that automates the process of downloading, configuring, compiling, and installing hundreds of Darwin packages (remember, Darwin is the version of Unix at the core of Mac OS X). By "package," we simply mean a piece of software along with its associated documentation and configuration files. Rather than your having to follow all the steps outlined in the previous section, Fink downloads, compiles, and installs a package with a single command (the Fink Web site at http://fink.sourceforge.net/ offers a variety of packages, from games to graphics, available for download, as does www.webmin.com).

⚠ See sidebar for late breaking news about Fink.

To install Fink, start by downloading the software. Fink comes precompiled, so you don't have to compile it to use it.

To install Fink:

1. From your Web browser, open the Fink download page:

   http://fink.sourceforge.net/download/

2. Click the link to download the latest version of the *installer disk image* (a file that, when mounted as a disk, contains the installation program for a particular piece of software).

   Figure 13.1 (showing how the Web page for downloading Fink appeared during production of this book) highlights the link to click.

Figure 13.1 The Fink download page. The file you want to download is the "installer disk image."

Late Breaking News about Fink

We have put updated information about Fink at http://www.peachpit.com/vqp/umoxhtml.

This chapter covers the installation and use of Fink version 0.4.0 which *only works with Mac OS X 10.1*, not with 10.2.

As we went to press, a newer, 10.2-friendly version of Fink (version 0.5.0) was not yet complete and available for testing; however, we expect it will available be by the time you read this, and we expect the installation and use to be substantially the same as Fink 0.4.0. Please check the Peachpit website and the Fink website (http://fink.sourceforge.net/) before proceeding with the installation of Fink.

Figure 13.2 When the download is complete, the Fink disk image is mounted as if it were a disk.

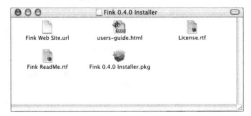

Figure 13.3 When you double-click the installer disk icon, you see the Fink installer and associated files.

Figure 13.4 Double-clicking the Fink Installer.pkg icon launches the installer program.

Figure 13.5 Clicking the lock icon in the first installation screen switches to an authentication screen, where your name is already filled in.

The installer disk image downloads to your computer. When the download is complete, Mac OS X automatically mounts the disk-image file as if it were a hard disk, so it appears in the Finder on your Desktop (**Figure 13.2**).

3. Double-click the Fink installer disk icon in the Finder.

   A Finder window opens, showing the Fink installer (the files whose names end in "Installer.pkg") and associated files (**Figure 13.3**).

4. Double-click the Fink Installer.pkg file to launch the Fink installation program (**Figure 13.4**).

5. Click the lock icon.

   The installation program switches to a screen asking you to enter an administrator name and password. Your name will already be filled in (**Figure 13.5**).

6. Enter your password.

   continues on next page

7. Click OK.

The installer moves to the introduction screen (**Figure 13.6**).

8. Click Continue.

The installer displays the Fink ReadMe.rtf file.

9. Read this file thoroughly, as it has the latest information about installing the version of Fink you have downloaded. You may even want to print it out using the Print button on the screen (**Figure 13.7**).

10. Click Continue.

The installer switches to the License screen (**Figure 13.8**).

11. Read the license agreement.

Fink is open-source software distributed under a license called the GNU General Public License. That means you may use Fink without any cost or obligation. However, if you redistribute Fink, then you are obligated to provide source code to all those to whom you distribute it.

Figure 13.6 After you enter your password in the installation screen and click OK, the installer switches to the introduction screen.

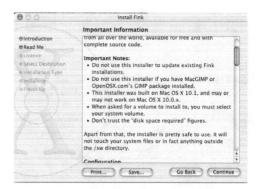

Figure 13.7 Clicking Continue in the Introduction screen brings up the README screen.

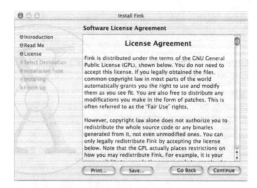

Figure 13.8 Clicking Continue on the README screen brings up the License screen.

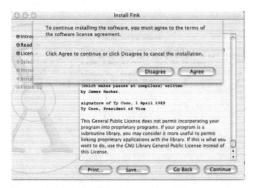

Figure 13.9 Clicking Continue on the License screen brings up a dialog box asking if you agree to the license terms.

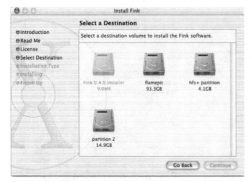

Figure 13.10 If you agree to the license terms, the Select Destination screen opens; you choose the installation disk for Fink here.

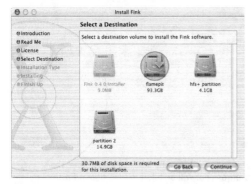

Figure 13.11 Selecting a disk or partition for installation causes it to be highlighted.

12. Click Continue.

A dialog box opens, asking if you agree to the license terms (**Figure 13.9**).

13. Click Agree if you agree to the license terms.

If you do not agree to the terms, then you may not use the software. Click Disagree and quit the installer.

If you agreed to the terms of the license, the installer switches to the Select Destination screen, which asks you to select a disk on which to install Fink (**Figure 13.10**).

14. Select a disk or partition on which to install Fink.

The disks displayed of course depend on what you have on your computer. The selected disk will be highlighted (**Figure 13.11**).

continues on next page

15. Click Continue.

The Easy Install screen opens (**Figure 13.12**).

16. Click Install.

The installer begins installing Fink. A progress bar appears (**Figure 13.13**).

When the installer has finished, the progress bar will be complete and the Close button will be highlighted (**Figure 13.14**).

17. Click Close to finish the installation.

The installer creates a new directory called sw on the partition you selected. If you selected the partition containing /, then Fink is installed in /sw. If you installed Fink on any partition other than your system startup partition, then you must make a symlink to /sw that points to the installed location. For example, if you installed Fink on a partition called Extra Disk, then you will create the symlink at the command line with

```
sudo ln -s "/Volumes/Extra Disk/
→sw" /sw
```

(Review Chapter 5, "Using Files and Directories," for details on symlinks.)

Fink is now installed. Next you must configure your command-line environment to use Fink, and then configure Fink itself.

The Fink program itself is located at /sw/bin/fink, and software you install using Fink will also be installed in /sw/bin. Man pages for Fink and the software it installs are located in /sw/share/man. The directory /sw/bin is not part of your PATH, and /sw/share/man is not in your MANPATH. You can change these manually, but a better way is to use a shell script provided with the Fink installation. The script will set several environment variables as well as some other settings that make using Fink easier. There are two versions of the script: /sw/bin/init.csh

Figure 13.12 The Easy Install screen; click Install to begin installation.

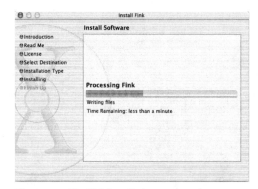

Figure 13.13 The Fink installation process shows a progress bar.

Figure 13.14 When the installation is done, the progress bar will be filled; click Close to finish.

and `/sw/bin/init.sh`. The first is for use with the `tcsh` or `csh` shell, and the second is for use with the `sh` or bash shell. The default shell on Mac OS X is `tcsh`.

To configure your shell to use Fink:

1. Add this line to your `~/.cshrc` file if you are using the `tcsh` shell:

   `source /sw/bin/init.csh`

   Or add this line to your `~/.bashrc` file if you are using the bash shell:

   `. /sw/bin/init.sh`

   (Review Chapter 7, "Configuring Your Unix Environment," for details on the `.cshrc` and `.bashrc` files.) The changes will take effect in the next Terminal window you open.

2. Log out of all open Terminal windows.

3. Open a new Terminal window.

   The shell for the new Terminal window will be configured properly to use Fink.

```
[localhost:~] vanilla% sudo fink configure
Password:
```

Figure 13.15 You are asked for your password to enable the `sudo` command.

The next step is to configure Fink as root from the command line. In order to automate the process of downloading, compiling, and installing software, Fink needs to know some things about how your computer is connected to the Internet.

To configure Fink:

1. `sudo fink configure`

   Fink must be configured as root, so you use the **sudo** command to run `fink configure` (see Chapter 11, "Introduction to System Administration"). You are asked for your password (**Figure 13.15**).

2. Enter your password, and press (Return).

   Fink asks a series of questions. The default answers will appear inside square brackets ([ ]). In most cases, you should simply accept the default answer by pressing (Return).

   Figure 13.16 shows the first question. You are asked in which directory Fink should look for *tarballs,* which are compressed **tar** archives (see Chapter 4, "Useful Unix Utilities").

   continues on next page

```
[localhost:~] vanilla% sudo fink configure
Password:

OK, I'll ask you some questions and update the configuration file in
'/sw/etc/fink.conf'.

In what additional directory should Fink look for downloaded tarballs?
[/Volumes/Data/FinkBase/src/]
```

Figure 13.16 Fink asks you about an additional directory to use to save downloaded files.

USING FINK TO INSTALL SOFTWARE

3. Accept the default by pressing Return.

You are asked if you want Fink to display verbose messages (**Figure 13.17**). The default is the uppercase letter N (for *no*). If you want Fink to display its messages when it is running, enter y for *yes*.

4. Press Return.

Fink now asks if you need to use an HTTP proxy server to get through a firewall on your network (**Figure 13.18**).

If you don't know what this is, you probably do *not* have one. If your computer is on an office network and you are not sure if you are using an HTTP proxy, ask your network administrator.

If you are using an HTTP proxy server, then you must enter its full URL—for example, http://proxy.bigcompany.net/. Most of you will accept the default ("none").

```
[localhost:~] vanilla% sudo fink configure
Password:


OK, I'll ask you some questions and update the configuration file in
'/sw/etc/fink.conf'.


In what additional directory should Fink look for downloaded tarballs?
[/Volumes/Data/FinkBase/src/]


Always print verbose messages? [y/N]
```

Figure 13.17 Fink asks if you want verbose messages.

```
[localhost:~] vanilla% sudo fink configure
Password:


OK, I'll ask you some questions and update the configuration file in
'/sw/etc/fink.conf'.


In what additional directory should Fink look for downloaded tarballs?
[/Volumes/Data/FinkBase/src/]


Always print verbose messages? [y/N]


Proxy/Firewall settings
Enter the URL of the HTTP proxy to use, or 'none' for no proxy. The URL
should start with http:// and may contain username, password or port
specifications. [none]
```

Figure 13.18 Fink asks if you have an HTTP proxy server.

5. Press ⟨Return⟩.

Fink asks if you're using an FTP proxy server (**Figure 13.19**). Again, unless you know you need to use one, simply accept the default.

6. Press ⟨Return⟩.

Fink asks you if it should "Use passive mode FTP transfers (to get through a firewall)?" (**Figure 13.20**). The default is Y (for *yes*) and should work in most cases. If you are not behind a firewall, then answer n (for *no*).

7. Press ⟨Return⟩.

Fink asks if you want to change the "Mirror selection" (**Figure 13.21**). This is a list of Internet sites from which Fink will download software. Accept the default (N, meaning you do not want to change the list).

8. Press ⟨Return⟩.

Fink tells you that it has updated its configuration file (**Figure 13.22**). You're finished configuring Fink and ready to use it to install software.

continues on next page

```
Enter the URL of the proxy to use for FTP, or 'none' for no proxy. The URL
should start with http:// and may contain username, password or port
specifications. [none]
```

Figure 13.19 Fink asks if you have an FTP proxy server.

```
Use passive mode FTP transfers (to get through a firewall)? [Y/n]
```

Figure 13.20 Fink asks if it should use passive mode for FTP.

```
Mirror selection
All mirrors are set. Do you want to change them? [y/N]
```

Figure 13.21 Fink asks if you want to change the list of mirror sites.

```
Writing updated configuration to '/sw/etc/fink.conf'...
```

Figure 13.22 Fink shows you that it is updating its configuration file.

USING FINK TO INSTALL SOFTWARE

✔ Tips

- Look at the Fink configuration file (/sw/etc/fink.conf) to learn more about how it works (**Figure 13.23**).

- Fink has good built-in help. Run

  `fink –help`

  to see it, and of course run man fink to see the Fink man page.

Now that you have Fink installed and configured, let's start using it.

Fink can show you all of the software packages available for installation. New software packages are added to the list frequently.

To list available packages:

- `fink list`

  brings up a list of all the available packages. (**Figure 13.24**). Packages that are already installed are marked with an *i*, such as the apt package.

One of Fink's most useful features is that it keeps track of all the software it has installed, so upgrading or removing software is easy.

```
# Fink configuration, initially created by
→ bootstrap.pl
Basepath: /sw
RootMethod: sudo
Trees: local/main stable/main stable/crypto
FetchAltDir: /Volumes/Data/FinkBase/src/
Mirror-cpan: ftp://cpan.cse.msu.edu/
Mirror-ctan: ftp://tug.ctan.org/tex-archive/
Mirror-gimp: ftp://ftp.gimp.org/pub
Mirror-gnome: ftp://ftp.gnome.org/pub/GNOME/
Mirror-gnu: ftp://ftp.gnu.org/gnu
MirrorContinent: nam
MirrorCountry: nam-us
ProxyPassiveFTP: false
Verbose: false
```

Figure 13.23 The Fink configuration file (/sw/etc/fink.conf) is where your choices are stored.

To list only installed packages:

- `fink list | grep "^ i"`

  gets you a list of only the installed packages. You are filtering the output of fink list by using grep to find only those lines of output that begin with a space followed by the letter *i* (**Figure 13.25**).

Now the fun part: actually installing a package using Fink. We'll install the wget program as an example. Wget is a command-line tool for retrieving files from Web sites and FTP sites. Mac OS X comes with a similar command, curl, but in our opinion wget is much easier to use. (We'll discuss wget more in Chapter 15, "More Open-Source Software" at www.peachpit.com/vqp/umox.) By the way, if you are unable to use Fink (see sidebar "Late Breaking News about Fink", above), then you can get wget from Apple at www.apple.com/downloads/macosx/unix_open_source/wget.html.

Fink and X Windows

Many of the packages available for installation with Fink rely on the X Windows system. X Windows is a large collection of software that provides a platform-independent graphical user interface (GUI) environment. Most Unix software that provides a GUI relies upon X Windows to handle the actual creation of windows, dialog boxes, and buttons.

See Chapter 15, "More Open-Source Software," for details on obtaining and installing X Windows.

```
(Listing in figure has been abbreviated.)

[localhost:~] vanilla% fink list
Reading package info...
Updating package index... done.
Information about 427 packages read in 31 seconds.
      a2ps          4.12-4      Any to PostScript filter.
  i   apt           0.5.4-1     Advanced front-end for dpkg
      aria          0.10.0-2    File downloader, similar to GetRight.
      audiofile     0.2.3-4     Audio File Library
      automake      1.5-1       Makefile generator
      aview         1.3.0rc1-3  Ascii art image viewer
  i   base-files    1.5-1       Directory infrastructure
      bash          2.05-3      The GNU Bourne Again SHell
      bison         1.29-1      Parser generator
      bitchx        1.0c18-3    IRC client
      bluefish      0.6-2       Web-oriented text editor
      bundle-gnome  1.4-3       GNOME convenience package
      bundle-tetex  20010808-4  Installs a complete TeX system including al...
  i   bzip2         1.0.2-1     Block-sorting file compressor
      canna         3.5b2-4     Japanese input system
      vim           6.0-2       Improved version of the editor "vi"
      vim-nox       6.0-4       Improved version of the editor "vi", no X11...
      vnc           3.3.3r2-4   Remote display system for X11.
      wget          1.8.1-1     Automatic web site retreiver
      wget-ssl      1.8.1-1     Automatic web site retreiver, with SSL support
      windowmaker   0.80.0-3    GNUstep (NeXT-like) Window Manager
      wmcalclock    1.25-1      Calendar clock dock app
      wmmoonclock   1.27-1      Moon cycle dock app
      zlib          1.1.4-1     Compression library
```

Figure 13.24 Fink shows a list of all available packages. (The listing has been abbreviated.)

```
[localhost:~] vanilla% fink list | grep "^ i"
  i   apt           0.5.4-1     Advanced front-end for dpkg
  i   base-files    1.5-1       Directory infrastructure
  i   bzip2         1.0.2-1     Block-sorting file compressor
  i   darwin        5.4-1       [virtual package representing the kernel]
  i   debianutils   1.15-4      Misc. utilities specific to Debian (and Fink)
  i   dpkg          1.9.20-1    The Debian package manager
  i   fink          0.9.11-1    The Fink package manager
  i   gettext       0.10.40-2   Message localization support
  i   gzip          1.2.4a-6    The gzip file compressor
  i   libiconv      1.7-3       Character set conversion library
  i   macosx        10.1.4-1    [virtual package representing the system]
  i   ncurses       5.2-6       Full-screen ascii drawing library
  i   tar           1.13.19-1   GNU tape archiver
```

Figure 13.25 You can see a list that only contains installed packages by using grep.

To install a package using Fink:

1. `sudo fink install wget`

   You must be root to install software with Fink, hence the use of **sudo**. Enter your password if prompted.

   Fink automatically downloads, compiles, and installs the software.

   You will see a great deal of output while this is happening. Fink is showing you the actual commands it is using while it's downloading, compiling, and installing the software. **Figure 13.26** shows just the start of the output.

   The amount of time involved will depend on the speed of your Internet connection and of your computer.

   You will get a shell prompt when Fink is done. The software is now installed.

2. Try using the newly installed software.

   If you are using the **tcsh** shell, then run the **rehash** command to update the shell's list of available commands.

   Then type

   `wget http://www.matisse.net/files/ glossary.html`

```
[localhost:~] vanilla% sudo fink install wget
Password:
Information about 427 packages read in 1 seconds.
curl -f -L -s -S -P - -O ftp://ftp.gnu.org/gnu/wget/wget-1.8.1.tar.gz
mkdir -p /sw/src/wget-1.8.1-1
tar -xzf /sw/src/wget-1.8.1.tar.gz
./configure –prefix=/sw –without-ssl –infodir=/sw/share/info –mandir=/sw/share/man
creating cache ./config.cache
configuring for GNU Wget 1.8.1
checking host system type... powerpc-apple-darwin5.4
checking whether make sets ${MAKE}... yes
checking for a BSD compatible install... /usr/bin/install -c
checking for gcc... no
checking for cc... cc
checking whether the C compiler (cc  -L/sw/lib) works... yes
checking whether the C compiler (cc  -L/sw/lib) is a cross-compiler... no
checking whether we are using GNU C... yes
checking whether cc accepts -g... yes
checking how to run the C preprocessor... cc -E
checking for AIX... no
checking for Cygwin environment... no
checking for mingw32 environment... no
checking build system type... powerpc-apple-darwin5.4
checking for ld used by GCC... /usr/bin/ld
checking if the linker (/usr/bin/ld) is GNU ld... no
```

Figure 13.26 Using Fink to download, compile and install software.

This retrieves my Glossary of Internet terms and saves it in your current directory as glossary.html (**Figure 13.27**) See `man wget` for details on wget.

✔ Tip

- Fink installs some informational files for each package in /sw/share/doc. In particular, there should be a README file for each package in a subdirectory named after the package:

  /sw/share/doc/wget/README

The database that Fink uses contains short descriptions of the available packages. You can see a package description with the `fink describe` command.

To show details about a package:

◆ fink describe *package*

  For example, to see the package description for the wget program,

  fink describe wget

  produces the output shown in **Figure 13.28**.

Figure 13.26 (continued)

```
checking for /usr/bin/ld option to reload object files... -r
checking for BSD-compatible nm... /usr/bin/nm -p
checking whether ln -s works... yes
checking how to recognise dependant libraries... file_magic Mach-O dynamically linked shared library
checking for object suffix... o
checking for executable suffix... no
checking command to parse /usr/bin/nm -p output... ok
checking for dlfcn.h... no
checking for ranlib... ranlib
checking for strip... strip
checking for objdir... .libs
checking for cc option to produce PIC... -fno-common
checking if cc PIC flag -fno-common works... yes
checking if cc static flag -static works... no
checking if cc supports -c -o file.o... /Volumes/partition 2/sw/src/wget-1.8.1-1/wget-1.8.1/conftest
yes
checking if cc supports -c -o file.lo... yes
checking if cc supports -fno-rtti -fno-exceptions... yes
checking whether the linker (/usr/bin/ld) supports shared libraries... yes
checking how to hardcode library paths into programs... unsupported
checking whether stripping libraries is possible... no
checking dynamic linker characteristics... darwin5.4 dyld
checking if libtool supports shared libraries... yes
checking whether to build shared libraries... yes
((rest of output deleted))
```

USING FINK TO INSTALL SOFTWARE

```
[localhost:~] vanilla% wget http://www.matisse.net/files/glossary.html
-20:52:49-  http://www.matisse.net/files/glossary.html
           => `glossary.html'
Resolving www.matisse.net... done.
Connecting to www.matisse.net[66.47.69.194]:80... connected.
HTTP request sent, awaiting response... 200 OK
Length: 71,409 [text/html]


100%[=====================================>] 71,409          1.48M/s    ETA 00:00


20:52:50 (1.48 MB/s) - `glossary.html' saved [71409/71409]


[localhost:~] vanilla%
```

Figure 13.27 Using the newly installed wget command to retrieve and save a document.

```
[localhost:~] vanilla% fink describe wget
Information about 427 packages read in 1 seconds.


wget-1.8.1-1: Automatic web site retriever
 GNU Wget is a free network utility to retrieve files from the World
 Wide Web using HTTP and FTP, the two most widely used Internet
 protocols.  It works non-interactively, thus enabling work in the
 background, after having logged off.
 .
 The recursive retrieval of HTML pages, as well as FTP sites is
 supported - you can use Wget to make mirrors of archives and home
 pages, or traverse the web like a WWW robot.
 .
 This package compiles wget without SSL (https) support. If you want
 SSL support, install wget-ssl instead.
 .
 Previous revisions by Christoph Pfisterer <chrisp@users.sourceforge.net>
 .
 Web site: http://www.gnu.org/software/wget/wget.html
 .
 Porting Notes:
 Uses libtool, but only for convenience libraries, so there is no need
 to update it.
 .
 Maintainer: Sylvain Cuaz <zauc@noos.fr>
```

Figure 13.28 Fink can provide a brief description of each available package.

Table 13.1

Updating and Removing Packages with Fink	
ACTION	COMMAND
Update a specific package	sudo fink update package
Update all installed packages	sudo fink update-all
Update Fink itself	sudo fink selfupdate
Remove a package	sudo fink remove package

More About Fink

The Fink Web site is at http://fink.sourceforge.net.

Fink has an HTML user's guide, which is included in the installation disk image. You can open the file with a Web browser. The user's guide is also available online at http://fink.sourceforge.net/doc/

You can find links to mailing lists about Fink at http://fink.sourceforge.net/lists/.

To search for packages by keyword:

◆ fink apropos *package*

To search for packages whose name or one-line description contains "audio," use

fink apropos audio

which produces output like that shown in **Figure 13.29.**

Updating and removing packages with Fink

One of the most excellent (dude!) features of Fink is the ease with which you can use it to update the frequent improvements in Unix software.

Updating a package in Fink is simply a matter of using the fink update command. You can update a single package by specifying a package name on the command line, but even cooler is the fact that you can update *all* installed packages with the fink update-all command.

Fink also makes it easy to have it update itself and to remove any package installed with it. **Table 13.1** summarizes the commands for updating and removing packages installed with Fink.

USING FINK TO INSTALL SOFTWARE

```
[localhost:~] vanilla% fink apropos audio
Information about 427 packages read in 2 seconds.
    agqt            0.9.1-1    6's Spiffy AudioGalaxy Query Tool
    audiofile       0.2.3-4    Audio File Library
    audiofile-bin   0.2.3-4    Audio File Library
    audiofile-shlib 0.2.3-4    Audio File Library
    gnome-audio     1.4.0-3    Audio files for Gnome.
    icecast         1.3.11-4   MP3 Audio Broadcasting System
    libvorbis       1.0rc3-3   The Vorbis General Audio Compression Codec
    libvorbis-shlib 1.0rc3-3   The Vorbis General Audio Compression Codec
    sdl-mixer       1.2.1-1    SDL multi-channel audio mixer library
[localhost:~] vanilla%
```

Figure 13.29 Searching for available packages by keyword.

Manually Installing from Source Code

Most of the Unix software you are likely to want to use is available via Fink, but as you get into more advanced uses of Unix, you will find that some software isn't available through Fink. You need to know how to compile and install software manually. The process for installing virtually all open-source Unix software is described here (except for Perl modules, which we describe later in this chapter).

For the following task we will use a sample program that is designed to demonstrate the process of manually downloading, compiling, and installing a Unix application from the command line. The program is the classic sample program `hello world`.

You use the `wget` program to download the software from the command line. If you haven't already installed `wget` using Fink, do that now (described in the previous section).

To manually install a package from source code:

1. `sudo -s`

   The installation process must be performed as root because you will be adding files to directories owned and writable only by root.

   To avoid typing "`sudo`" before every command, you are simply spawning a new shell as root. Notice that your shell prompt changes (**Figure 13.30**). Remember to exit from the new shell (with the `exit` command) after the installation is done. we'll remind you.

2. Enter your password, and press ⌈Return⌋.

   The next step is to create the directory where you are saving the source code.

   The conventional place for all user-installed software is in subdirectories of `/usr/local`.

   The source code goes in a subdirectory of `/usr/local/src`, and the actual program (the compiled executable file itself) goes in `/usr/local/bin`.

3. `mkdir -p /usr/local/src/hello`

   That command creates the directory `/usr/local/src/hello` and any intermediate directories that may not exist (such as the `src` directory).

4. `cd /usr/local/src/hello`

   This changes your current directory to `/usr/local/src/hello`.

```
[localhost:~] vanilla% sudo -s
Password:
[localhost:~] root#
```

Figure 13.30 Your shell prompt changes when you start a new shell as root.

5. wget ftp://gatekeeper.dec.com/
pub/GNU/hello/hello-1.3.tar.gz

The wget command retrieves the compressed tar file and saves it in the current directory (**Figure 13.31**).

Next you will unpack the compressed tar file.

continues on next page

```
[localhost:src/hello/hello-1.3] root# wget ftp://gatekeeper.dec.com/pub/GNU/hello/hello-1.3.tar.gz
–21:05:22–  ftp://gatekeeper.dec.com/pub/GNU/hello/hello-1.3.tar.gz
          => `hello-1.3.tar.gz'
Resolving gatekeeper.dec.com... done.
Connecting to gatekeeper.dec.com[204.123.2.2]:21... connected.
Logging in as anonymous ... Logged in!
==> SYST ... done.    ==> PWD ... done.
==> TYPE I ... done.  ==> CWD /pub/GNU/hello ... done.
==> PORT ... done.    ==> RETR hello-1.3.tar.gz ... done.
Length: 87,942 (unauthoritative)

100%[===================================>] 87,942        66.57K/s    ETA 00:00

21:05:23 (66.57 KB/s) - `hello-1.3.tar.gz' saved [87942]
[localhost:src/hello/hello-1.3] root#
```

Figure 13.31 Using wget to retrieve a compressed tar file of source code.

6. `tar xfvz hello-1.3.tar.gz`

This creates a new directory called `hello-1.3`.

The v option to `tar` causes it to display the name of each file and directory extracted from the archive (**Figure 13.32**).

7. `cd hello-1.3`

Now your current directory is the directory containing the actual source code. Check the files, looking especially for README and INSTALL files.

```
[localhost:src/hello/hello-1.3] root# tar xfvz hello-1.3.tar.gz
hello-1.3/hello.c
hello-1.3/version.c
hello-1.3/getopt.c
hello-1.3/getopt1.c
hello-1.3/alloca.c
hello-1.3/getopt.h
hello-1.3/COPYING
hello-1.3/ChangeLog
hello-1.3/NEWS
hello-1.3/Makefile.in
hello-1.3/README
hello-1.3/INSTALL
hello-1.3/hello.texi
hello-1.3/hello.cp
hello-1.3/hello.fn
hello-1.3/hello.ky
hello-1.3/hello.pg
hello-1.3/hello.tp
hello-1.3/hello.vr
hello-1.3/hello.cps
hello-1.3/gpl.texinfo
hello-1.3/configure
hello-1.3/configure.in
hello-1.3/mkinstalldirs
hello-1.3/texinfo.tex
hello-1.3/hello.info
hello-1.3/testdata
hello-1.3/TAGS
[localhost:src/hello/hello-1.3] root#
```

Figure 13.32 Using `tar` to extract files from the compressed archive.

MANUALLY INSTALLING FROM SOURCE CODE

8. `ls`

You will see that there are indeed both README and INSTALL files; read them both (**Figure 13.33**).

9. `less README`

The README file usually tells you what the program is for, who wrote it, where to find more information, and how to report bugs.

Learning More About Compiling Software

Almost all the Unix software you will download and install is written in the C programming language and uses a couple of common tools to manage the process of configuring the source code and compiling it.

The classic text on C is *The C Programming Language,* by Brian W. Kernighan and Dennis M. Ritchie (http://cm.bell-labs.com/cm/cs/cbook/).

The make program is widely used for managing software development, especially software written in C. The standard text on make is *Managing Projects with make,* 2nd Edition, by Andy Oram and Steve Talbott (www.oreilly.com/catalog/make2/).

10. `q`

This quits from the **less** program.

11. `less INSTALL`

The INSTALL file should tell you, in detail, how to install the software. INSTALL files can be quite complex because they try to address many different versions of Unix and the many options that someone might use. In general, as we noted at the beginning of this chapter, the basic instructions tell you to run

```
./configure
make
make test (in some cases)
make install
```

It is a good idea to read through the INSTALL files carefully the first dozen or so times you install software manually. After that, always read enough to confirm that nothing unusual is required for the installation.

One common option described in INSTALL files controls where you install the software. The convention is to use a prefix of /usr/local, so executables go in /usr/local/bin, man pages in /usr/local/man, software libraries in /usr/local/lib, and so on. Do not use something else unless you have a very good reason. Installing software in the default location keeps your system consistent with the rest of the world and makes for easier maintenance.

continues on next page

MANUALLY INSTALLING FROM SOURCE CODE

```
[localhost:src/hello/hello-1.3] root# ls
COPYING        TAGS          getopt1.c      hello.info     mkinstalldirs
ChangeLog      alloca.c      gpl.texinfo    hello.ky       testdata
INSTALL        configure     hello.c        hello.pg       texinfo.tex
Makefile.in    configure.in  hello.cp       hello.texi     version.c
NEWS           getopt.c      hello.cps      hello.tp
README         getopt.h      hello.fn       hello.vr
[localhost:src/hello/hello-1.3] root#
```

Figure 13.33 Using `ls` to see the files in the unpacked directory.

12. q

to quit from less.

In the case of this sample program, you will use the default configuration, so the next steps are very simple.

13. ./configure

This runs a script that probes your system and creates another script using the information found (**Figure 13.34**). You saw this happen automatically when you used Fink to install wget; now you are running the same process manually. The configure script creates a file called Makefile, which is used by the next command.

```
[localhost:src/hello/hello-1.3] root# ./configure
checking for gcc
checking how to run the C preprocessor
checking for install
checking for ANSI C header files
checking for string.h
checking for fcntl.h
checking for sys/file.h
checking for working alloca.h
checking for alloca
creating config.status
creating Makefile
[localhost:src/hello/hello-1.3] root#
```

Figure 13.34 The configure script probes your system and configures the source code for compilation.

```
[localhost:src/hello/hello-1.3] root# make
cc -c  -DSTDC_HEADERS=1 -DHAVE_STRING_H=1 -DHAVE_FCNTL_H=1 -DHAVE_SYS_FILE_H=1 -g hello.c
cc -c  -DSTDC_HEADERS=1 -DHAVE_STRING_H=1 -DHAVE_FCNTL_H=1 -DHAVE_SYS_FILE_H=1 -g version.c
cc -c  -DSTDC_HEADERS=1 -DHAVE_STRING_H=1 -DHAVE_FCNTL_H=1 -DHAVE_SYS_FILE_H=1 -g getopt.c
cc -c  -DSTDC_HEADERS=1 -DHAVE_STRING_H=1 -DHAVE_FCNTL_H=1 -DHAVE_SYS_FILE_H=1 -g getopt1.c
cc -g -o hello hello.o version.o getopt.o getopt1.o
/usr/bin/ld: warning unused multiple definitions of symbol _optind
getopt.o definition of _optind in section (__DATA,__data)
/usr/lib/libSystem.dylib(getopt.o) unused definition of _optind
/usr/bin/ld: warning unused multiple definitions of symbol _getopt
getopt.o definition of _getopt in section (__TEXT,__text)
/usr/lib/libSystem.dylib(getopt.o) unused definition of _getopt
/usr/bin/ld: warning unused multiple definitions of symbol _optarg
getopt.o definition of _optarg in section (__DATA,__data)
/usr/lib/libSystem.dylib(getopt.o) unused definition of _optarg
/usr/bin/ld: warning unused multiple definitions of symbol _opterr
getopt.o definition of _opterr in section (__DATA,__data)
/usr/lib/libSystem.dylib(getopt.o) unused definition of _opterr
/usr/bin/ld: warning unused multiple definitions of symbol _optopt
getopt.o definition of _optopt in section (__DATA,__data)
/usr/lib/libSystem.dylib(getopt.o) unused definition of _optopt
[localhost:src/hello/hello-1.3] root#
```

Figure 13.35 The make command runs the compilation process.

14. make

The make command reads Makefile, created by configure and runs a series of commands to compile the software. (Both configure and Makefile are plain text files—you can look inside them if you are curious.) **Figure 13.35** shows the output from make. In this case, you see some warnings (such as "warning unused multiple definitions of symbol _optind"), but the compilation process completes without any fatal errors, so we know it has worked. Depending on how large and complex the software is, the compilation process can take many minutes or even longer.

15. make test

Some software packages come with a set of tests to run after compiling the software but before installing it. In this case there are none, so you see an error message (**Figure 13.36**), but it doesn't hurt to try.

Up to now you have not changed anything on your disk outside the directory containing the source code. The next step is to actually install the software in the location where it will be available to all users on the system.

16. make install

The make program shows you what it does to install the software. In this case it uses the INSTALL program (/usr/bin/install), which has a man page you can read if you are curious (**Figure 13.37**). The software is now installed.

17. exit

This exits from the root shell you started in step 1. Your prompt changes back to your normal prompt. Note that your current directory reverts to whatever it was when you started the root shell (**Figure 13.38**).

If you are using the tcsh shell as your shell, type rehash so that tcsh will rebuild its list of available commands.

continues on next page

```
[localhost:src/hello/hello-1.3] root# make test
make: *** No rule to make target `test'.  Stop.
[localhost:src/hello/hello-1.3] root#
```

Figure 13.36 It doesn't hurt to see if there are any preinstallation tests.

```
[localhost:src/hello/hello-1.3] root# exit
[localhost:~] vanilla%
```

Figure 13.38 Exiting from the root shell brings you back to the directory you were in when you started it.

```
[localhost:src/hello/hello-1.3] root# make install
./mkinstalldirs /usr/local/bin /usr/local/info
/usr/bin/install -c hello /usr/local/bin/hello
/usr/bin/install -c -m 644 ./hello.info /usr/local/info/hello.info
[localhost:src/hello/hello-1.3] root#
```

Figure 13.37 The make install program performs the actual installation of the software.

MANUALLY INSTALLING FROM SOURCE CODE

Now you can try running the newly installed software. The new program has been installed as /usr/local/bin/hello, so you want to make sure that /usr/local/bin is in your PATH. See Chapter 7, "Configuring Your Unix Environment" to learn how to alter your PATH.

18. hello

The program produces output as shown in **Figure 13.39**.

19. You're done.

Congratulations.

✔ Tips

■ You can save a record of the compilation process to a file by redirecting the output of make to a file:

make > compilation.log

or

make install > install.log

■ You can remove all the files created in the source directory by the compilation process with

make clean

(If you want to remove files that have been installed with make install, you must remove them manually from their installed locations.)

■ The configure script saves the configuration it builds in another shell script, called config.status, which you can run to re-create the configuration, including any options you selected.

```
[localhost:~] vanilla% hello
Hello, world!
[localhost:~] vanilla%
```

Figure 13.39 Running the newly installed software to see what it does.

When Things Go Wrong

Sometimes running ./configure doesn't work smoothly. Usually, if something goes wrong with configure, it is because the script could not find something on your system that it needs.

Sometimes configure works, but compilation fails when you run make.

As you gain experience with compiling software, you may be able to fix the problem yourself, perhaps by installing a piece of software required by the one that didn't compile.

The first place to look for help is in the README and INSTALL files. Make sure you have read anything pertaining to Mac OS X or Darwin mentioned in those files. Look for references to other help resources, such as a Web site or mailing list. If you send a message to someone asking for help, be very respectful of his or her time. Make sure to include an exact copy of any error messages you received and any options you used when running configure.

Installing Perl Modules

If you've started using Unix a lot, there is a good chance you will also use Perl a lot. Perl is a powerful and easy-to-learn language that's well suited for both large and small programming tasks. A beginner can learn how to write a simple Perl script in a day, and an experienced programmer can use Perl to solve complex problems efficiently.

One of the things that make Perl so powerful is CPAN (Comprehensive Perl Archive Network). CPAN is a truly amazing collection of freely available Perl modules (we'll tell you where to find out more about CPAN later in the chapter).

A *Perl module* is a piece of software that adds features to Perl, such as the ability to do date and time arithmetic, to connect to databases, or to use strong encryption. Perl modules can be written in Perl, C, and other languages; most are written in C and/or Perl. The version of Perl installed with Mac OS X comes with more than 250 modules (the "standard modules") already installed. The CPAN system provides more than a thousand more.

You can download and build Perl modules using a series of steps very similar to the steps described above. The main difference is that instead of running a shell script (`./configure`) to build the makefile and configure the software for compilation, you run a Perl script with `perl Makefile.PL`. Also, Perl modules almost always come with tests that run when you do `make test`. But wait—there's more.

One of the standard modules included with Perl on Mac OS X is the CPAN module—essentially the Perl version of Fink (in fact, the CPAN module predates Fink by several years). As with Fink, your computer must be on the Internet to use the CPAN module.

Using the Perl CPAN module, you can easily install Perl modules in a couple of steps.

The first time you use the CPAN module, you must configure it.

To configure CPAN:

1. `sudo perl -MCPAN -e shell`

   That means: "As root, run Perl using the CPAN module and execute the expression shell." The CPAN module actually provides its own little shell interface—its prompt is `cpan>`, and it takes commands to search for and install Perl modules.

   You use `sudo` because the CPAN module will be making changes in system directories (it will save its configuration in `/System/Library/Perl/CPAN/Config.pm` and will install new modules in `/Library/Perl`).

   If this is the first time you have used the CPAN module, it will ask you to configure it (**Figure 13.40**).

2. Enter your password if asked.

The CPAN module asks if you are ready to manual configuration.

3. Accept the default ("yes") by pressing [Return].

The CPAN module asks you for the name of a directory where it will store files during installation. It creates the directory if it doesn't exist (**Figure 13.41**).

```
[localhost:~] vanilla% sudo cpan
Password:


/System/Library/Perl/CPAN/Config.pm initialized.


CPAN is the world-wide archive of perl resources. It consists of about
100 sites that all replicate the same contents all around the globe.
Many countries have at least one CPAN site already. The resources
found on CPAN are easily accessible with the CPAN.pm module. If you
want to use CPAN.pm, you have to configure it properly.

If you do not want to enter a dialog now, you can answer 'no' to this
question and I'll try to autoconfigure. (Note: you can revisit this
dialog anytime later by typing 'o conf init' at the cpan prompt.)


Are you ready for manual configuration? [yes]
```

Figure 13.40 Beginning the CPAN configuration process.

```
The following questions are intended to help you with the
configuration. The CPAN module needs a directory of its own to cache
important index files and maybe keep a temporary mirror of CPAN files.
This may be a site-wide directory or a personal directory.




First of all, I'd like to create this directory. Where?

CPAN build and cache directory? [/Users/vanilla/.cpan] /usr/local/CPAN
```

Figure 13.41 Choosing the directory in which CPAN will cache files during installations.

4. /usr/local/CPAN

This is one of the few places where you will enter something different from the default.

The module asks about the size of the cache it will keep of files used during installations. The default of 10 MB is a good choice (**Figure 13.42**).

5. Accept the default ("10") by pressing Return.

The module now asks if it should check the size of the cache when it starts up. The default ("atstart") is what you want. (**Figure 13.43**).

6. Accept the default by pressing Return.

The module asks if it should try to keep an index of information about modules (using another module called "Storable"). Again, accept the default ("yes") (**Figure 13.44**).

continues on next page

```
How big should the disk cache be for keeping the build directories
with all the intermediate files?

Cache size for build directory (in MB)? [10]
```

Figure 13.42 Selecting the size of the CPAN cache.

```
By default, each time the CPAN module is started, cache scanning
is performed to keep the cache size in sync. To prevent this,
disable the cache scanning with 'never'.

Perform cache scanning (atstart or never)? [atstart]
```

Figure 13.43 The CPAN module asks when to scan the cache to limit its size.

```
To considerably speed up the initial CPAN shell startup, it is
possible to use Storable to create a cache of metadata. If Storable
is not available, the normal index mechanism will be used.

Cache metadata (yes/no)? [yes]
```

Figure 13.44 The CPAN module asks if it should try to keep an index of information to speed startup.

INSTALLING PERL MODULES

7. Press ⟨Return⟩ to accept the default.

The module asks you about the character set supported by your terminal. Unless you are sure you know what you are doing, you should accept the default ("yes" indicates ISO-8859-1, the standard English character set) (**Figure 13.45**).

8. Press ⟨Return⟩. to accept the default.

Some modules depend on others' having already been installed. You can instruct the module to ask you before installing prerequisite modules ("ask"), to ignore prerequisites (not recommended), or to "follow" the requirements and install prerequisites when discovered.

The default is to ask before installing, but we suggest you change that to "follow" (**Figure 13.46**).

9. The module asks about a series of programs that it uses. You should accept the default for each of them by pressing ⟨Return⟩. (Don't worry if the lynx and ncftpget programs are not found—the module will work without them.)

10. Press ⟨Return⟩ for each program shown in **Figure 13.47**.

(Notice the wget program—you installed that using wget earlier in this chapter. You can also install lynx using Fink, if you like.)

The module asks about parameters for the perl Makefile.PL command. (**Figure 13.48**).

continues on next page

```
The next option deals with the charset your terminal supports. In
general CPAN is English speaking territory, thus the charset does not
matter much, but some of the aliens out there who upload their
software to CPAN bear names that are outside the ASCII range. If your
terminal supports UTF-8, you say no to the next question, if it
supports ISO-8859-1 (also known as LATIN1) then you say yes, and if it
supports neither nor, your answer does not matter, you will not be
able to read the names of some authors anyway. If you answer no, nmes
will be output in UTF-8.

Your terminal expects ISO-8859-1 (yes/no)? [yes]
```

Figure 13.45 The CPAN module asks about the character set supported by your terminal.

```
The CPAN module can detect when a module that which you are trying to
build depends on prerequisites. If this happens, it can build the
prerequisites for you automatically ('follow'), ask you for
confirmation ('ask'), or just ignore them ('ignore'). Please set your
policy to one of the three values.

Policy on building prerequisites (follow, ask or ignore)? [ask] follow
```

Figure 13.46 The CPAN module asks for your policy on building prerequisite modules. You tell it to "follow."

```
The CPAN module will need a few external programs to work properly.
Please correct me, if I guess the wrong path for a program. Don't
panic if you do not have some of them, just press ENTER for those. To
disable the use of a download program, you can type a space followed
by ENTER.

Where is your gzip program? [/sw/bin/gzip]
Where is your tar program? [/sw/bin/tar]
Where is your unzip program? [/usr/bin/unzip]
Where is your make program? [/usr/bin/make]
Warning: lynx not found in PATH
Where is your lynx program? []
Where is your wget program? [/sw/bin/wget]
Warning: ncftpget not found in PATH
Where is your ncftpget program? []
Where is your ncftp program? [/usr/bin/ncftp]
Where is your ftp program? [/usr/bin/ftp]
What is your favorite pager program? [/usr/bin/less]
What is your favorite shell? [/bin/tcsh]
```

Figure 13.47 The CPAN module asks about a series of programs it wants to use. You accept the default for each question.

```
Every Makefile.PL is run by perl in a separate process. Likewise we
run 'make' and 'make install' in processes. If you have any
parameters (e.g. PREFIX, LIB, UNINST or the like) you want to pass
to the calls, please specify them here.

If you don't understand this question, just press ENTER.

Parameters for the 'perl Makefile.PL' command?
Typical frequently used settings:

    POLLUTE=1        increasing backwards compatibility
    LIB=~/perl       non-root users (please see manual for more hints)

Your choice:  []
```

Figure 13.48 The CPAN module asks about options for the perl Makefile.PL command. You just press Return .

11. Don't supply any; just accept the default by pressing ⌈Return⌉.

The module asks for parameters for the make command (**Figure 13.49**).

If you have a dual-processor machine, enter

-j3

Otherwise, don't enter anything.

12. Press ⌈Return⌉.

You are asked about options for the make install command. The CPAN module offers an option to try to uninstall potentially conflicting packages, which is a good idea (**Figure 13.50**).

```
Parameters for the 'make' command?
Typical frequently used setting:


    -j3                 dual processor system


Your choice:   []
```

Figure 13.49 Options for the make command; enter -j3 if you have a dual processor, or don't enter anything.

```
Parameters for the 'make install' command?
Typical frequently used setting:


    UNINST=1         to always uninstall potentially conflicting files


Your choice:   [] UNINST=1
```

Figure 13.50 Options for the make install command. Select UNINST=1.

INSTALLING PERL MODULES

13. UNINST=1

The installation process for many modules involves asking you questions. You can tell the CPAN module how long to wait for an answer (in seconds) before stopping an installation process. The CPAN module recommends a setting of 0, which actually means "wait forever," so if you walk away from your computer during an installation, the module will wait until you come back (**Figure 13.51**).

14. Press [Return] to accept the default ("0").

The module now asks you about proxy servers. If your computer is set up behind a firewall, there may be one or more proxy servers you must use to access Web sites or FTP sites on the Internet.

Ask your network administrator if you are not sure. If you don't have a network administrator, then you almost certainly don't have proxy servers, so just accept the default (nothing) for each of the next three questions (**Figure 13.52**).

If you have a proxy server, then enter it in the form of a URL:

http://proxy.paranoid.sf.ca.us/

continues on next page

```
Sometimes you may wish to leave the processes run by CPAN alone
without caring about them. As sometimes the Makefile.PL contains
question you're expected to answer, you can set a timer that will
kill a 'perl Makefile.PL' process after the specified time in seconds.

If you set this value to 0, these processes will wait forever. This is
the default and recommended setting.

Timeout for inactivity during Makefile.PL? [0]
```

Figure 13.51 Setting the time-out period. The default ("0" for "wait forever") is a good choice.

```
If you're accessing the net via proxies, you can specify them in the
CPAN configuration or via environment variables. The variable in
the $CPAN::Config takes precedence.

Your ftp_proxy?
Your http_proxy?
Your no_proxy?
```

Figure 13.52 Press [Return] to accept the default ("nothing") for the proxy-server questions.

INSTALLING PERL MODULES

15. Press $\boxed{\text{Return}}$ for each of the proxy server questions to accept the default.

Now the module asks you about the sites from which it will download source code for Perl modules (**Figure 13.53**).

```
Your /usr/local/CPAN/sources/MIRRORED.BY is older than 60 days,
  I'm trying to fetch one
CPAN: Net::FTP loaded ok
Fetching with Net::FTP:
  ftp://ftp.perl.org/pub/CPAN/MIRRORED.BY


Now we need to know where your favorite CPAN sites are located. Push
a few sites onto the array (just in case the first on the array won't
work). If you are mirroring CPAN to your local workstation, specify a
file: URL.

First, pick a nearby continent and country (you can pick several of
each, separated by spaces, or none if you just want to keep your
existing selections). Then, you will be presented with a list of URLs
of CPAN mirrors in the countries you selected, along with previously
selected URLs. Select some of those URLs, or just keep the old list.
Finally, you will be prompted for any extra URLs - file:, ftp:, or
http: - that host a CPAN mirror.

(1) Africa
(2) Asia
(3) Central America
(4) Europe
(5) North America
(6) Oceania
(7) South America
Select your continent (or several nearby continents) [] 5
```

Figure 13.53 Telling the CPAN module what part of the world you are in.

16. Enter a number corresponding to the area of the world you are in so that you will download from servers closest to you.

Figure 13.53 shows 5 entered for North America.

The module gives you a list of countries to choose from (**Figure 13.54**).

17. Enter one or more numbers separated by spaces.

In Figure 13.54, we entered 2 and 3 for Mexico and the United States.

You will see a list of CPAN sites from your chosen countries, from which you are asked to select as many sites as you like (**Figure 13.55**). If the list is longer than what fits on your Terminal window, you can use the scroll bar to see the sites that scrolled off the top.

continues on next page

```
(1) Canada
(2) Mexico
(3) United States
Select your country (or several nearby countries) [] 2 3
```

Figure 13.54 The CPAN module asks you to choose from a list of countries.

```
(1) ftp://cpan.azc.uam.mx/mirrors/CPAN (Mexico)
(2) ftp://cpan.unam.mx/pub/CPAN (Mexico)
(3) ftp://ftp.msg.com.mx/pub/CPAN/ (Mexico)
(4) ftp://archive.progeny.com/CPAN/ (United States)
(5) ftp://carroll.cac.psu.edu/pub/CPAN/ (United States)
(6) ftp://cpan.cse.msu.edu/ (United States)
(7) ftp://cpan.digisle.net/pub/CPAN (United States)
(8) ftp://cpan.in-span.net/ (United States)
(9) ftp://cpan.llarian.net/pub/CPAN/ (United States)
(10) ftp://cpan.nas.nasa.gov/pub/perl/CPAN/ (United States)
(11) ftp://cpan.netnitco.net/pub/mirrors/CPAN/ (United States)
(12) ftp://cpan.pair.com/pub/CPAN/ (United States)
(13) ftp://cpan.teleglobe.net/pub/CPAN (United States)
(14) ftp://cpan.thepirtgroup.com/ (United States)
(15) ftp://cpan.uky.edu/pub/CPAN/ (United States)
(16) ftp://cpan.valueclick.com/pub/CPAN/ (United States)
(17) ftp://csociety-ftp.ecn.purdue.edu/pub/CPAN (United States)
(18) ftp://ftp-mirror.internap.com/pub/CPAN/ (United States)
(19) ftp://ftp.ccs.neu.edu/net/mirrors/ftp.funet.fi/pub/languages/perl/CPAN/ (United States)
(20) ftp://ftp.cise.ufl.edu/pub/mirrors/CPAN/ (United States)
```

Figure 13.55 You are asked to choose sites from which to download modules.

Figure 13.55 (continued)

```
(21) ftp://ftp.cpanel.net/pub/CPAN/ (United States)

(22) ftp://ftp.cs.colorado.edu/pub/perl/CPAN/ (United States)

(23) ftp://ftp.dc.aleron.net/pub/CPAN/ (United States)

(24) ftp://ftp.duke.edu/pub/perl/ (United States)

(25) ftp://ftp.epix.net/pub/languages/perl/ (United States)

(26) ftp://ftp.exobit.org/pub/perl/CPAN (United States)

(27) ftp://ftp.loaded.net/pub/CPAN/ (United States)

(28) ftp://ftp.lug.udel.edu/pub/CPAN (United States)

(29) ftp://ftp.mirrorcentral.com/pub/CPAN/ (United States)

(30) ftp://ftp.orst.edu/pub/CPAN (United States)

(31) ftp://ftp.ou.edu/mirrors/CPAN/ (United States)

(32) ftp://ftp.rge.com/pub/languages/perl/ (United States)

(33) ftp://ftp.stealth.net/pub/CPAN/ (United States)

(34) ftp://ftp.sunsite.utk.edu/pub/CPAN/ (United States)

(35) ftp://ftp.uwsg.iu.edu/pub/perl/CPAN/ (United States)

(36) ftp://mirror.csit.fsu.edu/pub/CPAN/ (United States)

(37) ftp://mirror.hiwaay.net/CPAN/ (United States)

(38) ftp://mirror.sit.wisc.edu/pub/CPAN/ (United States)

(39) ftp://mirror.telentente.com/pub/CPAN (United States)

(40) ftp://mirror.xmission.com/CPAN/ (United States)

(41) ftp://mirrors.cloud9.net/pub/mirrors/CPAN/ (United States)

(42) ftp://mirrors.kernel.org/pub/CPAN (United States)

(43) ftp://mirrors.netnumina.com/cpan/ (United States)

(44) ftp://mirrors.phenominet.com/pub/CPAN/ (United States)

(45) ftp://mirrors.phihost.com/CPAN/ (United States)

(46) ftp://mirrors.rcn.net/pub/lang/CPAN/ (United States)

(47) ftp://perl.secsup.org/pub/perl/ (United States)

(48) ftp://ruff.cs.jmu.edu/pub/CPAN/ (United States)

(49) ftp://uiarchive.uiuc.edu/mirrors/ftp/cpan.cse.msu.edu/ (United States)

Select as many URLs as you like,

put them on one line, separated by blanks [] 10 25 39
```

18. Enter three numbers separated by spaces.

In Figure 13.55, we entered 10, 25, and 39. Do not enter commas; just separate the numbers with spaces.

You can enter as few as one and as many as you like. Three is a good number. The CPAN module tries the first site first, and if it gets no answer, it tries the second, and so on.

The module then asks if you want to enter more sites (**Figure 13.56**).

19. Press [Return]. to move on to the next question.

```
Enter another URL or RETURN to quit: []
```

Figure 13.56 You are given a chance to enter more sites if you want to.

The module asks if you want to specify a WAIT server (**Figure 13.57**). WAIT is a network search protocol based on WAIS (Wide Area Information Server). You can get some documentation on using WAIT with the CPAN module by typing perl-doc CPAN::WAIT at a shell prompt (open another Terminal window if you want to do that now, or do it some other time).

20. Press [Return] to accept the default.

The CPAN module is now configured (**Figure 13.58**).

The module writes the configuration to /System/Library/Perl/CPAN/Config.pm (which is a text file—you can examine it if you are curious).

continues on next page

```
New set of picks:
  ftp://cpan.nas.nasa.gov/pub/perl/CPAN/
  ftp://ftp.epix.net/pub/languages/perl/
  ftp://mirror.telentente.com/pub/CPAN


WAIT support is available as a Plugin. You need the CPAN::WAIT module
to actually use it.  But we need to know your favorite WAIT server. If
you don't know a WAIT server near you, just press ENTER.

Your favorite WAIT server?
  [wait://ls6.informatik.uni-dortmund.de:1404]
```

Figure 13.57 The CPAN module shows the sites you picked and asks if you want to specify a WAIT server.

```
commit: wrote /System/Library/Perl/CPAN/Config.pm


cpan shell — CPAN exploration and modules installation (v1.59)
ReadLine support enabled


cpan>
```

Figure 13.58 The module shows you that is has saved the new configuration.

21. `quit`

This quits the CPAN shell (**Figure 13.59**). You have been using the CPAN module's shell interface—the **cpan>** at the end of Figure 13.58 is the CPAN module shell prompt, not to be confused with the shell prompt from your Unix shell.

✔ Tips

■ You can rerun the configuration process in the future by renaming the configuration file (so you have a backup copy) and then running the **CPAN** command again. For example, you could enter

```
cd /System/Library/Perl/CPAN
sudo mv Config.pm Config.pm.BACKUP
sudo perl -MCPAN -e shell
```

```
cpan> quit
Lockfile removed.
[localhost:~] vanilla%
```

Figure 13.59 Quitting the CPAN module and getting a CPAN module shell prompt.

■ Consider creating an alias or script called "cpan" so that you don't have to type "`perl -MCPAN -e shell`" every time you use CPAN. To learn about aliases, see Chapter 7, "Configuring Your Unix Environment"; for scripts see Chapter 9, "Creating and Using Scripts."

Now that you have configured the CPAN module, you can use it to install Perl modules.

To start the CPAN module:

1. `sudo perl -MCPAN -e shell`

2. Enter your password if asked.

You get the CPAN shell prompt:

`cpan>`

✔ Tip

■ You can quit by typing `quit` at the **cpan>** prompt.

The following tasks assume that you have started the CPAN module and are at a **cpan>** prompt.

```
cpan> i /date/
.
. (( output abridged ))
.
Module          CGI::Validate   (Z/ZE/ZENIN/CGI-Validate-2.000.tar.gz)
Module          Class::Date     (D/DL/DLUX/Class-Date-1.0.10.tar.gz)
Module          Date::Bahai     (Contact Author Rich Bowen <rbowen@rcbowen.com>)
Module          Date::Biorhythm (T/TB/TBONE/Date-Biorhythm-1.1.tar.gz)
Module          Date::Business  (D/DE/DESIMINER/Date-Business-1.2.tar.gz)
Module          Date::CTime     (Contact Author Graham Barr <gbarr@pobox.com>)
Module          Date::Calc      (S/ST/STBEY/Date-Calc-5.0.tar.gz)
Module          Date::Calc::Object (S/ST/STBEY/Date-Calc-5.0.tar.gz)
.
. (( output abridged ))
.
173 items found

cpan>
```

Figure 13.60 Searching module names for a keyword.

To search for a Perl module:

1. i /date/

This searches all the available module names for the string "**date**." In this case, you get a rather long list (**Figure 13.60**). Let's assume you know you want something to do date calculations, so the module Date::Calc seems appropriate.

2. You can get more information about the module:

i Date::Calc

From the description of the module (**Figure 13.61**), it looks as if we might want this one.

3. Or you can look at the README file for any module available through CPAN (even modules you have not installed), with the readme command:

readme Date::Calc

This retrieves the README file and displays it (using the less pager command described in Chapter 5, "Using Files and Directories") (**Figure 13.62**).

Upgrading the CPAN Module

When you start up the CPAN module, you may see a notice recommending that you upgrade the module to a newer version. Do this by typing:

install Bundle::CPAN

at a cpan> prompt.

In some cases, this process make take a very long time, possibly including downloading and installing a new version of Perl itself, so don't do this unless you are prepared to let the process run for an hour or more (depending on the speed of your Mac and your Internet connection.)

Furthermore, you may be asked to go through the CPAN configuration process again after an upgrade if new features have been added. The CPAN module generally remembers your previous configuration choices and presents them as defaults.

```
cpan> i Date::Calc
Module id = Date::Calc
    DESCRIPTION  Gregorian calendar date calculations
    CPAN_USERID  STBEY (Steffen Beyer <sb@engelschall.com>)
    CPAN_VERSION 5.0
    CPAN_FILE    S/ST/STBEY/Date-Calc-5.0.tar.gz
    DSLI_STATUS  Rdhh (released,developer,hybrid,hybrid)
    MANPAGE      Date::Calc - Gregorian calendar date calculations
    INST_FILE    /Library/Perl/darwin/Date/Calc.pm
    INST_VERSION 5.0


cpan>
```

Figure 13.61 Getting information about a specific module.

INSTALLING PERL MODULES

```
cpan> readme Date::Calc
Running readme for module Date::Calc
Fetching with Net::FTP:
  ftp://cpan.nas.nasa.gov/pub/perl/CPAN/authors/id/S/ST/STBEY/Date-Calc-5.0.readme

Displaying file
  /usr/local/CPAN/sources/authors/id/S/ST/STBEY/Date-Calc-5.0.readme
with pager "/usr/bin/less"
                  ===================================
                     Package "Date::Calc" Version 5.0
                  ===================================



This package is available for download either from my web site at

                 http://www.engelschall.com/u/sb/download/


or from any CPAN (= "Comprehensive Perl Archive Network") mirror server:

                 http://www.perl.com/CPAN/authors/id/S/ST/STBEY/



Abstract:
-----


This package consists of a C library (intended to make life easier for C
developers) and a Perl module to access this library from Perl.

The library provides all sorts of date calculations based on the Gregorian
calendar (the one used in all western countries today), thereby complying
with all relevant norms and standards: ISO/R 2015-1971, DIN 1355 and, to
some extent, ISO 8601 (where applicable).

The package is designed as an efficient (and fast) toolbox, not a bulky
ready-made application. It provides extensive documentation and examples
of use, multi-language support and special functions for business needs.
((output abridged))
```

Figure 13.62 Seeing a module's README file before installing the module.

The next step is to install the module. Again, to perform the following task, you must be at the **cpan>** prompt.

To install a Perl module:

◆ install Date::Calc

That's all there is to it. You will see a great deal of output as the install process proceeds (an abridged example is shown in **Figure 13.63**).

continues on next page

```
cpan> install Date::Calc
CPAN: Storable loaded ok
Going to read /usr/local/CPAN/Metadata
Running install for module Date::Calc
Running make for S/ST/STBEY/Date-Calc-5.0.tar.gz
CPAN: Net::FTP loaded ok
Fetching with Net::FTP:
  ftp://cpan.nas.nasa.gov/pub/perl/CPAN/authors/id/S/ST/STBEY/Date-Calc-5.0.tar.gz
Scanning cache /usr/local/CPAN/build for sizes
CPAN: MD5 loaded ok
Fetching with Net::FTP:
  ftp://cpan.nas.nasa.gov/pub/perl/CPAN/authors/id/S/ST/STBEY/CHECKSUMS
Checksum for /usr/local/CPAN/sources/authors/id/S/ST/STBEY/Date-Calc-5.0.tar.gz ok
Date-Calc-5.0/
Date-Calc-5.0/t/
Date-Calc-5.0/t/f023.t
Date-Calc-5.0/t/f006.t
Date-Calc-5.0/t/f025.t
Date-Calc-5.0/t/f008.t
Date-Calc-5.0/t/f027.t
Date-Calc-5.0/t/f029.t
Date-Calc-5.0/t/f011.t
.
. ((output abridged))
.


CPAN.pm: Going to build S/ST/STBEY/Date-Calc-5.0.tar.gz

Checking if your kit is complete...
Looks good
Writing Makefile for Date::Calc
Writing patchlevel.h for /usr/bin/perl (5.006)
```

Figure 13.63 Installing a module (abridged output).

Figure 13.63 (continued)

```
mkdir blib
mkdir blib/lib
mkdir blib/lib/Date
mkdir blib/arch
mkdir blib/arch/auto
mkdir blib/arch/auto/Date
.
. ((output abridged))
.

Running make test
PERL_DL_NONLAZY=1 /usr/bin/perl -Iblib/arch -Iblib/lib -I/System/Library/Perl/darwin -I/System/
→Library/Perl -e 'use Test::Harness qw(&runtests $verbose); $verbose=0; runtests @ARGV;' t/*.t
t/f000..............ok
t/f001..............ok
t/f002..............ok
t/f003..............ok
t/f004..............ok
t/f005..............ok
t/f006..............ok
t/f007..............ok
t/f008..............ok
t/f009..............ok
.
. ((output abridged))
.
All tests successful.
Files=47, Tests=2923, 26 wallclock secs (10.55 cusr +  1.16 csys = 11.71 CPU)
  /usr/bin/make test - OK
Running make install
.
. ((output abridged))
.
Installing /usr/share/man/man3/Carp::Clan.3
Installing /usr/share/man/man3/Date::Calc.3
Installing /usr/share/man/man3/Date::Calc::Object.3
Installing /usr/share/man/man3/Date::Calendar.3
Installing /usr/share/man/man3/Date::Calendar::Profiles.3
Installing /usr/share/man/man3/Date::Calendar::Year.3
Writing /Library/Perl/darwin/auto/Date/Calc/.packlist
Appending installation info to /System/Library/Perl/darwin/perllocal.pod
  /usr/bin/make install UNINST=1 - OK

cpan>
```

Using the Date::Calc Module

Since you've gone to the trouble of installing it, here's a little script that uses the Date::Calc module.

The code listing shown in **Figure 13.64** will prompt you for a date in U.S. format and a number of days to add, and will display the new date. To try the script, create a file, enter the text from Figure 13.64, make the file executable, and run the script. (You'll need the skills you learned in Chapter 5, "Using Files and Directories," and Chapter 8, "Working with Permissions and Ownership," to create the file and make it executable.)

✔ Tips

■ See the sidebar "Using the Date::Calc Module" for an example of using this module.

■ Perl modules have documentation built into their source code (which is different from how Unix man pages work). To read the documentation for an installed Perl module, use the **perldoc** command from a shell prompt (not from the **cpan>** prompt):

perldoc Date::Calc

In fact, on some Unix systems, including Mac OS X, you can use the **man** command to read the documentation for perl modules:

man Date::Calc

```perl
#!/usr/bin/perl
#
# Add days to a date. Get a date back.
############################################

use Date::Calc qw( Decode_Date_US Add_Delta_Days Date_to_Text_Long );

print "Enter a date in any US format (month, day, year): ";
$date = <STDIN>; # get input from user
chop $date;      # remove the newline character


( $y, $m, $d ) = Decode_Date_US( $date );


print "How many days to add? ";
$add_days = <STDIN>;
chop $add_days;


( $y, $m, $d ) = Add_Delta_Days( $y,$m,$d,$add_days );


$new_date = Date_to_Text_Long($y,$m,$d);


print "New date is $new_date\n";
```

Figure 13.64 Code listing of a Perl script that uses the Date::Calc module.

To see a list of all installed modules and their versions:

◆ autobundle

The CPAN module examines all the Perl modules installed on your system and compares their versions with the latest versions available. **Figure 13.65** shows an abridged version of the output. Notice that a few modules (such as CGI and Test::Harness) have new versions available. You could install them with

install CGI

and

install Test::Harness

✔ Tip

■ It bears repeating that you can read the documentation for any installed Perl module with

perldoc *ModuleName*

(Remember that the module name usually includes one or more pairs of colons—for example, Test::Harness.)

Learning More About CPAN

If you are going to do any Perl programming beyond the most basic level, then you should know how to find out more about CPAN.

Like all Perl modules, CPAN has built-in documentation; read it with perldoc CPAN.

The main CPAN Web site is www.cpan.org. The CPAN Frequently Asked Questions document (www.cpan.org/misc/cpan-faq.html) answers many questions, including "What is Perl?" and "What is CPAN?"

```
cpan> autobundle
CPAN: Storable loaded ok
Going to read /usr/local/CPAN/Metadata

Package namespace          installed   latest  in CPAN file
AnyDBM_File                    undef    undef  G/GS/GSAR/perl-5.6.1.tar.gz
Apache                          1.27     1.27  D/DO/DOUGM/mod_perl-1.26.tar.gz
Apache::Connection              1.00     1.00  D/DO/DOUGM/mod_perl-1.26.tar.gz
Apache::Constants               1.09     1.09  D/DO/DOUGM/mod_perl-1.26.tar.gz
Apache::Constants::Exports     undef    undef  D/DO/DOUGM/mod_perl-1.26.tar.gz
Apache::Debug                   1.61     1.61  D/DO/DOUGM/mod_perl-1.26.tar.gz
.
. (( output abridged ))
.
```

Figure 13.65 Using the CPAN autobundle command to see a list of all installed modules.

Figure 13.65 (continued)

Apache::Util	1.02	1.02	D/DO/DOUGM/mod_perl-1.26.tar.gz
Apache::httpd_conf	0.01	0.01	D/DO/DOUGM/mod_perl-1.26.tar.gz
Benchmark	1	1	G/GS/GSAR/perl-5.6.1.tar.gz
Bit::Vector	6.1	6.1	S/ST/STBEY/Bit-Vector-6.1.tar.gz
Bit::Vector::Overload	6.1	6.1	S/ST/STBEY/Bit-Vector-6.1.tar.gz
ByteLoader	0.03	0.04	G/GS/GSAR/perl-5.6.1.tar.gz
CGI	2.56	2.81	L/LD/LDS/CGI.pm-2.81.tar.gz

```
.
. (( output abridged ))
.
```

DBI::ProxyServer	0.2005	0.2005	T/TI/TIMB/DBI-1.21.tar.gz
DBI::Shell	11.02	11.02	T/TI/TIMB/DBI-1.21.tar.gz
DB_File	1.72	1.803	P/PM/PMQS/DB_File-1.803.tar.gz
Data::Dumper	2.101	2.102	G/GS/GSAR/perl-5.6.1.tar.gz
Date::Calc	5.0	5.0	S/ST/STBEY/Date-Calc-5.0.tar.gz
Date::Calc::Object	5.0	5.0	S/ST/STBEY/Date-Calc-5.0.tar.gz
Date::Calendar	5.0	5.0	S/ST/STBEY/Date-Calc-5.0.tar.gz

```
.
. (( output abridged ))
.
```

Test	1.13	1.20	M/MS/MSCHWERN/Test-1.20.tar.gz
Test::Harness	1.1604	2.22	M/MS/MSCHWERN/Test-Harness-2.22.tar.gz
Text::Abbrev	undef	undef	G/GS/GSAR/perl-5.6.1.tar.gz
Text::ParseWords	3.2	3.2	G/GS/GSAR/perl-5.6.1.tar.gz
Text::Soundex	1.0	2.20	M/MA/MARKM/Text-Soundex-2.20.tar.gz

```
.
. (( output abridged ))
.


Wrote bundle file
    /usr/local/CPAN/Bundle/Snapshot_2002_05_20_01.pm
```

INSTALLING AND CONFIGURING SERVERS

14

As you've probably gathered, managing servers is one of the most valuable—and most complex—aspects of running a Unix machine. It's something Unix does very well because of its reliability.

In this chapter we'll show you how to install and configure the basic server applications. We'll set up your machine's Internet domain name, activate file sharing using both AppleShare and FTP, and explain secure login. From there, you'll configure your Mac to be an email server, activate the Apache Web server, and add a simple CGI (Common Gateway Interface) script to the server.

After that, we'll show you how to install and configure the MySQL database engine. We even show you a simple Perl script that connects to and uses the database.

Some of these server applications are already installed in Mac OS X and can be activated with a mouse click. But of course we will show you how to do it all from the command line.

With this chapter in particular we are assuming that you have read the earlier chapters and are quite comfortable working at the command line and editing files.

You will need to be logged in as an administrative user for most of the tasks in this chapter, as almost all of them require that you perform tasks as root, using the sudo command.

Setting Your Machine's Hostname

In Chapter 10, "Interacting with Other Unix Machines," we explained that human beings refer to Internet hosts by their hostname, or their Fully Qualified Domain Name (FQDN) (such as www.peachpit.com), while machines on the Internet identify each other using IP addresses.

Throughout this chapter we talk about setting up server software on your computer so that other machines can connect to it using various network protocols (for example, to send email to your computer or to use a Web browser or FTP client to connect to your computer). If you want people to be able to connect to your server using an FQDN instead of an IP address, then you need to arrange for an FQDN to "point" to your machine's IP address.

FQDNs refer to specific machines and are created by whomever controls the domain involved. For example, the FQDN

www.matisse.sf.ca.us

refers to the machine that has the IP address 66.47.69.194. That FQDN is created by whomever controls the

.matisse.sf.ca.us

domain. The controller of a domain may create as many subdomains and FQDNs as he or she wishes.

If you are running your Mac in a large office environment, you should probably contact your office's network administrator to find out what the FQDN is for your machine, or have the administrator create one for you.

If you are a home- or small-office user, then your Internet service provider (ISP) has probably established FQDNs for the IP address(es) that it assigned to you. Unfortunately, the FQDN for your machine's IP address is probably something like "user135-walla-walla.high-speed.ispname.com."

You may also have reserved a new domain name through one of the many domain-name registries. You will need to contact that registry and ask it to set up the FQDN for you, giving it the FQDN you want and the IP address for your machine. It will often take several days or even weeks to get through the bureaucratic process.

So in order for your machine to have the FQDN that you want, you must arrange for the following.

◆ Your machine must have a static IP address. This is one that does not change each time you reboot the machine. Look in the Network panel of System Preferences, under the TCP/IP tab. The Configure method should be set to Manually (**Figure 14.1**). For an exception to this rule, see the sidebar, "Dynamic DNS."

Figure 14.1 The TCP/IP tab of the Network panel of System Preferences, where you set the Configure method to Manually for a static IP address.

◆ The owner of an Internet domain name must create a configuration entry that associates your IP address with a domain name (making it an FQDN).

Mac OS X tries to figure out the FQDN for your machine when it boots up, but if you want the operating system to set its hostname to an FQDN other than the one it finds automatically, you need to change a system-configuration file.

To see the hostname your Mac is using:

◆ hostname

This will show the FQDN that your Mac is currently using.

Technically, the hostname is only the leftmost part of the FQDN, and you can see that part alone by adding the -s option:

hostname -s

Dynamic DNS

Most home users of the Internet do not have static IP addresses. Instead, their Internet Service Providers assign a different address (from a pool of addresses) each time a customer connects.

There is a way that you can have an FQDN that points to a machine whose IP address changes each time it boots up. You arrange with a service that provides *dynamic DNS*. With this service, your computer contacts the dynamic DNS provider each time it gets a new IP address, and the dynamic DNS provider updates its database so your FQDN points to your current IP address.

See www.technopagan.org/dynamic/ for a list of dynamic DNS providers.

✔ Tip

■ Sometimes in a script you want to get the hostname part of the FQDN so that you can use it in the name of a log file or something similar. In a Bourne shell script you would use:

hostpart=`hostname -s`

and in a **tcsh** (**csh**) script you would use:

set hostpart=`hostname -s`

That sets **$hostpart** to contain only the host part of the FQDN.

The system of translating domain names to IP addresses (and vice versa) is handled by the Internet Domain Name System (DNS), a worldwide database of domain names and IP addresses. This distributed database is made up of tens of thousands of servers, called domain name servers, each of which is responsible for a small portion of the overall database. Each domain name is controlled by one server (the primary DNS server for that domain), with one or more backup servers (secondary DNS servers) that copy information from the primary one. In Chapter 15, at http://www.peachpit.com/vqp/umox.html, "More Open-Source Software," we show you how to configure your Mac to be a DNS server.

Running Your Own DNS Server

Mac OS X comes with the software necessary to run your own DNS server; we'll explain how to configure it in Chapter 15, "More Open-Source Software."

To effectively run your own DNS server for a particular domain, such as fuzzybears-are-cute.com, your Mac needs to be on all the time and have a static IP address. Also, you must notify the domain's registrar that you want your Mac to be the primary DNS server for the domain.

SETTING YOUR MACHINE'S HOSTNAME

Only the operator of a primary DNS server can create a new FQDN.

If the FQDN you intend to use for your machine is different from the one returned by the hostname command, then you must change a system-configuration file to tell your Mac to use the FQDN you want. The exact method of doing this varies among different versions of Unix, but here's the Darwin approach.

Note: For several tasks in this chapter, you'll have to become root, make a backup of your hostconfig file, and then edit it. We've listed the three steps of the task here, but later in the chapter we combine them, with a reference back here.

To change the /etc/hostconfig system-configuration file:

1. Become root:

   sudo -s

2. Make a backup copy of /etc/hostconfig:

   cp /etc/hostconfig /etc/hostconfig.
   → YYYYMMDD

   Use today's date for YYYYMMDD. The /etc/hostconfig file can be changed only by root.

   YYYYMMDD is the current year, month, and day from today's date. If you were doing this on July 23, 2003, the command line would read

   cp /etc/hostconfig /etc/hostconfig.
   → 20030723

3. Edit the file /etc/hostconfig using your favorite command-line editor—for example, using vi:

   vi /etc/hostconfig

Whenever you change a system-configuration file, you should always make a copy of it first. That way you can easily revert to whatever state the file was in before you messed it up ... um, before you changed it.

To set the machine's hostname on startup:

1. Per the task above, become root, back up /etc/hostconfig, and edit the file using vi.

2. Change the line that says

   HOSTNAME=-AUTOMATIC-

   to have your FQDN instead of -AUTOMATIC-. So if your FQDN is sailing.seas.uk, you would use

   HOSTNAME="sailing.seas.uk"

3. Save your changes, and quit the editor.

4. Restart networking services:

   sudo /System/Library/StartupItems
   →/Network/Network restart

   (The **stop** and **restart** arguments are ignored in Mac OS X 10.2.1 and earlier, but it won't hurt to use them, and future versions might require it. In Mac OS X 10.2.1 and earlier, there is no way to use the StartupItems script to restart networking. You will have to reboot.)

5. Test it:

   hostname

   should show the FQDN you entered.

Controlling the AppleShare Server

AppleShare is the Macintosh system for sharing files and disks across networks. Of course, you can activate AppleShare file sharing from the Sharing panel of System Preferences (under the Services tab) by selecting Personal File Sharing. But where's the fun in that?

The AppleShare file server listens on port 548. If you are using firewall software, make sure that access to port 548 is not blocked.

To activate AppleShare from the command line:

1. Per the task "To change the /etc/host-config system-configuration file," become root, back up `/etc/hostconfig`, and edit the file using `vi`.

2. Change the line that says

   `AFPSERVER=-NO-`

   to

   `AFPSERVER=-YES-`

3. Save your changes, and quit the editor (in vi, you press `Esc`:w and then :q).

4. Start AppleShare:

   `/System/Library/StartupItems/`
   `→AppleShare/AppleShare start`

   AppleShare is now active.

5. Stop being root:

   `exit`

   You should be back at your regular shell prompt.

✔ Tips

■ If you want to keep AppleShare from starting at boot time, reverse the change you made in step 2 above—that is, change `AFPSERVER=-YES-` back to `AFPSERVER=-NO-`.

■ Starting and stopping the AFP server from the command line does not update the display in the System Preferences GUI. So if you start AppleShare from the command line, and then open the Sharing tool in System Preferences and look at the Services tab, "Personal File Sharing" is off. If you try and start it from the GUI (after it has already been started from the command line), the GUI will act as if it is trying to start Personal File Sharing but will never finish. The GUI will say, "File sharing is starting up..." but never get past that. If you want to shut down the AppleShare server at that point, you must do it from the command line (see the next task).

You can turn AppleShare off from the GUI using the same Sharing panel in System Preferences that allows you to activate it, and you can also shut it down from the command line.

Once Apple updates the AppleShare StartupItems script to handle an argument of **stop**, you will be able to use that script to stop AppleShare. Until then, you can still do it with a few more steps. (As of Mac OS X 10.2.1, the AppleShare script still cannot stop or restart the AppleShare server.)

As with everything in Unix, there are many reasons for wanting to do something from the command line instead of through a graphical interface. For example, you might want to create a shell script to perform a task, or you might want to perform the task manually while logged in to your Mac at the command line from another machine on the Internet.

To shut down AppleShare from the command line:

1. Get the process ID number for the AppleFileServer:

   `ps -auxw | grep AppleFileServer`

   The output probably consists of two lines, one showing the `AppleFileServer` process itself and one showing the `grep` process. You want the line for the `AppleFileServer` process, which looks something like this:

   `root  6303  0.0  0.1  824  976 ??`
   `→Ss  8:47AM 0:00.15 AppleFileServer`

   The process ID number is the first number that appears in the line (6303 in this example).

2. `sudo kill pid`

   where *pid* is the process ID number—for example,

   `sudo kill 6303`

   That's it. The AppleFileServer stops.

Activating the SSH Server

Mac OS X comes with the **sshd** server, which provides secure log-in capability using the SSH (Secure Shell) protocol. We covered SSH in some detail in chapters 10 ("Interacting with Other Unix Machines") and 12 ("Security"). In an SSH connection all traffic between client and server is encrypted. Activating the SSH server enables other machines to connect to yours over the Internet using the SSH protocol. Review Chapter 10 for more on using **ssh**, **scp**, **sftp**, and other SSH-based tools.

You can deactivate the SSH server by going to the Sharing panel of System Preferences, clicking the Services tab, and deselecting the "Remote login" box, but here's the Unix way (actually, this is the Darwin way—most other Unix systems would use a different series of steps).

The SSH server listens on port 22. If you are using firewall software, make sure that access to port 22 is not blocked.

To activate the SSH server:

1. Per the task "To change the /etc/host-config system-configuration file," become root, back up **/etc/hostconfig**, and edit the file using **vi**.

2. Edit the file **/etc/hostconfig** by changing the line

   SSHSERVER=-NO-

   to

   SSHSERVER=-YES-

3. Save your changes, and quit the editor (in vi, it's (Esc):w :q).

4. Start the SSH server:

   /System/Library/StartupItems/SSH/
   →SSH start

5. Stop being root:

   exit

   You should be back at your regular shell prompt.

✔ Tips

■ As of Mac OS X 10.2.1, the SSH script ignores any arguments such as **start**, **stop**, or **restart**. It simply tries to start the SSH server every time the script is run. Hopefully this will be corrected in future versions of Mac OS X.

■ To keep the SSH server from starting at boot time, reverse the change in step 2 above. That is, change SSHSERVER=-YES- back to SSHSERVER=-NO-.

■ Incoming SSH connections are logged to /var/log/system.log.

You can also shut down the SSH server from the command line, but as of Mac OS X 10.2.1, you cannot use the /System/Library/StartupItems/SSH/SSH script to stop the SSH server. Hopefully this will also be corrected in the future.

To shut down the SSH server from the command line:

◆ sudo kill `cat /var/run/sshd.pid`
   Enter your password if prompted.

   When the SSH server starts up, it writes its pid number into the file /var/run/sshd.pid, so you can use that file to find the pid number and stop the server.

Configuring Sendmail — Internet Email Server

If your machine is connected to the Internet, you can use it to send email from the command line. If your machine is connected all the time ("24/7," as they say), then you can use it as a server to receive incoming email and store messages in mailboxes for each user on your system.

The Sendmail program (`/usr/sbin/sendmail`) has long been the standard Internet email server.

Sendmail actually provides two kinds of email services: It is both an MTA (Mail Transport Agent) and an MDA (Mail Delivery Agent). In its role as an MTA, Sendmail handles the exchange of email between MTAs across the Internet. In its role as an MDA, Sendmail takes incoming messages and stores them in the appropriate mailbox for each user. (In more complex configurations, Sendmail may also forward incoming mail to other machines for further processing.)

Fixing the permissions on the root directory so that Sendmail will work

Mac OS X comes with Sendmail already installed, but to make it function properly, you have to do a little more work.

The most basic use of Sendmail involves using it as an MTA, so when you use (for example) the `mail` command to send email from the command line, Sendmail figures out which Internet host handles email for the addressee and sends the message to the remote machine for delivery.

As installed in Mac OS X, Sendmail is almost set up to work as MTA. The incompleteness is a result of a conflict between the standard Sendmail configuration and a Mac OS X–specific change to the standard permissions on the root directory (/).

For security reasons, Sendmail normally wants the root directory and the directories containing its configuration files (`/etc` and `/etc/mail`) to be writable only by the root account.

In Mac OS X, the / directory is normally owned and writable by the admin group in order to allow Classic Mac applications to install files at the "top" or root level of the hard drive after software is installed—for example, the Late Breaking News file regarding updates that Apple sometimes inserts.

Normally in Unix, the permissions for the / directory are set at 755: read-write-execute for root and read-execute for everyone else (review modes in Chapter 8, "Working with Permissions and Ownership").

When Sendmail sees a group-writable / directory, it won't work. You could change the permissions on the / directory, but that might cause problems with some Classic applications or installers. Also, the next time you update the operating system, the permissions will be changed back to the Mac defaults. So you need to tell Sendmail that a group-writable directory is OK.

To activate the Sendmail server:

1. Per the task "To change the /etc/host-config system-configuration file," become root, back up `/etc/hostconfig`, and edit the file using `vi`.

2. In `/etc/hostconfig`, change the line

`MAILSERVER=-NO-`

to

`MAILSERVER=-YES-`

3. Save the file (type `:w` in `vi`).

4. Quit the editor (type `:q` in `vi`).

5. Use the StartupItems script to run Sendmail:

`/System/Library/StartupItems/Sendmail`
`→/Sendmail start`

If you get an error message that looks something like this:

`451 4.0.0 /etc/mail/sendmail.cf: line`
`→93: fileclass: cannot open`
`→'/etc/mail/local-host-names':`
`→Group writable directory`

then your Sendmail configuration suffers from the problem described above. You will need to perform one of the following tasks to correct the problem, and then come back and do this step again.

If you get no error message and only a response that says

`Starting mail services`

then Sendmail has started up and will automatically start if the system is rebooted.

6. Test sending email from the command line. Review Chapter 4, "Useful Unix Utilities," for instructions on how to send email from the command line.

7. Stop being root:

`exit`

If you got an error during step 6 of the previous task, then you need to perform either of the following two tasks to get Sendmail working.

The first approach is the quick-and-dirty way, but it does work; the subsequent task shows the more rigorous way to solve the problem.

To "correct" the permissions on the root directory:

◆ `sudo chmod g-w /`

This is just a quick hack. While it does restore the standard Unix permissions on the / directory, it may cause problems with some Classic applications or software installers, and you can expect the permissions to be reset the next time you do an operating-system update.

Sending Mail Addressed to an IP Address

It is perfectly valid to send email that is addressed to an IP address rather than a domain name. To do so, you must enclose the IP address in square brackets:

puffball@[198.137.241.43]

If you are doing this from the command line, make sure to escape the brackets:

`puffball@\[198.137.241.43\]`

because they would otherwise be interpreted by the shell as the `test` command. See `man test`: Looking carefully at the NAME line in the manual, see the `[` character? It's another name for the `test` command.

The right way to fix the problem is bit more involved.

To change the Sendmail configuration:

1. Become root, entering your password if prompted:

   ```
   sudo -s
   ```

2. `cd /usr/share/sendmail/conf/cf`

   This directory contains a collection of templates for Sendmail configurations in different operating-system versions. The one you will use is the generic-darwin.mc file.

3. Copy the generic Darwin configuration file:

   ```
   cp generic-darwin.mc MyConfig.mc
   ```

   (You may actually use any filename you like instead of MyConfig.mc, but we suggest that you make the name something meaningful to you and that it end with ".mc," for *macro file*.)

4. Change the permissions on MyConfig.mc to make it writeable:

   ```
   chmod 644 MyConfig.mc
   ```

5. Edit MyConfig.mc file. Add the following line to the end of the file:

   ```
   define(`confDONT_BLAME_SENDMAIL',
   `GroupWritableDirPathSafe')
   ```

   Figure 14.2 shows the complete file with the new line highlighted. (Figure 14.1 is based on version 1.3 of the generic-darwin.mc file. You may have a later version of the file, but the steps should be the same.)

6. Create a new Sendmail configuration file:

   ```
   m4 ../m4/cf.m4 MyConfig.mc >
   MyConfig.cf
   ```

```
divert(-1)
#
# Copyright (c) 1998, 1999 Sendmail, Inc. and its suppliers.
#       All rights reserved.
# Copyright (c) 1983 Eric P. Allman.  All rights reserved.
# Copyright (c) 1988, 1993
#       The Regents of the University of California.  All rights reserved.
#
# By using this file, you agree to the terms and conditions set
# forth in the LICENSE file which can be found at the top level of
# the sendmail distribution.
#
#


divert(0)dnl

###
# This file provides a very generic configuration for sendmail.
#
# To customize your configuration, you probably don't want to edit this file.
# See the files in /usr/share/sendmail/conf for more information on how to
# generate a new one with the features and values you want. The file README
# in that directory has instructions.
###
VERSIONID(`$Id: generic-darwin.mc,v 1.3 2002/04/12 18:41:47 bbraun Exp $')
OSTYPE(darwin)dnl
DOMAIN(generic)dnl
undefine(`ALIAS_FILE')
define(`PROCMAIL_MAILER_PATH',`/usr/bin/procmail')
FEATURE(`smrsh',`/usr/libexec/smrsh')
FEATURE(local_procmail)
FEATURE(`virtusertable', `hash -o /etc/mail/virtusertable')dnl
FEATURE(`genericstable', `hash -o /etc/mail/genericstable')dnl
FEATURE(`mailertable', `hash -o /etc/mail/mailertable')dnl
FEATURE(`access_db')dnl
MAILER(smtp)
MAILER(procmail)
define(`confDONT_BLAME_SENDMAIL', `GroupWritableDirPathSafe')
```

Version of the 'generic-darwin.mc' file. It is OK if your version is later.

Add this line.

Figure 14.2 Annotated code listing of MyConfig.mc showing the line to be added.

That creates MyConfig.cf from numerous template files, including the one you just edited.

7. Back up the current Sendmail configuration file:

```
cp /etc/mail/sendmail.cf /etc/mail/
→ sendmail.cf.backup
```

8. Install the new Sendmail configuration file:

```
cp MyConfig.cf /etc/mail/sendmail.cf
```

9. Activate and start Sendmail.

Go to the first task in this section, "To activate the Sendmail server," and follow the steps there.

If there seems to be a problem, you can copy the backup copies of the files onto the changed copies.

Spam Sucks

Spam email is unsolicited material, usually asking for money or selling products, sent to multiple email addresses (the name comes from the Monty Python sketch involving the seemingly endless repetition of the word spam).

Spam wastes bandwidth, and more important, it wastes the one thing none of us can ever get more of: time.

If you are running a mail server that is being hit with spam, you should look into anti-spam features. (The Mac OS X GUI email client, Mail, has anti-spam features you can use to help with your personal email account.)

Probably the premier anti-spam software for mail servers is SpamAssassin (http://spamassassin.org).

There is a Mac OS X how-to for Spam/Assassin at www.stupidfool.org/docs/sa.html.

---

10. Stop being root:

```
exit
```

You should be back at your regular shell prompt.

Congratulations—you have changed your Sendmail configuration and should be happily sending email from the command line.

Configuring Sendmail to receive email

Sending email is fine, but everybody loves to get email. Well, maybe not everybody, and maybe you don't love getting spam email, but receiving email is still the high point of many people's day.

Once you have activated the Sendmail server, you can immediately start receiving email sent directly to your Mac OS X machine, as long as it is addressed using your IP address—for example,

puffball@[198.137.241.43]

(see the sidebar "Sending Mail Addressed to an IP Address").

The odds are that you would like people to send email to you using a domain name, so they don't have to know your IP address.

Assuming that you have already activated the Sendmail server, and that you have arranged for an FQDN that points to your machine's IP address, there is one more step you need to take to receive email addressed to you at your FQDN.

CONFIGURING SENDMAIL— INTERNET EMAIL SERVER

To configure Sendmail to receive email addressed to your FQDN:

1. Become root, entering your password if prompted:

   ```
   sudo -s
   ```

2. Make a backup copy of /etc/mail/local-host-names:

   ```
   cp /etc/mail/local-host-names /etc
   →/mail/local-host-names.ORIGINAL
   ```

3. Add your FQDN to /etc/mail/local-host -names.

   The file may be empty to begin with, but that's OK.

   If your FQDN is rottweiler.gooddogs.com, then you add that to the file (which may end up having just that single line in it—that's fine).

   The file local-host-names has its permissions set to read-only. So if you are using vi to edit it, you must save your changes using :w! instead of the :w command you would normally use.

4. Restart the Sendmail server:

   ```
   /System/Library/StartupItems/Sendmail
   →/Sendmail restart
   ```

5. Stop being root:

   ```
   exit
   ```

   You should be back at your regular shell prompt.

6. Test the setup.

   Send yourself email from another system (or ask a friend to do it), using the FQDN for your Mac OS X machine.

✔ Tip

■ Watch the mail-server log file while testing. Type

   ```
   sudo tail -f /var/log/mail.log
   ```

   to see the mail server accept each incoming message.

Forwarding email to different addresses

Sometimes you want email that arrives for one address to be automatically forwarded to another address. There are a couple ways to do this. The way we describe here works when you want to forward email to an account that already exists on your system. It is also possible to set up virtual users—email addresses on your system that do not correspond to actual user accounts but rather to departments (for example, sales@bigthree. com). Setting up virtual users in Sendmail is beyond the scope of this book, but you can find instructions for doing it at Virtual Hosting with Sendmail (www.sendmail.org/ virtual-hosting.html).

More About Sendmail

The central source for information about Sendmail is www.sendmail.org. There you can find security announcements, the latest news, and links to many helpful resources such as email lists, books, and classes.

To forward email for an existing user account:

1. Create a file called `.forward` in the home directory of the user whose email is to be forwarded.

   The file should contain a single line: the email address you want to forward to. For example,

   ```
   sudo echo "user@newaddress.net" >
   ~user/.forward
   ```

where *user* is the user name of the user on your system and the address is whatever address you want to forward the mail to.

Enter your password if prompted for it.

If you want a copy of the forwarded email to stay on your system, use this format:

```
\user, user@newaddress.net
```

2. Set the ownership on the file:

   ```
   sudo chown user .forward
   ```

Providing Remote Access to Users' Email: IMAP and POP

Another kind of mail server allows users to connect and download or read their email from other machines. These servers provide remote access to users' mailboxes (kept in `/var/mail` on Mac OS X) and utilize either the complex and powerful IMAP (Internet Message Access Protocol) or the simpler but less capable POP (Post Office Protocol)

For information on IMAP, go to the IMAP Connection (www.imap.org). It has a searchable database of IMAP software, such as clients and servers (www.imap.org/products/database.php).

If you are considering setting up your Mac OS X machine to provide remote access to users' email, we suggest that you use an IMAP server. This will allow your users to read their mail from multiple remote machines (such as from home or the office), as well as provide better security, since IMAP servers can be configured to use encryption.

Two no-cost open-source IMAP servers:

◆ The University of Washington's IMAPd (IMAP daemon), available at the IMAP Information Center (www.washington.edu/imap/).

◆ The Cyrus IMAP server, which is designed for use on "email-only" servers where regular users are not permitted to log in (http://asg.web.cmu.edu/cyrus/imapd/).

Two commercial IMAP servers (which also handle POP):

◆ CommuniGate Pro (www.stalker.com/CommuniGatePro/). A free version is available, but it adds a line of advertising to each message.

◆ Post.Office, from Tenon Intersystems (www.tenon.com/products/post_office/).

Activating the FTP Server

FTP (File Transfer Protocol) is the oldest such protocol on the Internet and is still widely used. Virtually all Web browsers are capable of acting as clients with FTP servers, and there are several GUI and command-line clients for FTP (see Chapter 10, "Interacting with Other Unix Machines").

Mac OS X comes with an FTP server that can be activated from the Sharing panel of System Preferences.

To activate the FTP server using the GUI:

1. Open the Sharing panel of System Preferences and choose the Services tab (**Figure 14.3**).

2. Click the Start button or the "FTP Access" checkbox.

   The control panel shows the FTP server as running and the "Start" button changes to "Stop" (**Figure 14.4**).

   In the Unix layer of Mac OS X, two things happen: The file /etc/xinetd.d/ftp is changed (the "disable" entry changes from "yes" to "no"), and the xinetd server is restarted. Your FTP server is now running.

3. Test the server. Do this by logging in via FTP, preferably from another machine, or you can also do it from your own machine.

✔ Tip

■ Remember to deactivate any firewall rules that block access to ports 20 and 21. See Chapter 12, "Security," for more on firewalls.

Figure 14.3 The Sharing panel of System Preferences.

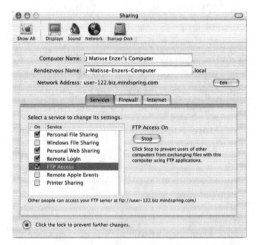

Figure 14.4 Dialog box for administrator authentication.

ACTIVATING THE FTP SERVER

Security Concerns About FTP

The FTP server in Mac OS X is not activated by default, and you should be careful about activating it, since FTP uses unencrypted passwords.

Review Chapter 12, "Security," for the dangers of passing unencrypted passwords over a network. See also "Reducing the security risks from an FTP server," later in this section.

At a minimum, you should add all admin users to the file /etc/ftpusers (the list of users forbidden from connecting to the FTP server) to prevent any admin-user passwords from being exposed to packet-sniffing attacks. See the sidebar "Security Concerns About FTP."

Of course, you can also activate the FTP server without ever leaving the command line.

To activate the FTP server from the command line:

1. Become root:

   sudo -s

   to get a root shell. Since all of the following steps need to be performed as root, it is easier to start a root shell than to add sudo to every command, but you can also do it that way. If prompted, enter your password.

2. Make a backup copy of /etc/xinetd.d/ftp:

   cp /etc/xinetd.d/ftp /etc/xinetd.d/
   ↪ftp.backup

3. Edit /etc/xinetd.d/ftp. Change the "disable" entry from "yes" to "no":

   vi /etc/xinetd.d/ftp

   Figure 14.5 shows /etc/xinetd.d/ftp and highlights the entry you must change.

4. Remember to save the changed file (in vi, [Esc]:w).

   continues on next page

```
                              Change "yes" to "no."

    service ftp
    {
            disable = yes
            socket_type    = stream
            wait           = no
            user           = root
            server         = /usr/libexec/ftpd
            server_args    = -l
            groups         = yes
            flags          = REUSE
    }
```

Figure 14.5 Annotated example of the /etc/xinetd.d/ftp file highlighting the line you change to activate FTP services.

ACTIVATING THE FTP SERVER

5. Quit the editor (type `:q` in `vi`).

6. Tell `xinetd` to reload its configuration:

`kill -HUP `cat /var/run/xinetd.pid``

That command line gets the process ID from `/var/run/xinetd.pid` and sends an HUP signal to it. The FTP server is now activated. You can stop being root now.

7. `exit`

to stop being root and get back to your own shell prompt.

✔ Tip

- Remember, if you have firewall rules blocking ports 20 and 21, you will need to change or remove the rules.

Allowing anonymous FTP access

Before there were Web sites, there were anonymous FTP sites.

An anonymous FTP server allows users who do not have an account on your system to download files. You can see how HTTP and Web servers have become the dominant tools for this role. Still, FTP is widely used to allow public downloading (and uploading) of files.

Anonymous FTP involves the user's logging in with a special account called "anonymous" (the user name "ftp" can also be used as a shorter alternative).

How the FTP Server Is Run by xinetd

Mac OS X comes with two versions of the `inetd` *super server* (both started from /System /Library/StartupItems/IPServices/IPServices), but it uses the more advanced `xinetd` to handle the FTP server. We expect the older `inetd` server to be removed from future versions of Mac OS X (see Chapter 12, "Security" for more about `inetd` and `xinetd` in the sidebar, "The Server of Servers: `inetd`").

The xinetd server uses the configuration files in the /etc/xinetd.d directory to determine which services it is responsible for. The file for the FTP server is `/etc/xinetd.d/ftp` which has a "server" entry of `/usr/libexec/ftpd` (**Figure 14.6**) this is the actual FTP server program that gets executed when `xinetd` receives a connection from an FTP client.

When an incoming FTP connection occurs, xinetd executes /usr/libexec/ftpd /usr/libexec/ftpd with the -l (logging enabled) option. The -l option comes from the "server_args" entry in the /etc/xinetd.d/ftp file.

Because of the -l option, every attempt to log in to your FTP server is logged in the file /var/log/ftp.log.

```
service ftp
{
        disable = yes
        socket_type     = stream
        wait            = no
        user            = root
        server          = /usr/libexec/ftpd
        server_args     = -l
        groups          = yes
        flags           = REUSE
}
```

Figure 14.6 Configuration file `/etc/xinetd.d/ftp` used by the `xinetd` server for FTP services.

Anonymous FTP log-ins do not need a password. It is traditional to use one's email address as a password.

The FTP server is designed to take special security precautions for anonymous log-ins to make sure that anonymous users cannot access anything outside the directory established for anonymous FTP use.

To allow anonymous FTP access (no password):

1. Create a new user with a short user name of "ftp." Refer to Chapter 11, "Introduction to System Administration," for instruction on adding new users.

    The full name for the account may be anything—we suggest "Anonymous FTP User."

    Even though the new account is called ftp, people accessing your server for anonymous FTP may use either of the log-in names ftp or anonymous.

    You can leave the password empty, because a password is not used for anonymous FTP access.

2. Become root:

    `sudo -s`

    The remaining steps must all be performed as root.

3. Change the user's log-in shell to `/usr/bin/false`

    This prevents the user from logging in at the command line. (Review Chapter 11 for instructions on changing a user's log-in shell.)

    If `/usr/bin/false` is not already listed in `/etc/shells`, you must add it by editing `/etc/shells` (**Figure 14.7**).

4. Change the ownership on ~ftp:

    `chown root.wheel ~ftp`

    The home directory of the new user should be owned by the root account and by group "wheel."

5. Create ~ftp/bin, ~ftp/etc, and ~ftp/pub:

    `mkdir ~ftp/bin ~ftp/etc ~ftp/pub`

    These subdirectories of the ftp user's home directory are used for various aspects of anonymous FTP access.

6. Copy `/bin/ls` into ~ftp/bin/:

    `cp /bin/ls ~ftp/bin/`

    For the FTP command `ls` to work, a copy of the `ls` command must be in the anonymous FTP account's bin directory.

7. Set the permissions on ~ftp:

    `chmod -R 555 ~ftp`

    continues on next page

```
# List of acceptable shells for chpass(1).
# Ftpd will not allow users to connect who are not using
# one of these shells.

/bin/bash
/bin/csh
/bin/sh
/bin/tcsh
/bin/zsh
# For FTP-only users to prevent sniffed password being used for shell login
/usr/bin/false
```

Figure 14.7 Contents of `/etc/shells` after adding `/usr/bin/false` as a valid shell for FTP access.

All of the directories and the `ls` command file should have permissions such that they are not writable by anyone, hence the 555 setting (review Chapter 8, "Working with Permissions and Ownership").

8. Copy `/etc/pwd.db` into `~ftp/etc/`:

```
cp /etc/pwd.db ~ftp/etc/
```

For the FTP `ls` command to show user and group ownership names, a copy of the `/etc/pwd.db` file must be placed in `~ftp/etc/`.

9. Your FTP server is ready for anonymous access.

The user names anonymous and ftp will both work. Accesses will be logged to the file `/var/log/ftp.log`.

10. Stop being root:

```
exit
```

This gets you back to you regular shell prompt.

Sometimes you want to allow anonymous FTP users to upload files as well as download them.

The proper way to do this involves creating a special directory (typically called "incoming") where FTP users can use the `put` command to upload files. When properly set up, the incoming directory does not allow users to see the files it contains (although if they can guess a filename, they can download it), and if they upload a file with the same name as an existing file, the new file is renamed by adding a ".1" to the filename (or ".2," or ".3," and so on).

The following task assumes that you have already set up anonymous FTP access.

To restrict FTP access to only anonymous access:

♦ Run `ftpd` with the `-A` (anonymous) option.

The default command used to start the FTP server (in `/etc/inetd.conf`) is

```
ftp -l
```

but if you change that to

```
ftp -lA
```

then only anonymous log-ins will be allowed.

To allow anonymous FTP users to upload files to your server:

1. Create a new directory called `~ftp/incoming`:

```
sudo mkdir ~ftp/incoming
```

Enter your password if prompted.

2. Set the permissions on `~ftp/incoming`:

```
sudo chmod 773 ~ftp/incoming
```

The permission mode 773 means that "others" may write and execute the directory but may not read it. This allows anonymous FTP users to `cd` into the directory and upload files but not to list the directory's contents.

✔ Tip

■ You may want to create a script that's run from `cron` to send email to someone whenever files are added to the `~ftp/incoming` directory. See the section "Running Regularly Scheduled Commands" in Chapter 11, "Introduction to System Administration," for instructions on setting up a cron job. **Figure 14.8** is a sample script you could set to run every 15 minutes (or whatever frequency seems convenient). If it's run as a cron job, the output from the script is emailed (by cron). The script produces output the first time it finds files in the ~ftp/incoming directory,

and it creates a marker file (just a file whose presence is an indication of something) to avoid sending email every time it runs (you remove the marker file to re-enable the script). See "Running Regularly Scheduled Commands" in Chapter 11 for an explanation of the cron utility.

```sh
#!/bin/sh
# Script for checking if files have been uploaded via Anonymous FTP
# This script should be run by root's crontab, perhaps every 15 minutes.
# It will produce output the first time it finds files in the
# ~ftp/incoming directory.
# After cleaning out the incoming directory you need to also remove
# the marker file so this script will send email again.


# Name of file that we use as a marker
NOTICE_FILE="incoming_has_files"


# cd to the ftp user home directory
cd ~ftp



# Get the contents of the incoming/ directory
contents=`/bin/ls incoming/`

if [ "$contents" != "" ] ; then
    if [ ! -e "$NOTICE_FILE" ] ; then
        echo "Anonymous FTP incoming files:"
        echo "$contents"
        # Create the notice file so we don't get email again
        # until someone clear it out.
        /bin/date > "$NOTICE_FILE"

        echo "Remember to remove ~ftp/$NOTICE_FILE"

        fi
fi


# Otherwise, remain silent
```

Figure 14.8 Code listing of a sample script to be used as a cron job, to send notification when files are added to the anonymous FTP upload directory.

ACTIVATING THE FTP SERVER

Reducing the security risks from an FTP server

Because of the security risk from password sniffing, you must assume that any user name and password used to access your FTP server can be obtained by an unauthorized person.

If you are running an FTP server to provide only anonymous access, then this is not an issue, since the account used for anonymous FTP is not one that people can use to log in to your machine.

You can reduce the risks that come from running an FTP server by treating all FTP log-ins in a manner similar to anonymous log-ins:

◆ Set up separate FTP-only accounts that cannot be used to log in on the command line.

◆ Configure the FTP server to place access restrictions on the FTP-only accounts so that they cannot access anything outside their home directories.

◆ Forbid any user except anonymous-access and the special FTP-only accounts from logging in via FTP.

See Chapter 12, "Security," for more Unix security information.

To increase the security restrictions when a user logs in via FTP:

◆ Add the user name to /etc/ftpchroot.

This prevents the user from accessing any files outside his or her home directory when logging in via FTP (chroot means "change the root directory the user sees"; see man chroot).

If the file /etc/ftpchroot doesn't exist, you must create it. You must be root (use sudo) to create or edit that file. It simply contains one user name per line. **Figure 14.9** shows an example.

```
# Users who get a chroot'd environment
# (See  man chroot )
puffball
mary
johnftp
xaos
jackftp
```

Figure 14.9 Example of a /etc/ftpchroot file.

Table 14.1

Files Used by ftpd	
FILE	USE
/usr/libexec/ftpd	The FTP server itself. See man ftpd.
/etc/ftpusers	List of users who may not connect to the FTP server.
/etc/ftpchroot	List of users whose use of FTP is restricted to their home directory. See man chroot.
/etc/ftpwelcome	Contents of this file are displayed when a user logs in via FTP.
/etc/nologin	If this file exists, it is displayed to users attempting to log in, and access is refused.
/var/log/ftp.log	Log of FTP connections and file transfers.
/var/log/ftpd	Log of file FTP connections.

Secure Alternatives to FTP

The primary secure alternatives to FTP are file transfers that use the SSH protocol. Chapter 10, "Connecting Over the Internet," covers the client side of these methods using the ssh and sftp commands.

One of the best things you can do to reduce the risks created by running an FTP server is allow only specially restricted FTP-only accounts to access your system via FTP.

To create FTP-only user accounts:

1. Create a new user account.

   This account will be configured so that it has access only via FTP. The password for this account should *not* be the same as the password for another account.

2. Change the user's shell to `/usr/bin/false`.

   Having `/usr/bin/false` as the log-in shell for an account means that as soon as someone logs in, he or she is instantly logged out.

   We want to prevent someone who obtains this account's password from logging in at the command line, where that user's opportunity for mischief is much greater than through FTP. Logging in via FTP and logging in to a command-line shell are two different things.

When a user logs in at the command line, the operating system executes his or her log-in shell—that is the program that accepts command-line input (review Chapter 2, "Using the Command Line"). The program `/usr/bin/false` is a tiny program that quits as soon as it is started and gives a code meaning "false" to whatever program ran it.

The FTP server will allow log-ins only from accounts whose log-in shell is listed in the file `/etc/shells`, so if this is the first FTP-only account you have created, you must add `/usr/bin/false` to the list of valid shells in the file `/etc/shells`. Figure 14.10 shows `/etc/shells` with the added entry.

3. Add the new user name to `/etc/ftpchroot`.

   If a user name is listed in the file `/etc/ftpchroot`, then the FTP server applies additional access restrictions to the account, preventing access to any file outside the account's home directory.

To prevent a user from connecting to the FTP server:

◆ Add the person's user name to `/etc/ftpusers`.

   Any user name listed in `/etc/ftpusers` is refused access by the FTP server before the user is even asked for a password. This is a good way of preventing certain users from sending their unencrypted passwords over a network where they could be sniffed.

ACTIVATING THE FTP SERVER

Apache: A Web Server

Apache is the most popular Web server on the Internet. It's easy to obtain and install, stable and secure, and reasonably easy to configure and modify; it handles both small and large Web sites; and it has a huge number of available options. Several common versions of Unix come with Apache already installed—including, of course, Mac OS X.

Apache gets its name from its history. Back at the dawn of the Web (circa 1993), the folks at the National Center for Supercomputing Applications (NCSA) at the University of Illinois, Urbana-Champaign, created the NCSA Web-server application, called HTTPD ("Hypertext Transfer Protocol daemon"). It was (and is) an open-source application, and many people contributed code for it, known as patches. So many patches were contributed that it became known as "a patchy server." "A patchy" morphed into "Apache."

Activating Apache

As with AppleShare and the SSH server, you can activate and deactivate the Apache Web server from the Sharing panel of System Preferences, under the File & Web tab, by clicking the Start/Stop button for Web Sharing.

Web servers listen on port 80 by default. If you are using firewall software, make sure that access to port 80 is not blocked.

Here's the command-line version. Astute readers will note that these tasks are almost identical to the ones for the SSH server.

Apache Documentation

Mac OS X comes with the complete Apache documentation in HTML format.

Start with `/Library/Documentation/Services/apache/index.html.html`.

(Yes, "html" appears twice in the filename.)

The main Apache-configuration file is `/etc/httpd/httpd.conf`. Every directive in the file is documented in the supplied documentation, starting in `/Library/Documentation/Services/apache/mod/directives.html`.

More documentation, as well as specific how-to documents, are available through the Apache HTTP Server Project (http://httpd.apache.org/docs-project). The site contains a document on performance tuning, for example (http://httpd.apache.org/docs/misc/perf-tuning.html).

To activate Apache from the command line:

1. Per the task "To change the /etc/host-config system-configuration file," become root, back up /etc/hostconfig, and edit the file using vi.

2. Change the line that says

   WEBSERVER=-NO-

   to

   WEBSERVER=-YES-

3. Save your changes, and quit the editor (in vi, it's Esc :w and type :q).

4. Start the Apache server:

   /System/Library/StartupItems/Apache
   →/Apache start

   The Apache Web server is now active.

5. Stop being root:

   exit

   You should be back at your regular shell prompt.

✔ Tips

■ To keep the Apache server from starting at boot time, reverse the change from step 2 above. That is, change WEBSERVER=-YES- back to WEBSERVER=-NO-.

■ Apache logs all connections to /var/log /httpd/access_log, and error-message and startup/shutdown events to /var /log/httpd/error_log.

APACHE: A WEB SERVER

To browse your Web server:

◆ Enter the URL for your Web server into your favorite Web browser.

◆ If you are browsing from the same machine the server is on, you can simply use
http://localhost/

◆ If you want to browse your machine from another machine, you need to know your machine's FQDN or IP address:
http://www.mozilla.org/
or
http://207.200.81.215/

✔ Tips

■ The main HTML directory for your Web server is `/Library/WebServer/Documents`, which is defined in the Apache-configuration file (`/etc/httpd/httpd.conf`) by the `DocumentRoot` directive.

■ Mac OS X automatically creates a separate Apache-configuration file for each user you create, through the Accounts panel in System Preferences. The user-configuration files are in `/etc/httpd/users` and are named after each user—for example, `/etc/httpd/users/puffball.conf`

The last line of the main Apache-configuration file reads all the files in the `/etc/httpd/users` directory when Apache starts up. The default is for each user to have his or her own directory of HTML pages, which is the Sites directory in each user's home directory. The URL for a user's personal Web page is http://domainname/~username/. For user puffball, it would be
http://localhost/~puffball/
or
http://domain.name/~puffball/

More About the Apache Startup Script

The Apple-supplied StartupItems script, `/System/Library /StartupItems /Apache/Apache`, actually executes the standard Apache startup script, `apachectl`.

On Mac OS X, `apachectl` is installed as `/usr/sbin/apachectl`. It is a Bourne shell script—you can look at it with any text editor to see how it works.

On most Unix systems where Apache is installed, the `apachectl` script itself is used to start (and stop) Apache, because that script handles arguments of `start`, `stop`, `restart`, and others. There is a man page for `apachectl` showing all of its options.

You can use `apachectl` directly (ignoring `/etc/hostconfig`), if you want.

On Mac OS X, it will be perfectly effective for you to start Apache with

`sudo apachectl start`

and to stop it with

`sudo apachectl stop`

You can also shut down the Apache server from the command line.

To shut down the Apache server from the command line:

◆ `sudo apachectl stop`

   Enter your password if prompted.

   When the Apache server starts up, it writes its process ID (pid) number into the file `/var/run/httpd.pid`. The `apachectl` script uses that file to find the pid number and stop the server. See the sidebar "More About the Apache Startup Script."

Adding a CGI script

One of the most important—and exciting—things you can do with Apache is build your first Common Gateway Interface (CGI) script.

CGI is the standard for how Web servers communicate with other software. A CGI program can be written in any language, as long as it adheres to the CGI standard.

Basically, CGI works this way: The Web server is configured to treat certain requests as CGI requests. Typically, these requests begin with `/cgi-bin`, but they can begin with anything the person doing the configuration decides. In Mac OS X, the Apache server is configured so that any request starting with `/cgi-bin` is a CGI request, and Apache looks for the CGI program to execute in the directory `/Library/WebServer/CGI-Executables`.

continues on next page

APACHE: A WEB SERVER

So if Apache gets a request for
/cgi-bin/shopping.pl, it will execute the file

/Library/WebServer/CGI-Executables
→/shopping.pl

When the Web server gets a CGI request, it executes a program instead of simply sending back an HTML page. The CGI program then does ... something. It might contact a database or send some email. (A CGI program can be written to do anything any other program can do.) It then sends a response back to the Web server, which in turn passes that response back to the Web browser. Often that response is an HTML document generated on the fly, perhaps based on a database connection.

The process of installing your first CGI program involves creating the program (we will use a simple script in this case), and telling the Web server where the CGI programs are and which requests to treat as CGI requests.

We'll use a simple script as an example. This Perl script produces an HTML page that shows all the environment variables present at the time the script is run. Apache sets a large number of environment variables when it executes a CGI script. These environment variables contain a great deal of information about the Web server and the request, so a script like this is very useful for troubleshooting and debugging.

To create a CGI script:

1. Copy the script from **Figure 14.10** into a new file called test.pl.

2. Put the file in the directory
   /Library/WebServer/CGI-Executables
   The URL for this script will be
   http://localhost/cgi-bin/test.pl

   You do not need to be root for this step, but you must be in group admin (you already are if you have been using the sudo command to become root).

3. Make the script executable:
   chmod 755 test.pl

continues on page 466

Learning More About CGI

The CGI standard has been very stable, but it is still evolving.

You can read about the effort to formalize the CGI 1.1 specification at the Common Gateway Interface—RFC Project Page (http://cgi-spec.golux.com).

An introductory book for creating CGI programs with Perl is Perl and CGI for the World Wide Web: Visual QuickStart Guide, Second Edition, by Elizabeth Castro (www.peachpit.com/books/).

```perl
#!/usr/bin/perl
# Simple CGI test script
# Displays environment variables in HTML format
# Save as /Library/WebServer/CGI-Executables/test.pl
################################################################

# Anything printed out gets sent back to the Web server
# and then to the Web browser.

# Print everything up until the line that starts with BUNNY
print <<"BUNNY";
Content-type: text/html

<html>
<head>
<title>CGI Test Output</title>
</head>

<body bgcolor="#ffffff">
<h1>CGI Test Output</h1>

<table>
<tr>
  <th>Variable<th>
  <th>Value</th>
</tr>
BUNNY

# Iterate over all the environment variable names.
foreach $variable ( sort keys %ENV ) {
    print <<"BUNNY";
        <tr>
        <td><font color="blue">$variable</font></td>
        <td><font color="red">$ENV{$variable}</font></td>
        </tr>
BUNNY
}

print <<"BUNNY";

</table>
</html>
BUNNY
```

Figure 14.10 Code listing of a simple CGI script that displays its environment variables.

4. Test the script from the command line:

`./test.pl`

You should get output similar to that in **Figure 14.11**.

5. Test the script from a Web browser.

To test from the same machine, you can use the URL

http://localhost/cgi-bin/test.pl

You can also use your IP address instead of "localhost," and that should work from anywhere on the Internet. Of course, if your machine has an FQDN, you can use that, too.

continues on next page

```
[g4-cube:/Library/WebServer/CGI-Executables] vanilla% ./test.pl
Content-type: text/html

<html>
<head>
<title>CGI Test Output</title>
</head>

<body bgcolor="#ffffff">
<h1>CGI Test Output</h1>

<table>
<tr>
  <th>Variable<th>
  <th>Value</th>
</tr>
        <tr>
        <td><font color="blue"> ENV_SET</font></td>
        <td><font color="red"> </font></td>
        </tr>
        <tr>
        <td><font color="blue"> GROUP</font></td>
        <td><font color="red"> staff</font></td>
        </tr>
        <tr>
        <td><font color="blue"> HOME</font></td>
        <td><font color="red"> /Users/matisse</font></td>
.
.
. Output continues...
.
```

Figure 14.11 Abbreviated output from the CGI test script at the command line.

Figure 14.12 A Web browser showing output from the CGI test script.

```
<Directory "/Users/vanilla/Sites/">
    Options Indexes MultiViews
    AllowOverride None
    Order allow,deny
    Allow from all
</Directory>


ScriptAlias "/~vanilla/cgi-bin/"
→ "/Users/vanilla/Sites/cgi-bin/"
```

Figure 14.13 Code listing of user vanilla's Apache-configuration file (`/etc/httpd/users/vanilla.conf`) after adding a line to enable a cgi-bin directory.

Figure 14.12 shows the output from the script in a browser window, so we know it works.

6. Congratulations—you've created a CGI script and are hosting dynamically generated HTML pages.

If you want to install a CGI script somewhere besides the default location, you will need to make a change to the Apache-configuration file.

To install a CGI program in your personal Sites directory:

1. Create a cgi-bin directory inside your Sites directory:

    `mkdir ~/Sites/cgi-bin`

2. Put the CGI program inside the cgi-bin directory. Copy the script from Figure 14.28 into the cgi-bin directory.

    ◆ If you already created a script in the previous task, you can just copy that file.

    ◆ If you are creating the script as a new file, be sure to make its mode executable when you are done.

3. Become root, entering your password if prompted:

    `sudo -s`

4. Edit the Apache-configuration file.

    You will be editing the Apache configuration for just your one user. For example, for the user vanilla:

    `vi /etc/httpd/users/vanilla.conf`

    Add the following line to the file:

    `ScriptAlias "/~vanilla/cgi-bin/"`
    `→ "/Users/vanilla/Sites/cgi-bin/"`

    Figure 14.13 shows the resulting file. Be sure to save the changes.

    If you are using a command-line editor such as vi, be sure to quit.

    continues on next page

APACHE: A WEB SERVER

467

5. Test the Apache-configuration file:

`apachectl configtest`

The `apachectl` command checks all of the Apache-configuration files for errors (the main configuration file and those for each user); the output looks like that in **Figure 14.14**.

6. Restart the Apache server:

`apachectl graceful`

The `apachectl` command has two ways of restarting the server. The argument `graceful` allows any current connections to finish before the server restarts, while the argument **restart** kills all current connections before the server restarts.

7. Stop being root:

`exit`

You should be back at your normal shell prompt.

8. Test the CGI through a Web browser. Assuming you logged in as the user vanilla's account, the URL is http://localhost/~vanilla/cgi-bin/test.pl

You should get almost exactly the same result as in the previous task, only the values of some of the environment variables will be different (have a look at REQUEST_ URL, SCRIPT_FILENAME, and SCRIPT_NAME in particular).

Apache Version 1.3.x vs. 2.x

Mac OS X 10.2 comes with version 1.3.26 of Apache. In May 2002, though, Apache version 2.0 was released.

The 2.x family of Apache is a major rewrite of Apache, offering significantly improved speed on some systems (for the geeks in the audience, Apache 2.x supports POSIX threads). The new features in Apache 2 are listed at httpd.apache.org/docs-2.0/new_features_2_0.html

Apache 2 has been slow to catch on, mostly because Apache 1.3.x is so good, and some of the more popular add-on modules for Apache 1.3 have not yet been rewritten for Apache 2. Still, Apache 2 is the future, and if you are thinking of being heavily involved in managing a Web site, you should look into Apache 2.

```
[g4-cube:/Users/vanilla/Sites/cgi-bin] root# apachectl configtest
Processing config directory: /private/etc/httpd/users
 Processing config file: /private/etc/httpd/users/howard.conf
 Processing config file: /private/etc/httpd/users/matisse.conf
 Processing config file: /private/etc/httpd/users/puffball.conf
 Processing config file: /private/etc/httpd/users/vanilla.conf
Syntax OK
[g4-cube:/Users/vanilla/Sites/cgi-bin] root#
```

Figure 14.14 Using the `apachectl` command to check the Apache-configuration files for syntax errors.

The MySQL Database Server

Databases are everywhere these days. It's all part of the increasing role of information in society. There is more information, and more need to organize it. Even your cell phone has a database.

MySQL is a relational database management system (RDBMS) that understands Structured Query Language (SQL) (pronounced either by saying the letters individually or the word "sequel"). The ideas of tracking relationships within a database and being able to query it for information have been around for 20 years and are fundamental precepts to the way almost all corporate databases run today.

MySQL is a powerful, stable, open-source RDBMS that you can use without cost, but you can also purchase commercial support for it from the developers at MySQL (www.mysql.com).

If a database engine (that's another name for an RDBMS) understands SQL, then other applications can talk to it in a standardized fashion. Software written to communicate with one SQL database can usually communicate with any other with only minimal changes.

An RDBMS can contain many databases, such as one for "purchases" and one for "sales." Each database in turn may have many tables, identifying "customers," "invoices," and "invoice line items." A table is a collection of data entries that all have exactly the same list of headings, called columns or fields. Each table can have many columns, such as "ID number," "name," "address," and "phone."

A database is essentially a tool for organizing information. Relational databases are databases that can contain several tables of information, which can be linked to each other. A database of purchase histories might contain one table that lists customers (the "customer table"), another that lists invoices (the "invoice table"), and a third that lists invoice line items (the "invoice line items table"). An entry in the invoice table might have only the invoice number, customer number, and invoice date. Thus, an entry in the invoice table is not actually a complete invoice; rather, it holds only the information that is unique to one invoice. This avoids the necessity of keeping a copy of the customer address for every invoice. The customer's ID number is in the invoice table and is used to look up the customer address for each invoice in the customer table. This connection between the tables is called a *relationship*.

To produce a complete invoice, the system would need to pull a record from the invoice table and then pull information from the two related tables (the customer table and the invoice line items table).

This is possible because each record in the invoice table has a customer ID number (which is used to find a customer), and an invoice ID. Each record in the invoice line items table has an invoice ID, so by finding all the records in the invoice line items table with a particular invoice ID, the database can find all the line items for one invoice.

Figure 14.15 is a diagram showing the relationships between the tables in a sample database.

Learning how to use a database, totally apart from setting one up, is quite a project. But you have to have a database in order to start learning, and installing an industrial-strength database on Mac OS X is actually very easy.

Installing MySQL

We are going to show you how to install MySQL from source code, using the methods described in Chapter 13, "Installing Software from Source Code."

Installing MySQL puts more than a dozen programs on your system (listed in **Table 14.3**). These programs will be installed in

/usr/local/mysql/bin and you should add /usr/local/mysql/bin to your PATH (see Chapter 7, "Configuring Your Unix Environment"). You also want to alter your MANPATH environment variable to add the directory where the MySQL Unix man pages are installed. If you are using the tcsh shell, add this line at the end of .tcshrc file in your home directory:

```
setenv MANPATH "${MANPATH}:/usr/local/
→mysql/man"
```

If you are using the bash shell, add this line at the end of your .bash_profile file:

```
export MANPATH=${MANPATH}:/usr/local/
→mysql/man
```

THE MySQL DATABASE SERVER

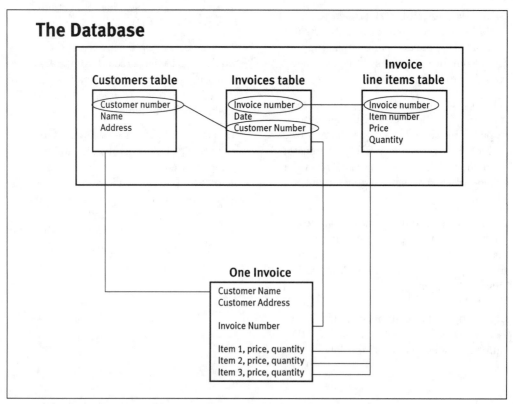

Figure 14.15 Diagram showing the relationships between tables in a relational database.

Table 14.3

What Gets Installed with MySQL?

All commands are described in Unix man pages and in the MySQL user's manual. See the INSTALL.log file you create in step 15 of the installation process for more details.

WHAT	WHERE AND WHY
Unix man pages	There are man pages for all the commands listed in this table. The man pages are installed in /usr/local/mysql/man, so you should add that directory to your MANPATH environment variable.
user's manual	See the sidebar "The MySQL User's Manual."
isamchk	/usr/local/mysql/bin/isamchk
	Used to check and repair MySQL database files.
isamlog	/usr/local/mysql/bin/isamlog
	Used to produce reports from MySQL log files.
msql2mysql	/usr/local/mysql/bin/msql2mysql
	Utility program for migrating from mSQL, an older, simpler SQL database, to MySQL.
mysql	/usr/local/mysql/bin/mysql
	The command-line client program for connecting to and manipulating MySQL databases.
mysql_zap	/usr/local/mysql/bin/mysql_zap
	A Perl script used to kill processes. Not used by any standard part of MySQL.
mysqlaccess	/usr/local/mysql/bin/mysqlaccess
	A Perl script for creating MySQL users.
mysqladmin	/usr/local/mysql/bin/mysqladmin
	A utility program for various administrative tasks, including setting the MySQL root password and creating/deleting databases.
mysqld	/usr/local/mysql/sin/mysqld
	The actual MySQL engine. This is the daemon that actually manages the databases you create.
mysqld_multi	/usr/local/mysql/bin/mysqld_multi
	Perl script for managing multiple MySQL servers.
mysqldump	/usr/local/mysql/bin/mysqldump
	Very useful utility program for dumping a MySQL database to a text file. Creates a file containing all the SQL commands needed to re-create the database.
mysqlshow	/usr/local/mysql/bin/mysqlshow
	Utility program for seeing the structure of a MySQL database. ·
perror	/usr/local/mysql/bin/perror
	Utility program for translating system error messages.
replace	/usr/local/mysql/bin/replace
	Utility program used by msql2mysql; does fast search-and-replace of strings in large files.
safe_mysqld	/usr/local/mysql/bin/safe_mysqld
	Bourne shell script used for starting mysqld. Performs a variety of safety checks and will restart mysqld if it crashes.

THE MYSQL DATABASE SERVER

Compiling MySQL takes almost half an hour on a 400 MHz G4, so set aside at least an hour to download, install, and configure MySQL.

To install MySQL:

1. Create a `mysql` group.

See "To create a new group:" in Chapter 11, "Introduction to System Administration."

The new group should be called mysql. The gid property can be any number not in use by another group. In step 3, below we'll assume you are using a gid of 74.

2. `sudo -s`

Enter your password if prompted. You need to be root for the rest of this task.

3. Create a `mysql` user.

We know we told you Chapter 11 that you should create new users using the GUI tool, but in this case the new user is one that no one will ever actually log in as. So following these instructions creates a user that will work for the database but that cannot be used like a regular account.

4. `nireport / /users uid`

Make note of the numbers in the resulting list. You need to pick a new uid number that is not already in use. We are assuming you are picking a uid of 74 (it is nice, but not at all required, that the new uid be the same as the new gid you created in step 2 above).

```
niutil -create / /users/mysql
niutil -createprop / /users/mysql uid 74
niutil -createprop / /users/mysql gid 74
niutil -createprop / /users/mysql realname "MySQL Server"
niutil -createprop / /users/mysql passwd \*
niutil -createprop / /users/mysql change 0
niutil -createprop / /users/mysql expire 0
niutil -createprop / /users/mysql home /var/empty
niutil -createprop / /users/mysql shell /dev/null
```

5. Download the software.

The source code for the MySQL database server is available as a free download from www.mysql.com and also from http://sourceforge.net/projects/mysql/.

Besides the source code, you can also download a pre-compiled version of MySQL.

The file you download will have a name like this:

mysql-3.23.53.tar.gz

The exact file name depends on the version you are downloading. We have installed and tested MySQL version 3.23.53 on Mac OS X 10.2.1.

Make a note of where you save the downloaded file. You will be moving it in step 7 below.

Make sure to check that you are downloading the source code.

One reason we recommend installing the software from source code is that having source code makes it easier to install other software that is designed to connect to the MySQL server. We'll show an example of this later in this chapter when we show you how to make a perl script that connects to the MySQL database.

6. `mkdir -p /usr/local/src/mysql`

This simply creates a directory where you will store and compile the source code.

7. `cd /usr/local/src/mysql`

This changes your current directory to the one you just created.

8. Move the downloaded source code into `/usr/local/src/mysql`.

For example, if you saved the downloaded source code package on the Desktop of user vanilla, you would move it with:

```
mv ~vanilla/Desktop/
→mysql-3.23.53.tar.gz .
```

9. Unpack the source code.

`tar xfvz mysql-3.23.53.tar.gz`

This creates a new directory containing the uncompressed source code.

10. Change into the unpacked source code directory.

`cd mysql-3.23.53`

11. `less README`

It is always a good idea to read the README file included with the source code because this is where the developers put notes they expect you to see before you install the software.

12. `./configure --prefix=/usr/`
`→local/mysql`

You are telling the `configure` script that you are installing the software in `/usr/local/mysql`.

The `configure` script performs a large number of checks on your system and configures the source code for compiling. This will take a few minutes.

continues on next page

THE MySQL DATABASE SERVER

13. make

This command starts the actual compiling of the software. You see a great deal of output on your screen and it takes a while for the process to complete — several minutes at least. On a 400Mhz G4, it took us around twenty four minutes.

14. make test

This runs a long series of tests (one hundred and twenty six of them for MySQL 3.23.53) on the software that you just compiled. The process takes several minutes and you may see some error message that look like this:

```
Error: Could not start master,
→exit code 1
```

```
Error: Could not start slave,
→exit code 1
```

You can ignore those. As long as the process finishes by saying:

```
All 136 tests were successful.
```

you are fine. If any of the tests do fail, check the README file again to see if you overlooked any special notes about the version you are installing, and to see how to notify the developers about the problem you experienced.

15. make install > INSTALL.log

This installs the software in /usr/local/mysql (creating many subdirectories within that directory). By redirecting the output of make install into a file (INSTALL.log), you save a record of what exactly is installed and where — you can read that file to see all the things that were installed. Even with the redirect, you still see a good deal of output on the screen, but you can ignore it.

16. ./scripts/mysql_install_db

Running this script creates the initial set of database tables used by MySQL itself (much of MySQL's configuration is stored in its own database).

17. chown -R mysql /usr/local/mysql/var

This sets the ownership of the /usr/local/mysql/var directory and all its contents to be owned by the mysql user you created earlier. /usr/local/mysql/var is where MySQL stores the actual database data.

18. chgrp -R mysql /usr/local/mysql

This sets the group ownership on the /usr/local/mysql/var directory and its contents.

19. Stop being root.

exit

The MySQL installation process is now complete.

Next you will need to configure your MySQL installation. Proceed to the next tasks.

✔ Tips

- The MySQL installation comes with extensive documentation. See the sidebar "The MySQL User's Manual."

- If Fink has problems downloading any of the packages, try updating Fink itself, and then retry the MySQL installation:

  `sudo fink selfupdate`

  If that doesn't help, try

  `sudo fink selfupdate-cvs`

  which updates to the latest version of Fink (which might be a beta version). This command can take a long time to finish—more than 2 hours.

The MySQL User's Manual

Besides man pages for all the MySQL utility programs, the MySQL installation includes a comprehensive user's manual in plain-text, HTML, and PostScript formats.

The MySQL user's manual includes a tutorial, performance-tuning tips, and detailed reference material on all aspects of MySQL.

The user's manual's files are installed in the Docs directory of the source code directory; for example, `/usr/local/src/mysql/mysql-3.23.53/Docs`.

The HTML version of the manual comes in two files: the table of contents (manual_toc.html) and the full manual (manual.html).

If you have access to a PostScript printer, you can print out the PostScript version, manual.ps. Be warned that it is more than 200 pages long.

There is also a plain-text version of the full manual, manual.txt.

- MySQL listens on port 3306. If you are running firewall software, be sure to configure it to allow access to this port if you want other machines to be able to connect to your MySQL server. If you are only using MySQL from your own machine, then you do *not* need to allow access to port 3306.

Configuring and starting MySQL

Configuring MySQL involves seven steps: creating a root password for MySQL, starting the `mysqld` program itself, learning how to use the `mysql` command-line tool, creating one or more MySQL users, creating a MySQL database, setting the access controls for the new database, and creating tables in the new database. Once all this is done, you can insert and retrieve data from the tables in the new database. Though this is more detail than we've gone into for most tasks in this book, we feel that it's appropriate because database mastery is a key asset for knowledgeable Unix users.

MySQL has its own list of users, which are totally separate from the user accounts on your system. When you install MySQL, it has one user already installed—root. This can be a bit confusing—the MySQL root account is totally different from the Unix root account. It can—and should—have a different password and is used only for managing MySQL.

The MySQL root account starts off with no password, so the first thing you should do is to set a password for the MySQL root account.

For the following tasks, we are assuming you have added the directory /usr/local/mysql/bin to your PATH. If you haven't done that, do it now (see Chapter 7 for instructions).

To set the mysql root password:

1. Become root:

   sudo -s

   Enter your Unix password if prompted. You need to be the Unix root user to start MySQL.

2. safe_mysqld &

   The safe_mysqld script starts the mysqld daemon after performing some checks and puts it "in the background." Safe_mysqld also restarts the daemon if it crashes.

   The mysqld daemon must be running in order to set a password for the MySQL root account.

   Figure 14.16 shows what this looks like. The output includes the process ID number for the mysqld daemon and tells you that the directory /usr/local/mysql/var is where the actual database data files are stored.

```
[g4-cube:~] root# safe_mysqld &
[1] 7724
[g4-cube:~] root# Starting mysqld daemon with databases from /usr/local/mysql/var
```

Figure 14.16 Starting the mysqld daemon using the safe_mysqld command.

Notice how the output appears to include your shell prompt—that is because when you put the command "in the background" with the &, the shell gives you a prompt again without waiting for the safe_mysqld command to finish running. As a result, the two lines of output from safe_mysqld get mixed in with the shell prompt—the line with the process ID for mysqld appears first, then your shell prompt, and then the second line of output from safe_mysqld.

You can clear things up and get a fresh shell prompt by pressing ⟨Return⟩.

3. mysqladmin -u root -p password
→ 'newpassword'

That sets the MySQL root password to *newpassword*. Note that the new password is enclosed in single quotes.

For example, to set the MySQL root password to Gr56%kQ, the command is

mysqladmin -u root -p password
→ 'Gr56%kQ'

You will be prompted for a password, but there isn't one to enter yet.

From now on, when you use the mysqladmin command, you need to enter the password you just created.

4. Shut down mysqld:

mysqladmin -u root -p shutdown

You are prompted for a password.

5. Enter the new MySQL root password, and press ⟨Return⟩.

Mysqld shuts down. You see

020730 09:45:59 mysqld ended
[1] + Done   safe_mysqld

(That first line is the date and time that mysqld shut down, in YYMMDD format.)

6. Clear the password out of your shell's command history. Because your command history (see Chapter 2, "Using the Command Line") is written to disk, when your shell exits, you want to ensure that the password you just typed doesn't get written where someone might be able to see it.

◆ If you are using the default shell (tcsh):

history -c

◆ If you are using the bash shell:

unset HISTFILE

7. Stop being root:

exit

You should be back to your regular shell prompt.

To start MySQL from the command line:

1. Become root, entering your password if prompted:

   `sudo -s`

2. `safe_mysqld &`

   The `safe_mysqld` script starts the MySQL RDBMS (Figure 14.16). Later in this section we tell you how to have MySQL start up when the machine boots up. (Remember, we are assuming you have added `/usr/local/mysql/bin` to your PATH.)

3. Stop being root:

   `exit`

   That should bring you back to your regular shell prompt.

✔ Tips

■ The "right" way to start `mysqld` is to create a StartupItems script, as we describe in the task "To create a StartupItems script for MySQL," later in this section. Then you can use that script, with an argument of **start**, **stop**, or **restart** to perform those three functions.

■ The reason we have you start a root shell instead of using

   `sudo safe_mysqld &`

   is that using **sudo** to put a command in the background doesn't work properly if you need to enter your password for **sudo** (if you have exceeded the grace period since your last use of **sudo**). What happens is that the whole command line goes into the background, and so **sudo** itself is no longer "in the foreground" when its password prompt appears. So you type your password but **sudo** isn't listening for it, and the background job just hangs, waiting for you.

To shut down MySQL from the command line:

1. `mysqladmin -u root -p shutdown`

   You are prompted for a password.

2. Enter the MySQL root password.

   The `mysqld` shuts down.

MySQL has dozens of available options. You put options into a configuration file called my.cnf, which can be located in one of two places: `/etc/my.cnf`, which is read first by any of the MySQL programs, or `/usr/local/mysql/var/mysql/my.cnf`. If an option appears in both files, the setting in `/usr/local/mysql/var/mysql/my.cnf` overrides the setting in `/etc/my.cnf`.

Four sample configuration files are provided in `/usr/local/mysql/share/mysql`, each corresponding to how heavily used your MySQL server will be: my-huge.cnf, my-large.cnf, my-medium.cnf, and my-small.cnf.

The files contain some documentation about the various options, and the MySQL manual covers them in section 4.1.2 (see the sidebar "The MySQL User's Manual," above).

To install a MySQL configuration file:

1. Choose one of the sample configuration files from `/usr/local/mysql/share/mysql`.

2. Copy the file to `/usr/local/mysql/var/my.cnf` or `/etc/my.cnf`.

   For example,

   `sudo cp /usr/local/mysql/share/`
   `→mysql/my-medium.cnf/etc/my.cnf`

3. Edit the file to adjust the options to your liking. You need to be root in order to edit the file.

4. Start or restart `mysqld`.

Connecting to MySQL

The main way to manage MySQL is to connect to the mysqld daemon using the mysql command-line utility. (See also the sidebar "Using a Web Browser to Manage MySQL," later in this section.)

Most of the commands you use inside the mysql utility are SQL commands, called statements. The MySQL manual has a complete tutorial in section 3, "Introduction to MySQL: A MySQL Tutorial," and extensive coverage of SQL in section 6, "MySQL Language Reference."

In the following tasks, we use two databases that are created when you install MySQL. One is called "mysql"—it's the "master database" containing information about MySQL itself, as well as all the databases, users, and access-control information. The other is called "test"; it's an empty database used for—you guessed it—testing.

When you connect to MySQL, you must do so as a MySQL user. Until you create more MySQL users, the only one that exists is the MySQL root user, so we use that user in this task.

We strongly recommend that you read and perform the tutorial shown in section 3 of the MySQL user's manual.

You do *not* need to be root to perform the following task. You are logging into the MySQL server as the MySQL root user, which is not the same as the Unix root user (it just has the same name in order to confuse you).

To use the mysql utility to connect to the mysqld daemon:

1. mysql -u root -p

2. Enter the MySQL root password.

   You are now connected to mysqld. **Figure 14.17** shows the command line for connecting, and then the output and prompt from the mysql utility.

   The mysql utility is an interactive program, like the ftp command. Mysql provides its own prompt where you type commands to it. You can think of it as a shell program just for MySQL.

   continues on next page

```
[your-hostname:~] vanilla% mysql -u root -p
Enter password:
Welcome to the MySQL monitor.  Commands end with ; or \g.
Your MySQL connection id is 1 to server version: 3.23.53

Type 'help;' or '\h' for help. Type '\c' to clear the buffer.

mysql>
```

Figure 14.17 Connecting to mysqld using the mysql command-line utility.

3. show databases;

This shows a list of all the databases that mysqld is managing (**Figure 14.18**).

You can enter commands in the mysql utility (called *SQL statements*) on multiple lines. That is, you can press Return in the middle of an SQL statement because the SQL statement doesn't actually end (and get executed) until you enter one of the following and press Return:

;

\g

\G

The first two have the same meaning. The third one, \G, does a nice job of formatting output that is too wide for your screen when using either of the first two forms.

```
[your-hostname:~] vanilla% mysql -u root -p
Enter password:
Welcome to the MySQL monitor.  Commands end with ; or \g.
Your MySQL connection id is 1 to server version: 3.23.49

Type 'help;' or '\h' for help. Type '\c' to clear the buffer.

mysql>mysql> show databases;
+------+
| Database |
+------+
| mysql    |
| test     |
+------+
2 rows in set (0.00 sec)

mysql>
```

Figure 14.18 Using the show databases command in the mysql utility to display a list of all MySQL databases.

4. `use mysql;`

This tells the `mysql` utility that you want to communicate with the MySQL database (**Figure 14.19**).

5. `show tables;`

This command lists all the tables in the currently selected database—in this case, the MySQL database (**Figure 14.20**).

continues on next page

```
mysql> use mysql;
Reading table information for completion of table and column names
You can turn off this feature to get a quicker startup with -A

Database changed
mysql>
```

Figure 14.19 Telling the `mysql` utility which database you want to communicate with.

```
mysql> show tables;
+---------+
| Tables_in_mysql |
+---------+
| columns_priv  |
| db            |
| func          |
| host          |
| tables_priv   |
| user          |
+---------+
6 rows in set (0.00 sec)

mysql>
```

Figure 14.20 Using the `show tables` command to see all the tables in the currently selected database.

6. `DESCRIBE user;`

This command (which need not be capitalized) describes all the fields (or columns) in the user table. **Figure 14.21** shows the output. The output shows the column ("Field") name, the data type for the column, whether the column can contain NULL (empty) values, whether the column is indexed (in which case the "Key" column has a value in it), and finally the column's default value (which is "N" for all but three fields in this example).

7. `quit`

This exits the `mysql` utility, taking you back to your shell prompt. Notice that you did not need a semicolon at the end of that command.

✔ Tips

■ Commands, table names, and field (column) names are not case-sensitive, so `describe` and `DESCRIBE` mean the same thing. We show SQL commands in uppercase for clarity only.

```
mysql> DESCRIBE user;
+-----------+-----------------+------+-----+---------+-------+
| Field     | Type            | Null | Key | Default | Extra |
+-----------+-----------------+------+-----+---------+-------+
| Host           | char(60) binary | | PRI |   |   |
| User           | char(16) binary | | PRI |   |   |
| Password       | char(16) binary | |     |   |   |
| Select_priv    | enum('N','Y')   | |     | N |   |
| Insert_priv    | enum('N','Y')   | |     | N |   |
| Update_priv    | enum('N','Y')   | |     | N |   |
| Delete_priv    | enum('N','Y')   | |     | N |   |
| Create_priv    | enum('N','Y')   | |     | N |   |
| Drop_priv      | enum('N','Y')   | |     | N |   |
| Reload_priv    | enum('N','Y')   | |     | N |   |
| Shutdown_priv  | enum('N','Y')   | |     | N |   |
| Process_priv   | enum('N','Y')   | |     | N |   |
| File_priv      | enum('N','Y')   | |     | N |   |
| Grant_priv     | enum('N','Y')   | |     | N |   |
| References_priv| enum('N','Y')   | |     | N |   |
| Index_priv     | enum('N','Y')   | |     | N |   |
| Alter_priv     | enum('N','Y')   | |     | N |   |
+-----------+-----------------+------+-----+---------+-------+
17 rows in set (0.00 sec)

mysql>
```

Figure 14.21 Using the `DESCRIBE` command to see the descriptions of all the fields in the user table.

- You can specify which database to connect to on the command line when you run the `mysql` utility—for example,

  `mysql -u root -p test`

  starts the `mysql` program and connects to the test database right away.

- The `mysql` tool has a command history much like your Unix shell. You can use the up arrow and down arrow keys to scroll through command lines you have entered.

Creating a new database

When you create a new database in MySQL, it has no access controls whatsoever, unless you have put them in place before creating the database. So the process we show you for creating a new database in MySQL involves first setting up the access controls, and then actually creating the empty database.

To set up the access controls, connect to the MySQL master database, mysql. That is the database where MySQL keeps information about itself and any databases you create.

Once again, we are assuming you have added `/usr/local/mysql/bin` to your PATH.

At the end of this chapter, we show you a simple Perl script that connects to MySQL. The script assumes you have created the sample database and user described below.

To create a new database in MySQL:

1. `mysqladmin -u root -p create dbname`

   where *dbname* is the name of the new database. For example, to create a database called sample:

   `mysqladmin -u root -p create sample`

2. Enter the MySQL root password.

   The database now exists but has no tables or access control. See the next two tasks to set up access control and create tables in the database.

Access control in MySQL can be quite complex. The simple version we show you here creates a single MySQL user with its own password. The user is allowed to connect to one database and will have a great deal of access to the database, but not total access. The user is able to retrieve information from the database ("SELECT" data) and to add, delete, and change records in the database. He or she is only able to connect to the database from the same machine that MySQL is running on (localhost) and can create and remove—but not alter—the structure of tables in the database.

Section 4 of the MySQL user's manual goes into great detail about MySQL access control. Section 4.3 in particular covers MySQL user-account management.

The Web interface for MySQL provided by the Webmin application simplifies much of MySQL administration. (See the sidebar "Using a Web Browser to Manage MySQL," at the end of this section.)

Properly setting up a new database in MySQL involves first creating its access controls. This ensures that a new database never exists even for a moment without access control.

To configure access control for a database:

1. If `mysqld` is not already running, then start it.

2. `mysql -u root -p mysql`

   You are connecting to the "master" database, mysql, as user root.

3. Enter the MySQL root password.

4. Create a new MySQL user.

   Commands in the `mysql` tool can be many lines long.

   continues on next page

The following command inserts a new row into the user table, creating a MySQL user named "daffy":

```
INSERT INTO user SET
Host='localhost', User='daffy'
```

To execute the command, enter a semicolon and press Return, as shown in **Figure 14.22**:

```
;
```

The above command is an SQL statement. In this case, you are inserting data into a table called "user" in the mysql database.

```
mysql> INSERT INTO user SET
    -> Host='localhost', User='daffy'
    -> ;
Query OK, 1 row affected (0.00 sec)

mysql>
```

Figure 14.22 Creating a new MySQL user named "daffy."

```
mysql> SELECT * FROM user WHERE
    -> User='daffy'
    -> \G
*************************** 1. row ***************************
            Host: localhost
            User: daffy
        Password:
     Select_priv: N
     Insert_priv: N
     Update_priv: N
     Delete_priv: N
     Create_priv: N
       Drop_priv: N
     Reload_priv: N
   Shutdown_priv: N
    Process_priv: N
       File_priv: N
      Grant_priv: N
 References_priv: N
      Index_priv: N
      Alter_priv: N
1 row in set (0.00 sec)

mysql>
```

Figure 14.23 Using an SQL SELECT statement to view a record from the database.

The new user is added and is set to be allowed to connect only from this machine (that's the localhost setting) and to have no permissions to do anything yet (the default).

5. Look at the record ("row") for the new user:

SELECT * FROM user

WHERE User='daffy'

\G

The * means that we are asking for all the fields in the record.

We use the \G end-of-command code here because otherwise the output would not fit nicely on the screen (**Figure 14.23**).

```
mysql> UPDATE user SET
    -> Password=password('d**kb0y')
    -> WHERE User='daffy';
Query OK, 1 row affected (0.00 sec)
Rows matched: 1  Changed: 1  Warnings: 0

mysql>
```

Figure 14.24 Using an SQL UPDATE statement to set the user's password.

```
mysql> SELECT User,Password FROM user
    -> WHERE User='daffy';
+-------+------------+
| User  | Password   |
+-------+------------+
| daffy | 4f2a21332a72df7a |
+-------+------------+
1 row in set (0.00 sec)

mysql>
```

Figure 14.25 Using a SELECT statement to retrieve only two fields from a record.

Notice how all of the fields except the Password field have something in them. When you created this record in step 4, you set the values for the User and Host fields, and the default values (from Figure 14.21) were filled in for all the fields you did not set. One field, the Password field, has no default, so it is empty.

6. Set the user's password.

The following SQL statement updates the user table, setting the contents of the field "Password" to an encrypted version of "d**kb0y"—you should use a different password, of course, but just remember what you use!

UPDATE user SET Password=password
→('d**kb0y') WHERE User='daffy';

The value put into the Password field is the result of using the MySQL password() function to encrypt the supplied password (**Figure 14.24**).

7. Check that the update worked:

SELECT User,Password FROM user

WHERE User='daffy';

In this case, you are asking for only two fields from the record: the User field and the Password field (**Figure 14.25**).

continues on next page

THE MySQL DATABASE SERVER

8. DESCRIBE *db*

This shows all the column (field) descriptions in the db table (**Figure 14.26**).

9. Create an entry for the new database.

Here's how to create an entry for a new database called "sample." The database doesn't exist yet—you are simply preparing access controls for it first.

INSERT INTO *db*

VALUES ('localhost','sample','daffy',

'Y','Y','Y','Y','Y','Y','N','N','N',

→ 'N');

```
mysql> DESCRIBE db;

+---------------+-----------------+------+-----+---------+-------+
| Field         | Type            | Null | Key | Default | Extra |
+---------------+-----------------+------+-----+---------+-------+
| Host          | char(60) binary |      | PRI |         |       |
| Db            | char(64) binary |      | PRI |         |       |
| User          | char(16) binary |      | PRI |         |       |
| Select_priv   | enum('N','Y')   |      |     | N       |       |
| Insert_priv   | enum('N','Y')   |      |     | N       |       |
| Update_priv   | enum('N','Y')   |      |     | N       |       |
| Delete_priv   | enum('N','Y')   |      |     | N       |       |
| Create_priv   | enum('N','Y')   |      |     | N       |       |
| Drop_priv     | enum('N','Y')   |      |     | N       |       |
| Grant_priv    | enum('N','Y')   |      |     | N       |       |
| References_priv| enum('N','Y')  |      |     | N       |       |
| Index_priv    | enum('N','Y')   |      |     | N       |       |
| Alter_priv    | enum('N','Y')   |      |     | N       |       |
+---------------+-----------------+------+-----+---------+-------+
13 rows in set (0.00 sec)

mysql>
```

Figure 14.26 Output from DESCRIBE *db* showing the column descriptions for the db table.

See **Figure 14.27**.

Here you have given the user daffy permission to connect to the sample database from the local machine (not over the Internet) and have granted the user select, insert, update, and delete privileges. The six 'Y' values correspond to the fourth, fifth, sixth, seventh, eight, and ninth fields listed in Figure 14.26.

```
mysql> INSERT INTO db
    -> VALUES ('localhost','sample','daffy',
    -> 'Y','Y','Y','Y','Y','Y','N','N','N','N');
Query OK, 1 row affected (0.01 sec)

mysql>
```

Figure 14.27 Inserting a new record into the db table.

Using this form of the INSERT statement, you must supply exactly the right number of values, one for each column. Otherwise, you will get an error message like this:

```
ERROR 1136: Column count doesn't
→match value count at row 1
```

10. Check that the new record looks OK:

SELECT * FROM db
WHERE User='daffy'\G

as shown in **Figure 14.28**.

11. Quit the mysql tool:

quit (or exit)

You're back at a shell prompt.

12. Tell MySQL to reload its access controls:

mysqladmin -u root -p reload

MySQL now knows about the access controls you just created.

continues on next page

```
mysql> SELECT * FROM db
    -> WHERE User='daffy'\G
*************************** 1. row ***************************
          Host: localhost
            Db: sample
          User: daffy
   Select_priv: Y
   Insert_priv: Y
   Update_priv: Y
   Delete_priv: Y
   Create_priv: Y
     Drop_priv: Y
    Grant_priv: N
References_priv: N
    Index_priv: N
    Alter_priv: N
1 row in set (0.00 sec)

mysql>
```

Figure 14.28 Selecting a record from the db table.

THE MYSQL DATABASE SERVER

13. Connect to the new database as user daffy:

```
mysql -u daffy -p sample
```

14. Enter daffy's password.

You are now connected to the sample database as the MySQL user daffy (**Figure 14.29**).

15. Quit the `mysql` utility:

```
quit
```

To add a table to a database:

1. Connect to the database.

To connect to the sample database as the user daffy:

```
mysql -u daffy -p sample
```

2. Enter the MySQL user's password (Figure 14.29).

3. Create the table.

The following SQL statement creates a table called "table_one" with three fields. The name field will hold up to 20 characters, the address field up to 30, and the phone field up to 20; and the id field will hold an integer (a number) that will be automatically filled in each time a record is added. The `PRIMARY KEY` instruction tells MySQL to use the id field as a sort of master index for the table. Searching the table based on that field will go faster than a search based on other fields.

```
CREATE TABLE table_one (

name char(20),

address char(30),

phone char(15),

id int NOT NULL auto_increment,

PRIMARY KEY(id)

);
```

```
[your-hostname:~] vanilla% mysql -u daffy -p sample
Enter password:
Welcome to the MySQL monitor.  Commands end with ; or \g.
Your MySQL connection id is 11 to server version: 3.23.53


Type 'help;' or '\h' for help. Type '\c' to clear the buffer.


mysql>
```

Figure 14.29 Connecting to the sample database as the user daffy.

Figure 14.30 shows the result, and also the result of the next step. Section 6.5.3 of the MySQL user's manual covers the CRE-ATE TABLE syntax in detail.

4. show tables;

   This shows that the new table has been created.

   If you want to see how mysql describes your table, use

   DESCRIBE table_one;

5. Quit the mysql utility:

   quit

```
mysql> CREATE TABLE table_one (
    -> name char(20),
    -> address char(30),
    -> phone char(20),
    -> id int NOT NULL auto_increment,
    -> PRIMARY KEY (id)
    -> );
Query OK, 0 rows affected (0.01 sec)

mysql> show tables;
+----------+
| Tables_in_sample |
+----------+
| table_one    |
+----------+
1 row in set (0.00 sec)

mysql>
```

Figure 14.30 Creating a new table with a CREATE statement.

✔ Tip

- You can see the SQL statement used to create any table with the special SQL statement

  show create table *tablename*\G

  This can be a useful way to learn how tables are constructed.

For the following tasks, we assume that you are connected to the sample database as the user daffy, as described above.

About the SQL WHERE clause

Many of the SQL statements we show you here use the SQL WHERE clause to limit which records are affected by the SQL statement. The options for using a WHERE clause are varied, but usually you specify a column and the value it must contain for the SQL statement to "catch" a record. Section 3.3.4 of the MySQL user's manual has some good examples of using a WHERE clause in an SQL statement.

To add a new record (row) to a table:

♦ Use an INSERT statement.

  There are three forms of the INSERT statement. Section 6.4.2 of the MySQL user's manual covers INSERT syntax in detail. Here is one way to insert a new row into a table:

  INSERT INTO table_one
  SET name = 'Margaret',
  address='Constantinople';

  In this case, even though you did not specify a value for the id column, it will be filled in automatically, because it is an auto_increment field. The phone field remains empty.

THE MYSQL DATABASE SERVER

To change the values in an existing record:

◆ Use an UPDATE statement.

Section 6.4.4 of the MySQL user's manual covers UPDATE in detail. Here is an example of changing Margaret's address to "Istanbul":

```
UPDATE table_one
SET address='Istanbul'
WHERE name='Margaret';
```

That is OK, unless there is more than one Margaret in the table, in which case they would *all* get moved to Istanbul—maybe not what they wanted.

In our sample table, the id field was designated as a PRIMARY KEY, which means that no two rows will ever have the same value in that column. So if you know that the record you want to update has an id of 1, you would use

```
UPDATE table_one
SET address='Istanbul'
WHERE id=1;
```

Because the id field is an integer field, you do not enclose its value in single quotes.

How would you know that the record had an id of 1? You would have had to SELECT that data from the table first. See the next task.

To select data from a table:

◆ Use a SELECT statement.

The SELECT statement is covered in section 6.4.1 of the MySQL user's manual.

We are covering this after the INSERT and UPDATE statements so that you will have some data to select! But SELECT statements are actually the most common in using databases.

The following SQL statement selects the name, address, and id fields for all records from table_one:

```
SELECT name,address,id
FROM table_one;
```

Figure 14.31 shows the result (we cheated and added two more records when you weren't looking). We can see that there are two Margarets—one in Constantinople with id 1, and one in Pompeii, with id 3.

If you do not include a WHERE clause in the SELECT statement, it fetches every record in the table.

To do the same SELECT statement, but to find only records where the name is Margaret, you would use

```
SELECT name,address,id
FROM table_one
WHERE name='Margaret';
```

```
mysql> SELECT name,address,id
    -> FROM table_one;
+----------+---------------+----+
| name     | address       | id |
+----------+---------------+----+
| Margaret | Constantinople |  1 |
| Larry    | Ohio          |  2 |
| Margaret | Pompeii       |  3 |
+----------+---------------+----+
3 rows in set (0.02 sec)

mysql>
```

Figure 14.31 Using a SELECT statement to select only the name, address, and id columns.

```
mysql> DELETE FROM table_one
    -> WHERE name='Margaret'
    -> AND address='Pompeii';
Query OK, 1 row affected (0.00 sec)

mysql>
```

Figure 14.32 Using a DELETE statement to delete a record.

Learning More About SQL

Obviously, there is a great deal more to SQL than we show you here. The MySQL user's manual is a good reference (especially sections 3 and 6).

An online tutorial for beginners is available at www.sqlzoo.net.

The MySQL Web site maintains a list of books about SQL and MySQL (www.mysql.com/portal/books/html/book-5-1.html).

To delete a row from a table:

◆ Use a DELETE statement.

Unless you want to delete every row in a table, always include a WHERE clause in your DELETE statements. DELETE is covered in section 6.4.5 of the MySQL user's manual.

To delete the Margaret who lives in Pompeii:

```
DELETE FROM table_one
WHERE name='Margarget'
AND address='Pompeii';
```

as shown in **Figure 14.32**.

Having the mysql server start up at boot time

As with other servers covered in this chapter, the right approach here is to create a StartupItems script as described in Chapter 11, "Introduction to System Administration."

To create a StartupItems script for MySQL:

1. Become root.

2. Add `MYSQL=-YES-` to `/etc/hostconfig`.

3. `mkdir /Library/StartupItems/MySQL`

4. `cd !$`

   That's a little trick. The `!$` is shorthand for "the last argument of the last command," so in this case the `!$` gets replaced with

   `/ Library/StartupItems/MySQL`

   and the command line is shorthand for

   `cd Library/StartupItems/MySQL`

   continues on next page

THE MySQL DATABASE SERVER

5. Create a new StartupItems script.

The script must be named MySQL (same as the directory it is in).

Figure 14.33 is a code listing of a sample script.

Note that as of version 3.23.53 of MySQL, there is no easy way in Mac OS X to shut down MySQL without

using the `mysqladmin` tool, and that requires using the MySQL root password. The sample script in Figure 14.33 includes code to use `mysqladmin`, but you should make the script readable *only* by root if you enable that feature; otherwise, the MySQL root password could be obtained by people without root privileges who read the file.

continues on page 494

```
#!/bin/sh
# Darwin/Mac OS X StartupItem script for MySQL
# This script should be saved as /Library/StartupItems/MySQL/MySQL


# Read in common system configuration stuff
# Among other things this will cause /etc/hostconfig to be read
#
. /etc/rc.common


# /etc/hostconfig should have   MYSQL=-YES-
# If $MYSQL has not been set then we set it to -NO-
# If  $MYSQL is not -YES- then we exit and skip everything else.
if [ "${MYSQL:=-NO-}" != "-YES-" ] ; then
    exit
fi



# If we get here then /etc/hostconfig has MYSQL=-YES-

BASE_DIR="/usr/local/mysql"

# Command to start MySQL
MYSQL_START="$BASE_DIR/bin/safe_mysqld"

StartService ()
{
        ConsoleMessage "Starting MySQL"
        $MYSQL_START &
}
```

Figure 14.33 Code listing of a sample StartupItems script for MySQL.

Figure 14.33 (continued)

```
StopService ()
{
        ConsoleMessage "Stopping MySQL"
        # As of MySQL version 3.23.53 there is no clean way to
        # shutdown the MySQL server without using the msqladmin
        # tool, which requires the MySQL root password.
        # If you decide to use this part, make this file readable
        # ONLY by root (chmod 700 MySQL) then uncomment the last line
        # of this function and fill in the MySQL root password
        # where the XXXXXXXX is. There must not be any spaces between
        # the -p and the password.

        # /usr/local/mysql/bin/mysqladmin -u root -pXXXXXXXX shutdown
}


RestartService ()
{
   StopService
   sleep 3 ; # wait 3 seconds
   StartService
}

RunService "$1"
```

6. Create the StartupParameters.plist file. Copy the code from **Figure 14.34** into a file called StartupParameters.plist.

7. Test the script from the command line. You should be able to start MySQL with
/Library/StartupItems/MySQL/MySQL
→start

8. If you want, reboot the machine to fully test that the script works on boot-up.

✔ Tip

■ For the StartupParameters.plist you could copy a similar file and modify it: The file for the SSH server is /System/Library /StartupItems/SSH/ StartupParameters. →plist.

```
{
    Description    = "MySQL SQl Database
Engine";
    Provides       = ("MySQL");
    Requires       = ("Resolver");
    OrderPreference = "None";
    Messages =
    {
        start = "Starting MySQL";
        stop  = "Stopping MySQL";
    };
}
```

Figure 14.34 Sample StartupParameters.plist file for MySQL.

Using a Web Browser to Manage MySQL

The Webmin application, described in Chapter 11, "Introduction to System Administration," includes a module for managing MySQL.

Figure 14.35 shows the Webmin interface for managing MySQL user permissions, and **Figure 14.36** shows the Webmin interface for editing the fields in a table.

If you want to use MySQL and just don't have the time to learn how to manage it from the command line, Webmin will be your new best friend.

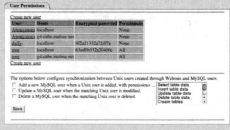

Figure 14.35 The Webmin interface for managing MySQL user permissions.

Figure 14.36 The Webmin interface for editing the fields in a table.

Creating a script that uses SQL

Now that you have that lovely new database running, we are going to show you a very simple Perl script that uses MySQL.

The script uses the popular Perl DBI (Data-Base Independent) module, which allows Perl scripts to be written to work with a variety of SQL databases. You add a second Perl module for the particular database engine you are using. So our script will also use the DBD::mysql module.

If this sort of thing interests you (and who would not be fascinated by such an enthralling subject?), then we suggest you have a look at the book Programming the Perl DBI, co-authored by Alligator Descartes and the creator of the Perl DBI module, Tim Bunce (www.oreilly.com/catalog/perldbi).

Installing Perl modules is covered in Chapter 13, "Installing Software from Source Code."

Learning More About MySQL

Besides all the documentation we keep telling you to read, the MySQL Web site is the best place to start looking (www.mysql.com).

There are links there to training, books, and email lists.

PostGreSQL: Another SQL Database

Another very popular open-source SQL database is PostgreSQL (pronounced "Post-gres-Kew-el") (www.postgresql.org).

To prepare for installing the Perl DBI and DBD::mysql modules:

1. Install the MySQL database server.

2. Make sure the MySQL server is running.

   Now you can use the instructions in Chapter 13 to install the DBI and DBD::mysql modules. The short version for the DBI module is:

   ```
   sudo perl -MCPAN -e'install DBI'
   ```

   For the DBD::mysql module, you need to use the CPAN shell as described in Chapter 13, and add a little extra command. The short version would be:

   ```
   sudo perl -MCPAN -eshell
   ```

   Then at the cpan> prompt:

   ```
   o conf makepl_arg -testuser=test
   install DBD::mysql
   ```

   The DBD::mysql install process performs several hundred tests. Sometimes a few of the tests will fail but the module is still usable. You can force CPAN to install the module in spite of the test failures by using this command at the cpan> prompt:

   ```
   force install DBD::mysql
   ```

   (We had to do this for DBD::mysql version 2.1020, which failed two tests.)

Once you have installed the Perl modules, you can create a simple script that will talk to the MySQL database engine. The script in the following task assumes you have created the 'sample' database described earlier.

To create a Perl script that uses MySQL:

1. Copy the code from **Figure 14.37** into a file called database.pl.

2. Make the file executable, but not readable by others:

   chmod 700 database.pl

```perl
#!/usr/bin/perl
# Simple script that uses MySQL
#
#########################################################################

# Tell Perl we want to use the DBI module
use DBI;

# Ask the user for a name to search the database for.
print "Enter a name: ";
$name = <STDIN>;
chop $name;   # strip the newline character

# Items needed to connect to MySQL
$database = 'sample';
$user     = 'daffy';
$password = 'd**kb0y';
$hostname = 'localhost';

# dsn is the "Distiguished Service name". It includes the name of the
# DBD module we are using (mysql)
$dsn = "DBI:mysql:database=$database;host=$hostname";

# dbh is the "Database handle"
$dbh = DBI->connect($dsn, $user, $password);

# Here's SQL statement we'll use
$sql = "SELECT id,name,address,phone FROM table_one WHERE name=?";
```

Figure 14.37 Code listing of a Perl script that searches a database for a name supplied by the user.

The file contains a MySQL user name and password, so you make it executable for yourself but not readable by others; that way, they can't find the password. If the MySQL user whose password is in the script has only SELECT privileges on the database, then it would be safe to let others see the password (assuming that there is no private information in the database).

continues on next page

Figure 14.37 (continued)

```
# These lines check the SQl statement for errors
$sth = $dbh->prepare($sql);
$sth->execute($name);


# Here we actually fetch the data
$found_rows = $sth->fetchall_arrayref( {} );


$sth->finish;  # tell the database we are done with this request


# If we didn't find anything, give a message and quit
unless ( @{$found_rows} ) {
    print "Didn't find anyone with the name $name\n";
    exit;
}


# If we get this far we found at least one row.
# Print our all the found rows.
foreach $row ( @{$found_rows} ) {
    print "ID: $row->{id}\n";
    print "Name: $row->{name}\n";
    print "Address: $row->{address}\n";
    print "Phone: $row->{phone}\n";
    print "\n";  # extra blank line
}
```

THE MySQL DATABASE SERVER

3. Test the script:

`./database.pl`

You are prompted for a name. Type one that you know is in the database, and press [Return]. **Figure 14.38** shows what happens when the script finds something, and when it doesn't.

```
[hostname:~] vanilla% ./database.pl
Enter a name: Johnny
Didn't find anyone with the name Johnny
bash-2.05$ ./database.pl
Enter a name: Margaret
ID: 1
Name: Margaret
Address: Constantinople
Phone:


ID: 4
Name: Margaret
Address: Ithaca
Phone: 000-333-1111


[hostname:~] vanilla%
```

Figure 14.38 Using the Perl script to search the database.

Even More Servers

Chapter 15, "More Open-Source Software," describes several more servers (although in less detail) that you may want to experiment with. You'll find it on the web at http://www.peachpit.com/vqp/umox.html.

Even if the subject of running servers on your Mac OS X machine is not of great interest to you, we suggest that you study chapters 11 ("Introduction to System Administration"), 12 ("Security"), and 13 ("Installing Software from Souce Code") thoroughly, and follow up on the additional resources mentioned in each of those chapters. It will be especially helpful for you to connect with other Unix users, as they will be the most valuable sources of assistance in all your Unix endeavors.

FOR MORE
INFORMATION

This appendix gathers together almost all of the Web sites and books mentioned in this book. We've organized them by subject matter so that, for example, all the Perl resources are listed together inside the "Languages and Programming" section.

About Darwin

These resources relate specifically to the Darwin operating system, which forms the Unix foundation of Mac OS X.

Apple's Darwin Project

(http://developer.apple.com/darwin/)

Apple's official Darwin Project site, where you can download source code and find links to other related projects.

Darwinfo

(http://darwinfo.org)

General-purpose site about Darwin, including links to mailing lists.

Darwin Mailing Lists

(http://developer.apple.com/darwin/
mail.html)

Apple hosts a number of email lists on the Darwin operating system. The Darwin-UserLevel and DarwinOS-Users lists are most likely to be useful to a new Unix user.

Darwin NetInfo HOWTO

(http://developer.apple.com/techpubs/
macosx/Darwin/howto/netinfo/
netinfo.html)

Apple documentation for the NetInfo system.

The GNU-Darwin Distribution

(http://gnu-darwin.sourceforge.net)

Web site that "aims to be the most free Darwin-based Unix distribution."

About Open-Source and Free Software

These resources deal with the general principles of open-source and free software ("free" as in "freedom," not as in "free beer").

GNU (GNU's Not Unix!)

(www.gnu.org)

> The Free Software Foundation's site dedicated to the GNU Project.

GNU GPL (GNU General Public License)

(www.gnu.org/licenses/licenses.html)

> The most famous of the various open-source software licenses. The GNU GPL requires that people who modify the source code make their modifications available to others under the same terms as the GPL.

ISC (Internet Software Consortium)

(www.isc.org)

> Nonprofit corporation "dedicated to developing and maintaining production quality Open Source reference implementations of core Internet protocols."

Open Source Initiative (OSI)

(www.opensource.org)

> Nonprofit corporation dedicated to promoting open-source software.

ABOUT OPEN-SOURCE AND FREE SOFTWARE

General Help Resources

There's only one entry in this section, but it's a big one. The WELL (Whole Earth 'Lectronic Link) is an intense online discussion system—of stored messages, not live chat—covering hundreds of subject areas. The Macintosh and Unix areas alone have more than 300 ongoing discussion topics between them. Because people must use their real names on The WELL, the general level of discourse is much higher than on most online systems.

WELL

(www.well.com)

> The Macintosh and Unix discussion areas are of extremely high quality and worth the $10 per month fee all by themselves. Most of the people who helped us with this book are WELL users. Registration is only available via the Web, but registered users may use ssh to log in from the command-line interface.

Languages and Programming

All of the languages mentioned here are programming languages, except for HTML, which is a markup language.

AppleScript

(www.apple.com/applescript/)

This is the main Apple Computer Web site for AppleScript.

AppleScript for Applications: Visual QuickStart Guide, by Ethan Wilde

(Peachpit Press; www.peachpit.com)

Covers AppleScript for Mac OS 9 and Mac OS X.

Bourne Shell scripting

(http://unix.about.com/library/course/ blshscript-outline.htm)

(http://steve-parker.org/sh/sh.shtml)

Two online tutorials for learning how to program using the Bourne shell.

"The Development of the C Language"

(http://cm.bell-labs.com/cm/cs/who/dmr/ chist.html)

Paper written by Dennis M. Ritchie, father of the C programming language.

HyperText Markup Language (HTML) Home Page

(www.w3c.org/MarkUp/)

The HTML standard is coordinated by the World Wide Web Consortium (W3C).

Mastering Regular Expressions, Second Edition, by Jeffrey E. F. Friedl

(O'Reilly; www.oreilly.com)

This book goes into great depth about the use of the "regular expression" pattern-matching system, which shows up in many Unix programs such as grep, vi, awk, and perl.

The Practice of Programming, by Brian W. Kernighan and Rob Pike

(Addison Wesley; www.awl.com)

An excellent general-purpose guide for computer programming. Sort of an *Elements of Style* for computer programming.

Perl

The following resources are all about the Perl programming language.

Learning Perl, Third Edition, by Randal L. Schwartz and Tom Phoenix

(O'Reilly; www.oreilly.com)

An essential resource for beginning Perl programmers.

Perl and CGI for the World Wide Web: Visual QuickStart Guide, Second Edition, by Elizabeth Castro

(Peachpit Press; www.peachpit.com)

Beginner's guide for creating CGI scripts with Perl. Uses the classic Peachpit task-oriented approach.

Perl Mongers' Perl Fast Facts

(www.perl.org/press/fast_facts.html)

Start here if you have never heard of Perl.

Programming Perl, Third Edition, by Larry Wall, Tom Christiansen, and Jon Orwant

(O'Reilly; www.oreilly.com)

The definitive programmer's guide to Perl.

Programming the Perl DBI, by Alligator Descartes and Tim Bunce

(O'Reilly; www.oreilly.com)

The Perl DBI (DataBase Independent Module) is the standard Perl module for working with databases. It was created by Tim Bunce.

Mac OS X in General

These resources all focus on the Macintosh and the Mac OS X operating system, as opposed to Unix or Darwin.

Apple Discussion Forums

(http://discussions.info.apple.com)

Apple's official Mac OS X discussion forums are found here.

"The Challenges of Integrating the Unix and Mac OS Environments"

(www.mit.edu/people/wsanchez/papers/ USENIX_2000/)

An excellent paper on some of the technical problems Apple had to deal with in creating Mac OS X.

Mac OS X Apps

(www.macosxapps.com)

This Web site provides a large and growing collection of Mac OS X applications.

Mac OS X Hidden Files & Directories

(www.westwind.com/reference/OS-X/ invisibles.html)

Table describing the different types and purposes of hidden files and directories in Mac OS X.

Mac OS X Hints

(www.macosxhints.com)

A Web site devoted to tricks, hints, help, and arcana about Mac OS X. Includes extensive discussion forums. Created and run as a labor of love by Rob Griffiths. If you find the site useful, consider donating $10.

People

The people listed here are all mentioned in the book or in other resources we refer to.

Matisse Enzer

(www.matisse.net)

> As the author of this book, he gets to list his own Web site.

Bill Joy

(www.sun.com/aboutsun/media/ceo/mgt_joy.html)

> His official Sun Microsystems biography.

Jon Postel

(www.postel.org/jonpostel.html)

> Jon Postel made major contributions to the development of the Internet, including managing the assignment of IP addresses for many years. His philosophy was encapsulated in his statement "Be liberal in what you accept, and conservative in what you send." See the "Protocols and Standards" section.

Dennis M. Ritchie

(www.cs.bell-labs.com/who/dmr/)

> Home page of the coinventor of Unix and the C programming language.

Wilfredo Sánchez

(www.mit.edu/people/wsanchez/)

> One of the technical leads for Mac OS X. Also did a great deal of development work on the tcsh shell.

Richard M. Stallman

(www.stallman.org)

> Personal Web page of the founder of the Free Software Foundation and inventor of the GNU General Public License.

Linus Torvalds

(www.cs.helsinki.fi/u/torvalds/)

(www.tuxedo.org/~esr/faqs/linus/)

> The home page and the unofficial Linus Torvalds FAQ, respectively, for the developer of Linux.

PEOPLE

Protocols and Standards

CIFS (Common Internet File System)

(http://ubiqx.org/cifs/)

A detailed guide to CIFS.

Domain Names: Implementation and Specification

(www.ietf.org/rfc/rfc1035.txt)

The official Internet Engineering Task Force explanation of DNS (the Domain Name System).

HTTP Made Really Easy

(www.jmarshall.com/easy/http/)

Introduction to the HTTP protocol.

HTTP Pocket Reference, by Clinton Wong

(O'Reilly; www.oreilly.com)

Compact, terse reference guide to the HTTP protocol.

IANA (Internet Assigned Numbers Authority)

(www.iana.org)

The ultimate authority for the assignment of blocks of IP addresses.

The IMAP Connection

(www.imap.org)

Web site devoted to IMAP (Internet Message Access Protocol).

NAT (Network Address Translation)

(www.ietf.org/rfc/rfc1631.txt)

(www.ietf.org/rfc/rfc2766.txt)

These are the main RFCs for NAT. (See RFC, below.)

RFC (Request for Comments)

(www.ietf.org/rfc)

The Internet Engineering Task Force (IETF) coordinates the documents that establish the technology standards used on the Internet. The IETF's motto is "Rough Consensus and Running Code."

XML for the World Wide Web: Visual QuickStart Guide, by Elizabeth Castro

(Peachpit Press; www.peachpit.com)

A beginner's guide to XML (Extensible Markup Language).

Security

Here we have gathered a collection of resources about Unix and Macintosh security.

Apple security information for developers

(http://developer.apple.com/internet/macosx/securityintro.html)

Information for people developing software for Mac OS X.

Apple Security Updates

(www.info.apple.com/usen/security/security_updates.html)

A list of the frequent security updates provided by Apple.

BugTraq mailing lists

(http://online.securityfocus.com/archive/1)

"BugTraq is a full disclosure moderated mailing list for the *detailed* discussion and announcement of computer security vulnerabilities: what they are, how to exploit them, and how to fix them." (From the BugTraq Web site.)

Building Your Own Personal Firewall

(http://wopr.norad.org/articles/firewall/)

Article by Stefan Arentz covering the use of `ipfw`, which comes with Mac OS X.

The CERT Advisory Mailing List

(www.cert.org/contact_cert/certmaillist.html)

CERT (which originally stood for "Computer Emergency Response Team") advisories are the primary central source of Internet security notifications.

CERT Unix Security Checklist

(www.cert.org/tech_tips/usc20_essentials.html)

A good checklist for securing a Unix system, with links to more resources; compare with our checklist in Chapter 12, "Security."

Common Vulnerabilities and Exposures (CVE) email list

(http://cve.mitre.org/cve/)

The CVE list is a dictionary of security issues that seeks to present standardized descriptions of security problems.

FreeBSD Handbook: Firewalls section

(www.freebsd.org/doc/en_US.ISO8859-1/books/handbook/firewalls.html)

The Darwin layer of Mac OS X is based largely on FreeBSD, so Mac OS X users may be interested in this online manual.

Mac-specific security sites

SecureMac.com (www.securemac.com)

MacSecurity.org (www.macsecurity.org)

Two Web sites devoted entirely to Macintosh security.

Privacy.org

(www.privacy.org)

Web site for news about information privacy issues.

Books on Unix Security

Building Internet Firewalls, Second Edition, by Elizabeth D. Zwicky, Simon Cooper, and D. Brent Chapman

Practical UNIX & Internet Security, Second Edition, by Simson Garfinkel and Gene Spafford

(Both from O'Reilly; www.oreilly.com)

Both books are written by people who are well regarded in the Unix community and who have many years of experience in the Unix security field.

Security-Related Software

ettercap

(http://ettercap.sourceforge.net)

A packet-sniffer/logging program that can be installed using fink.

Firewalk

(www.pliris-soft.com/products/firewalkx/)

A low-cost commercial Mac OS X package for setting up a firewall.

Kerberos

(http://web.mit.edu/kerberos/www/)

Software for creating secure connections between systems.

Nmap

(www.insecure.org/nmap/)

An open-source network-mapping tool.

RBrowser

(www.rbrowser.com)

Aqua software for secure file transfer. Shareware version handles both FTP and secure transfers; freeware version handles only FTP.

Snort

(www.snort.org)

An intrusion-detection system. Documentation and source code are online.

OpenSSH

(www.openssh.org)

The SSH (Secure Shell) tool facilitates secure connections between computers.

Swatch

(www.stanford.edu/~atkins/swatch/)

A tool for automating the watching of system log files, written in Perl.

Tripwire

(www.tripwire.com)

A commercial security tool capable of monitoring hundreds (or even thousands) of servers.

Virtual Private Network Daemon

(http://sunsite.dk/vpnd/)

Web site for vpnd, software for creating secure connections between two or more networks, across the public Internet.

System Administration

Where to find more information about Unix system administration.

Boot Sequence for Mac OS X

(http://developer.apple.com/techpubs/ macosx/Essentials/SystemOverview/ BootingLogin/The_Boot_Sequence.html)

Describes the various pieces of software that execute, in order, when Mac OS X boots up.

Creating new StartupItems

(http://developer.apple.com/techpubs/ macosx/Darwin/howto/system_starter_ howto/system_starter_howto.html)

The Apple documentation on creating StartupItems.

Essential System Administration, Third Edition, by Aileen Frisch

(O'Reilly; www.oreilly.com)

Comprehensive book covering all aspects of Unix system administration. Describes many variants of Unix, showing how to perform the same task on different Unix systems. Does not yet specifically cover Darwin or Mac OS X.

System Administration with Webmin, by Joe Cooper

(www.swelltech.com/support/webminguide/)

Users' guide for the Web-based system-administration software, Webmin.

UNIX System Administration Handbook, Third Edition, by Evi Nemeth, Garth Snyder, Scott Seebass, and Trent R. Hein

(www.admin.com)

Widely used reference guide for Unix system administration. While comprehensive in its approach, the book does not (yet) specifically cover Darwin or Mac OS X.

Backups

Meta Object

(www.metaobject.com/Community.html)

From here you can download a version of hfstar, a version of gnutar for Mac OS X that supports archiving HFS+ specific information such as resource forks, type and creator codes as well as other finder flags.

Howard Oakley's Web Page

(http://homepage.mac.com/howardoakley/)

From here you can download hfspax, another solution for archiving HFS-based file systems.

Mac OS X Labs

(www.macosxlabs.org/rsyncx/rsyncx.html)

RsyncX is an implementation of the rsync synchronization tool with HFS+ support and configuration through a command line or graphical user interface.

PocketBackup

(Pocket Software; www.pocketsw.com)

Minimalist Aqua software for automated backups.

Retrospect

(www.dantz.com)

Dantz's full-featured commercial Aqua software for performing automated backups.

The Domain Name System

DNS HOWTO

(www.tldp.org/HOWTO/DNS-HOWTO.html)

Online how-to guide for DNS and BIND ("BIND" is the Berkeley Internet Name Daemon; it is the full name for the standard version of named.)

DNS and BIND, Fourth Edition, by Paul Albitz and Cricket Liu

(O'Reilly; www.oreilly.com)

The definitive book on managing DNS software.

Quick DNS

(www.menandmice.com/products/ quickdnspro/)

Nice commercial Mac OS X Aqua application (free trial version available).

Unix in General

These are general-purpose Unix resources, not focusing on any particular version of Unix.

"The Challenges of Integrating the Unix and Mac OS Environments"

(www.mit.edu/people/wsanchez/papers/ USENIX_2000/)

Delivered by Wilfredo Sánchez at a Unix professionals convention in 2000. Describes several of the issues Apple faced in building Mac OS X on top of Unix.

CrackMonkey History of Unix

(http://crackmonkey.org/unix.html)

A history of the operating system, including a discussion of its important flavors, including Linux.

"The Evolution of the Unix Time-Sharing System"

(http://cm.bell-labs.com/cm/cs/who/dmr/ hist.html)

Unix coinventor Dennis M. Ritchie offers a technical and social history of Unix.

The Open Group

(www.opengroup.org)

The nonprofit organization that currently owns the trademark on "Unix."

UGU Unix Flavors

(www.ugu.com/sui/ugu/show?ugu.flavors)

A good list of dozens of versions of Unix.

Unix/Darwin Software

The software in this section all works without the Aqua graphical interface. It's all command-line Unix software (although many of the packages also have versions for Windows and/or other operating systems).

See the "Security" section in this appendix for software specifically used for security purposes.

Apache Web server

(www.apache.org)

By far the most popular Web server in the world, Apache provides a huge variety of configuration options and can be altered easily to add new ones. Mac OS X comes with Apache (see Chapter 14, "Installing and Configuring Servers").

CPAN (Comprehensive Perl Archive Network)

(www.cpan.org)

A vast collection of add-on modules for Perl. See also the Perl entries in the "Languages and Programming" section.

Fink

(http://fink.sourceforge.net)

The Fink program makes it easy to download and install Unix software from a constantly growing collection of packages configured to build on Mac OS X.

The FreeBSD Ports Collection

(www.freebsd.org/ports/)

A collection of software packages for the FreeBSD version of Unix. Since Darwin is based on FreeBSD, most of these will work on Mac OS X.

Managing Projects with make, Second Edition, by Andy Oram and Steve Talbott

(O'Reilly; www.oreilly.com)

The make program is widely used for managing software development, especially software written in C.

OpenSSH

(www.openssh.org)

The SSH (Secure Shell) tool facilitates secure connections between computers.

Samba

(www.samba.org)

The primary Web site for Samba, which provides Windows file sharing for Unix systems.

Sed & awk, Second Edition, by Dale Dougherty and Arnold Robbins

(O'Reilly; www.oreilly.com)

The standard reference for these two venerable Unix utility programs.

Sudo

(www.sudo.ws)

Web site devoted to the sudo program.

Database Software

A Gentle Introduction to SQL

(www.sqlzoo.net)

An online tutorial that takes you step-by-step through learning basic SQL.

MySQL

(www.mysql.com)

PostgreSQL

(www.postgresql.org)

The two most popular open-source SQL database engines.

Email software

IMAP servers—commercial

(www.stalker.com/CommuniGatePro/)

(www.tenon.com/products/post_office/)

> Two commercial IMAP servers: Stalker Software's CommuniGate Pro and Tenon Intersystems' Post.Office, respectively.

IMAP servers—no-cost

(www.washington.edu/imap/)

> (http://asg.web.cmu.edu/cyrus/imapd/)
> The University of Washington and Cyrus IMAP servers, respectively.

Majordomo—email list manager

(www.greatcircle.com/majordomo/)

> The Majordomo Web site.

Pine—text-only email client

(www.washington.edu/pine/)

> The University of Washington's Pine Information Center.

Sendmail—email server

(www.sendmail.org)

> Web site for the most commonly used Unix email server.

SpamAssassin—anti-spam software

(http://spamassassin.org/)

> Anti-spam software for mail servers.

SpamAssassin how-to for Mac OS X

(www.stupidfool.org/docs/sa.html)

> Describes how to install SpamAssassin on Mac OS X.

Printing software

CUPS Home Page (Unix/Darwin)

(www.cups.org)

> The Common UNIX Printing System (CUPS) is a cross-platform printing solution for all UNIX environments. It is based on the "http://www.pwg.org/ipp" and provides complete printing services to most PostScript and raster printers.

Gimp-Print Project (Unix/Darwin)

(gimp-print.sourceforge.net/MacOSX.php3)

> Information about the latest versions of this printing software for Mac OS X 10.2 and related drivers.

The vi editor

vi Cheat Sheet #1

(www.kcomputing.com/vi.html)

Has a link to an excellent PDF cheat sheet that is very graphically oriented. Highly recommended.

vi Cheat Sheet #2

(http://cac.uvi.edu/miscfaq/vi-cheat.html)

A text-based cheat sheet that covers many commands. Created by the University of the Virgin Islands, Center for Administrative Computing.

vi Cheat Sheet #3

(www.tufts.edu/as/medept/compstudio/vihelp.html)

A short, text-based cheat sheet, created by the folks at the Tufts University Computational Mechanics Studio.

Vim—(Vi Improved)

(www.vim.org)

This improved version of the vi editor has several features that make it easier to use.

Unix shells

Bash:

The Bash Reference Manual

(www.gnu.org/manual/bash/)

A complete reference manual for the popular bash shell.

Bash tutorial

(www-106.ibm.com/developerworks/library/bash.html)

This is at IBM's developer Web site.

Learning the bash Shell, Second Edition, by Cameron Newham and Bill Rosenblatt

(O'Reilly; www.oreilly.com)

A comprehensive guide to learning and using the bash shell.

Ksh, tcsh, zsh:

The KornShell (ksh)

(www.kornshell.com).

Ksh is widely used for programming. It is now open-source software, although you must agree to AT&T's license to install it.

The tcsh shell

(www.tcsh.org)

The standard shell in Darwin/Mac OS X.

The zsh shell

(www.zsh.org)

An alternative Unix shell with many features designed for programming.

X Windows

The XFree86 Project

(www.xfree86.org)

Web site for the version of X Windows that forms the basis for XonX.

X.org

(www.x.org)

Main X Windows Web site.

UNIX/DARWIN SOFTWARE

Miscellaneous

These are the resources that didn't fit into any of the other categories. Fun stuff, oddments, and trivia.

BBEdit text editor

(www.barebones.com).

> An Aqua program designed for editing text files such as HTML pages, shell scripts, Perl scripts, and files in other programming languages.

Calculating the difference between two squares

(www.mste.uiuc.edu/users/dildine/sketches/Diff2sq.htm)

> A classic algebraic equation: $A^2 - B^2 = (A - B)(A + B)$.

Distributed Computing

(www.distributed.net)

> Web site for worldwide projects coordinating the use of hundreds of thousands of computers to work on the same problem.

Einstein on $E = mc2$ (the special theory of relativity)

(www.aip.org/history/einstein/voice1.htm)

> Audio files of Einstein stating the basic premises of the special theory of relativity.

RPN (Reverse Polish Notation)

(www.hpmuseum.org/rpn.htm)

> You thought it was folklore? Nope, real math. Invented by Jan Lukasiewicz in the 1920s.

Search for Extraterrestrial Intelligence

(http://setiathome.ssl.berkeley.edu)

> SETI@home is a scientific experiment that uses Internet-connected computers in the Search for Extraterrestrial Intelligence (SETI). You can participate by running a free program that downloads and analyzes radio telescope data.

GLOSSARY

. Special filename for the current directory. See also *current directory*.

.. Special filename for the directory "one step closer to / from here."

Aqua The graphical user interface used in Mac OS X.

argument A piece of information passed to a command, function, or method. An argument usually tells a command what to act upon. For example, in the command line

ls -l /etc

-l is an option and /etc is an argument. See also *option*.

CGI (Common Gateway Interface) A set of rules that describe how a Web server communicates with another piece of software (the CGI program) on the same machine, and how the other piece of software talks to the Web server. Any piece of software can be a CGI program if it handles input and output according to the CGI standard.

client A software program used to contact and obtain data from a server software program on another computer, often across a network. Each client program is designed to work with one or more specific kinds of server programs, and each server requires a specific kind of client. A Web browser is a specific kind of client. See also *server*.

command line A written instruction given to a computer. A Unix command line always begins a specific command and may also contain modifers for the command (called "options") and/or a list of things for the command to act upon (called "arguments").

comment, comment out *Comment* refers to text included solely for the benefit of humans in a file that is read by a computer program. Comments never affect the execution of the program that reads them—they are skipped. To *comment out* a chunk of code in a computer program or configuration file means to turn it into a comment, usually by adding the appropriate characters to the code so that the portion being commented out is no longer executed. See also *uncomment*.

current directory The current location in the file system. This is like the Macintosh concept "Which folder are you in?" See also *directory*.

daemon A program that runs continuously, waiting to be called upon to perform some service. Most server software programs on Unix systems run as daemons, and so they often have command names ending in "d" for *daemon*; for example, ftpd is the daemon that provides the FTP service. See also *FTP*.

Darwin The specific version of Unix that forms the foundation of Mac OS X. Darwin is a variant of an earlier version of Unix called FreeBSD.

directory The Unix name for what Mac users call a "folder." In Unix, a directory is a special kind of file that contains the names of the files (and directories) that are "inside" it.

DNS (Domain Name System) The entire system of servers and software that associate domain names, such as www.peachpit.com, with IP addresses, such as 165.193.123.104. See also *IP address*.

GLOSSARY

domain name The unique name that identifies an Internet site. Domain names always have two or more parts, separated by dots. The part on the left is the most specific, and the part on the right is the most general. A given machine may have more than one domain name, but a given domain name points to only one machine. For example, the domain names

matisse.net

mail.matisse.net

workshop.matisse.net

might all refer to the same machine, but each domain name can refer to no more than one machine.

Usually, all of the machines on a given network will have the same right-hand portion of their domain name (matisse.net in the examples above). It is also possible for a domain name to exist but not be connected to an actual machine. This is often done so that a group or business can have an Internet email address without having to establish a real Internet site. In these cases, a real Internet machine must handle the mail on behalf of the listed domain name.

escape To remove the special meaning from a character in a string of text. For example, the space character has a special meaning on the Unix command line. It is used to separate the parts of the command line, so a command line like this:

```
ls My Projects
```

would normally be interpreted as having three parts. If you are trying to list the contents of a directory called My Projects, then you can fix the problem by escaping the space with the \ character:

```
ls My\ Projects
```

Now the `ls` command is passed only one argument instead of two.

FAQ (Frequently Asked Questions) FAQs are documents that list and answer the most common questions on a particular subject. There are hundreds of FAQs on subjects as diverse as pet grooming and cryptography. FAQs are usually written by people who have tired of answering the same question over and over.

filesystem, file system A *filesystem* is a single partition of a disk. On the other hand, *file system* correctly refers to the entire logical structure of all the disk space available to the user. For example, "Making backups of your entire file system is important." See also *partition*.

firewall A system designed to separate a network into two or more parts in order to reduce to a strictly controlled list the kinds of connections that can occur between the two parts.

flag See *option*.

FQDN (fully qualified domain name) A domain name that contains all the parts needed to translate it into an IP address. Top-level domain names such as ".com" are never FQDNs. In common usage, people say "domain name" when what they mean is "fully qualified domain name."

FTP (File Transfer Protocol) A common method of moving files between two Internet sites.

FTP is a way to log in to another Internet site in order to retrieve and/or send files. Many Internet sites have established publicly accessible repositories of material that can be obtained using FTP by logging in with the account name "anonymous"; these sites are called *anonymous FTP servers*.

FTP was invented and used prevalently long before the advent of the World Wide Web, and originally it was always used from a text-only interface.

host Any computer on a network that is a repository for services available to other computers on the network. It is quite common to have one host machine provide several services, such as SMTP (email) and HTTP (Web).

HTTP (Hypertext Transfer Protocol)
The protocol for moving hypertext files across the Internet. Requires an HTTP client program on one end (such as a browser) and an HTTP server program on the other end. HTTP is the most important protocol used on the World Wide Web.

hypertext Generally, any text that contains links to other documents—words or phrases in the document that, when selected, cause another document to be retrieved and displayed. See also *HTTP*.

IMAP (Internet Message Access Protocol)
IMAP is gradually replacing POP as the main protocol used by email clients in communicating with email servers. Using IMAP, an email client program not only can retrieve email but also can manipulate messages stored on the server, without having to actually retrieve them. Users can delete messages or change their status, or manage multiple mail boxes. See also *POP*.

Internet Evolved from the ARPANET of the late '60s and early '70s, the Internet is a global collection of tens of thousands of networks that are connected using the TCP/IP protocols. It is undoubtedly the largest wide area network (WAN) in the world. See also *network*.

IP (Internet Protocol) address Also called an *IP number*. A unique number consisting of four parts separated by dots—for example:

165.113.245.2

Every machine on the Internet has a unique IP address. If a machine does not have an IP address, it is not connected to the Internet. Many machines (especially servers) also have one or more domain names that are easier for people to remember. See also *domain name*.

Linux A widely used open-source Unix-like operating system. Linux was first released by its inventor, Linus Torvalds, in 1991. There are versions of Linux for almost every available type of computer hardware, from desktop machines to IBM mainframes. The inner workings of Linux are open and available for anyone to examine and change as long as the changes are available to the public. This has resulted in thousands of people working on various aspects of Linux and adaptation of Linux for a huge variety of purposes, from servers to TV-recording boxes. See also *open-source software*.

log-in, log in As a noun *(log-in)*: The account name used to gain access to a computer system. Not a secret (in contrast to *password*). As a verb *(log in)*: The act of connecting to a computer system by giving your credentials (usually your user name and password). See also *password, user name*.

network Any time you connect two or more computers together so that they can share resources, you have a computer network. Connect two or more networks together and you have an internetwork. The Internet is the world's largest internetwork. See also *Internet*.

open-source software Software for which the underlying programming code is available to users so that they may read it, make changes to it, and build new versions of the software incorporating their changes. There are many types of open-source software, mainly differing in the licensing terms under which altered copies of the source code may (or must be) redistributed.

GLOSSARY

operator As part of a command line, an operator is a character such as > or & that alters the behavior of the entire command line. For example, the >, or *redirect,* operator takes whatever input it receives (from the commands on its left) and redirects them into the file whose name appears on its right:

```
ls -l /etc/ > output.txt
```

option Also called a *flag* or a *switch,* an option is a piece of information passed to a command that turns on or off a behavior of that command. For example, in the command line

```
ls -l /etc
```

the -l option tells the ls command to produce the "long-format" listing. (Frequently, but not always, the option name works as an abbreviation of the action.) See also *switch.*

partition As a noun: A portion of a disk configured to be used by the operating system as if it were a physically separate disk. All disks have at least one partition (which can be the full size of the disk). The Macintosh concept of "volume" is the same as a partition. As a verb: The act and process of creating a partition. For example, "You must partition the disk before you can use any of the partitions."

password A code used to gain access (log in) to a locked system. Good passwords contain letters and nonletters, and are not simple combinations, such as "virtue7." A good password might be "5%df(29)." But don't use that one! See also *log in* and *user name.*

path The location of a file in the file system. Paths may be *full* or *relative.* A full path always begins with / and gives the exact location of the file in the file system, showing all the directories in the path. For example,

```
/Users/vanilla/Music/lyrics.txt
```

A relative path never begins with /, and it gives the location of a file relative to the current directory. The special filenames . and .. are often used in relative paths, such as

```
../Music/lyrics.txt
```

See also . , .. , *filename,* and *file system.*

pipe The | operator is used in command lines to pass the output of a command as input to another command. This is called "piping the output" into the other command. For example,

```
grep ipfw /var/log/system.log | grep Deny
```

The output of the first grep command is "piped into" a second grep command. See also *operator.*

POP (Post Office Protocol) Post Office Protocol refers to a way that email client software, such as Eudora, gets mail from a mail server. When you obtain an account from an Internet service provider, you almost always get a POP account with it, and it is this POP account that you tell your email software to use to get your mail. Another protocol, called IMAP, is replacing POP for email. See also *IMAP.*

port Every service on an Internet server listens on a particular port number on that server. Most services have standard port numbers; for instance, Web servers normally listen on port 80. See also *server.*

redirect To change where the output of a command goes or where its input comes from. For example, the input redirect operator (<) changes where a command gets its input.

```
mail hello@dolly.com < message.txt
```

causes the `mail` command to take its input from the file message.txt, and the output redirect operator (>) changes where a command's output goes. For example,

```
grep sudo /var/log/system.log > fishy.txt
```

causes the output of the `grep` command to be redirected into the file fishy.txt. See also *operator.*

server A computer or a software package that provides a specific kind of service to client software running on other computers. The term can refer to a particular piece of software, such as a Web server, or to the machine on which the software is running. For example, "Our mail server is down today—that's why email isn't getting out."

A single server machine can (and often does) have several different server software packages running on it, thus providing many different servers to clients on the network. See also *client* and *network.*

shell A program that provides a (usually text-only) interface to a user, interpreting commands, passing them to the operating system, and displaying the commands' output. Although the term technically can apply to some graphical interfaces, it is commonly used to mean a command-line interface. See also *command line* and *shell prompt.*

shell prompt The text presented to the user by a shell when it is ready and waiting for input. See also *shell.*

switch See *option.*

uncomment To reverse the process of commenting-out code. See also *comment.*

Unix The general name for the family of computer operating systems that have evolved from the work of Dennis Ritchie, Ken Thompson, et al. in 1969-70. Unix was designed from the start as an environment for collaborative computing and is inherently suited to use by multiple, simultaneous users running multiple programs.

unpack An informal term usually meaning to extract the contents of a compressed archive of files, as with the `tar` command.

user name The name used to identify a user on a multi-user operating system like Unix. Mac OS X documentation sometimes means a user's full name when it says "user name" and sometimes means the user's shorter "short user name". In Mac OS X a user's "short user name" is in fact his or her Unix user name —all lower-case and without spaces. See also *log-in* and *password.*

XML (Extensible Markup Language) A specification for the creation of Web-ready data structures. Data stored in a format defined according to the XML standard is very easy for a computer to read, even if it is very complex.

INDEX

Symbols

INDEX

X–Z

asked for it.
U got it.

Unix Utilities

Unix Utilities for Mac OS X is an essential toolbox for the OS X power user. Unix Utilities includes XFree86, the traditional Unix GUI, and seamlessly integrates Unix applications with your OS X desktop. Many applications are also included: a graphic editor, word processor, IRC client, fast web browser, and dozens of other useful programs.

This CD contains everything you need to turn your Mac OS X desktop into a full-fledged Unix workstation.

15% off ! Just enter this code "UnixUtil15" in your order.
http://bsdmall.com/unixutils.html